University of North Carolina

Sketches of the History of the University of North Carolina

Together with a Catalogue of Officers and Students, 1789-1889

University of North Carolina

Sketches of the History of the University of North Carolina
Together with a Catalogue of Officers and Students, 1789-1889

ISBN/EAN: 9783337035716

Printed in Europe, USA, Canada, Australia, Japan

Cover: Foto ©ninafisch / pixelio.de

More available books at **www.hansebooks.com**

SKETCHES OF THE HISTORY

OF THE

UNIVERSITY OF NORTH CAROLINA,

TOGETHER WITH A

CATALOGUE

OF

OFFICERS AND STUDENTS,

1789-1889.

PUBLISHED BY THE UNIVERSITY.
1889.

UNIVERSITY OF NORTH CAROLINA,
CHAPEL HILL, N. C., *April* 8th, 1889.

I wish it to be understood that the following sketches of the University of North Carolina are not intended as a grave history for the public, but chiefly for the gratification of the students, old and new. I have been compelled to prepare them hastily, even hurriedly, while much engrossed with other duties. I have not hesitated to use extracts from my published addresses, now out of print. Fragmentary and imperfect as the sketches are, I venture to hope that they will be of interest, not only to those for whom they are especially designed, but to all friends of our University.

KEMP P. BATTLE.

OLD EAST BUILDING—UNIVERSITY OF NORTH CAROLINA

SKETCHES OF THE HISTORY

OF THE

UNIVERSITY OF NORTH CAROLINA.

By President Kemp P. Battle.

It might be claimed that the Centennial year of American Independence was likewise the Centennial year of the University of North Carolina, although the charter was not granted until 1789.

In December, 1776, a Convention, then called Congress, of enlightened men met at Halifax to form a Constitution for the new free State of North Carolina, under whose protection the people could maintain the Independence they had declared a few months before.

Without an army or navy, they had entered on a war for existence with a nation powerful, populous and wealthy, having the tradition of invincibility, which had, under Marlborough, within the century, broken the power of the Great Louis of France—had, with heavy hand, crushed the fortunes of the Pretender at Culloden—had sent Wolfe to storm the Heights of Quebec; had swept the seas with her fleets. The Revolution, if it failed, was Rebellion. The penalty of defeat was the doom of traitors. The State had barely two hundred thousand inhabitants, widely scattered and badly armed, and divided in sentiment. But notwithstanding these odds, this Congress, with wisdom unparalleled and faith approaching sublimity, provided for the interests of unborn children. They knew that those children would not be capable of freedom without education. They knew there could be no education without teachers. They knew that teachers could not be procured without colleges, and they made the requirement of the University a part of the fundamental law. In the month of December, 1776, in the Constitution of the new State, then first adopted, are found these golden words, written amid storms and thunderings, to be made good when the sun shone on a free and united people: "ALL USEFUL LEARNING SHALL BE DULY ENCOURAGED AND PROMOTED IN ONE OR MORE UNIVERSITIES."

It was an act of sagacity and courage and far-seeing statesmanship, prompted by the bold men of Mecklenburg, who, smarting under the repeal of the charter of Queen's College, instructed their delegates, John Phifer, Robert Irwin, Zaccheus Wilson, Hezekiah Alexander, and lastly, but most prominent, Waightstill Avery, when cannon were booming and banners were flying and soldiers marshalling for the great death-struggle, to use all their endeavors for the establishment of a University and its endowment and maintenance.

The Revolutionary Fathers went to their honored graves. Generation after generation grew up and passed away. The old Constitution, after conferring the blessing of good government for many decades, was amended to suit the wants of a growing West. A great civil war desolated our land and destroyed institutions woven into the fabric of society. A race of slaves was suddenly made a part of the governing voting element of the State. A Constitution, superseding the old Constitution of 1776, was adopted to carry into effect this great change, and by a singular coincidence, exactly one hundred years after the adoption of the old Constitution, the people of the State amended the new, giving it a shape which will probably remain essentially unchanged to a distant period. But in all these vicissitudes and changes, showing the settled determination of the people of North Carolina, which no anxieties or disasters could banish from their minds, is still the substance of those golden words of 1776; or rather the execution of the mandate of the old Constitution, *in part*, is assumed, and the General Assembly is directed to go on and provide for rearing up, to the full magnitude of its usefulness, the University of the State.

While the Revolution was progressing, as might be anticipated, the mandate of the Constitution lay dormant. *Inter arma silent leges.* When Caswell was beating McDonald at Moore's Creek Bridge, and Campbell, Shelby, Cleveland, Sevier, Williams and McDowell were capturing Ferguson's forces at King's Mountain, and Cornwallis and Greene were wrestling for the victory at Guilford, and Fanning was carrying as prisoner from Hillsboro the Governor of our State, and the momentous question whether our ancestors were patriots or traitors was still undecided, there was no time for erecting universities. And after the war, industry must have time for restoring plenty to wasted lands and statesmanship to form a settled government in the place of a nerveless confederacy. In the month of November, 1789, our State, after first a stern refusal and then a coy hesitation of a year, entered the American Union. In the next month of December, as if forming part of a comprehensive plan, the charter of the University, under the powerful advocacy of Davie, was granted by the General Assembly. The Trustees under the charter comprised the great men of the State, the good men of the State, the trusted leaders of the people.

The first named and chairman was Samuel Johnston, who, in legislative, executive and judicial station, in war and peace, left the impress of his wise conservatism on the State. There were James Iredell, one of the earliest Judges of the Supreme Court of the United States, and Alfred Moore, his successor in this high office. There were the first Federal District Judge, Colonel John Stokes, and John Sitgreaves, his successor. There was Hugh Williamson, the historian, and signer of the Constitution of the United States, a delegate to the Convention of 1787, and a long array of men who were to become Governors: Samuel Ashe and William Richardson Davie and Richard Dobbs Spaight, Benjamin Williams and Benjamin Smith. There were military men, who had been conspicuous fighters in the Revolution: General Joseph Graham, scarred with wounds in the defence of Charlotte under Davie, the father of the revered statesman, William A. Graham, the last exertions of whose honored life were spent for the revival of the University; General Thomas Person, whose hatred of injustice began with the disastrous struggles of the Regulation. There were Colonels William Lenoir and Joseph McDowell, who aided in thwarting the plans of Cornwallis by the capture of Ferguson at King's

Mountain. Of the State Judiciary we find the three Judges under the Court law of 1777—Samuel Spencer, John Williams, and Samuel Ashe, already mentioned, whose name is worthily represented by his descendants, Thomas Samuel Ashe, of Anson, and Samuel A. Ashe, of Raleigh; and of others distinguished in the history of the State—Archibald McLaine and Willie Jones, bold and active patriots, Stephen Cabarrus, long Speaker of the House of Commons, and John Haywood, the popular State Treasurer. Of the national House of Representatives, were Charles Johnson, grandfather of the late distinguished physician, Charles E. Johnson, of Raleigh, Joseph Dixon, James Holland and Alexander Mebane.

At the same session the General Assembly granted to the University all escheats and certain debts due by tax collectors during the Revolutionary war, called arrearages. All sheriffs realize that claims nearly ten years old of the nature of these arrearages were likely to remain in a state of suspension for many years and so indeed they have, even to this day.

The grant of escheats under the act of 1789 was of real value, and by the energy and good management of the Trustees, after a long period was the source of the endowment of the University. Many denizens of foreign birth left no heirs, citizens of North Carolina, and under the law as it stood until 1871, their lands escheated to the State; and in like manner obscure soldiers, to whom land warrants were granted for their services in the war, died leaving no heirs to inherit their claims. Of course the revenue from this source naturally diminished as the years rolled away from the Revolution, and it was still further diminished by acts of the Legislature giving the lands to a remoter heir, being a citizen, when the next heir is an alien, and giving the widow all the estate if her husband should die without an heir. At this day the chances of an escheat are worth but little, as an alien stands on the same footing with a citizen in regard to the possession of real estate.

It was not from parsimony but hard necessity that the long services of our patriot-soldiers, in hunger, and thirst, and cold, and nakedness, were paid for in a paper currency, like that of which the conquered Confederates have had such bitter experience. To this meagre dole was added for faithful service warrants for land to be located in a country of great fertility, but the home of bears and panthers and not friendly Indians, the western region of Tennessee, then a part of the domain of North Carolina. To a private was given 640 acres, to a Lieutenant 2,560, to a Captain 3,840, to a Major 4,800, to a Colonel, or Lieutenant-Colonel Commanding, 7,200, to a Brigadier-General 12,000 acres. To the great General Greene, who had by his genius retrieved the fortunes of the war after Gates' disastrous failure, they gave 25,000 acres.

The gift of the unclaimed land warrants was to the University like the cool waters near the parched lips of Tantalus. North Carolina, in 1789, ceded all its territory of Tennessee to the United States. The new State, after its admission into the Union in 1796, claimed all the rights of sovereignty, and refused to give effect to the grants made by North Carolina.

The State of North Carolina would never have secured an acre of these lands. No argument but that they were to be used for education, had any weight with the legislators of Tennessee. The Trustees sent to plead their cause one of the most enlightened members and most skilled in the arts of managing men, Judge Archibald Murphy. Even he, with all his eloquence and address, was forced to a hard compromise. Two-thirds of the warrants were given to the College of East Tennessee and the College of Cumberland, and one-third to the University of North Carolina. It was not until 1835, after suffering untold privations, staggering under a debt of nearly $40,000 to the banks, that funds were gathered from this source and the donations of Smith, Gerrard and others, to lift its head above the waters.

It is pleasant to note that by the providence of our ancestors the enemies of our country's freedom contributed, albeit unwillingly, to the enlightenment of our people. But it is of pathetic interest to know that the ignorant soldiers of America, who, after countless sufferings, filled uncoffined graves, were not only gaining liberty for their country but, unintentional benefactors, were building a great institution of learning. They did glorious work, those "unnamed demigods of history," as Kossuth calls them, blindly suffering martyrdom for a cause they dimly understood, but that cause triumphant and leading to never ending blessings of free institutions and liberal education.

With the exception of $10,000 loaned by the State for erecting buildings (afterwards converted into a gift), all the benefactions of the General Assembly were only of such interests as could be of little, if any, advantage to the State. This is expressed in the preamble of one of the acts: "*Whereas*, The State possesses certain funds from which no profit is yielded, but which by the zeal, activity and united exertions of the Trustees of the University, might be rendered productive," &c. The abortive gift of uncollected taxes has been mentioned.

The gift of confiscated property was likewise of this nature, though at one time great revenues were expected from it. The Trustees had collected a handsome sum from debts due Henry Eustice McCulloch, the agent of Lord Granville, for lands sold by him prior to the Revolution, when behold, our Conference Court, then the Supreme tribunal, decided in accordance with the Treaty of Peace of 1783, that these debts could not be taken from McCulloch, and the University was forced by the Legislature to disgorge —a rare instance of a corporation performing an act so disagreeable and "contrary to nature."

The Trustees met for organization on the 18th of December, 1789, Charles Johnson being chairman. The journal kept by one of the earliest Treasurers, Walter Alves, written with wonderful neatness and accuracy, gives the names of the subscribers. The largest donations were by William Cain of the Orange District, and Alfred Moore of the Cape Fear, great-grandfather of a distinguished son of the University, Alfred Moore Waddell. The charter was accepted and steps were taken to solicit subscriptions. Davie cheered the hearts of the Trustees by announcing the gift by Benjamin Smith of warrants for 20,000 acres of land.

The second meeting was likewise in Fayetteville, November 15th, 1790.

Col. William Lenoir, a hero of King's Mountain, the Speaker of the Senate, on the nomination of the Speaker of the House, Stephen Cabarrus, was made President of the Board. James Taylor, of Rockingham, was elected Secretary, while to the position of Treasurer, the State Comptroller, John Craven, was appointed. Death had invaded their ranks. The old heroes were dropping off. The venerable Robert Dixon was succeeded by

James Kenan, grandfather of our Attorney General, and battle-scarred Judge Winston by Alex. Martin, who, like our Vance, had been Governor in times of war, and after a long interval in times of peace, occupied the executive chair. James Hogg proceeded to the welcome duty of presenting to the Board patents for the 20,000 acres of land, donated at the preceding meeting by Governor Smith. On the resignation, by Col. Lenoir, of the chairmanship, Governor Alexander Martin was chosen as his successor. It was agreed that the places of future meetings should be selected by ballot. Hillsborough was the choice of the Board for the next meeting, and also for that of August, 1792. It was at this meeting that steps were taken for the purpose of locating the institution. The attendance of members proved the interest taken in the question. There were present 25 trustees out of 40, the largest proportion ever known. The largest number in these days of easy railroad travelling, is 39 out of 80, in 1885, when six professors were elected. Such patriotic sacrifice of comfort in the heated dog-days deserves to be recorded. Those who answered to the roll-call were:

Alex. Martin, Governor, of Guilford; Hugh Williamson, the historian, of Chowan; Benjamin Williams, afterwards Governor, of Moore; John Sitgreaves, Judge United States District Court, of Craven; Fred. Hargett, State Senator, of Jones; Richard Dobbs Spaight, the elder, elected Governor that year, of Craven, who was afterwards killed in a duel by John Stanly; Wm. H. Hill, member of the Legislature and of Congress, of New Hanover; James Hogg, merchant, of Cumberland; Samuel Ashe, then Judge, afterwards Governor, New Hanover; John Hay, lawyer, Cumberland; Wm. Barry Grove, member of Congress, Cumberland; Col. Wm. Polk, member of the Legislature, then of Mecklenburg; Judge John Williams, Granville; Alexander Mebane, afterwards member of Congress, Orange; Joel Lane, member of Senate, Wake; Alfred Moore, then member of the Legislature, afterwards Judge Supreme Court, Brunswick; Willie Jones, Halifax; Benjamin Hawkins, Senator in Congress, Warren; John Haywood, State Treasurer, then of Edgecombe; Rev. Dr. Samuel E. McCorkle, a distinguished preacher and teacher, Rowan; Wm. Richardson Davie, afterwards Governor, Halifax; Joseph Dixon, State

Senator, afterwards member of Congress, Lincoln; Joseph McDowell, Jr., member of the Legislature, Burke; Wm. Porter, member of the Legislature, Rutherford; Adlai Osborne, Clerk of the Superior Court of his county, a well-read and influential man, Rowan.

According to localities, counting New Hanover as an Eastern county, and Cumberland, Warren and Guilford as Middle counties, there were ten Eastern, nine Middle, and six Western Trustees.

Willie Jones submitted a motion, which was adopted, that the Board would not select any particular spot, but would choose by ballot a place with liberty of locating within fifteen miles thereof. This was all the more proper because the charter provided that the site should not be within five miles of the permanent seat of government or any court house—an incidental proof of the drunkenness and rowdyism of the country during court week, horrible specimens of which may be witnessed to this day.

The places in nomination were as follows: Raleigh, in Wake county; Williamsboro, in Granville county; Hillsboro, in Orange county; Pittsboro, in Chatham county; Cyprett's Bridge, over New Hope, in Chatham; Smithfield, in Johnston county; Goshen, in Granville county.

The Board proceeded to ballot, and Cyprett's, or Cipritz, Bridge, now Prince's Bridge, on the great road from Newbern by Raleigh to Pittsboro, was chosen. The choice was a natural one. The fifteen miles radius allowed a range over wide areas of Chatham, Wake and Orange, from the highlands of New Hope to the hills of Buckhorn, from the Hickory Mountain to the eminences overlooking our beautiful capital on the west. The same influences which secured that the capital should be located within ten miles of Isaac Hunter's plantation, in Wake county, that is, as near the centre of the State as possible, carried this vote.

On the 4th of August, 1792, the Board adopted an ordinance to carry into effect the selection of the University site within the circle described. One commissioner from each Congressional District was appointed by ballot. There were from the Morganton District, Wm. Porter, of Rutherford; the Salisbury District, John Hamilton, of Guilford; the Hillsboro District, Alex. Mebane, of Orange; the Halifax District, Willie Jones, of Halifax; the Edenton District,

David Stone, of Bertie; the Newbern District, Frederick Hargett, of Jones; the Wilmington District, Wm. H. Hill, of New Hanover; the Fayetteville District, James Hogg, of Cumberland. They were to meet in Pittsboro on November 1st, 1792, prepared to visit in person all places deemed eligible.

At the appointed time a majority convened in Pittsboro, viz:— Hargett, Mebane, Hogg, Hill, Stone and Jones. It was an excellent committee. Senator Hargett had already assisted as Commissioner in locating and laying out the city of Raleigh. Alexander Mebane had been a member of the Convention which framed the State Constitution and a useful officer of the Revolutionary army. He long served the county of Orange in the State Legislature and the year after this was elected to the Congress of the United States. He was father of James Mebane, first President of the Dialectic Society, who attained the honor of the Speakership of the House of Commons, and grandfather of another alumnus of the University, the respected Giles Mebane, once Speaker of the Senate. James Hogg was an influential merchant, afterwards of Hillsborough, among whose descendants are the Binghams, Norwoods and Webbs of Orange, and Dr. Wm. Hooper, an eminent professor of the University. Wm. H. Hill, a descendant of Governor Yeamans, was an able lawyer of Wilmington, afterwards State Senator and member of Congress. David Stone, then a member of the House of Commons from Bertie, afterwards Governor and Senator of the United States, was a well educated and accomplished young man. Willie Jones was one of the most active and influential men of the Revolutionary and post-revolutionary periods, as chairman of the Committee of Safety, wielding executive authority in 1776, a member of the Continental Congress.

We have the journal of the proceedings of these Commissioners as, in the beginning of November, ninety-seven years ago, they started from Pittsboro to view the various points offered for their choice. Great efforts were made for the location at Haywood, in the forks of Haw and Deep rivers, likewise a competitor with Raleigh for the seat of government. An offer was made of six hundred and forty acres of land to secure the selection of the Cross Roads in Wake, near Cary, where then lived Nathanael Jones, called of White Plains, to distinguish him from Nathanael

Jones of Crabtree. Ten other places were tendered, mainly in the county of Chatham, but in far-sighted liberality, the men of Chapel Hill and its vicinity exceeded all others. I give their names, because they should be had in especial remembrance by the lovers of the University:

Colonel John Hogan, two hundred acres; Benjamin Yergan, fifty-one; Matthew McCauley, one hundred and fifty; Alexander Piper, twenty-six; James Craig, five; Christopher Barbee, two hundred and twenty-one; Edward Jones, two hundred; Mark Morgan, one hundred and seven; John Daniel, one hundred and seven; Hardy Morgan, one hundred and twenty. Total, one thousand one hundred and eighty acres, of which eight hundred and forty were in one body.

Let me describe the spot more particularly, as it appeared to the eyes of the Commissioners.

The construction of railroads has made a wonderful change in the relative importance of our public highways. In the old days those who made tobacco rolled it away to Petersburg, the hogsheads being at once the wagon and the wheels for carriage. Those who made corn, generally converted it into hogs and drove them on foot to Philadelphia or Charleston. Wheat was ground into flour and sent by wagon to distant markets—to Fayetteville, Wilmington, Newbern and Petersburg. The corn and rye not fed to swine was changed to whisky and the fruit into brandy, and that which escaped the capacious throats of the neighborhood drinkers, was peddled along the road side to the rural drinkers or sold in bulk to the village shops. In violation of all rules of political economy, a man was at the same time an agriculturist, a manufacturer, a transporter, a wholesale merchant, a retailer, and a voracious consumer.

The returning wagons carried home supplies of molasses and sugar, iron and salt, shot and powder and flints, not forgetting the ribbons and combs and such paraphernalia, that ladies in all ages will obtain to gild the refined gold of their personal charms. They were the vehicles also of the news of the day, there being no post-office nearer than Tarboro. The wondering neighbors heard from these drivers what was going on in the big world—that Washington had consented to accept a second term of the Presidency, that

GERRARD HALL—UNIVERSITY OF NORTH CAROLINA.

the heads of the King and Queen of France had rolled into the guillotine basket, that the allied armies had been driven back from the Rhine; and then what has proved to be of more importance than all the victories of armies or the crownings of kings, that a Yankee schoolmaster, named Whitney, had invented a machine for picking seed out of cotton, and every old lady paused in the musical whirr of her spinning wheel to listen to the astounding intelligence, not more than three months old, that in the old country a man named Arkwright was spinning yarn by water power, and more incredible still, a preacher named Cartwright was weaving cloth by wood and iron instead of human muscles.

From these causes the roads of those days, though over them rolled no modern carriages or effeminate buggies, or bicycles, picturesque but unsociable, frequently resounded with the heavy wheels of the covered wagons, and the Cross Roads were places of importance, where wagoners and the neighbors met for business and social enjoyments, listened to political speeches, and more rarely to homely but heart-stirring sermons.

The great roads from Petersburg to Pittsboro and the country beyond, and from Newbern toward Greensboro and Salisbury, crossed on this eminence. At the north-east corner of the cross was a chapel of the Church of England, a sad relic of the futile efforts to establish a church in North Carolina. It was called New Hope Chapel and the eminence was called New Hope Chapel Hill, or the Hill of New Hope Chapel. The eminence is a promontory of granite, belonging to the Laurentian system, and extends into the sandstone formation to the east, which was once the bed of a long sheet of water stretching from near New York to the centre of Georgia. We have in our Museum pieces of rock formed from the mud and sand at the bottom of this old bay on which are ripple marks of the waves and prints of the plants and animals which grew in its shallows. It was on this plateau, elevated 250 feet above the country on the east, then as now celebrated for its magnificent forests of oak and hickory, its springs of cool and purest water, its pleasant, mudless, dustless soil, its genial, healthful climate, on whose hillsides the mountain flora blossom, that the home of the University was fixed.

The report of the Commissioners was submitted by their chairman, Hargett, to the Board, and was referred to a committee consisting of Gov. Davie, Rev. Dr. McCorkle, Willie Jones, Judge Ashe and Judge Sitgreaves. Jones reported an ordinance ratifying their action, which was unanimously adopted. Davie offered an ordinance for appointing commissioners to erect buildings and lay off a town. The building was to accommodate fifty students, not to cost over $5,000.

The corner stone of this building, the "Old East," was laid on the 12th of October, 1793.

We have fortunately an account of the proceedings of this day so memorable, written by Davie himself, the chief actor. I will endeavor to take the veil off this picture of long ago, and wipe off the dust which obscures it.

The Chapel Hill of 96 years ago was vastly different from the Chapel Hill of to-day. It was covered with a primeval growth of forest trees, with only one or two settlements, and a few acres of clearing. Even the trees on the East and West Avenue, named Cameron by the Faculty in recognition of the wise and skilful superintendence, by Mr. P. C. Cameron, of the extensive repairs of our buildings prior to the re-opening in 1875, were still erect. The sweet-gums and dogwoods and maples were relieving in the autumnal sun, with their russet and golden hues, the general green of the forest. A long procession of people for the first time are marching along the narrow road, afterwards to be widened into a noble avenue. Many of them are clad in the striking, typical insignia of the Masonic Fraternity, their Grand Master arrayed in the full decorations of his rank. They march with military tread, because most of them have seen service, many scarred with wounds of horrid war. Their faces are serious, for they feel that they are engaged in a great work. They are proceeding to lay the foundations of an institution which for weal or woe is to shape the minds of thousands of unborn children; whose influence will be felt more and more, ever widening and deepening as the years roll on, as one of the great forces of civilization.

Let us transport ourselves in imagination and look on this strange procession and see if we can recognize any of them as they step firmly in the pleasant sunshine of the autumnal sun.

The tall commanding figure most conspicuous, in the Grand

Master's regalia, is that of William Richardson Davie. He is no common man. He had been a gallant cavalry officer in the Revolution. He had been a strong staff on which Greene had leaned. He had been conspicuous in civil pursuits; an able lawyer, an orator of vast influence. With Washington and Franklin, and other great men, he had assisted in evolving the grandest government of all ages, the American Union, out of an ill-governed and disintegrating confederacy. He was beyond his times in the advocacy of a broad, generous education. His portrait has been drawn by a masterly hand, Judge Archibald Murphy, one of the most progressive and scholarly men our State has known. In his speech before the two Societies at Chapel Hill he says: "Davie was a tall, elegant man in his person, graceful and commanding in his manners. His voice was mellow, and adapted to the expression of every passion; his mind comprehensive yet slow in its operations, when compared with his great rival; his style was magnificent and flowing; he had a greatness of manner in public speaking which suited his style, and gave to his speeches an imposing effect. He was a laborious student, arranged his discourses with care, and where the subject merited his genius, poured forth a torrent of eloquence that astonished and enraptured his audience."

Judge Murphy says: "I was present in the House of Commons when Davie addressed that body upon the bill granting a loan of money to the Trustees for erecting the buildings of the University, and although more than thirty years have since elapsed, I have the most vivid recollection of the greatness of his manner and the powers of his eloquence on that occasion." General Davie was afterwards Governor of the State and Envoy of the United States to the Court of France. I find him styled in the Journal of the University in 1810, "the Father of the University," and he well deserved the title.

Who is that distinguished looking man, "small in stature, neat in his dress, elegant in his manner," next to Davie? It is Davie's great rival, Alfred Moore. Judge Murphy gives us a vivid picture of him also: "His voice was clear and sonorous, his perception quick, and judgment almost intuitive. His style was chaste and manner of speaking animated. Having adopted Swift for his model, his language was always plain. The clearness and energy of his mind enabled him almost without an effort to disentangle the most intricate subject and expose it in all its parts to the simplest understanding. He spoke with ease and with force, enlivened his discourse with flashes of wit, and where the subject required it, with all the bitterness of sarcasm. His speeches were short and impressive. When he sat down every one thought he had said everything he ought to have said." His learning and acquirements secured for him a seat on the bench of one of most august tribunals in the world, the Supreme Court of the United States.

In that procession appeared too one who had highest reputation among his contemporaries as an enlightened lawyer, William H. Hill, heretofore described, father of the brilliant young man whose death filled the whole State with grief, Joseph A. Hill.

We next see one who was for many years the most popular man in North Carolina, John Haywood. For forty years—1787 to 1827—he was Treasurer of the State. His hospitality was unbounded. He made it a rule to invite specially to an entertainment at his house, at each session of the General Assembly, which then met annually, every member. His kindness and charity were absolutely inexhaustible. In reading over the University records, I find that for over thirty years he scarcely missed a meeting of the Board, whether held at Chapel Hill or at Raleigh. His name is perpetuated not only by distinguished sons now living, but by one of our loveliest mountain counties and by a neighboring town, which once aspired to be the capital of the State, and site of the University.

Marching with Haywood was Gen. Alexander Mebane, of the old Scotch-Irish stock, who settled the Haw Fields in Alamance, something of whose history has been given.

In that procession was also John Williams, founder of Williamsboro in Granville county, whose strong, sturdy sense enabled him to step with short interval from the bench of the carpenter to the bench of the Judge of the first court under the Constitution of 1776. He was likewise a member of the Congress of the Confederacy.

Thomas Blount, member from Edgecombe, soon to enter Congress and to become an attached colleague of Nathaniel Macon, was likewise present.

Prominent in the procession was the venerable Hargett, Senator from Jones, plain, solid, but eminently trustworthy. His name, as well as Blount's, is commemorated by principal streets of Raleigh.

After these came other Trustees. Who they were, with the exception of McCorkle, we have no record.

The orator of the day, Dr. Samuel E. McCorkle, was one of the most noted educators of that period. He was one of the sturdy Scotch-Irish, who made the North of Ireland famous throughout all lands for triumphs of intelligent industry and thrift, whose glorious defence of Londonderry stands unrivalled in the annals of human valor and endurance; who gave to North Carolina many of its leaders in war and in peace—Grahams and Jacksons, Brevards, Alexanders, Mebanes and hosts of others, but above all most of its faithful and zealous instructors of youth, such as Dr. Caldwell of Guilford, and Dr. Caldwell of the University, Dr. Ker and Harris, its first Professors, and that noble progenitor of a long line of able and cultured teachers, and founder of a school eminent for nearly a century for its wide-spread and multiform usefulness, William Bingham, the first.

Dr. McCorkle was among the foremost of these. He was beyond his generation as a teacher. His school at Thyatira, six miles west of Salisbury, spread abroad not only classical learning but sound religious training. He attached to it a department specially for teachers, the first Normal School, I feel sure, in America. The first class which graduated at our University consisted of seven members; six of them had been pupils of Dr. McCorkle. And it is gratifying that one of the first graduates of the revived University was a relative of his, George McCorkle of Catawba, the Chief Marshal of 1876.

The name, Zion-Parnassus, which he gave to his school at Thyatira, shows how he combined the culture of the Bible and the culture of the muses. The first Board of Trustees of the University was composed of the greatest men of the State, and among them—Senators, Governors, Judges of the Supreme Court of the United States and of the State—was Dr. McCorkle, the solitary preacher and solitary teacher. He was one of the best friends the University had; worked for it, begged for it, preached for it.

The Trustees, in December, 1795, tendered him the chair of Moral and Political Philosophy with the chairmanship of the Faculty, which was not accepted. It was most fitting that he should deliver the first address at the University, to be followed by a long line of eminent men.

After the Trustees march State officers, not Trustees; among them Judge Spruce McKoy of Salisbury, and doubtless John Taylor, the clerk of the Superior Court of Orange, ancestor of one of our professors; and then followed the gentlemen of the vicinity, the McCauleys and Barbees and Hogans and Daniels and Pipers and Craigs and Yeargins and Morgans, and among them Patterson of Chatham, the contractor for the building. Since that day we have had processions, year by year, on our commencement days, and in their columns, Presidents and Governors and Senators and great divines, men learned and distinguished in all the pursuits of life, but never has there been a procession more imposing than that which laid the corner-stone of the Old East, on the 12th of October, 1793.

We have a report of the address made by Dr. McCorkle under the blue sky of that autumn day. It is replete with wisdom and noble thoughts, and fully proves that the estimation placed on him by the men of that day was fully earned. An extract is given:

"It is our duty to acknowledge that sacred Scriptural truth, 'Except the Lord do build the house their labor is but in vain that build it.' The happiness of a nation depends on national wealth and national glory and cannot be gained without them. They in like manner depend on liberty and good laws. Liberty and laws call for general knowledge in the people. . . . . How can glory or wealth be procured or preserved without liberty and laws? They must check luxury, encourage industry and protect wealth. They must secure me the glory of my actions and save me from a bow-string or a bastile, and how are those objects to be gained without general knowledge? Knowledge is wealth, it is glory; whether among philosophers, ministers of state or religion, or among the great mass of the people."

We thank thee for thy golden words, thou venerable father of education in North Carolina. On this foundation the University desires to rest. The enlightenment of the people, their instruction not alone in secular learning but in religious truth, leading up to and sustaining liberty by demanding and shaping beneficent laws, under which wealth may be accumulated and individual happiness and national glory secured, all sanctified by the blessing of God; these are the objects, these the methods, these are the good rewards of the University.

But the beginnings of the University were in troublous times. Its struggles were not only with want and penury, but with ignorance and prejudice and a wild spirit of lawlessness.

All the world was in a ferment. The passions of the era flamed across the ocean and enkindled sympathetic passions in our midst. Furious efforts were made to force the United States into alliance with the French Republic. The vision of the sister democracies of the Old World and the New, marching shoulder to shoulder to plant in every capital the standard of Universal Freedom, and conquering together a Universal Peace, aroused every sentiment of romantic philanthropy and quixotic gratitude.

The rage of parties was strong in North Carolina as elsewhere. It stood in the way of all measures for the advancement of the public good. It stimulated bad passions, prevented coöperation, divided the people into hostile camps. In the general excitement the cause of education was little regarded, and but for the wisdom of such men as Davie, and Moore, and Mebane, and Haywood, and Hill, the new-born University would have been strangled in its infancy.

The population of the State was only about 400,000, of whom about 100,000 were slaves. The permanent seat of government had just been chosen. The city of Raleigh was located in 1792, the State-house was not finished until 1794. The inhabitants of the State lived remote from one another, and mutual intercourse was prevented not only by long distances but by the execrable roads and the almost entire absence of spring vehicles. The two-wheeled sulky and stick-back gig were possessed by the better class, while only a few of the wealthiest could boast of the ancient lumbering coach. Most traveling was on horseback, it being quite the fashion for the lady to sit behind the gentleman, and steady herself by an arm around his waist.

The diffusion of intelligence through most of the regions of the

State was by the chance traveler or the wagoner. In 1790 there were only 75 post-offices in all the Union, there are now 50,000. There were only 1,875 miles of post roads in all the Union, now there are over 300,000. Then there was only one letter to 17 people, now there are over 20 letters to each person. Then there were only 265,500 letters carried in a year, now there are over 1,000,000,000 letters. Then the postage was from 7 to 33 cents according to distance, now for 2 cents a letter will go with great certainty to the shores of the Pacific, even to distant Alaska among the frozen latitudes. In his message to the Legislature of 1790, Gov. Alexander Martin complains that there is only one mail route in the State and that runs only through the seaboard towns, that only a few inhabitants derive advantage from that establishment in comparison to the general bulk of the people of the interior country. Five years afterwards Prof. Harris, when a weekly mail had been established, writes, "our news at this place (Chapel Hill) has given us more trouble and disappointment than information. I joined Mr. Ker, acting President, in getting Browne's daily paper, but it has not arrived by the two last posts, and if it does not come more regularly we must discontinue it." The old records show that it was a common practice to send a special messenger, called an "express," when important communication became necessary between the University authorities and the Trustees.

The state of education was at a low ebb. There were no public schools and few private schools. I am fortunately able to give information on this subject from Judge Archibald Murphy, an early student of the University; after his graduation, one of its professors. He says: "Before this University came into operation in 1795, there were not more than three schools in the State in which the rudiments of a classical education could be acquired. The most prominent and useful of these schools was kept by Mr. David Caldwell, of Guilford county. He initiated it shortly after the close of the war, and continued it more than thirty years. The usefulness of Dr. Caldwell to the literature of the State will never be sufficiently appreciated, but the opportunities of instruction in the school were very limited. There was no library attached to it. His students were supplied with a few of the Greek and Latin

Classics, Euclid's Elements of Mathematics, and Martin's Natural Philosophy. Moral Philosophy was taught from a syllabus of lectures by Dr. Witherspoon in Princeton College. The students had no books on history or miscellaneous literature. There were very few indeed in the State, except in the libraries of lawyers who lived in the commercial towns. I well remember that after completing my course of studies under Dr. Caldwell, I spent nearly two years without finding any books to read except some old works on theological subjects. At length I accidentally met with Voltaire's History of Charles XII of Sweden, and an odd volume of Smollett's Roderick Random and an abridgement of Don Quixote. These books gave me a taste for reading which I had no opportunity of gratifying until I became a student of the University in 1796. Few of Dr. Caldwell's students had better opportunies of getting books than myself, and with those slender opportunities of instruction, it is not at all surprising that so few have become eminent in the liberal professions. At this day (1827) when libraries are established in all our towns, when every professional man and every respectable gentleman has a collection of books, it is difficult to conceive the inconvenience under which young men labored thirty or forty years ago." And yet there were men who, like Judge Murphy, conquered all these difficulties and rose, conspicuous for learning and science.

The *North American Review*, in 1821, said that, "in an ardent and increasing zeal for the establishment of schools and academies for several years past, we do not believe North Carolina has been outdone by a single State. The Academy at Raleigh was founded in 1804, previously to which there were only two institutions of the kind in the State. The number at present is nearly fifty, and is rapidly increasing. Great pains are taken to procure the best instructors from different parts of the country, and we have the best authority for our opinion, that in no part of the Union are the interests of education better understood and under better regulation than in the middle counties of North Carolina. The schools for females are particularly celebrated and are much resorted to from Georgia, South Carolina and Virginia. In the year 1816, the number of students at academies within the compass of forty miles amounted to more than one thousand. This space comprised the counties of Warren, Granville, Orange, Wake, Franklin, and two or three others adjoining."

In those days the University was the only institution of higher learning in North Carolina, and when we contrast the general darkness in 1795 with the rapid improvement, as shown by the extract from the *North American Review*, in twenty-five years, cannot the University say with triumph: These schools were my children? I am their *Alma Mater*—their creative and fostering author, they are the fruit of my labors.

THE BUILDINGS.

It is convenient now to give a connected history of the various buildings of the University, commencing with the "Old East," of whose beginning we have spoken.

The bricks of this, as of all the other buildings, except those in Memorial Hall, which were obtained from the Penitentiary, were burnt on University land. The lime used in the mortar of the early structures was obtained from shells brought from Wilmington by boat, thence by wagon. There is recorded a donation of fifty bushels of such shells by Mr. Richard Bennehan, grandfather, as the royal charters say, of "our well-beloved cousin and trusted counsellor," Paul C. Cameron.

The Old East continued in its primitive condition until 1824, when its roof was adorned by a third story nearer to the skies. At the same time the Old West was built of a corresponding size. In 1848 the length of both was extended towards the north so as to admit new Society Halls and Libraries.

The first President of the Dialectic Society, James Mebane, already mentioned as son of one of the Trustees who selected the site, was present at the ceremonies attending the removal into the new Halls, and he, with President Battle, then a Senior and President of the Society, jointly presided over the body.

The lots of the village of Chapel Hill were sold on the same 12th of October, 1793, the price for all, about $3,000, being considered highly satisfactory. It was pressingly necessary to provide a residence for the President, or presiding Professor, and also a Steward's Hall, wherein the students of the period might obtain

their subsistence. The President's Mansion is the house on the avenue west of the New West building, which is now in the occupancy of our Professor of Physics. In that house were sheltered David Ker and Joseph Caldwell and Dr. Chapman, then it passed into the possession of Dr. Elisha Mitchell. President Caldwell, after his marriage to Mrs. Wm. Hooper in 1809, removed to the lot owned by her and bought by the University after his death. The dwelling house, which had the honor of sheltering three Presidents of the United States, as well as Presidents Caldwell and Swain, was accidently burned on Christmas Day, 1886. The old President's house contained, in the small room at the head of the stairs, the library of the institution.

The Steward's Hall was situate nearly opposite the east end of the New East building in the centre of Cameron avenue. It was there that most of the students for many years boarded at Commons, paying for the first year $30, or $3 per month; for the next four years $40 per year, or $4 per month; in 1800 rising to $57 per year; in 1805 to $60; in 1814, under the inflated war prices, to $66.50; in 1818 to $95, or $9.50 per month; in 1839 to $76, when the system was abandoned. It was in this building that the "balls" of the old days were given, at which tradition hath it, venerable Trustees and Faculty, even the great President himself, together with their pupils, with hair powdered and plaited into "pigtails," and legs encased in tight stockings and knees resplendent with buckles, mingled in the dance with the beauteous damsels of the day.

At the Commencement of 1881 we had a most eloquent and instructive address to the students by a classmate of President Polk, an excellent specimen of the old school, an octogenarian, Gen. E. J. Mallett, of New York, lately called to his final home. He was introduced as having received his diploma sixty-three years before that day, and it was stated that for seventy years he had never taken a glass of ardent spirits, and, *therefore*, that he had still the inestimable blessing of *mens sana in corpore sano*, and that other still greater blessing, *mens sibi conscia recti*. In his autobiography, printed only for his relatives—a copy being donated to our Historical Society, we find an account of the ball given in compliment to his class, when graduating. The following description of his dress is interesting.

"The style of costume," said Gen. Mallett, "and even the manners of the present generation are not, in my opinion, an improvement on a half century ago. The managers would not then admit a gentleman into a ball-room with boots, or even a frock coat; and to dance without gloves was simply vulgar. At Commencement ball (when I graduated, 1818), my coat was broadcloth of sea-green color, high velvet collar to match, swallow-tail, pockets outside with lapels, and large silver-plated buttons; white satin damask vest, showing the edge of a blue undervest; a wide opening for bosom ruffles, and no shirt collar. The neck was dressed with a layer of four or five three-cornered cravats, artistically laid, and surmounted with a cambric stock, pleated and buckled behind. My pantaloons were white canton crape, lined with pink muslin, and showed a peach-blossom tint. They were rather short, in order to display flesh-colored silk stockings, and this exposure was increased by very low cut pumps with shiny buckles. My hair was very black, very long and queued. I should be taken for a lunatic or a harlequin in such costume now."

PERSON HALL—THE OLD CHAPEL.

Having provided dormitories for sheltering the students and food for their bodily sustenance, and halls for their mental instruction, the Trustees next addressed themselves to provision for their religious and moral training. The old ante-Revolutionary Chapel of the Church of England, from which the place took its name, had gone to decay. A building under the control of the Trustees must be erected. When it was barely above the ground the treasury ran low.

An old bachelor, one of that class, which, having no immediate claims on its bounty, sometimes redeems by beneficence to public objects their failures in social duty, came to their relief. His name was Thomas Person. He had been an ardent lover of liberty, had sympathized with the Regulators in their abortive effort to shake off colonial oppressors, and had suffered from the ravages of Tryon's army. He was prominent in resisting the exactions of the British Government, which led to the war of Independence. He appeared at Newbern as a Delegate from Granville to the first Assembly held in defiance of the royal authority in August, 1774, of which that noble patriot, John Harvey, was moderator. He was one of the thirteen Council of Safety which was the supreme Provisional Government, after the end of the Royal authority. He assisted in 1776, as a member of the Congress at Halifax, in forming our State constitution, in which was the provision requiring the establishment of the University. He was the first Brigadier-General of the District of Hillsborough. He was among the band of forty of the greatest men the State had in 1789—the first Board of Trustees of the University. As Senator from Granville he gave his vote for the new institution. He did more. He gave a sum in money very liberal for that day for the completion of the Chapel. In grateful memory of his services to the State the General Assembly gave his name to a county carved out of old Orange. In gratitude for his generous gift the Trustees called the new Chapel after him, Person Hall, or as it appeared until lately on the diplomas, *Aula Personica*.

In this hall Faculty, students and villagers worshipped for nearly forty years. It was likewise used on commencement occasions. In it Judge Murphy delivered the first address before the two Societies in 1827, and, among other eloquent orators, Judge Gaston made his memorable speech in 1833, which has gone through three editions, notwithstanding that it contained a hope for the abolition of slavery.

Although this building is named Person *Hall*, yet, because of its use as a church on Sundays and for morning and evening prayers, it gained the name of "the Chapel," and when Gerrard Hall was built, the former was called, and is so known to this day by old students, "the Old Chapel."

About 1840 it was divided by partitions into four recitation rooms. It was restored to a single room in 1877 for the use of the Professor of Chemistry; the wood-work was accidentally destroyed by fire in the same year and immediately rebuilt. In 1885 chemical laboratories were added on its western side.

GERRARD HALL

was begun in 1822. It was called after another Revolutionary hero, Major Charles Gerrard,—not a bachelor, but childless. He was a native of Carteret, but long a resident of Edgecombe. He served in the war of the Revolution from the beginning to the end. As a soldier he was "brave, active and persevering." His character as a citizen, husband, friend and neighbor was justly admired. His rank in the army (Lieutenant) entitled him to a grant of 2,560 acres, which he located at the junction of Yellow Creek with Cumberland river, not far below the city of Nashville.

This tract, the fruit of his toil and suffering and blood, he regarded with peculiar affection, and when he bequeathed this, with some 10,000 acres additional, which he had purchased, he requested in his will that it should perpetually remain the property of the University. For thirty-five years the Trustees regarded this wish as sacred. But after losses from the neglect and perfidy of agents and the onerous charges of taxes, while the black cloud of debt hung over the institution, they concluded with sorrow to authorize its sale. Two of their ablest lawyers, William Gaston and George E. Badger, after examination reported the following resolution:

"WHEREAS, The Trustees of the University of North Carolina have been compelled to direct a sale of a valuable tract of land, bequeathed by Major Charles Gerrard, with the request that the same might be perpetually retained by the University; and

"WHEREAS, They are solicitous not only to manifest their own sense of the liberality of the donor, but as far as may be practicable to perpetuate its remembrance;

"*Resolved*, Therefore that $2,000, part of the purchase money of said land shall be applied to the finishing of the new Hall at the University, and that the same shall be called by the name of 'Gerrard Hall.'"

Five years afterwards this resolution was carried into effect. The spelling given is according to the original will of Major Gerrard. Judges Gaston and Badger, in reporting the foregoing resolutions, adopt the same. Afterwards the name was wrongly confounded with that of the founder of Girard College.

When this Hall was built it was intended to have a broad avenue running along the southern wall, east and west. Hence the porch on the south side of the building. The merchants of the village claimed that this would injure their trade by diverting travel from Franklin Street, and the plan was abandoned.

SOUTH BUILDING, UNIVERSITY OF NORTH CAROLINA

THE SOUTH BUILDING.

We will now turn to what we call the South, but what was known for many years as the "Main" Building. The European plan of a quadrangle—in old times a veritable prison in which the students were locked at night, was adopted, probably at the suggestion of Dr. Caldwell and Prof. Harris, who were educated at Princeton. Its corner-stone was laid in 1798. Its walls reached the height of a story and a half, and then remained roofless for years. Dr. Wm. Hooper, in his "Fifty Years Since," a most interesting and amusing production, tells how the students of that day packed in the East Building four in a room, built cabins in the corner of the South in order to secure greater privacy for devotion to their books, and how, "as soon as spring brought back the swallows and the leaves, they emerged from their den and chose some shady retirement, where they made a path and a promenade," like the Peripatetics of ancient Greece. He states moreover, what sounds strange to us, that holidays were sometimes given for the curious reason that the inclemency of the weather *prevented study*.

To finish this building was the great problem of the young University. The Trustees in despair did not hesitate to practise what was common in old times, even for building churches and denominational schools, but which the sounder morals of our day make a criminal offence, the raising of money by lotteries. Their circular of 1802 announces with sanctimonious gravity that "the interests of the University of North Carolina and of learning and science generally, are concerned in the immediate sale of these tickets." The highest prize was $1,500, and was drawn by Gen. Lawrence Baker, of Gates. The lucky number, 1138, was announced as an important item by the metropolitan journal, the Raleigh *Register*.

Still the building was unfinished, and still the intellectual squatters of the University sat *sub divo*, as the Professor of Latin would say. President Caldwell mounted with heroic energy his stick-back gig and painfully traveled over the State in 1809, and again in 1811, soliciting subscriptions.

It would be interesting to contrast his journeys with those of the present day, when one can dine in Goldsboro and breakfast next morning in Asheville. The battle of New Orleans occurred on the 8th of January, 1815. The news did not reach Raleigh until the 17th of February. Prof. Charles W. Harris writes in 1795 to Dr. Caldwell, at Princeton, that his best way of reaching Chapel Hill is to buy a horse and sulky and thus travel in his own conveyance, selling the same at Chapel Hill. He is confident that the trip can be made in *thirty days*. His baggage was sent by water to Petersburg and thence hauled by a passing wagon. The President of the present day can, without losing a night's rest, journey luxuriously from New York to Chapel Hill in less than one day. It was doubtless the achings and weariness of the flesh of these journeys which caused Dr. Caldwell, twenty years after, to astonish the State by his eloquent and practical Carlton letters, advocating the N. C. Railroad from the Tennessee line to Beaufort. His labors for the University were successful. He secured about $12,000, and while our people were going crazy over the naval victories of 1814, the rejoicing students moved into the completed "South Building." The corner-stone was laid the year when the great Napoleon gained the victory of the Pyramids, the year before he usurped the power of First Consul; it was finished the year when he laid down the imperial title for a petty throne in Elba, the year before his final ruin at Waterloo.

It was one of the grandest buildings in North Carolina in those days. It furnished for a third of a century halls and libraries for the two societies, which, before its erection, were forced to meet by turns in Person Hall. It should have been called in honor of the Father of the University, Gen. Davie. The omission thus to recognize his great services has been rectified by the happy thought of a gifted lady, on whom the Muses of History and Poesy have benignly breathed, Mrs. C. P. Spencer. She has named the historic tree which sheltered the venerable Commissioners, when, under its shade, they located the site of the University, and which, in spite of a century's storms and the fierce assault of the thunderbolt, still rears its majestic head above the neighboring oaks, the *Davie Poplar*.

SMITH HALL.

In 1852 the Trustees did tardy honor to the first benefactor of the University. As has been stated Governor Benjamin Smith, of Brunswick, made the first donation for the cause of higher education in North Carolina, namely, warrants for 20,000 acres of land in Tennessee. It is true they were not immediately available. They were afterwards surrendered to the Chickasaws and subsequently repurchased by the Government. It was forty years before they were made available. They were ultimately sold for $14,000, after being broken up by the severest earthquake which has afflicted America since its discovery, into lakes and hills. The proceeds went into the endowment and were swallowed up by the great civil war, which, with more terrible voracity than a hundred earthquakes, engulfed so much of the wealth and population of the Southern country.

Benjamin Smith was a man of mark. He was in youth an aide-de-camp of Washington in the disastrous defeat of Long Island. He was conspicuous for his gallantry under Moultrie. By his fiery eloquence the militia of Brunswick volunteered to serve under him in the threatened war against France. He was fifteen times Senator from Brunswick. He was chosen Governor in 1810. His county called its capital, Smithville, in his honor. His name survives too in the bleak and stormy island at the mouth of the Cape Fear. The land he gave us, as was also the land of Gerrard, was won by valor and blood in the war for freedom. Their sacrifices were not useless. Their monuments are far more enduring than brass or marble. Centuries will come and go. Families will grow great and be extinguished. Fortunes will be made and lost. Offices will be struggled for and ambitious hopes realized, but the names of the victors will vanish as if written on the sands of the sea-shore. Reputations blazing in pulpit, or forum, and senate chamber will fade as rapidly as the meteor's path. But the blessings of the gifts of Person, Gerrard and Smith will never cease. For nearly a century they have planted learning and sound principle in the minds of men over all our Southern land. In all the ages to come their work will go on.

The thousand young men, who will have their mental panoply supplied from the University armory to engage in life's varied conflicts, will hold their names in honor. As long as the University lasts they will never be forgotten, *and the University will last forever!*

New East—New West.

Prior to 1850 the highest number of students was 170. After the discovery of the California gold mines, and consequent increase in the supply of the circulating medium, there ensued wonderfully prosperous times for all the world, and especially for our Southern States. The old North Carolina families who had carried their *lares* and *penates* into the fertile regions of the southwest sent back their sons to their native State for education. Students swarmed into the University. They overflowed the old buildings and were camped in little cottages all over the town from Couchtown to Craig's. In 1858 there were as many as 461, of whom 178 were from other States than North Carolina. The New East and New West were built for their accommodation, finished in 1859. The two societies aided in a considerable degree in the construction and adornment of their beautiful halls and library rooms. Probably no societies in America have superior accommodations in these respects, and I am bound to say that in my opinion no societies by intelligent and honest devotion to the purposes of their creation better deserve them. Long may they flourish.

The Gymnasium is the property of a corporation, whose stockholders are friends and alumni of the University. It was ready for use in June, 1885.

The Memorial Hall

was erected to the memory of David L. Swain, for thirty years President, and of all the departed good and great—Trustees, Professors, Alumni—who have aided and honored the University. It is a Memorial too of those gallant Alumni who, at the call of our State, gave up their lives in the great civil war. Though God gave them not the victory, and though we will not question the wisdom of the decision of the All-Wise, yet we must always honor

MEMORIAL HALL—UNIVERSITY OF NORTH CAROLINA.

the courage, the devotion to duty, the high resolve and the willing sacrifice of our Confederate Dead.

The tablets on the walls not only show the widespread usefulness of the University, but call to mind every important epoch in our State history, from the Provisional Government of 1775 to the threshold of the present day, as appears from the following statement:

The Provisional Government of 1775–'76 is illustrated by the name of Samuel Johnston, who was the President of the Provincial Council, and therefore the first acting Governor of the State; also by Archibald MacLaine, member of the Committee of Safety for Wilmington, and by Waightstill Avery, signer of the Mecklenburg Declaration of May, 1775.

The Constitution of 1776 *and the War of the Revolution* are called to mind by the three above named, of whom Avery was the first Attorney-General of the State and, with MacLaine, was on the committee which reported the Constitution to the body which adopted it. Besides these are Benjamin Hawkins, aide-de-camp to Washington, Wm. Richardson Davie, Wm. Lenoir, Joseph Winston and Joseph Graham, all gallant fighters for freedom, and Richard Dobbs Spaight, Sr., likewise a soldier, but more famous as a member of the Continental Congress.

The adoption of the Constitution of the United States is illustrated by Spaight and Davie, members of the Convention which adopted it; by Samuel Johnston and Benjamin Hawkins, the first two Federal Senators from North Carolina, and by Wm. Lenoir, a member of the Conventions of our State, of 1788 and 1789, one of which refused, and the other agreed to adopt it.

The threatened French war is called to mind by Davie, who was appointed a General in the army, proposed for waging it, and was one of the Commissioners to France, who succeeded in averting it.

The war of 1812 is well commemorated by Wm. Hawkins, Governor, and Duncan Cameron, one of his aids; by Joseph Graham, a General in the expedition against the Creeks; by David Stone, United States Senator from North Carolina; and Wm. Gaston, a prominent member of the House of Representatives.

The acquisition of Florida is called to mind by Wm. D. Mosely, Governor of the Territory.

The first inauguration of Internal Improvements is especially noted by Archibald D. Murphy and Rev. Dr. Joseph Caldwell, the first and most earnest advocates of canal and railroad building.

The great Eastern and Western agitation, leading to the Convention of 1835, is brought to mind by the names of Wm. Gaston, David L. Swain, John Owen, Bartlett Yancey, Duncan Cameron, Willie P. Mangum, Calvin Graves, James W. Bryan, James Mebane, Wm. B. Shepard.

The hot controversies of *Jackson's time* are peculiarly commemorated by James K. Polk, Bedford Brown, Willie P. Mangum, John Owen, Wm. B. Shepard and others.

The important period of the *acquisition of Texas and the Mexican war* is revived by the tablets of James K. Polk, President, Wm. A. Graham, Governor, Michael Hoke, George E. Badger, Willie P. Mangum, Bedford Brown, Daniel M. Barringer, John M. Morehead, Burton Craige, Romulus M. Saunders and the three brothers, Wm. B., Charles B. and James B. Shepard.

The internal improvement era of 1848 is called up by the names of John M. Morehead, Calvin Graves, Haywood W. Guion, William A. Graham, Waightstill Avery, Jr., Romulus M. Saunders, Jonathan Worth, John D. Hawkins, Dr. Joseph W. Hawkins.

The compromise of 1850 *and the period preceding the Civil War* are called to mind by Graham, Badger, Morehead, W. Avery, Jr., R. M. Saunders, Jacob Thompson, Lewis Thompson, Patrick H. Winston.

Secession and the Civil War are largely represented on the walls of the Hall by civilians as well as soldiers, prominent in council or field. Among the civilians are Thomas Ruffin, Graham, Worth, W. Avery, Jr., Gov. Henry T. Clark, Walter F. Leak, Burton Craige, Jacob Thompson.

Of the military are Gen. Bryan Grimes, Gen. James Johnston Pettigrew, Gen. George B. Anderson, Col. W. Avery, Col. Clark M. Avery, Col. Isaac E. Avery, Major Joseph A. Engelhard, Major Joseph H. Saunders, Col. John L. Bridgers, Lieut. Wm. Preston Mangum.

The period of reconstruction is commemorated by Gov. Worth, Gov. Tod R. Caldwell, Lewis Thompson, Patrick H. Winston, Matthias E. Manly.

The Judicial history can be almost read from the tablets. It begins with Samuel Johnston, a Judge before the organization of the Supreme Court under the Act of 1818.

Of the Supreme Court, there are tablets to Chief Justices Leonard Henderson, Thomas Ruffin, Frederick Nash and Richmond M. Pearson, and to Associate Justices Wm. Gaston, Wm. H. Battle, Matthias E. Manly.

Of the Superior Court Judges are Archibald D. Murphy, John R. Donnell, Willie P. Mangum, Duncan Cameron, George E. Badger, David L. Swain, John M. Dick, R. M. Pearson, W. H. Battle, M. E. Manly, David F. Caldwell, James W. Osborne, Jesse G. Shepherd.

Of the Federal Courts is Judge John A. Cameron of the District Court of Florida.

There is a long list of Governors represented, beginning with Samuel Johnston, Chairman of the Provincial Council in 1775, and Governor in 1787; Richard Dobbs Spaight, Sr., 1792–'95; Wm. Richardson Davie, 1798–'99; David Stone, 1808; Wm. Hawkins, 1812; John Owen, 1828; David L. Swain, 1833–'35; Richard Dobbs Spaight, Jr., 1835; John M. Morehead, 1840–'44; Wm. A. Graham, 1844–'48; Henry T. Clark, 1861–'63; Jonathan Worth, 1866–'68; Tod R. Caldwell, 1870–'74.

The National Congress, before the adoption of the Constitution, has Richard Dobbs Spaight, Sr., Samuel Johnston, Benjamin Hawkins, Wm. R. Davie.

Senators of the United States are Samuel Johnston, Benjamin Hawkins, David Stone, Willie P. Mangum, Wm. A. Graham, George E. Badger, and M. E. Manly, the latter elected but not allowed to take his seat.

Representatives in Congress are Joseph Winston, Richard Dobbs Spaight, Sr., Alexander Mebane, David Stone, Wm. Gaston, James S. Smith, John H. Bryan, John Owen, Bartlett Yancey, R. D. Spaight, Jr., Wm. B. Shepard, Charles B. Shepard, Ebenezer Pettigrew, James K. Polk, D. M. Barringer, R. M. Saunders, Richard S. Donnell, Jacob Thompson.

Ministers to Foreign Nations are Wm. R. Davie, D. M. Barringer, R. M. Saunders.

Attorney-Generals of North Carolina are Waightstill Avery, Sr., R. M. Saunders, Bartholomew F. Moore, and Wm. A. Jenkins.

The Financial History of the State is illustrated by Thomas Ruffin and Duncan Cameron, Presidents of the leading early banks, and by Samuel Johnston, John Haywood, Jonathan Worth, State Treasurers.

The Teachers are largely represented. There are Presidents Joseph Caldwell and David L. Swain, Professors A. D. Murphy, Wm. Bingham, Wm. Hooper, Elisha Mitchell, James Phillips, J. DeB. Hooper, Ralph H. Graves, the elder, Carey D. Grandy, Wm. M. Green. Of these Wm. Hooper was afterwards President of Wake Forest College, and Bishop Green, Chancellor of the University of the South.

The great schools of the State are represented by Wm. Bingham, Wm. J. Bingham, his son, and Col. Wm. Bingham, his grandson, Alexander Wilson, Ralph H. Graves, the elder, J. DeB. Hooper, James B. Slade, the pioneer of higher female education in Georgia.

The Clergy has most able representatives: Charles Pettigrew, elected in 1795 first Bishop of the Episcopal church in North Carolina, Wm. Hooper, Wm. M. Green, Elisha Mitchell, Alexander Wilson, James Phillips, James Morrison, Francis L. Hawks, Joseph H. Saunders, the elder, Wm. Barringer.

The Medical Profession is abundantly honored by Simmons J. Baker, John B. Baker, James H. Dickson, James S. Smith, Joseph W. Hawkins, Frederick D. Lente, of New York.

The Legal Profession. It is unnecessary to repeat the names of those illustrating the legal profession. Of course the Judges and Attorney-Generals belong thereto, and most of those named as having held official stations. It may be well to name some who devoted themselves mainly to the bar. For example, B. F. Moore, Francis L. Dancy, James W. Bryan, H. W. Guion, Robert Strange, P. H. Winston, of Bertie, R. S. Donnell, Wm. F. Dancy.

Authors and Scientists are slimly, though ably represented. Lewis von Schweinitz, the great Botanist, Francis L. Hawks, Joseph Caldwell, Elisha Mitchell, David L. Swain, Wm. A. Graham, Haywood W. Guion.

Enlightened and successful men of business, but little engaged in public life, are here commemorated, viz. :

Richard Bennehan, Thomas D. Bennehan, James C. Johnston, Bryan Grimes, the elder, Richard Henry Lewis, James S. Battle, Edward J. Mallett, Wm. Peace, John D. Hawkins, Joseph H. Saunders, the younger.

There is a tablet to the *Donors of Land, embracing the site of the University,* and recently a tablet has been inserted to the memory of Miss Mary R. Smith, who donated a valuable tract of land in Chatham county for the education of students at the University.

The Hall was designed by Samuel Sloan, architect, and is one of the handsomest college buildings in the Union, its roof supported by semi-circular arches, from basement wall to basement wall, 128 feet in diameter, with not a column to break the view. Its seating capacity is 2,450, while, by making the aisles available, 4,000 people can be accommodated.

This noble building was dedicated on the 3rd of June, 1885. Rev. A. W. Mangum, D. D., Professor of Moral Philosophy, read the dedication Ode, adapted by himself. Rev. Charles Phillips, D. D., Professor Emeritus of Mathematics, offered up a most appropriate prayer, and Mr. Paul C. Cameron, Chairman of the Building Committee, in behalf of himself and associates on the committee, at the request of the Faculty, delivered an address on the University, very able and instructive. It is noticeable that Mr. Cameron had been an alumnus of the institution for sixty years. The Trustees unanimously passed a resolution of thanks to him for his personal supervision of the work, and for a timely loan of $8,000 needed for its completion. Resolutions of thanks to Governor Thos. J. Jarvis were also unanimously adopted for his valuable services while Governor in behalf of the University, in many directions, particularly in aiding the erection of this building.

DONATIONS AND APPROPRIATIONS.

The donations of Smith, Gerrard and Person have been mentioned, as also the contributions raised by President Caldwell for completing the South Building. Prior to 1797 sundry persons subscribed the sum of $7,648 for the purpose of erecting buildings.

In 1802 the ladies of Raleigh and Newbern contributed a pair of globes, a compass and a quadrant. The escheated land warrants granted by the State in 1789 realized to the University in 1836 about $150,000, which was lost during the civil war by reason of the insolvency of the bank, in the stock of which the endowment was invested. Other smaller amounts were received from time to time from escheats in North Carolina, balances unclaimed in hands of executors, etc., arrearages confiscated, etc., amounting to $134,000. This was used for current expenses, including building.

In 1875, at the solicitation of President Battle, then Secretary and Treasurer, a number of persons, principally alumni, contributed about $18,000 for the purpose of repairing the buildings, and subsequently a like amount was contributed for building the Memorial Hall. Soon afterwards the ladies of Raleigh and of Hillsborough contributed about $500 towards the purchase of apparatus.

The Land Grant.

In 1866 the General Assembly granted to the University 270,000 acres of land scrip with the obligation to establish at least two professorships, in which the leading object should be, as stated in the Act of Congress of July 2, 1862, without excluding other scientific and classical studies and including military tactics, to teach such branches of learning as are related to Agriculture and Mechanic Arts, in such manner as the General Assembly may prescribe, in order to promote the liberal and practical education of the industrial classes in the several pursuits and professions in life. It was further provided that the county court of each county should have the privilege to select one student, a native of the State and resident in such county, of good moral character and capacity for usefulness, and without means of his own, free of all charges for tuition and room-rent; and further that students should be admitted to this department without any requirements of previous education sufficient to enter the regular college course.

The scrip was sold in 1867 at the then market price of fifty cents per acre. Ten thousand dollars of the proceeds were used on account of the real estate of the University. The residue was invested in North Carolina bonds, partly special tax. In 1875, as the State had, in accepting the Land Grant, bound itself to keep the fund intact, the General Assembly gave its certificate for the original principal ($125,000), and directed the public Treasurer to pay the interest, $7,500 a year, regularly. This act enabled the institution to be reopened in 1875. The Trustees proceeded to carry into effect the above recited clause of the Act devoting the scrip, by paying special attention to Industrial and Agricultural Chemistry, Botany, Physiology, Zoölogy, Physics, Mechanics, Surveying, etc., pains being taken to make the instruction in these branches as practical as possible, while "other scientific and classical studies" were also taught. In the place of one laboratory the University had now five, viz: Chemical (quantitative as well as qualitative), Physical, Biological, Botanical, and Mineralogical. While classes were exercised in the field for purposes of instruction in those departments and also in surveying and engineering, the small amount, $7,500 per annum, which was not supplemented by grants from the State or other source, did not suffice for carrying on agricultural or mechanical works, or performing experiments for the benefit of the public.

In 1887 the General Assembly concluded to establish a separate Agricultural and Mechanical College at Raleigh, and ordered the $125,000 to be delivered to that institution as soon as it should be prepared to begin the work of instruction.

In 1867 the General Assembly granted the University $7,000 for the purpose of paying arrears due the Faculty.

In 1881 the Assembly made an appropriation of $5,000 per annum, and in 1885 of $15,000 per annum, for the support of the institution.

Hon. B. F. Moore, LL.D., of Raleigh, N. C., in 1878 bequeathed $5,000 in United States five per cent. bonds, the interest of which is to be applied to paying the tuition of students, to be appointed by his heirs, or, failing such appointment, by the Trustees of the University.

In 1880 Rev. Chas. F. Deems, D.D., LL.D., established a fund to be loaned, on security, to indigent students for defraying their expenses at the University of North Carolina. Mr. W. H. Vanderbilt added to it in 1881, and the amount of the principal is now

$13,300. The fund is of very great benefit to the poor young men of the State. Already 130 students have been assisted by it in obtaining higher education.

In 1885 Miss Mary Ruffin Smith, living near Chapel Hill, died, leaving to the University a valuable plantation in Chatham county, called Jones' Grove, the rent of which, or the interest of the proceeds if sold, is to be used in the education of such students as the Faculty may nominate. The fund is to be called the Francis Jones Smith Fund, after her brother from whom she inherited the land. The property is worth about $14,000 or $15,000.

The earliest donations of books to the Library were made by Judge John Williams, James Reid, of Wilmington, Gov. Wm. R. Davie, Prof. David Ker, Richard Bennehan, Abram Hodge, the Centre Benevolent Society, Francis N. W. Burton, Wm. H. Hill, Edward Jones, Joseph Gautier, Joseph B. Hill, Calvin Jones. The most considerable donation in recent years was by Mrs. Cornelia P. Spencer, about one thousand volumes from the library of her father, Rev. Dr. James Phillips.

Plan of Instruction.

As soon as the corner-stone was laid, the Trustees took steps for organizing a plan of instruction in the University. The committee appointed for the purpose on the 4th of December, 1792, was an able one. The chairman was the Rev. Dr. Samuel McCorkle. Associated with him were David Stone, Alfred Moore, Samuel Ashe, Hugh Williamson and John Hay, an eminent lawyer of Fayetteville, whose name survives in Haymount. Of these McCorkle and Stone were graduates of Princeton; Williamson, a graduate and ex-professor of the University of Pennsylvania. Moore's education at Boston was interrupted by the Revolutionary War, but he was a well read and accomplished man. Hay was distinguished for his literary acquirements.

The committee reported through Dr. McCorkle on the 5th of December, 1792, that "taking into consideration the financial condition of the University, the pursuits of literature and science should be confined to the following objects: . . . The study of languages, particularly the English; the acquirement of historical knowledge,

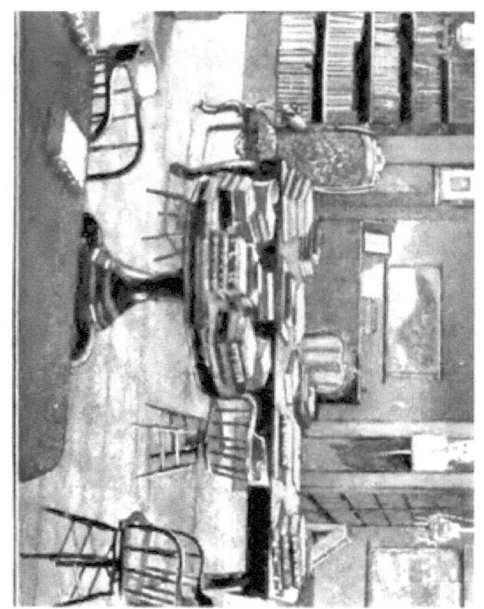
SECTION OF LIBRARY—UNIVERSITY OF NORTH CAROLINA.

ancient and modern; the study of the Belles-Lettres, Mathematics and Natural Philosophy; the improvement of the intellectual powers, including a rational system of Logic and Moral Philosophy; information on Botany, to which should be added a competent knowledge of the theory and practice of agriculture best suited to the climate and soil of this State; the principles of architecture."

They further recommended the purchase of apparatus for experimental Philosophy and Astronomy. In this they would include a set of globes, barometer, thermometer, microscope, telescope, quadrant, prismatic glass, electrical machine and an airpump. The committee recommended the purchase of a library, the selection of the books to be left to the Faculty.

The report is remarkable for the great prominence of scientific studies, and those of a practical nature. The scheme is almost identical with that adopted by Congress for the colleges to be formed under what is known as the Agricultural and Mechanical College Land Grant Act of 1862. Not many years elapsed, however, before classical studies were given the prominence usual in the colleges of the day.

On the 21st of December, 1793, the committee made an additional report, recommending the election of a "presiding professor," and if the receipts from tuition should justify it, one assistant. The style of the presiding officer was "Professor of Humanity." This term expressive of the widely ramifying duties of the new professor, signified "mental cultivation befitting man"—such intellectual panoply as the perfect man should possess; and as from mediaeval traditions still dominant in the higher institutions of learning, modern science was little known and less regarded, this mental panoply was held mainly to include languages, and grammar, and rhetoric, and poetry, and especially the study of the ancient classics.

It was carefully provided in the strongest terms that neither the professor nor his assistant should have any claim, right or preference to the Presidency of the University.

The doors of the Institution were ordered to be opened on the 15th of January, 1795, and the session was to continue for eleven months, with only one week's vacation in summer, beginning with the 10th of July.

The tuition was graded according to the studies taken. For Reading, Writing, Arithmetic, and Book-keeping, $8 per year; for the Latin, Greek, and French Languages, English Grammar, Geography, History, and Belles-Lettres, for any or all, $12.50; for Geometry, with its practical branches, Astronomy, Natural and Moral Philosophy, Chemistry and the principles of Agriculture, for all or any of them, $15.

The salary of the Professor of Humanity was $300 per annum and two-thirds of the tuition fees. If an assistant should be found necessary, he was to be paid $200 and the other one-third of the fees.

The Professor of Humanity was elected by ballot. As showing to some extent who were prominent in educational circles in that day, the names of those nominated are given. They were Rev. Dr. Samuel McCorkle, Dr. David Ker, the Rev. George Micklejohn, Rev. Robert Archibald, Mr. John Brown, Rev. James Tate, and Andrew Martin.

The friends of Dr. McCorkle expected his election, as in their opinion he was eminently suitable by reason of his learning, experience, and enthusiasm for the new institution. But I find that General Davie was opposed to him, probably on account of his deficiency in business qualifications, and Davie's influence was potent.

Rev. David Ker was a graduate of Trinity College, Dublin. He was pastor of the Presbyterian Church in Fayetteville, and was principal of a school as well. He was a man of ability and learning, but held his office for only one year. After leaving the University he studied law, and was appointed by Jefferson at the instance of David Stone, then Senator, Judge of the Mississippi Territory, in which position he died in 1810, leaving the reputation of an able and faithful officer. He is said to have exchanged his calvinistic tenets for a mild form of infidelity.

Professor Charles W. Harris, who was soon afterwards chosen at a salary of $200 per annum and one-third of the fees, was a native of Cabarrus, one of that excellent family which for about a century has been among the best and most intelligent in the country. He was a graduate of Princeton, and was evidently a superior man. After the resignation of Dr. Ker he was placed in charge of the

University, though not styled President. He was a young man, evidently fond of politics—was reading law while at the University. He, too, was for awhile tinctured with the prevailing Voltaireism of the day, but soon, it is said, he returned to the true faith. He seems to have enjoyed the entire confidence of the Trustees. He would doubtless have won a high position in our State if he had not been cut off by early death from pulmonary consumption. It was his sagacity which caused the election of Joseph Caldwell, his college-mate at Princeton, as his successor in the chair of mathematics, an election which gave the University what it needed—an able, energetic and wise leader.

The *North Carolina Journal*, of February 23rd, 1795, gives a spirited account of the opening day of the new institution, on which Providence did not smile. The Governor of the State, Richard Dobbs Spaight, accompanied by several members of the General Assembly and by the Trustees of the University, rode in state over the muddy mid-winter road. The clouds gathered and wept cold tears over the melancholy scene. The editor's imagination warms at the idea of the number who would have been present on the " much desired occasion" but for "the unfavorable state of the weather." The Governor and his cortege found for their inspection under the gloomy sky and among the giant trees, waving their leafless branches in the icy wind, an unfinished two-story building of new brick, splashed with mortar; the red hole in the ground which marked the site of the future Chapel; an unpainted President's house and steward's hall of wood; a village without houses, and with its streets overgrown with forest trees; a solitary professor and not a single student.

The coming of students was delayed by the inclement winter, and the impassable state of the roads, bridges being seldom found over streams ordinarily fordable. It was the 12th of February when the first student arrived. He was from Wilmington—his name, Hinton James. The Faculty records show that he was faithful and successful. For several years students were required to read original compositions on Saturdays, and those deemed especially meritorious were posted in an honor book. The name of Hinton James occurs often on this roll. His subjects show that he had a bias towards science, such as " The Uses of the Sun," the " Commerce of Britain," "The Motions of the Earth." He became afterwards a civil engineer, an assistant of Fulton in his work on our rivers. Some results of their labors may be still seen on the Cape Fear. He served his county for several terms as Senator in the General Assembly.

The next students who arrived were Alfred and Maurice Moore, sons of Judge Moore, both of whom served in the General Assembly afterwards, the former attaining the dignity of Speaker of the House; John Taylor, who became Clerk of the Superior Court of Orange; Hutchings G. Burton, who became Governor of this State; and Robert Burton, his brother, afterwards a Judge of the Superior Court. In four months there were forty-one students in attendance, and by the end of the year about one hundred, many of whom were in the preparatory department.

Mr. James mentions that no uniform dress was used in his day. In 1827 the Trustees prescribed a uniform of dark gray in summer and blue in winter, but six months afterwards changed the winter color to dark gray, so that it is probable that our boys were the first in our State to wear the dress which is so intimately associated in Southern minds with the tenderness and pathos and heroism of the Lost Cause. A solemn ordinance was adopted at the same time, which sounds strange in our ears, "The wearing of boots by the students is positively prohibited." This law was passed doubtless on account of the financial panic of 1825, but, like all sumptuary laws, was regularly circumvented. We have it on the authority of the late Judge Battle, who graduated in 1820, that the College servant, known as "Brad," owned a pair of these objectionable articles, which he rented to students for a handsome sum whenever they particularly desired to shine in the eyes of the ladies. The Seniors, during the commencement in which they graduated, were exempt from the prohibitory boot law by special exception to the ordinance, and it was not long before ambitious Juniors, Sophomores and Freshmen obtained the distinguished privilege.

THE STEWARD.

The number of inhabitants of the village of Chapel Hill was so small that at the beginning and for many subsequent years a

NEW EAST BUILDING—UNIVERSITY OF NORTH CAROLINA

steward was appointed, who gave bond and security for furnishing the students their table board. It is interesting to inspect the bill of fare of 1795, provided at $3 per month.

For breakfast: milk or coffee and tea, or chocolate and tea, one warm roll, or loaf of bread, or corn bread and butter.

For dinner: that noble Anglo-Saxon dish, which has built more railroads, dug more canals, fought more battles, and felled more forests than any other ration in history, namely: bacon and greens. For this might be substituted beef and turnips. With these must be furnished fresh meat and fowl, for which the steward could substitute puddings and tarts.

For supper, the ration was either coffee, or tea, or milk, and bread or biscuit—not any butter.

In addition to the above, potatoes and other vegetable food usual in North Carolina were prescribed. It was expressly understood that when milk was furnished, neither coffee, nor tea, nor chocolate was required, "unless for boys who eat no milk." By an amendment to the agreement the supplying with milk was delayed until the 1st day of May, and wheat bread and biscuit until the 1st of August. For the months of January, February and March thereafter, the wheat bread was allowed to be cold, but well risen. The ration of butter was limited to one ounce, and in place of butter meat might be substituted by permission of the Faculty. For supper, milk was required from May 15th to September 15th, coffee, or tea, or chocolate afterwards. These amendments were in favor of the steward, but a great concession was won by the students, which must have tended to increase their respect for the Sabbath, namely, that during January, February and March, puddings and tarts on Sundays were obligatory.

It is noticeable that the hours for meals were at 8 o'clock a. m., 1 o'clock p. m., and supper "before or after candlelight, as the Faculty may prescribe."

If the steward had faithfully complied with the terms of this contract in spirit and letter, it is clear that all things needful for the body were supplied, but the records show that there was interminable wrangling both about the quantity and quality of the food furnished. Some of the wealthier students preferred to walk from one and a half to two miles to houses in the country for their meals, and it was the rule for the others to supplement their rations at commons by night suppers, sometimes fairly paid for, sometimes captured in nocturnal hunts for persimmon-loving opossums, sometimes obtained by illicit raids on gardens and poultry yards. The tradition of this latter practice led a juvenile Juvenal, who was a student nearly fifty years ago—now one of the most distinguished lawyers of all our alumni—in a satirical description of Chapel Hill, to write of it as a place

> "Where demand and supply,
> Your all-conquering law,
> Robs barrels and hen-roosts
> From Pinhook to Haw."

Old students will remember that Pinhook was a cross-roads not far from the town of Durham.

The plan of "living at commons," though necessary in the early days on account of the want of boarding houses, was finally abandoned about 1840. Long before this large numbers of the students refused to patronize the official table, and paid higher prices elsewhere. About six years afterward Steward's Hall was sold and removed from the campus.

THE CURRICULUM.

The experience of the first year demonstrated that a number of the students, owing to the paucity of good schools in the State, were not prepared for collegiate instruction. In December, 1796, there was established a Preparatory department, which arrangement continued for a number of years.

At the same time a curriculum, or course of studies for the University proper, was adopted. The plan called for five professorships, namely: 1. Rhetoric, and Belles-Lettres; 2. Moral and Political Philosophy, and History; 3. Natural Philosophy; 4. Mathematics; 5. Languages.

The ancient classics were made optional, the degree of Bachelor of Arts (A. B.) being obtainable without the study of either. In 1800, doubtless through the influence of Professor Caldwell, who was a strong advocate of the classics, Latin was made a required study, and the year afterwards either French or Greek was also made essential. In 1804 Greek was made obligatory, thus inaugurating the course which dominated the University exclusively until 1875, over seventy years.

It is true a "School for the application of Science to the Arts" was inaugurated in 1854, two professorships being added, namely, that of Civil Engineering and that of applied Chemistry, in which the degree of Bachelor of Science was obtainable, but as the science students could obtain their Bachelor of Arts degree one year before that of Bachelor of Science, the course leading to the latter was in effect post-graduate, and the number pursuing it was small.

In 1875 the University was reorganized on the basis of largely increased liberty of election and much greater proportion of scientific and linguistic studies. Three courses lead to degrees: one to that of Bachelor of Arts (A. B.), including both Latin and Greek; another to that of Bachelor of Philosophy (Ph. B.), with Latin or Greek replaced by French or German; and the third replacing both the classics with French, German, and scientific studies. Besides these, students are allowed to take an optional course, leading to no degree, but in number of hours employed equivalent to the regular courses. Teachers' certificates are given to those completing a course of two years specially prescribed. The classical course is "the old curriculum," but with a larger proportion of scientific studies. The degrees of Doctor of Philosophy (Ph. D.), Master of Arts (A. M.), and Master of Science (M. S.), are conferred upon students who have completed post-graduate studies prescribed by the Faculty. The first (Ph. D.) requires the equivalent of two years' study in two departments, and the others, the equivalent of one year's study in three departments. Special certificates are given for proficiency in any department.

The classical course, corresponding to that inaugurated in 1804, has still its hold on those seeking higher education, the number of graduates for the last ten years being 110, while those who took one ancient language number 64, and those who took neither of them number 20. There is, however, even in the classical course, much greater attention paid to scientific studies and those included under the general name of English studies than formerly.

EARLY STRUGGLES.

The University had in its early days severe struggles for success. Its income was exceedingly small. The people of the State had little money on account of the difficulty of getting crops to market over the long and rough roads. It was almost impossible to obtain competent professors on the meagre salaries offered, and when obtained, they soon resigned their places for better compensation elsewhere. Acting President Ker left the institution after only one year's teaching; Prof. Samuel A. Holmes, after two years; Prof. W. E. Webb, one year; Prof. Charles W. Harris served one year; Judge Murphy, one year; Prof. Wm. Bingham, four years; Prof. Gillespie, two years. Dr. Joseph Caldwell was the only early professor who determined to burn his ships and make the care of the University his life work. His indomitable perseverance and dauntless pluck often saved the tottering fabric from ruin.

Not only was there a paucity of numbers, but the violence and unruliness of spirit among the few students in attendance show that there was little scholarly spirit in the land. Fights, often with knives and pistols, shown if not used, were common. Drunkenness and riots were frequent. Infidelity was the fashion of the day and invaded the Faculty as well as the student body.

Another great obstacle to success was the defective mode of government. The Trustees, although meeting seldom and engrossed in other pursuits, deemed it their duty to claim a large share in regulating the discipline, often as an appellate tribunal reversing the sentences of the Faculty. There was no one of them who could give that continuous supervision, so absolutely necessary to secure good results. Davie did a great work in inaugurating the institution, but his home was in Halifax, several days' journey from Chapel Hill. He was much engaged in an extensive law practice, and in gubernatorial and legislative duties. In 1799 he was long absent from the country on his peace mission to France, and in 1805, after a heated canvass for Congress, in which he was overwhelmed by the rising tide of Republicanism, he transferred his home to South Carolina. It was not until after many years' proof of fitness for the task that the Trustees gave to Dr. Caldwell and

PHILANTHROPIC SOCIETY HALL—UNIVERSITY OF NORTH CAROLINA.

his Faculty that power and responsibility which must be possessed by those in authority in every business in order to secure its proper conduct.

The catalogue of students proves clearly how slowly the institution progressed on its upward path. The first class of graduates, in 1798, contained seven; the second, nine; the third, three. In each of the years 1800, 1802, 1803 and 1805 there were only three. The sky brightened in 1808 when there were thirteen. But two years afterward an unfortunate effort was made to force students habitually to inform on one another, which caused the reduction of the senior class to one in 1811.

After this there was a constant though irregular progress; for the ten years prior to 1830 averaging about thirty, then declining until 1840. From 1840 to 1850 there was an average of over thirty. From 1850 to 1860 was the period of greatest prosperity, the number of graduates reaching ninety-six in 1858, and the highest number of matriculates being 461 in that year.

The prosperity of the University has, of course, always been dependent on the financial condition of the country. In the good times of 1821 to 1825 the attendance was nearly equal to that in Governor Swain's time of 1837 to 1850.

Doctor Caldwell.

President Caldwell was an extraordinary man. The pen portraits drawn of him by such able observers as Paul C. Cameron, Walker Anderson and others, show us a character, brave and strong, full of energy and courage; a scholar, yet a man of action; genial and kindly, yet stern in discipline; a true Christian; a courteous, high-toned gentleman. His benevolence extended beyond the sphere of his daily duties. His labors for popular education and for the building of a railroad from the Tennessee line to the Atlantic, show broad and enlightened views.

For thirty years he was the Atlas on whose shoulders our University world rested. The Trustees and Faculty learned to confide not only in his sincerity of purpose, which all admitted, but in his skill as a teacher, and wisdom as an executive officer. The students, although often smarting under the severity of his censures, carried into their maturer life a profound respect for him—in most cases veneration and love. Among them were many leaders of the people in all the States south of the Potomac, comprising a President and Vice-President of the United States, members of the cabinet and foreign ministers, National and State Senators and Representatives, judges of the highest courts, Governors, professors in colleges and eminent teachers, great divines—in fact, men eminent in all the pursuits of life.

President Caldwell's prosperity culminated in 1824, when the financial condition of the University was so good as to allow the Trustees to send him to Europe for the purchase of scientific apparatus and books, appropriating $6,000 for the purpose. Mr. Cameron gives a glowing account of the illumination of the buildings in honor of his return. It was only two years after this when the effects of the financial crisis of 1825 were felt in the diminution of students and of income. As usual in such cases, the Trustees, hoping for a favorable change, postponed the reduction of the Faculty, borrowing money to meet deficiencies, incurring a debt of nearly $40,000. It was then, and long afterwards, generally thought that all of the property of the institution was liable to be sold for its debts and the doors could be closed. This direful evil was threatened, and while the good President's heart was torn by anxiety on this acccount, he was attacked by a most painful and lingering disease. His sun went down in the deepest gloom, after nine years of bodily and mental suffering, on the 27th of January, 1835, at the age of sixty. A cast was taken of his head after death, and the bust in the Philanthropic Hall, executed by this means, preserves faithfully his features. He is buried at the old monument, near the Dialectic Hall, with his second wife and his stepson, Dr. William Hooper, sleeping by his side. When President Polk visited Chapel Hill at the commencement of 1847, the project for erecting a more handsome monument of marble was inaugurated. He has a nobler monument still in the county named in his honor by a grateful and admiring Legislature.

Dr. Caldwell's specialty was Mathematics. He was the author of a book on Geometry, in which, as an appendix, is a treatise on Trigonometry. He was particularly partial to Astronomy. Prof.

James L. Love has shown in a well-written monograph that he is entitled to the credit of having built the first Astronomical Observatory in America, connected with a college. It was on a knoll a few hundred yards southeast of the campus. In it were a meridian transit instrument, a zenith telescope, a refracting telescope, an astronomical clock, a sextant, a reflecting circle, and a Hadley's quadrant. Observations were made for several years, in 1832 and afterwards, by him and Professors Mitchell and Phillips. The instruments were removed after his death on account of leakage in the roof, and the abandoned building was soon destroyed by fire.

Dr. Caldwell was Professor of Mathematics and Chairman of the Faculty from 1798 to 1804, then President until 1812, teaching Mathematics at the same time; then at his earnest request he was relieved of the Presidency. His successor was Rev. Robert Hett Chapman, D. D., a good and learned man, but not successful as an executive officer. The records show that his difficulties chiefly came from the intensity of political feeling in those war times. He was a Federalist and nearly all the students were Republicans. Their hostility to him culminated in contemptuous injury to his property. Dr. Caldwell obtained a warrant against the perpetrators and forced the students to divulge the names of the guilty parties under process of law. Dr. Chapman resigned after a troublous incumbency of four years, and Dr. Caldwell was forced reluctantly to resume the headship, only to lay it down with his life.

TENNESSEE LANDS SOLD.

The echoes of Dr. Caldwell's funeral bell had hardly died away when the dark clouds passed from the sky of the University. The escheated lands of the Revolutionary soldiers, who had died without heirs, located in West Tennessee, belonging to the University, were bringing little profit to the institution. The Secretary, Charles Manly, was sent by the Trustees, in conjunction with their agent, Samuel Dickens, to sell the whole, including the 20,000 acres donated by Governor Smith in 1790. Speculation in western lands was buoyant, purchasers were readily found, and an endowment, after paying all debts, of about $150,000 was received. $100,000 of this was invested in bank stocks, drawing eight per cent. dividends, and a total income of about $12,000 yearly, in addition to tuition receipts, was received. An assured salary could be offered to a new President, and additional professors employed.

Governor Swain.

The choice of the Trustees for the Presidency fell on David L. Swain, who, at the age of thirty-four, had filled with honor the offices of Solicitor, Judge and Governor, besides being a member of the General Assembly and Convention. In his busy life he had not been able to read many books, but he had great knowledge of men, a large brain, a powerful memory, a genial temper, and kindly heart, ready wit and unfailing tact. While his person was ungainly, his manner was imposing, and he was a most effective speaker. His administrative powers were of a high order. He had the prestige of success. He had large acquaintance with North Carolina, and has left valuable monographs on various portions of its history.

The procurement of an endowment and the election of a popular ex-Governor as President, caused an immediate accession of matriculates. The number rose from 89 in 1836 to 142 in 1837, and 169 in 1838. For the first twelve years of Swain's administration the attendance averaged somewhat larger than during the best years of Caldwell's. The increase was not, however, in proportion to the increase of population, nor to the better facilities for travelling. This was the result of the extreme low prices of agricultural products during this period. Cotton was as low as five cents per pound in 1844 and 1845. After 1850, owing to rapid increase of prosperity in the South by extension of the cotton culture, combined with the increase of slaves, and to the completion of railroads, making travelling more easy, the number rapidly grew. In 1853–'54 there were 281, of whom 220 were from North Carolina; in 1857–'58 and 1858–'59 the maximum was reached; 461 in the former year, of whom 168 were from other states, and in the latter 456, of whom 178 were from beyond our borders. Then the effects of the panic of 1857, and the apprehensions of the coming war began to be felt. In 1859–'60 there were 430; in 1860–'61 only 376.

Being a Southern Institution, the sons of the University rushed into the war with all the *élan* of Southern character. Trustees, alumni, professors, tutors, students, ceased reading of the old wars of Greece and Rome, ceased disputing about the conflicts of chemical atoms, ceased pondering over the solution of mathematical problems, threw aside their books and their studies, gave up fair hopes and scholarly leisure and life itself, without grudging the magnitude of the sacrifice. Into that great vortex were plunged the largest portion of our wealth and much of the best youth of our country; but none who died left a wider remembrance or more sincere mourners than the sons of the University, the victims of the great civil war.

The University was one of the few Southern institutions which kept its light burning throughout that dark and bitter period. The perseverance of President Swain and the elders of his coadjutors (his younger associates had gone to the war), kept that light in steady radiance until Kilpatrick's cavalry tramped through the streets of Chapel Hill.

The terrible blow to higher education by the disastrous struggle may be gathered from the simple facts that out of the 95 Freshmen who matriculated in 1857-'58 only 10, out of the 80 Freshmen of 1858-'59 only 1, and out of the 68 Freshmen of 1859-'60 only 5, remained to receive their diplomas at graduation. Taking the three classes together, 227 out of 243 lost their opportunity of higher education; nearly all of them enlisting in the army. The tablets in Memorial Hall contain 260 names of our alumni who lost their lives in the Confederate cause, beginning with Lieutenant-General, Bishop Polk, who matriculated in 1821, and ending with John R. Haughton and Frederick Nash, matriculates of 1862, James J. Phillips, of 1863, and Wm. H. C. Webb, of 1864. The researches of Dr. Stephen B. Weeks have added at least ten to the mournful list.

As the personal and official prosperity of Dr. Caldwell culminated in 1824, so that of Governor Swain culminated in 1859. He had been recently honored with the degree of LL. D., by Yale University. The commencement of that year was a most brilliant occasion. President Buchanan was present, with Secretary Thompson, and many of the most distinguished citizens of the State. The University was in a most prosperous condition. Its income largely exceeded its expenditures. The General Assembly, as a favor, had granted it the right to subscribe for $200,000 in the new Bank of North Carolina. Half of the stock was paid for, and it had money owing it by individuals sufficient, with a few years' savings, to pay for the other half. Thus would be secured $16,000 a year, which, added to tuition receipts, would make a total annuity of over $35,000.

From that year the troubles of the worthy President began—troubles, personal and official. His sense of hearing became more and more dull. The numbers of the University began to fall off as the mutterings of the coming storm were heard.

War began, and for four years the institution he loved so well was the object of the most painful solicitude. While he had private means sufficient for his own support, his professors found it difficult to live on their salaries, paid in depreciated currency. But for the liberty given them by the Trustees, to cut fuel from the University lands, they would have been compelled to resort to other pursuits in order to procure the necessities of life. At the end of 1862 a professor's salary was worth 60 barrels of flour; at the end of 1863, 20 barrels; at the end of 1864, 9 barrels; and in the spring of 1865, about 4 barrels. The number of students dwindled to 60, with a Junior class of two. By the destruction of the value of the Confederate and State treasury notes and bonds, the close of the war found the bank stock of the University worthless. The endowment was gone, but the debts remained—about $100,000, the major part incurred for the worthless stock. The salaries of the professors could not be paid out of the meagre tuition receipts of only 76 students in 1865, 107 in 1866, and 86 in 1867. The General Assembly granted $7,000 for one year, but the relief was partial only. By the exertions of President Swain, the Agricultural College land scrip was issued to the State, and transferred to the University, but, except for a small amount, the proceeds could be made available only after long delay. A thorough reorganization was deemed advisable, and to that end the members of the Faculty placed their resignations in the hands of the Trustees. A scheme of reorganization, more in accordance with modern ideas, very much like that now prevailing, reported by a committee of Trustees, Messrs. K. P. Battle, William A.

NEW WEST BUILDING—UNIVERSITY OF NORTH CAROLINA

Graham, and S. F. Phillips, through Mr. Battle, the chairman, was adopted to go into operation in the fall of 1868. At the Commencement of that year, it was apparent that the Trustees would soon lose their places in pursuance of the changes in the mode of appointing Trustees, ordained by the constitution adopted under the Reconstruction Acts of Congress. They therefore refused to accept the resignations of the Faculty, and directed the exercises to be resumed, as was accustomed after the usual vacation.

As was expected the old Trustees were removed in July, 1868, and others appointed in their stead. These at once vacated the chairs of all the members of the Faculty. President Swain claimed that, as by the new Constitution the President of the University was made *ex-officio* a Trustee of the same, his office was placed beyond the authority of the Board. This claim was not allowed, and he did not appeal to the courts. Soon afterwards he was so severely wounded by being thrown from his carriage by a runaway horse, that he died on the 27th of August, his last thoughts, like Caldwell's, being on the apparent ruin of an institution he loved better than his life.

NOTES ABOUT THE PROFESSORS.

Among the coadjutors of Caldwell and Swain, the following are specially mentioned on account of the length and faithfulness of service, or because of their attaining distinction in other fields.

Professors Ker, Harris and Archibald D. Murphy, of the early professors, have already been described. Rev. Wm. Bingham, a learned and most faithful professor, founder of the Bingham School, which has been continued with eminent ability by his son, William J., and his grandsons, Col. William and Major Robert Bingham, was an emigrant from North Ireland, in the latter part of the last century.

Ethan A. Andrews, LL. D., and Denison Olmsted, LL. D., were called back to Yale College, and were the authors of valuable text-books in their respective departments of Latin and Natural Philosophy. While in North Carolina Prof. Olmsted made a report on the Geology of the State, said to be the first in point of time in the Union.

Rev. Elisha Mitchell, D. D., LL. D., a native of Connecticut, was an indefatigable and successful worker in the development of the Botany, Geology and Mineralogy of North Carolina. He was the author of many monographs on these subjects of great value, including text-books in Chemistry and Geology. After the death of Dr. Caldwell, he was Chairman of the Faculty until the arrival of Governor Swain, and frequently acted in that capacity in the absence of the latter from Chapel Hill. He had a very great brain, and if he had confined himself to a specialty, would have won world-wide distinction. He began his service for the University as Professor of Mathematics. After eight years in this department he was transferred to the chair of Chemistry, Geology and Mineralogy, but he extended his reading into all departments, including theology, and even law. The stone walls around the campus and other University lands are monuments to his memory at Chapel Hill, while he sleeps on the summit of the highest peak of the Black, named in his honor, in exploring which he lost his life on June 16th, 1858. He and Olmsted and Andrews were graduates of Yale University.

Rev. James Phillips, D. D., was a native of England. He died at the post of duty, suddenly, on the Chapel rostrum, as he was about to conduct morning prayers one day in 1867, after having faithfully served the institution for forty-one years. He was a preacher of great force and fervor, and was a profound scholar, especially in pure and applied mathematics and in theology. He was succeeded by his son, Rev. Charles Phillips, D. D., LL. D., who gained great reputation in the South, both as an instructor and preacher. After being superseded as heretofore mentioned in 1868, he served as Professor of Mathematics in Davidson College until 1875, when he was invited to resume his chair at the University, serving during that year as Chairman of the Faculty. Three years later he was forced by ill health to tender his resignation of his professorship, but consented, at the request of the Trustees, to allow his name to continue in the list of the Faculty as Professor Emeritus. He has recently removed to Birmingham, Ala.

Professor Walker Anderson embraced the profession of the law and became Chief Justice of Florida.

Wm. M. Green, D. D. LL. D., was the Protestant Episcopal Bishop of Mississippi, and Chancellor of the University of the South. He was one of the last survivors of the class of President Polk (1818), dying in 1887, leaving Rev. Dr. Robert Hall Morrison the sole survivor and oldest living graduate.

Rev. Wm. Hooper, D. D., was a grandson of Wm. Hooper, a signer of the Declaration of Independence. He was at one time President of Wake Forest College, at another, Professor in the University of South Carolina. He was an elegant writer, as his published sermons and addresses show. He was engaged in the instruction of youth, male or female, for sixty-six years.

His cousin and son-in-law, John DeBerniere Hooper, was a teacher for forty-one years. He was an accurate and well-read scholar and was possessed of an elegant style as a writer.

Rev. Charles F. Deems, D. D. LL. D., born in Maryland, is Pastor of the Church of the Strangers, New York, and is the author of several able and popular religious works, viz.: "Who Was Jesus," "The Home Altar," "Weights and Wings," etc. He is a preacher of great power, and in that capacity, and as President of the American Institute of Christian Philosophy, and editor of *Christian Thought,* exercises a wide influence.

Wm. H. Battle, LL. D., was Judge of the Superior Court of North Carolina from 1840 to 1852 and of the Supreme Court from 1852 to 1868. He was at one time Reporter of the decisions of the Supreme Court, and reprinted with annotations volumes of old reports, which had become out of print. He was also one of the authorized compilers of the Revised Statutes, and sole compiler of Battle's Revisal.

His associate in the School of Law, Samuel Field Phillips, son of Rev. Dr. James Phillips, held under this State the positions of Reporter, of Auditor, and of Speaker of the House of Commons; and under the United States, the office of Solicitor General.

Rev. Albert M. Shipp, D. D., LL. D., after leaving the University, was President of Wofford College, and Dean of the Theological department of Vanderbilt University. He was a very able preacher.

Manuel Fetter, a native of New York, was Professor of Greek for thirty years, and then a teacher of boys for twenty years longer, making fifty years spent in teaching. He had a peculiar hold on the affections of those who studied under him at the University.

Rev. Fordyce M. Hubbard, D. D., born in Massachusetts, was master of an elegant style, and was author of various historical and literary essays of great merit. He was very learned in classical and English literature.

Nicholas M. Hentz was distinguished for his learning as an entomologist, and published an exhaustive monograph on spiders. He was the husband of the authoress, Mrs. Caroline Lee Hentz.

Rev. John Thomas Wheat, D. D., was widely known as a minister of the gospel for about sixty years. His work lay chiefly in Tennessee, Virginia, and this State.

Rev. Andrew D. Hepburn, D. D., LL. D., a native of Pennsylvania, after leaving the University became President of Davidson College, and a professor in Miami College, in Ohio. He has published an excellent text-book on Rhetoric. He is a learned and accurate scholar, especially in mental and moral philosophy.

Prof. William J. Martin, LL. D., a native of Virginia, was a meritorious officer (Colonel), of the Confederate war. He has been about twenty years Professor of Chemistry at Davidson College, and has acted as President with great acceptability.

Prof. Benjamin S. Hedrick, after leaving North Carolina, was for many years chemical expert in the Patent Office at Washington, D. C.

Of the Tutors, John M. Morehead and Wm. D. Mosely became Governors, the former of North Carolina, the latter of Florida; M. E. Manly became Judge of the Superior and Supreme Courts of the State; Anderson Mitchell and James Martin, Judges of the Superior Courts; Giles Mebane, Speaker of the Senate; Jacob Thompson attained Cabinet positions in the United States, and then the Confederate States; Gavin Hogg was a leader of the bar of the State; Lewis Williams was for years member of the House of Representatives; H. C. Jones, Reporter of the Supreme Court of the State; Edward D. Sims, Professor of the University of Georgia; James H. Otey, Protestant Episcopal Bishop of Tennessee; R. H. Graves, Principal of prominent schools for males.

The Board of Trustees.

The Board of Trustees, under the Constitution of 1868, was composed of one from each county, appointed by the Board of Education, with the members of the latter *ex-officio* Trustees of the University. The Board thus constituted elected new professors, with Rev. Solomon Pool, D. D., President. The doors of the institution were opened, and in 1869–'70 a catalogue was published, showing a list of 35 students. As the attendance was not satisfactory, and there was no endowment for the support of the Faculty, the Trustees in 1872 ordered the exercises to be indefinitely suspended.

In 1873 a Constitutional Amendment was adopted by a vote of the people, giving the management of the University to the General Assembly. That body in 1874 provided for the election of 64 Trustees by joint ballot of the Senators and Representatives, to serve for eight years, but so classified that one-fourth go out of office every two years. In 1877 the number was increased to 72, and in 1884 to 80. Ten constitute a quorum. In order still further to remedy the difficulties resulting from the government being vested in so numerous a body of men, scattered over the State, an Executive Committee of seven is annually appointed by the Board, who have all powers not prohibited. Thus are secured such promptness and continuity of management as are necessary to success in all matters of business.

The new Trustees lost no time in meeting for the purpose of reopening the institution. Governor Tod R. Caldwell was requested to preside, but he refused to do so, alleging that the Board had not been appointed in accordance with the Constitution. Dr. Pool, who had charge of the University buildings, likewise declined to surrender possession of the same.

Hon. Alexander McIver, Superintendent of Public Education, with whom had been deposited for safe keeping the University seal and record books of the University, consented to become defendant in a friendly suit for the purpose of deciding the question. The Supreme Court gave their decision in favor of the new Board, and on May 4th, 1875, they met at the Executive office, Governor Curtis H. Brogden presiding, and Kemp P. Battle, being appointed Secretary. A committee, consisting of Messrs. Kemp P. Battle, John Manning, James A. Graham, J. J. Davis and Rev. C. B. Hassell, on motion of Mr. P. C. Cameron was appointed to report a scheme of reorganization at an adjourned meeting next day. The committee accordingly submitted a scheme embracing six colleges or departments. The plan was adopted, and at an adjourned meeting on the 16th of June ensuing an amendment was adopted, providing for an adjunct professorship of Latin and German. The following Professors were chosen: Rev. Charles Phillips, D. D., LL. D., Professor of Mathematics; J. DeBerniere Hooper, A. M., Professor of Greek and French; Rev. Adolphus W. Mangum, A. M., Professor of Moral Philosophy and English Literature; Alexander Fletcher Redd, Professor of Physics and Chemistry; Ralph H. Graves, B. Sc., C. & M. E., Professor of Engineering; John Kimberly, A. M., Professor of Agriculture; George Tayloe Winston, Adjunct Professor of Latin and German. Of these Dr. Phillips and Professors Hooper and Kimberly had been members of the Faculty in former times; Messrs. Graves and Winston had been students of the University, but had completed their education elsewhere, the latter at the United States Naval Academy and Cornell University, the former at the University of Virginia; Prof. Mangum was a graduate of Randolph-Macon College, and Prof. Redd was an alumnus of the Virginia Military Institute. Dr. Phillips was, by authority of the Board of Trustees, elected by the Faculty Chairman.

As has already been stated, money was contributed, mainly by alumni, for repairs which were most judiciously made under the personal supervision of Mr. P. C. Cameron. By aid of these contributions and the interest on the Land Grant, which the General Assembly at the request of the Trustees ordered to be paid, the doors were opened on the 6th of September, 1875, the attendance in the first year reaching 69; in the second, 112; and in the third, 160. In the following week, on the 15th, were had the formal ceremonies of the reopening. A procession of students, citizens of the village, visitors, Alumni, Faculty, and Trustees of the University, and the chaplain and orators of the day marched from the South Building into Gerrard Hall. Addresses were delivered by Governor Curtis H. Brogden, President *ex-officio* of the

DIALECTIC SOCIETY HALL—UNIVERSITY OF NORTH CAROLINA.

Board of Trustees, and by Hon. William H. Battle, a graduate of 1820, at the request of the Faculty. A hymn composed by Mrs. C. P. Spencer for the occasion was sung. A most feeling prayer was offered by Rev. Dr. Wm. Hooper, who had graduated sixty-eight years before.

IMPROVEMENTS SINCE THE REOPENING.

The improvements in the University, since the reopening in 1875, have been marked, as the following statement will show. When we consider the poverty of the State, and the frequent failures in crops, they have been very gratifying.

The numbers have for the last six years averaged 207, nearly all being from North Carolina. This is more than was had from the opening in 1795 to the year 1852. In 1853-'54 the number from this State was only 220, and in 1854-'55, only 230. There was then however a considerable attendance from other states, especially those south of us, on account of their unparalleled prosperity, and their having been settled by North Carolina families. In addition to the impoverishment and sundering of old ties caused by the long war, and the closing of this University for so many years, these states have well endowed and well manned institutions which are all free, except in the case of the University of South Carolina, which was once free, but now charges $40 per annum for tuition.

The prosperity of our University has stimulated the other colleges of our State, so that the departure from our borders of young men for higher education, other than those pursuing specialties, has almost ceased. Up to the reopening in 1875, not a dollar of annual appropriation had ever been secured from the State. The $7,500 interest on the Land Grant fund cannot properly be considered an appropriation, as it is merely interest paid on an honest obligation, and this has been ordered to be transferred to the Agricultural and Mechanical College at Raleigh. Independently of this, the University has by the Act of 1881 $5,000, and by the Act of 1885 $15,000, making a regular income of $20,000 from the State. This amount with the receipts from tuition and interest on endowments, enables the University to employ a teaching force substantially equal to that had in its palmiest days. In 1860, counting the President, there were eleven professors and five assistants; in 1888, eleven professors and three assistants.

The University has kept step with the general educational tendency of the age in the direction of more practical and scientific studies, while holding high its classical and mathematical standard. A full professorship is given to the English language and literature. Quantitative and qualitative analysis in chemistry are provided for in ample laboratories, built as an extension to Person Hall, instead of the ill-ventilated and darkened basement under Smith Hall. A separate laboratory is assigned for work in mineralogy and another large one for work in botany, and dissection and study of animals. Graduates in Chemistry of this University, since 1875, are at the head of the State Experiment and Fertilizer Control Station, and of various other enterprises requiring such scientific knowledge. Funds have been provided for the purchase of large additions to the apparatus and appliances for teaching in the departments of Physics, Chemistry and Natural History, including such instruments and models as are needed to illustrate the most recent discoveries in electricity, &c. A large collection has been made of mineralogical specimens, as well as woods and medicinal plants, and the specimens, previously owned by the University, have been relabelled in accordance with modern scientific nomenclature and properly displayed. A nearly complete collection of the skins of birds of the State and a very large collection of insects and other animals have been made.

In the department of Physics and Engineering, there is a great progress in the acquisition of apparatus, &c., needed for instruction. Besides purchases made from time to time the Trustees have recently appropriated $1,500 for this department alone, and the physical laboratory will soon be supplied with a dynamo and other instruments, requisite for showing experimentally the most recent discoveries. Much practical work is required in the use of surveying and engineering instruments, and in projection drawing.

In Pure Mathematics constant drilling is had in the lower classes, and the higher, being elective, and only entered by the best students, are carried much further than was possible in miscellaneous classes.

The other departments are not behind the scientific in the best methods and appliances of teaching. In that of Political Economy and Constitutional Law much attention is given to the history of the great questions involved, and an elective course in the Constitutional History of England has been added. In Mental and Moral Philosophy there is increased study of Christian Evidences, and an elective course in the History of Philosophy and Natural Theology is given.

In the Classics it is aimed to make the students able to read at sight the standard authors, and to appreciate the beauties of thought and language. They are constantly practised in Greek and Latin Composition, and made to study the Histories of Greece and Rome. A course in Comparative Philology is given in these departments.

In the department of English much attention is paid to the History of English Literature, to the criticism of the best authors at various epochs, to the beauties of style and language, and to the formation of good style. Historical Grammar is carefully studied. Much parallel reading is required. There is an elective class in Anglo-Saxon, in addition to the regular work of the department.

French and German are taught by a full professor, a native of a neighboring State, who has spent years in both France and Germany, and has the proper pronunciation of those languages and thorough acquaintance with their idioms. Attention is paid to the history and development of the literature of those countries.

In all these departments, post-graduate courses are provided, as has been stated, giving the students advanced instruction of a high order. This is done in addition to the regular work of the professors, and there is no charge for tuition.

Besides the above, the President and professors offer for three months in each year during the session, special instruction in their departments, suitable to the teachers of the State. For this no tuition is charged. Among the studies thus offered is the Science and Art of Teaching, thereby giving the advantages of the Summer Normal Schools, which have been abolished.

Shorter courses of study, requiring only two years for their completion, are offered to those who have not time nor money nor the previous preparation to enable them to complete one of the full four-year courses. One of these courses is arranged for the education of teachers, another for physicians and pharmacists, a third for the training of business men, merchants, farmers, manufacturers, mechanics, &c. And provision is made for those wishing to pursue special studies in Chemistry, Natural History, &c.

The Law School has been placed on a much more satisfactory basis, the professor in charge devoting nearly all his time to instruction.

Arrangements have been made for the addition to the University, beginning at the opening of the next fall term, of a well equipped and well manned Medical and Pharmaceutical department, in which students can get thorough preliminary training in all studies pertaining to those professions.

The literary and scientific activity of the students is quickened by various societies, conducted jointly by Faculty and students.

The Elisha Mitchell Society is for the promotion of scientific research. Other scientific workers in the State are members. A Journal is published, which is exchanged for the publications of more than two hundred similar learned bodies. Thus a valuable scientific library is being collected.

Another society is the Shakspere Club, for the critical study of Shakspere and other dramatists. Carefully prepared papers are read, and addresses made. The nucleus of a Shakspere library is formed.

The North Carolina Historical Society is engaged in the study of our State history, and the collection of documents and materials for its illustration. Public meetings are sometimes held for this, as well as the other societies, and papers read.

The Seminary of Literature and Philology has for its object promotion of research along special lines of literary work. The professors, besides guiding and assisting in the regular work, present, from time to time the results of their own labors. The character of the topics may be gathered from the following list of subjects on the programme: 1. Lyric Poetry; 2. The Historians; 3. Sacred Literature; 4. Words; 5. The Drama; 6. The Supernatural in Literature; 7. The Alphabet; 8. Epic Poetry.

The spirit and intelligence shown by the students in these societies are very encouraging, and the professors are stimulated to increased ardor in their respective specialties.

The University is entitled to the distinction of having inaugurated the plan of Summer Normal Schools. The first was held in the University buildings in June and July, 1877, and was wonderfully successful in arousing enthusiasm and introducing the best methods of teaching into the State. The President and several of the professors gave a large portion of their vacations to the work without pecuniary compensation. This Normal School was the parent of those held in various parts of North Carolina, and was imitated in Virginia, South Carolina, and nearly every Southern State. Although now discontinued in North Carolina, their influence will be felt in the Teachers' Institutes recently inaugurated by Act of Assembly, under the management of two of our recent graduates.

The erection of the addition to Person Hall, the Gymnasium and the Memorial Hall, has been since the re-opening in 1875. These cost nearly $50,000, while repairs and changes in the old buildings have been made, costing nearly $20,000 more. The greater portion of this money (about $70,000) has been contributed by the alumni and friends of the institution.

The branch railroad to Chapel Hill was secured chiefly by the exertions of Governor Jarvis, Col. A. B. Andrews, Gen. R. H. Hoke, and the officers of the University.

In addition to the amount above stated, as donated for buildings and repairs, Rev. Dr. C. F. Deems has provided a fund, to which the late Mr. W. H. Vanderbilt made a handsome addition, for aiding students by loans, amounting to over $13,000; the late B. F. Moore, $5,000; and the late Mary R. Smith, a plantation worth about $15,000, for paying the tuition of needy students; and Mrs. Cornelia P. Spencer made an addition to the library of about 1,000 volumes,—in all nearly $50,000. It may be safely estimated that over $75,000 have been donated to the University since its re-opening in 1875, besides the procurement of the annual appropriation of $20,000. When we consider the exceedingly distressed financial condition of our people, this statement shows that the friends of the institution have not been sleeping.

The improvement in the religious condition of the student body is shown by the great interest taken in the work of the Young Men's Christian Association. Its meetings are regularly attended and conducted with true devotional spirit and fervor. The members have recently fitted up, with neatness and taste, their Hall on the first floor of the South Building, and the room adjoining it on the west, the latter as a reading-room. The Association has a great and increasing influence for good among the students.

LIBRARIES.

There are three libraries, one belonging to the University, and one to each of the Literary Societies, each containing about 8,000 volumes. These by recent action have been combined, and thus a most valuable collection of over 20,000 volumes is accessible to the students every day in the week except Sundays, in the spacious, well lighted, and well ventilated room, called Smith Hall. Adjoining the library is a well equipped reading-room.

LITERARY SOCIETIES.

There are only two Literary Societies of the students in the University, the Dialectic and Philanthropic. Both were established in 1795, the former having a brief priority in time. The latter was for a few months called the Concord Society. The motto of the former is "Love of Virtue and Science," and its color is blue, the emblem of truth. The motto of the latter is "Virtue, Liberty, and Science," and its color is white, the emblem of purity. As has been said, James Mebane was the first President of the Dialectic Society. Richard Eagles, whose name survives in Eagles' Island, opposite Wilmington, was the first President of the Philanthropic Society. The students, until a few years ago, selected one or the other from social or other personal motives. Lately there has grown up the custom, not founded on any law, that those from the western counties shall join the Dialectic, and those from the eastern counties, the Philanthropic Society. The dividing line is not fixed, but well enough understood to prevent disputes. Some of the central counties are considered debatable territory but etiquette forbids active effort to influence the decisions of those coming from this territory.

Occasionally, too, for special reasons, the rule is broken and occasions no permanent ill-feeling. The relative numbers vary from year to year, as the larger wave of students happens to flow from the East or the West.

The exercises of the Societies consist in debating, declamation, and English composition. The meetings are secret. They are conducted, as a rule, with great decorum, and the members perform their duties with much diligence and spirit. Many alumni, who have achieved great success in life, have borne testimony to the advantages they derived from practice in speaking and writing, and in the conduct of deliberative assemblies.

The Societies, alternately, select a distinguished man to deliver an oration before the University on the day preceding the annual Commencement day. This usage has existed since 1826. It is suspended for the present year, owing to the Centennial Celebration, the orators being chosen by a committee of the Alumni Association and by the Faculty.

Three Representatives, chosen after competition by judges appointed by the Faculty, deliver original speeches during Commencement week. The Marshals must likewise be members of the Societies.

No other societies are allowed except with the permission of the Trustees. Such permission has been granted to a number of "Greek letter fraternities."

The Dialectic and Philanthropic Societies have each very handsome halls. They each have about twenty oil portraits of their eminent members, life size. These are the best collections in the State, perhaps not excelled in the South. Some of these are donations, the majority have been painted at the expense of the Societies.

OFFICERS AND STUDENTS
OF THE
UNIVERSITY OF NORTH CAROLINA.
1789-1889.

TRUSTEES.

PRESIDENTS OF THE BOARD OF TRUSTEES.

[Since 1810 the Governors of the State have been *ex officio* Presidents of the Board.]

WILLIAM LENOIR	1790–'92
ALEXANDER MARTIN	1792–'93
RICHARD DOBBS SPAIGHT	1793–'95
SAMUEL ASHE	1795–'99
BENJAMIN WILLIAMS	1799–1802
WILLIAM POLK	1802–'05
NATHANAEL ALEXANDER	1805–'07
BENJAMIN WILLIAMS	1807–'09
DAVID STONE	1809–'10
BENJAMIN SMITH	1810–'11
WILLIAM HAWKINS	1811–'14
WILLIAM MILLER	1814–'17
JOHN BRANCH	1817–'20
JESSE FRANKLIN	1820–'21
GABRIEL HOLMES	1821–'24
HUTCHINS G. BURTON	1824–'27
JAMES IREDELL	1827–'28
JOHN OWEN	1828–'30
MONTFORD STOKES	1830–'32
DAVID LOWRY SWAIN	1832–'35
RICHARD DOBBS SPAIGHT, JR	1835–'37
EDWARD B. DUDLEY	1837–'41
JOHN M. MOREHEAD	1841–'45

William A. Graham	1845–'49
Charles Manly	1849–'51
David S. Reid	1851–'54
Warren Winslow	1854–'55
Thomas Bragg	1855–'59
John W. Ellis	1859–'61
Henry T. Clark	1861–'63
Zebulon B. Vance	1863–'65
William W. Holden	1865–'66
Jonathan Worth	1866–'68
William W. Holden	1868–'70
Tod R. Caldwell	1870–'74
Curtis H. Brogden	1874–'77
Zebulon B. Vance	1877–'79
Thomas J. Jarvis	1879–'85
Alfred M. Scales	1885–'89
Daniel G. Fowle	1889–

Secretaries of the Board.

James Taylor	1790–'91
Robert Burton	1791–'92
Thomas Rogers	1792–'95
Hugh Williamson	1795–1801
Gavin Alves	1801–'09
Robert Williams	1809–'21
Charles Manly	1821–'48
Charles Lewis Hinton	1848–'50
Charles Manly	1850–'69
R. W. Lassiter	1869–'74
Kemp P. Battle	1874–'76
Seaton Gales	1876–'77
William L. Saunders	1877–

Treasurers.

John Craven	1790–'95
Walter Alves	1795–'99
Gavin Alves	1799–1809
Robert Williams	1809–'21
Charles Manly	1821–'48
Charles Lewis Hinton	1848–'50
Charles Manly	1850–'69
R. W. Lassiter	1869–'74
Kemp P. Battle	1874–'76
Seaton Gales	1876–'77
William L. Saunders	1877–

MEMBERS OF THE BOARD OF TRUSTEES.

[NOTE.—Until 1804, the Trustees filled vacancies occurring in their Board; from 1804 to 1868, members were elected by the General Assembly; from 1868 to 1874, they were appointed by the Board of Education; and since 1874, they have been elected by the General Assembly.]

TERM BEGAN.		APPOINTED FROM.	TERM EXPIRED.
1789	SAMUEL JOHNSTON, LL.D.	Chowan	1801
"	JAMES IREDELL	Chowan	1790
"	CHARLES JOHNSON	Chowan	1792
"	HUGH WILLIAMSON, LL.D	Chowan	1801
"	STEPHEN CABARRUS	Chowan	1792
"	RICHARD DOBBS SPAIGHT	Craven	1802
"	WILLIAM BLOUNT	Craven	1793
"	BENJAMIN WILLIAMS	Moore	1802
"	JOHN SITGREAVES	Craven	1802
"	FREDERICK HARGETT	Jones	1796
"	ROBERT WHITEHURST SNEAD	Granville	1799
"	ARCHIBALD MACLAINE	New Hanover	1791
"	SAMUEL ASHE	New Hanover	1798
"	ROBERT DIXON	Duplin	1790
"	BENJAMIN SMITH	Brunswick	1824
"	SAMUEL SPENCER, LL.D.	Anson	1793
"	JOHN HAY	Cumberland	1809
"	JAMES HOGG	Cumberland	1802
"	HENRY WILLIAM HARRINGTON	Richmond	1795
"	WILLIAM BARRY GROVE	Cumberland	1818
"	SAMUEL MCCORKLE, D.D.	Rowan	1801
"	ADLAI OSBORNE	Rowan	1814
"	JOHN STOKES	Stokes	1790
"	JOHN HAMILTON	Guilford	1802
"	JOSEPH GRAHAM	Mecklenburg	1790
"	JOHN WILLIAMS	Granville	1799
"	THOMAS PERSON	Granville	1795
"	ALFRED MOORE	Brunswick	1807
"	ALEXANDER MEBANE	Orange	1795
"	JOEL LANE	Wake	1795
"	WILLIE JONES	Halifax	1799
"	BENJAMIN HAWKINS	Warren	1798
"	JOHN HAYWOOD, SR	Edgecombe	1827
"	JOHN MACON	Warren	1792
"	WILLIAM RICHARDSON DAVIE, LL.D	Halifax	1807
"	JOSEPH DIXON	Lincoln	1795
"	WILLIAM LENOIR	Wilkes	1804
"	JOSEPH MCDOWELL, SR	Burke	1790
"	JAMES HOLLAND	Rutherford	1795
"	WILLIAM PORTER	Rutherford	1798

TERM BEGAN.		APPOINTED FROM.	TERM EXPIRED.
1790	Alexander Martin, LL.D.	Guilford	1807
"	James Kenan	Duplin	1799
"	James Glasgow	Glasgow	1801
"	Charles Pettigrew, D.D.	Tyrrell	1793
"	Joseph McDowell, Jr.	Burke	1794
"	William Polk	Wake	1834
1791	William H. Hill	New Hanover	1809
1792	David Stone	Bertie	1818
"	Thomas Blount	Edgecombe	1812
1793	John Louis Taylor	Craven	1818
"	Thomas Wynns	Hertford	1825
"	Josiah Collins	Chowan	1795
1795	John Moore	Lincoln	1809
"	John Skinner	Perquimans	1797
"	William P. Little	Granville	1818
"	William Hinton	Wake	1799
"	Walter Alves	Orange	1813
"	Waightstill Avery	Burke	1804
"	Wallace Alexander	Lincoln	1804
"	John Williss	Robeson	1801
1796	John Gray Blount	Beaufort	1802
1798	John Haywood, Jr.	Halifax	1807
"	Alexander Duncan Moore	New Hanover	1807
1799	Joshua Granger Wright	New Hanover	1811
"	Henry Potter	Cumberland	1856
"	Evan Alexander	Rowan	1809
"	John Hill	New Hanover	1812
"	Richard Bennehan	Orange	1804
1800	Charles Wilson Harris	Cabarrus	1803
1801	Gabriel Holmes	Sampson	1804
"	Durant Hatch	Jones	1807
"	Henry Seawell	Wake	1835
"	Nathanael Alexander	Mecklenburg	1808
"	Robert Montgomery	Hertford	1808
1802	Duncan Cameron	Orange	1838
"	Calvin Jones	Wake	1832
1802	Archibald Debow Murphy	Orange	1832
"	Blake Baker	Warren	1804
"	John Churchill Osborne, M. D.	Rowan	1807
"	William Gaston, LL.D	Craven	1844
1803	William Hawkins	Warren	1819
"	Robert Williams	Wake	1841
1804	Joseph Caldwell, D.D.	Orange	1835
"	Edward Jones	Chatham	1841
"	Robert Troy	Anson	1807
"	William Cherry	Bertie	1809
"	James Wellborn	Wilkes	1814

TERM BEGAN.		APPOINTED FROM.	TERM EXPIRED.
1805	JOHN STEVELEY	Burke	1812
"	PETER FORNEY	Lincoln	1808
"	MONTFORT STOKES	Rowan	1838
"	JESSE FRANKLIN	Surry	1817
"	SAMUEL LOWRIE	Mecklenburg	1817
"	THOMAS DAVIS	Cumberland	1808
"	ROBERT COCHRAN	Cumberland	1821
"	BRYAN WHITFIELD	Lenoir	1808
"	EDWARD HARISS	Craven	1813
"	WILLIAM HARDY MURFREE	Hertford	1818
"	WILLIAM SLADE	Chowan	1813
"	WILLIAM WILLIAMS	Halifax	1812
"	RICHARD W. FREEAR	Northampton	1808
"	JOSEPH THOMAS RHODES	Duplin	1812
"	THOMAS KING	Sampson	1813
1807	ARCHIBALD MCBRYDE	Moore	1837
"	ROBERT WILLIAMS, M. D	Pitt	1820
"	JOSEPH WINSTON	Stokes	1813
"	JOHN DAVIS HAWKINS	Warren	1857
"	BENJAMIN WOODS	Craven	1808
"	WILLIE WILLIAM JONES	Halifax	1812
"	FREDERICK NASH, LL.D.	Orange	1857
"	JAMES RHODES	Wayne	1810
1808	ROBERT HILL JONES	Warren	1832
"	JOHN SPENCE WEST	Craven	1817
"	JOHN WINSLOW	Cumberland	1820
"	ISRAEL PICKENS	Burke	1817
"	SAMUEL RUSSELL JOCELYN	New Hanover	1816
"	JEREMIAH SLADE	Martin	1824
"	NATHANAEL JONES (of White Plains)	Wake	1815
1809	FRANCIS LOCKE	Rowan	1823
"	WILLIAM EDWARDS WEBB	Halifax	1818
"	JOSEPH HUNTER BRYAN	Bertie	1817
"	THOMAS LOVE	Haywood	1834
"	THOMAS BROWN, JR	Bladen	1826
"	ATLAS JONES	Moore	1825
1810	JAMES WALLIS	Mecklenburg	1820
1811	JAMES MEBANE	Orange	1856
1812	ROBERT HETT CHAPMAN, D. D	Orange	1817
"	WILLIAM MCPHEETERS, D. D	Wake	1842
"	JOHN STEELE	Rowan	1815
"	SIMMONS JONES BAKER, M. D	Martin	1853
"	JAMES WEBB, M. D	Orange	1850
"	THOMAS D. BENNEHAN	Orange	1847
"	JOSEPH BLOUNT LITTLEJOHN	Chowan	1817
1813	JAMES WEST CLARK	Edgecombe	1844
"	JAMES IREDELL (the younger)	Chowan	1853

TERM BEGAN.		APPOINTED FROM.	TERM EXPIRED.
1813	Lewis Williams	Surry	1842
"	Thomas Ruffin, LL.D	Orange	1831
1814	William Caldwell Love	Rowan	1818
"	John Briggs Mebane	Chatham	1819
1817	John Branch	Halifax	1844
"	William Miller	Warren	1826
"	John Stanly	Craven	1833
"	Leonard Henderson	Granville	1828
"	Kemp Plummer	Warren	1826
"	Bartlett Yancey	Caswell	1828
"	John Witherspoon, D. D.	Orange	1834
"	Gabriel Holmes	Sampson	1829
"	Alfred Moore, (the younger)	Brunswick	1837
1818	Enoch Sawyer	Camden	1827
"	James Cathcart Johnson	Chowan	1863
"	George Edmund Badger, LL.D.	Craven	1844
"	Joseph Blount Skinner	Pasquotank	1851
"	Willie Person Mangum, LL.D	Orange	1859
"	William Dozier Martin	Pasquotank	1834
"	John Burgess Baker	Gates	1838
"	John D. Toomer	Cumberland	1855
1819	Lewis von Schweinitz, LL.D	Surry	1822
"	Romulus Mitchell Saunders	Caswell	1864
1820	John Owen	Bladen	1841
"	Thomas Pollock Devereux	Wake	1827
1821	Richard Dobbs Spaight (the younger)	Craven	1850
"	Louis D. Henry	Cumberland	1846
"	Francis Lister Hawks, D.D., LL.D.	Orange	1828
"	Solomon Graves	Surry	1860
"	James Strudwick Smith, M. D.	Orange	1852
"	Leonard Martin	Hertford	1826
"	Thomas Wharton Blackledge	Beaufort	1830
"	Thomas Burgess	Halifax	1833
"	Archibald Roane Ruffin	Stokes	1829
1823	James Martin, Jr.	Rowan	1836
"	Daniel Morgan Forney	Lincoln	1834
"	John Herritage Bryan	Craven	1868
1824	John Scott	Orange	1836
"	Joseph Hawkins	Warren	1827
1826	Nathanael Macon	Warren	1828
"	Charles Manly	Chatham	1868
"	James Fauntleroy Taylor	Chatham	1828
"	William Augustus Blount	Beaufort	1867
"	Thomas Settle	Rockingham	1857
"	Isaac Croom	Lenoir	1836
1827	William Julius Alexander	Mecklenburg	1856
"	Nicholas John Drake	Nash	1831
"	William Robards	Granville	1843

TERM BEGAN.		APPOINTED FROM.	TERM EXPIRED.
1827	EMANUEL SHOBER	Forsyth	1846
1828	HUGH WADDELL	Orange	1864
"	JOHN GILES	Rowan	1847
"	JOHN MOTLEY MOREHEAD	Guilford	1866
"	JOHN LANCASTER BAILEY	Pasquotank	1868
"	WILLIAM SPIVEY MHOON	Wake	1835
"	JOHN ROBERT DONNELL	Craven	1864
1831	THOMAS GILCHRIST POLK	Rowan	1839
"	JOSEPH ALSTON HILL	New Hanover	1835
"	JOHN BRAGG	Warren	1835
"	WILLIAM DUNN MOSELEY	Lenoir	1839
"	DAVID LOWRY SWAIN, LL.D	Buncombe	1868
1832	DANIEL MOREAU BARRINGER	Cabarrus	1868
"	DANIEL WILLIAMS COURTS	Surry	1839
"	CHARLES LEWIS HINTON	Wake	1860
1833	WILLIAM HORN BATTLE, LL.D	Louisburg	1868
"	JOHN REAVES JONES DANIEL	Halifax	1868
"	HUGH MCQUEEN	Orange	1845
1834	HENRY SELBY CLARKE	Beaufort	1854
"	WILLIAM ALEXANDER GRAHAM, LL.D	Orange	1868
"	OWEN HOLMES	New Hanover	1840
"	PLEASANT WILLIAMS KITTRELL	Granville	1836
1835	FREDERICK JONES HILL, M. D	Brunswick	1860
"	JAMES WEST BRYAN	Craven	1855
"	MATTHEW EVANS MANLY, LL.D	Craven	1868
"	WILLIAM BELVIDERE MEARES	New Hanover	1841
"	SAMUEL FINLEY PATTERSON	Caldwell	1868
1836	ANDREW JOYNER	Halifax	1856
1838	CHARLES CHALMERS, M. D	Moore	1857
"	GEORGE FRANKLIN DAVIDSON	Iredell	1868
"	WILLIAM EATON, JR	Warren	1868
"	ROBERT BALLARD GILLIAM	Granville	1868
"	MICHAEL HOKE	Lincoln	1844
"	JAMES TURNER MOREHEAD	Guilford	1868
"	WILLIAM BIDDLE SHEPARD	Pasquotank	1852
"	LEWIS DICKEN WILSON	Edgecombe	1840
1840	BURGESS SIDNEY GAITHER	Burke	1868
"	WESTON RALEIGH GALES	Wake	1848
"	CADWALLADER JONES, JR	Orange	1857
"	GEORGE CAMERON MENDENHALL	Guilford	1859
"	BARTHOLOMEW FIGURES MOORE, LL.D	Halifax	1868
"	JOHN CAMPBELL WILLIAMS	Cumberland	1868
"	PATRICK HENRY WINSTON	Anson	1864
"	JONATHAN WORTH	Randolph	1868
1842	THOMAS SAMUEL ASHE, LL.D	Anson	1868
"	THOMAS BRAGG, LL.D	Northampton	1868
"	JOHN MCCLINTOCK DICK	Guilford	1860

TERM BEGAN.		APPOINTED FROM.	TERM EXPIRED.
1842	GEORGE WASHINGTON JEFFREYS	Person	1848
"	THOMAS RUFFIN, LL.D	Orange	1868
"	WILLIAM WALTON CHERRY	Bertie	1843
1844	CALVIN GRAVES	Caswell	1868
"	NICHOLAS LANIER WILLIAMS	Surry	1868
"	WILLIAM HENRY WASHINGTON	Craven	1860
1846	THOMAS NASH CAMERON, M. D	Cumberland	1851
"	DANIEL WILLIAMS COURTS	Rockingham	1868
"	JOHN ADAMS GILMER	Guilford	1868
"	JOHN KERR, LL.D	Caswell	1868
"	WALTER FRANCIS LEAK	Richmond	1868
"	GILES MEBANE	Orange	1868
1848	JAMES COCHRAN DOBBIN	Cumberland	1857
"	DAVID S. REID	Rockingham	1868
"	CUSHING BIGGS HASSELL	Martin	1868
"	LEWIS THOMPSON	Bertie	1867
1851	WILLIAM WAIGHTSTILL AVERY	Burke	1864
1852	WALTER L. STEELE	Richmond	1868
"	SAMUEL P. HILL	Caswell	1868
1854	JOHN G. BYNUM	Rutherford	1857
"	JOHN W. CUNNINGHAM	Person	1868
1857	RICHARD DILLARD, M. D	Chowan	1868
"	JAMES F. E. HARDY, M. D	Buncombe	1868
"	WILLIAM W. HOLDEN	Wake	1866
"	THOMAS SETTLE, JR	Rockingham	1868
1858	ROBERT R. BRIDGERS	Edgecombe	1868
"	PAUL C. CAMERON	Orange	1868
"	ROBERT D. HART	Granville	1868
"	JOSEPH J. JACKSON	Chatham	1868
"	WILLIAM LANDER	Lincoln	1867
"	THOMAS D. MCDOWELL	Bladen	1860
"	RUFUS L. PATTERSON	Forsyth	1868
"	MATT W. RANSOM, LL.D	Northampton	1868
"	ALFRED M. SCALES	Rockingham	1868
"	DE WITT C. STONE	Franklin	1863
"	JAMES M. TAYLOR	Nash	1868
1862	KEMP P. BATTLE, LL.D	Wake	1868
"	NEILL MCKAY, D. D	Harnett	1868
"	JESSE G. SHEPHERD	Cumberland	1868
"	FRANCIS E. SHOBER	Rowan	1868
"	LEONIDAS F. SILER	Macon	1868
"	EDWARD WARREN, M. D., LL.D	Wake	1863
"	MASON L. WIGGINS	Halifax	1868
1864	DAVID M. CARTER	Beaufort	1868
"	MONTFORD MCGEHEE	Person	1868
"	SAMUEL F. PHILLIPS, LL.D	Orange	1868
"	JOHN POOL	Bertie	1864

TERM BEGAN.		APPOINTED FROM.	TERM EXPIRED.
1865	LUKE BLACKMER	Rowan	1868
"	WILLIAM P. BYNUM	Lincoln	1868
"	JOHN W. CAMERON	Richmond	1866
"	DENNIS D. FEREBEE	Camden	1868
"	SEATON GALES	Wake	1868
"	WILLIAM A. JENKINS	Warren	1868
"	WILLIAM N. H. SMITH, LL.D.	Hertford	1868
1869	R. V. MICHAUX	Burke	1870
"	VICTOR C. BARRINGER	Cabarrus	1870
"	CALVIN C. JONES	Caldwell	1870
"	J. J. MOTT, M. D.	Catawba	1870
"	BENJAMIN I. HOWZE	Chatham	1870
"	FELIX AXLEY	Clay	1870
"	JOHN A. MAULTSBY	Columbus	1870
"	ROBERT F. LEHMAN	Craven	1870
"	RALPH P. BUXTON	Cumberland	1870
"	P. A. LONG	Davie	1870
"	JOHN NORFLEET	Edgecombe	1870
"	THOMAS P. HOFFLER	Gates	1870
"	JEFFERSON M. LOVEJOY	Halifax	1870
"	ANDERSON MITCHELL	Iredell	1870
"	R. W. KING	Lenoir	1870
"	WILLIAM F. CRAIGE	McDowell	1870
"	WILLIS L. MILLER	Mecklenburg	1870
"	WILLIAM NICHOLSON, M. D.	Perquimans	1870
"	W. H. HOWERTON, M. D.	Rowan	1870
"	A. H. JOYCE	Stokes	1870
"	JAMES FONT. TAYLOR	Wake	1870
"	R. DON WILSON	Watauga	1870
"	GEO. W. BLOUNT	Wilson	1870
"	JOHN R. FRENCH	Chowan	1872
"	JOSEPH W. ETHERIDGE	Currituck	1872
"	WILLIAM F. HENDERSON	Davidson	1872
"	WILLIAM E. HILL	Duplin	1872
"	MADISON NOLAND	Gaston	1872
"	NEILL MCKAY, D.D.	Harnett	1872
"	W. G. B. GARRETT	Haywood	1872
"	DAVID A. BARNES	Hertford	1872
"	J. A. HASKELL	Jones	1872
"	R. M. HENRY	Macon	1872
"	J. W. BOWMAN	Mitchell	1872
"	A. R. MCDONALD	Moore	1872
"	EDWARD CANTWELL	Nash	1872
"	JOHN ROBINSON	Onslow	1872
"	ROBERT L. ADAMS	Polk	1872
"	J. R. BULLA	Randolph	1872
"	ALFRED DOCKERY	Richmond	1872

TERM BEGAN.		APPOINTED FROM.	TERM EXPIRED.
1869	ORLIN S. HAYES	Robeson	1872
"	G. W. LOGAN	Rutherford	1872
"	E. W. JONES	Washington	1872
"	C. H. BROGDEN	Wayne	1872
"	J. H. BOWDITCH	Yancey	1872
"	JOHN M. CARSON, M. D.	Alexander	1874
"	A. W. TOURGEE	Alleghany	1874
"	DIXON INGRAM	Anson	1874
"	WILLIAM LATHAM	Ashe	1874
"	A. T. DAVIDSON	Cherokee	1874
"	D. H. STARBUCK	Forsyth	1874
"	RICHARD INGE WYNNE	Franklin	1874
"	W. D. WHITTED, M. D.	Henderson	1874
"	WILLIAM CARTER	Hyde	1874
"	E. W. POU	Johnston	1874
"	W. P. BYNUM	Lincoln	1874
"	GEORGE A. GRAHAM	Montgomery	1874
"	J. C. ABBOTT	New Hanover	1874
"	SOLOMON POOL, D. D.	Orange	1874
"	C. C. POOL	Pasquotank	1874
"	EDWIN G. READE, LL.D.	Person	1874
"	THOMAS SETTLE	Rockingham	1874
"	JOHN M. CLOUD	Surry	1874
"	R. H. DUCKWORTH	Transylvania	1874
"	G. W. BROOKS	Tyrrell	1874
"	HUGH DOWNING	Union	1874
"	JOHN READ	Warren	1874
"	HENRY A. BADHAM	Alamance	1874
"	WILLIAM B. RODMAN	Beaufort	1874
"	JOHN POOL	Bertie	1874
"	ABIEL W. FISHER	Bladen	1874
"	DANIEL L. RUSSELL, JR.	Brunswick	1874
"	JAMES L. HENRY	Buncombe	1874
"	MATCHET TAYLOR	Camden	1874
"	C. R. THOMAS	Carteret	1874
"	MONTFORD MCGEHEE	Caswell	1874
"	DECATUR GRIGG	Cleveland	1874
"	R. W. LASSITER	Granville	1874
1870	WM. P. GRIMSLEY	Greene	1874
"	R. P. DICK, LL.D.	Guilford	1874
"	R H. CANNON	Jackson	1874
"	G. W. GAHAGAN	Madison	1874
"	S. W. WATTS	Martin	1874
"	WILLIAM BARROW, M. D.	Northampton	1874
"	BYRON LAFLIN	Pitt	1874
"	J. C. MONK, M. D.	Sampson	1874
"	J. C. KROWZE, M. D.	Stanly	1874

TERM BEGAN.		APPOINTED FROM.	TERM EXPIRED.
1870	CALVIN J. COWLES	Wilkes	1874
"	RICHMOND M. PEARSON, LL.D	Yadkin	1874

Trustees Ex-Officio, 1869–1874.

W. W. HOLDEN, *Governor* (1869–'70).
TOD R. CALDWELL, *Lieutenant Governor* (1869–'70).
TOD R. CALDWELL, *Governor* (1870–'74).
H. J. MENNINGER, *Secretary of State.*
HENDERSON ADAMS, *Auditor.*
C. L. HARRIS, *Superintendent of Public Works.*
WILLIAM M. COLEMAN, *Attorney General.*
L. P. OLDS, *Attorney General.*
S. S. ASHLEY, *Superintendent of Public Instruction.*
SOLOMON POOL, D. D., *President of the University.*

[NOTE.—The terms of those of the foregoing Trustees appointed under the provisions of the Constitution of 1868, which did not expire sooner, were terminated in 1874 by an amendment to the Constitution.]

1875	JAMES S. AMIS	Granville	1885
"	REV. WILLIAM C. BOWMAN	Mitchell	1878
"	DAVID M. CARTER	Wake	1878
"	DAVID D. COLEMAN	Buncombe	1878
"	C. L. COOK, M. D	Wilkes	1878
"	WILLIAM H. DAY	Halifax	1877
"	JAMES L. DUSENBURY, M. D	Davidson	1879
"	WILLIAM J. EWING, M. D	Montgomery	1885
"	RUFUS FRAZIER	Randolph	1877
"	*FORNEY GEORGE	Columbus	1878
"	*CUSHING B. HASSELL	Martin	1880
"	WILLIAM H. JOHNSTON	Edgecombe	1885
"	PAUL B. MEANS	Cabarrus	—
"	WILLIAM L. SAUNDERS	New Hanover	—
"	JOHN H. THORP	Nash	1885
"	GEORGE B. WETMORE, D. D	Rowan	1877
"	MILLS L. EURE	Gates	1879
"	WILLIAM T. FAIRCLOTH	Wayne	—
"	JOHN A. GILMER	Guilford	—
"	*WILLIAM A. GRAHAM, LL.D	Orange	1876
"	J. F. GRAVES	Surry	1879
"	G. H. HAMILTON	Ashe	1879
"	LOUIS HILLIARD	Pitt	1877
"	JOHN F. HOKE	Lincoln	1879
"	*JOHN D. HYMAN	Henderson	1876
"	JOHN MANNING, LL.D	Chatham	—
"	JOHN McIVER, M. D	Moore	1879

*Died before expiration of term of office.

TERM BEGAN.		APPOINTED FROM.	TERM EXPIRED.
1875	R. W. MILLARD	Duplin	1879
"	ROBERT B. PEEBLES	Northampton	—
"	ARCHIBALD PURCELL	Robeson	1879
"	MARMADUKE ROBBINS	Randolph	1879
"	WILLIAM L. TWITTY	Rutherford	1879
"	JOSEPH J. DAVIS, LL. D	Franklin	—
"	BENJAMIN S. HARDY	Greene	1881
"	J. DeBERNIERE HOOPER	Orange	1881
"	EDMUND W. JONES	Caldwell	1876
"	*JOHN KERR, LL. D.	Caswell	1880
"	JAMES C. MARSHALL	Anson	1881
"	*WILLIAM F. MARTIN	Pasquotank	1880
"	THOMAS D. McDOWELL	Bladen	1880
"	NEILL McKAY, D. D.	Harnett	—
"	*BARTHOLOMEW F. MOORE, LL. D	Wake	1878
"	*RUFUS L. PATTERSON	Forsyth	1880
"	WILLIAM B. SHAW	Currituck	1881
"	WALTER L. STEELE	Richmond	—
"	SAMUEL McD. TATE	Burke	—
"	H. CLAY THOMAS	Davidson	1881
"	JOSEPH WILLIAMS	Yadkin	1888
"	*WILLIAM H. BATTLE, LL. D	Wake	1879
"	KEMP P. BATTLE, LL. D	Wake	—
"	CHARLES W. BROADFOOT	Cumberland	—
"	PAUL C. CAMERON	Orange	—
"	E. HAYNE DAVIS	Iredell	—
"	JOHN E. DUGGER	Warren	1883
"	*SEATON GALES	Wake	1878
"	BENJAMIN F. GRADY	Sampson	—
"	JAMES A. GRAHAM	Alamance	—
"	LOUIS C. LATHAM	Washington	1883
"	*MATHIAS E. MANLY, LL.D	Craven	1881
"	WILLIAM N. MEBANE	Rockingham	—
"	ZEBULON B. VANCE, LL.D	Mecklenburg	—
"	SAMUEL H. WALKUP	Union	1877
"	*CALVIN H. WILEY, D.D	Forsyth	1886
"	PATRICK H. WINSTON, JR	Bertie	1883
1877	JOHN W. GRAHAM	Orange	—
"	STUART L. JOHNSON	Washington	1879
"	*JAMES L. ROBINSON	Macon	1886
"	G. N. FOLK	Caldwell	—
"	*THOMAS S. ASHE, LL.D	Anson	1883
"	R. McBRAYER	Cleveland	1885
"	JULIAN S. CARR	Durham	—
"	JOHN S. HENDERSON	Rowan	1885
"	WILLIAM E. HILL	Duplin	—

* Died before expiration of term of office.

TERM BEGAN.		APPOINTED FROM.	TERM EXPIRED.
1877	*L. R. McAboy, D.D.	Polk	1884
"	Montford McGehee	Person	—
"	M. H. Pinnix	Davidson	1885
"	Charles Price	Davie	—
"	Daniel A. Long, D. D.	Alamance	1887
"	William B. Lynch	Alamance	1879
"	John D. Cameron	Orange	—
"	George V. Strong	Wake	—
"	*Bryan Grimes	Beaufort	1880
"	*David M. Carter	Wake	1879
"	*Thomas Sparrow	Beaufort	1883
1879	Eugene Grissom, M. D., LL. D.	Wake	—
"	A. Haywood Merritt	Chatham	—
"	Richard H. Battle, Jr.	Wake	—
"	A. M. Lewis	Wake	—
"	*A. D. Betts	N. C. Conference	1889
"	*R. R. Bridgers	New Hanover	1888
"	Ralph P. Buxton	Cumberland	1887
"	George Davis, LL. D.	New Hanover	—
"	N. P. Foard	Surry	1887
"	F. M. Johnston	Davie	1887
"	James M. Leach	Davidson	1887
"	D. P. McEachern	Robeson	1887
"	*W. J. Yates	Mecklenburg	1888
"	George Williamson	Caswell	1887
1881	Charles M. Cooke	Franklin	—
"	C. W. Hollowell	Martin	—
"	Robert B. Vance	Buncombe	—
"	William J. Hawkins, M. D.	Warren	—
"	A. S. Merrimon, LL. D.	Wake	1885
"	*David T. Tayloe, M. D.	Beaufort	1882
"	*H. F. Grainger	Wayne	1883
"	*Lewis Hanes	Davidson	1882
"	*H. B. Short	Columbus	1885
"	Isaac R. Strayhorn	Orange	—
"	J. L. Stewart	Sampson	—
"	C. R. Thomas	Burke	—
"	*N. H. D. Wilson, D. D.	Guilford	1888
1883	Kerr Craige	Rowan	—
"	Thomas J. Jarvis, LL. D.	Wake	—
"	James S. Battle	Nash	—
"	Robert S. Beall, M. D.	Caldwell	—
"	Henry R. Bryan	Craven	—
"	Thomas S. Kenan	Wilson	—
"	James T. Morehead	Guilford	—
"	Fabius H. Busbee	Wake	—

* Died before expiration of term of office.

TERM BEGAN.		APPOINTED FROM.	TERM EXPIRED.
1883	W. H. K. BURGWYN	Vance	—
"	THOMAS M. HOLT	Alamance	—
"	WALTER W. LENOIR	Watauga	—
"	J. EDWIN MOORE	Martin	—
"	E. R. PAGE	Jones	1885
"	DANIEL L. RUSSELL	Brunswick	1885
1885	H. A. GUDGER	Buncombe	—
"	JAMES M. MULLEN	Halifax	1886
"	JOHN E. WOODARD	Wilson	—
"	A. B. ANDREWS	Wake	—
"	JOSEPH A. BITTING	Forsyth	—
"	JOHN M. GALLOWAY	Rockingham	—
"	JAMES H. HORNER	Granville	—
"	GEORGE HOWARD	Edgecombe	—
"	LEE S. OVERMAN	Rowan	—
"	JAMES PARKER	Gates	—
"	THOMAS H. PRITCHARD, D. D.	New Hanover	—
"	JOHN C. SCARBOROUGH	Johnston	—
"	WILLIAM H. CHADBOURN	New Hanover	—
"	THOMAS W. MASON	Northampton	—
1887	ALPHONZO C. AVERY	Burke	—
"	H. D. WILLIAMSON, M. D.	Columbus	—
"	JOHN W. FRIES	Forsyth	—
"	S. M. FINGER, (ex officio)	Catawba	—
"	CHARLES A. COOK	Warren	—
"	A. LEAZAR	Iredell	—
"	W. S. LONG	Alamance	—
"	HAMILTON C. MCMILLAN	Robeson	—
"	SOLOMON C. WEILL	New Hanover	—
"	FRANK D. WINSTON	Bertie	—
1889	W. S. BLACK, D. D.	Wake	—
"	J. H. CORDON	N. C. Conference	—
"	JOHN D. CURRIE	Bladen	—
"	RUFUS A. DOUGHTON	Alleghany	—
"	WILLIAM JOHNSTON	Mecklenburg	—
"	HAMILTON C. JONES	Mecklenburg	—
"	CHARLES D. MCIVER	Wake	—
"	PATRICK L. MURPHY, M. D.	Burke	—
"	ROBERT W. SCOTT	Alamance	—
"	GEORGE N. THOMPSON	Caswell	—

FACULTY.

PRESIDENTS.

DAVID KER, D. D., 1795-1796, Presiding Professor; **CHARLES W. HARRIS, A. M.**, 1796-1797, Presiding Professor; **JOSEPH CALDWELL, D. D.**, 1797-1804, Presiding Professor; **JOSEPH CALDWELL, D. D.**, 1804-1812; **ROBERT HETT CHAPMAN, D. D.**, 1813-1816; **JOSEPH CALDWELL, D. D.**, 1816-1835; **DAVID LOWRY SWAIN, LL. D.**, 1835-1868; **SOLOMON POOL, D. D.**, 1869-1874; **KEMP PLUMMER BATTLE, LL. D.**, 1876-.

PROFESSORS.

Ancient Languages (Latin and Greek): **DAVID KER**, 1794-1796; **SAMUEL ALLEN HOLMES**, 1796-1798; **WILLIAM EDWARDS WEBB**, 1799-1800; **ARCHIBALD DEBOW MURPHY**, 1800-1801; **WILLIAM BINGHAM**, 1801-1805, **ANDREW RHEA**, 1806-1814; **WILLIAM HOOPER**, 1817-1822; **ETHAN ALLEN ANDREWS**, 1822-1828; **WILLIAM HOOPER**, 1828-1837; **MANUEL FETTER**, 1838; **ASHBEL GREEN BROWN**, Adjunct, 1855-1856.

Latin Language and Literature: **JOHN DEBERNIERE HOOPER**, 1838-1848; **FORDYCE MITCHELL HUBBARD**, 1849-1868; **D. S. PATRICK**, 1869-1870; **GEORGE TAYLOE WINSTON**, 1875-.

Greek Language and Literature: **MANUEL FETTER**, 1838-1868; **FISK P. BREWER**, 1869-1870; **J. DEBERNIERE HOOPER**, 1875-1885; **SOLOMON COHEN WEILL**, Acting Professor, 1885-1886; **EBEN ALEXANDER**, 1886-.

Mathematics: **CHARLES WILSON HARRIS**, 1795-1796; **JOSEPH CALDWELL**, 1796-1817; **ELISHA MITCHELL** (Mathematics and Natural Philosophy), 1817-1825; **JAMES PHILLIPS**, (Mathematics and Natural Philosophy), 1826-1867; **CHARLES PHILLIPS**, 1861-1868; **SOLOMON POOL**, Adjunct, 1860-1868; **ALEXANDER McIVER**, 1869-1870; **CHARLES PHILLIPS**, 1875-1879; **RALPH HENRY GRAVES**, 1879-; **JAMES LEE LOVE**, Associate Professor, 1885-; **MANSFIELD T. PEED**, Assistant Professor, 1889-.

Engineering: **CHARLES PHILLIPS**, 1854-1860; **RALPH HENRY GRAVES**, 1875-1880; **JOSHUA WALKER GORE**, 1882-.

Natural Philosophy: **JAMES SMILEY GILLESPIE**, 1797-1799; **WALKER ANDERSON**, 1833-1836; **CAREY D. GRANDY**, 1879-1882; **JOSHUA WALKER GORE**, 1882-.

Chemistry: **DENISON OLMSTED**, 1817-1825; **ELISHA MITCHELL**, 1825-1857; **WILLIAM JOSEPH MARTIN**, 1858-1867; **ALEXANDER FLETCHER REDD**, 1875-1880; **CAREY D. GRANDY**, Assistant Professor, 1875-1879; **FRANCIS PRESTON VENABLE**, 1880-.

Modern Languages (French and German): **NICHOLAS MARCELLUS HENTZ**, 1826-1831; **JOHN DEBERNIERE HOOPER**, 1836-1838; **CHARLES MAREY**, Instructor, 1838-1839; **JOHN JONES ROBERTS**,

1841–1842; **JOHN DeBERNIERE HOOPER**, 1843–1848; **ALBERT M. SHIPP**, 1850–1853; **HENRY HENRISSE**, Instructor, 1853–1856; **HILDRETH HOSEA SMITH**, 1856–1868; **JOHN DeBERNIERE HOOPER**, (French), 1875–1885; **GEORGE TAYLOE WINSTON**, (German), 1875–1885; **WALTER D. TOY**, 1885–.

Rhetoric and Logic: **SHEPARD KOSCIUSKO KOLLOCK**, 1819–1825; **WILLIAM HOOPER**, 1825–1828; **WALKER ANDERSON**, 1833; **WILLIAM MERCER GREEN**, 1838–1849; **CHARLES FORCE DEEMS**, Adjunct, 1842–1848; **JOHN THOMAS WHEAT**, 1850–1859; **ANDREW DOZ HEPBURN**, 1860–1867.

History: **ALBERT MICAJA SHIPP**, 1849–1860.

Law: **WILLIAM HORN BATTLE**, 1845–1868, and 1876–1879; **SAMUEL FIELD PHILLIPS**, 1854–1859; **KEMP P. BATTLE**, 1879–1881; **JOHN MANNING**, 1881–.

Political Science: **DAVID LOWRY SWAIN**, 1835–1868; **KEMP PLUMMER BATTLE**, 1876–.

Mental and Moral Science: **ADOLPHUS W. MANGUM**, 1875–.

Agricultural Chemistry: **BENJAMIN S. HEDRICK**, 1853–1858; **JOHN KIMBERLY**, 1856–1866, and 1875–1876; **GEORGE DIXON**, 1869.

Agricultural Chemistry and Metallurgy: **WILLIAM B. PHILLIPS**, 1885–1888.

Natural History: **WILLIAM H. SMITH**, 1876–1877; **FREDERICK WILLIAM SIMONDS**, 1877–1881; **W. C. KERR** (Lecturer), 1877–1882; **JOSEPH AUSTIN HOLMES** (Natural History and Geology), 1881–; **EMILE A. VON SCHWEINITZ**, Assistant Professor, 1884–1885; **GEORGE F. ATKINSON**, Associate Professor, 1885–1888.

English Language and Literature: **JAMES A. MARTLING**, 1869; **ADOLPHUS W. MANGUM**, 1875–1885; **THOMAS HUME, JR.**, 1885–.

Theory and Art of Teaching: **NELSON B. HENRY**, 1885–1888.

Medicine: **THOMAS W. HARRIS**, 1878–1885.

TUTORS AND ASSISTANTS.

ARCHIBALD DEBOW MURPHY, 1799–1800; **P. CELESTINE MOLIÉ**, 1802; **RICHARD HENDERSON**, 1800–1804; **ATLAS JONES**, 1804–1806; **JAMES MARTIN**, 1806–1807; **GAVIN HOGG**, 1808; **ABNER WENTWORTH CLOPTON**, 1809–1810; **LEWIS WILLIAMS**, 1810–1812; **WILLIAM HOOPER**, 1810; **ABNER STITH**, 1814–1816; **JAMES MORRISON**, 1814–1817; **JOHN HARPER HINTON**, 1814–1815; **JOHN PATTERSON**, 1816–1817; **JOHN MOTLEY MOREHEAD**, 1817; **PRIESTLEY HINTON MANGUM**, 1817; **ROBERT RUFUS KING**, 1817–1818, and 1819–1820; **WILLIAM DUNN MOSELEY**, 1817–1818; **HAMILTON CHAMBERLAIN JONES**, 1818; **SIMON PETER JORDAN**, 1818–1821; **JAMES HERVEY OTEY**, 1820–1821; **ANDERSON MITCHELL**, 1821–1823; **JOSEPH HUBBARD SAUNDERS**, 1821–1825; **GEORGE SHONNARD BETTNER**, 1823–1826; **ELISHA YOUNG**, 1824–1825; **MATTHIAS EVANS MANLY**, 1825–1826; **EDWARD DROMGOOLE SIMS**, 1825–1827; **OLIVER WOOLCOTT TREADWELL**, 1826–1829; **JOHN JENKINS**

WYCHE, 1826–1828; SILAS MILTON ANDREWS, 1827–1828; LORENZO LEA, 1828–1829; THOMAS BIRD, 1829–1831; HENRY GRATTAN SMITH, 1830–1832; JOHN ALLEN BACKHOUSE, 1830–1831; JOHN DEBERNIERE HOOPER, 1831–1833; JACOB THOMPSON, 1831–1833; GILES MEBANE, 1832–1833; JAMES HOGG NORWOOD, 1833–1834; THOMAS LAPSLEY ARMSTRONG, 1833; WILLIAM NELSON MEBANE, 1833–1834; SAMUEL RICHARDSON BLAKE, 1834–1835; WILLIAM PUGH BOND, 1835; HARRISON WALL COVINGTON, 1835; ABRAHAM FORREST MOREHEAD, 1835; DAVID MCALLISTER, 1835–1836; WILLIAM HENRY OWEN, 1835–1843; RALPH HENRY GRAVES, 1837–1843; ASHBEL GREEN BROWN, 1844–1855; CHARLES PHILLIPS, 1844–1854; KEMP PLUMMER BATTLE, 1850–1854; WILLIAM HENRY JOHNSTON, 1851–1852; RICHARD HINES, 1853–1854; SOLOMON POOL, 1854–1860; JOSEPH BLOUNT LUCAS, 1854–1858; RICHARD HENRY BATTLE, 1855–1858; WILLIAM ROBARDS WETMORE, 1855–1858; PETER EVANS SPRUILL, 1856–1858; SAMUEL SPENCER JACKSON, 1856–1860; THADDEUS CHARLES COLEMAN, 1856–1857; CHARLES ANDREWS MITCHELL, 1857; JOHN WASHINGTON GRAHAM, 1858–1860; WILLIAM LEE ALEXANDER, 1858–1859; ROBERT WALKER ANDERSON, 1859–1861; WILLIAM CAREY DOWD, 1859; EDWARD GRAHAM MORROW, 1859; FREDERICK AUGUSTUS FETTER, 1860–1863; GEORGE PETTIGREW BRYAN, 1860–1863; GEORGE BURGWYN JOHNSTON, 1860–1863; IOWA ROYSTER, 1860–1863; ISAAC E. EMERSON, 1878–1879; LOCKE CRAIG, 1879–1880; ALBERT LUCIAN COBLE, 1879–1880 and 1883–1885; ROBERT PAINE PELL, 1879–1881; ROBERT WATSON WINSTON, 1880–1881; ANGUS ROBERTSON SHAW, 1881–1882; NUMA FLETCHER HEITMAN, 1881–1882; THOMAS RADCLIFFE, 1882–1883; BENJAMIN FRANKLIN WHITE, 1883–1884; BERRIE CHANDLER MCIVER, 1883–1885; JAMES LEE LOVE, 1883–1884; AUGUSTUS WHITE LONG, 1884; SOLOMON COHEN WEILL, 1884–1885; JAMES RANDLETTE, 1885; CLAUDIUS DOCKERY, 1887–1888; STEPHEN BEAUREGARD WEEKS, 1887–1888; HUNTER L. HARRIS, 1888–1889; JOSEPH V. LEWIS, 1888–1889.

NOTE.

For the following Catalogue the University is chiefly indebted to Mrs. Cornelia P. Spencer, of Chapel Hill, who has been employed upon it for several years, giving much time and pains to the work. The difficulties have been such as only compilers of similar catalogues can appreciate.

It contains the names of all matriculates, so far as known, from 1795 to 1889 inclusive. Being the first of its kind to be issued by this University, it must contain many errors, and is now published in order that one more perfect may be made possible. It is earnestly requested that corrections and additions of any kind be sent to President Battle, at Chapel Hill. Valuable material has already been furnished by Dr. S. B. Weeks.

The plan of the Catalogue explains itself. Immediately after each name is placed the town or county from which the student came to the University; then his degree, with the year of graduation, or, in the case of non-graduates, the years of entrance and departure; following this, the occupation, etc.; then the latest known address, if different from that first given. Where no State is named, North Carolina is understood, except in such cases as plainly imply what State is meant.

Students known to be dead have been so recorded.

CATALOGUE OF STUDENTS.
1795-1889.

ABERNETHY, BENJAMIN FRANKLIN, Rialto, Chatham Co.: 1882–'83.
ADAMS, BENJAMIN B., Eatonton, Ga.: 1859–'61. Born 1841. C. S. A. Planter. Baldwin Co., Ga.
ADAMS, JAMES M., Yorkville, S. C.: 1859–'62.
ADAMS, JOSEPH HENRY, Augusta, Ga.: 1860–'61. Sergeant C. S. A. Born 1843, killed at Santa Rosa Island, Fla., 1861.
ADAMS, NATHANIEL, Wilmington: 1801.
ADAMS, PETER HENRY, Greensboro: 1861–'65. Scout C. S. A. West Point, Va.
ADAMS, ROBERT B., Yorkville, S. C: A. B., 1860.
ADAMS, SAMUEL B., Little Rock, Ark.: 1864–'65.
ADAMS, WILLIAM, Greensboro: A. B., 1858. Capt. C. S. A. Killed in battle, 1862.
ADAMS, WILLIAM GALES, Iredell Co.: 1878–'82. Teacher. West Tenn.
ADAMS, WILLIAM JACKSON, Carthage: A. B., 1881.
ADAMS, WILLIAM W., Petersburg, Va.: A. B., 1866.
ADERHOLDT, JOHN D. W., Dallas, Gaston Co.: 1886–'87.
ADNEY, EDWIN TAPPAN, Pittsboro: 1881–'82.
ALBERTSON, ROBERT BROOKE, Raleigh: Ph. B., 1881. Lawyer. Seattle, Washington.
ALBRIGHT, JAMES ALEXANDER, Graham: 1877–'78.
ALDERMAN, EDWIN ANDERSON, Wilmington: Ph. B., 1882. Pres. N. C. Teachers' Assembly. Supt. of Goldsboro Schools. Supt. of State Institutes, 1889–. Goldsboro.
ALDERMAN, WALTER WILLIAMS, Pender Co.: 1877–'79. Leasburg, Caswell Co.
ALDERMAN, WILLIAM COLIN, Fayetteville: 1877–'79.
ALDERMAN, WILLIAM F., New Hanover Co.: A. B., 1856. Prof. Math., Greensboro Female Coll. Greensboro.
ALEXANDER, CHARLES EATON, Boydton, Va.: A. B., 1825. Planter. Born 1805, died 1827.
ALEXANDER, CHARLES TAYLOR, Rutherford Co.: 1880–'84. Prin. of Institute. McKinney, Texas.

ALEXANDER, CHARLES WILSON HARRIS, Mecklenburg Co.: A. B., 1827. Dead.
ALEXANDER, CYRUS ADAMS, Mecklenburg Co.: A. B., 1820. Physician. Dead.
ALEXANDER, EDMUND, Plymouth: 1885–'86. Lawyer. Columbia.
ALEXANDER, ELAM, Mecklenburg Co.: A. B., 1825. Minister. Dead.
ALEXANDER, JOHN WILSON, Charlotte: 1884–'86. Merchant.
ALEXANDER, JOSEPH L. H., Mecklenburg Co.: 1847–'49. Dead.
ALEXANDER, JUNIUS M., Mecklenburg Co.: 1846–'47. Dead.
ALEXANDER, LAWSON HENDERSON, Lincoln Co.: A. B., 1816. Dead.
ALEXANDER, MARK, Boydton, Va.: A. B., 1811. Planter. Gen. Assem. of Va. M. C., 1819–'33. Mem. Va. Convention, 1829–'30. Born 1792, died July 6, 1883.
AEXANDER, NATHANIEL WASHINGTON, Mecklenburg Co.: A. B., 1821. Dead.
ALEXANDER, RICHARD HENDERSON, Mecklenburg Co.: A. B., 1817. Dead.
ALEXANDER, SAMUEL MIDGET, Creswell, Washington Co.: 1880–'81.
ALEXANDER, SYDENHAM B., Charlotte: A. B., 1860. Gen. Assem. Capt. C. S. A. Pres. Farmers' Alliance.
ALEXANDER, WILLIAM J., Plymouth: 1815.
ALEXANDER, WILLIAM JULIUS, Mecklenburg Co.: A. B., 1816. Gen. Assem. Speaker H. of Commons, 1829–'30.
ALEXANDER, WILLIAM LEE, McDowell Co.: A. B., 1854. Capt. C. S. A. Dead.
ALFORD, WILLIAM L., Normal College, Randolph Co.: A. B., 1861. Dead.
ALLEN, ALBERT VINE, New Berne: A. B., 1825. Lawyer. Born 1807, died 1829.
ALLEN, ALVIS WALDO, Grissom, Granville Co: Ph. B., 1882. Dead.
ALLEN, DAVID CHARLES, Brunswick Co: 1855–'57. Gen. Assem. Col. C. S. A. Lawyer. Planter. Armour, Columbus Co.
ALLEN, EDWARD L., Fayetteville, Tenn.: A. B., 1858. Died 1877.
ALLEN, ETHAN ARCHIBALD, Newton Grove, Sampson Co.: 1883–'84. Lawyer.
ALLEN, JOHN, Pitt Co.: 1810. Physician. Dead.
*ALLEN, NATHANIEL H., Leasburg, Caswell Co.: 1835–'36.
ALLEN, NATHANIEL MOORE, Chatham Co.: 1853–'56.
ALLEN, ROBERT L., Granville Co.: 1854–'56. C. S. A. Dead.
ALLEN, THOMAS TURNER, Windsor, Bertie Co.: A. B., 1861. Lawyer. Dead.
ALLEN, VINE, New Berne: A. B., 1853. A. M. Lawyer. Born 1831, died 1860.
ALLEN, WALTER N., Halifax Co.: 1855–'56. Lawyer.
ALLEN, WILLIAM HENRY, Greenville, Pitt Co.: 1886–'87.
ALLEN, WILLIAM MARSHALL, Polkton: 1888–.
ALLEN, WILLIAM T., Oxford: 1856–'58. Lieut. C. S. A. Planter.
ALLISON, JOHN A., Iredell Co.: 1849–'51.
ALLISON, JOHN R., Iredell Co: A. B., 1824. Planter. Physician. Dead. Columbus, Miss.

ALLISON, JULIUS F., Orange Co.: A. B., 1854. Dead.
ALLISON, RICHARD, Iredell Co.: A. B., 1820. Dead.
ALLISON, RICHARD M., Iredell Co.: 1841–'42. Dead.
ALLISON, ROBERT GRIER, Iredell Co.: A. B., 1827. Teacher. Died 1877.
ALSTON, ALEXANDER S., Edenton: 1826. Dead.
ALSTON, ALFRED, Warren Co.: 1810. Dead.
ALSTON, ALFRED, Warren Co.: A. B., 1847. Planter. Warrenton.
ALSTON, ALFRED T., Warren Co.: 1865–'66. Planter.
ALSTON, ARCHIBALD D., Warren Co.: 1834–'35.
ALSTON, AUGUSTUS A., Sparta, Ga.: 1821–'25.
ALSTON, BENJAMIN HARDY, Edenton: A. B., 1824. Physician. Dead.
ALSTON, CHARLES, Chatham Co.: 1838–'39.
ALSTON, EDWARD JONES, Warrenton: A. B., 1852. C. S. A. Dead.
ALSTON, JOHN J., Chatham Co.: 1808. Dead.
ALSTON, JOHN W., South Carolina: 1809. Dead.
ALSTON, JUNIUS A., Chatham Co.: 1848–'49.
ALSTON, KEMP PLUMMER, Warren Co.: A. B., 1838. Planter.
ALSTON, NATHANIEL MACON, Chatham Co.: 1854–'56. Dead.
ALSTON, NICHOLAS F., Warren Co.: 1841–'43. Dead.
ALSTON, NORMAN, Chatham Co.: 1853–'54.
ALSTON, PHILIP G., Warren Co.: 1855–'57. C. S. A. Warrenton.
ALSTON, PHILIP K., Chatham Co.: 1830–'32. Planter. Born 1811, died 1852.
ALSTON, PHILIP WHITNELL, Edenton: A. B., 1829. Minister. Dead.
ALSTON, SOLOMON W., Warren Co.: 1855–'56. Surgeon C. S. A. Died 1862.
ALSTON, WILLIAM C., Halifax Co.: 1795. Dead.
ALSTON, WILLIS, Halifax Co.: A. B., 1867. A. M. Physician. Littleton.
ALSTON, WILLIS WILSON, Sparta, Ga.: 1820–'24. Dead.
ALSTON, WILLIS W., Halifax Co.: A. B., 1824. Dead.
ALVES, JAMES, Orange Co.: 1807. Dead.
ALVES, JOHN, Kentucky: 1811. Dead.
ALVES, SAMUEL JOHNSTON, Orange Co.: A. B., 1821. Dead.
ALVES, WALTER, Kentucky: A. B., 1825. Physician. Dead.
ALVES, WILLIAM J., Orange Co.: 1807. Dead.
AMBROSE, SHERIDAN A., Hertford, Perquimans Co.: 1884–'85. Died 1886.
AMICK, THOMAS CICERO, Liberty: 1887–'88.
AMIS, JAMES SANDERS, Granville Co.: A. B., 1846. Lawyer. Oxford.
AMIS, JOHN D., Halifax Co.: 1802. Dead.
AMIS, LEWIS, Granville Co.: 1839–'40.
AMIS, RUFUS, Granville Co.: 1853–'54. Capt. C. S. A. Gen. Assem., 1879–'80. Journalist. Henderson.
AMIS, THOMAS GALE: A. B., 1801. Dead.
ANDERSON ADOLPHUS, Laurens District, S. C.: 1853–'54.
ANDERSON, ALBERT GALLATIN, Caswell Co.: A. B., 1834. Minister.
ANDERSON, CAMERON, Pensacola, Fla.: 1840–'41. Lawyer. Paymaster, U. S. N. Died 1852.
ANDERSON, EDWIN ALEXANDER, Wilmington: 1830–'31. A. B. Yale, 1835. A. M. M. D. Yale, 1837. Pres. N. C. Med. Society.

ANDERSON, GEORGE BURGWYN, Wilmington: 1847–'48. U. S. Mil. Acad. Lieut. U. S. A. Brig. Gen. C. S. A. Born 1830, killed at Sharpsburg, 1862.
ANDERSON, JACOB MARCUS, Pleasant Grove, Alamance Co.: 1885–'88.
ANDERSON, JAMES LATON, Winton, Hertford Co.: A. B., 1861.
ANDERSON, LAWRENCE M., Tallahassee, Fla.: A. B., 1860. Capt. C. S. A. Born 1841, killed at Shiloh, 1862.
ANDERSON, MONROE, Lebanon, Tenn.: 1859–'60.
ANDERSON, ROBERT WALKER, Wilmington: A. B., 1858. C. S. A. Born 1838, killed at the Wilderness, 1864.
ANDERSON, THOMPSON, Nashville, Tenn.: 1867–'68. Merchant.
ANDERSON, WALKER, Petersburg, Va.: A. B., 1819; A. M., 1822; LL. D., 1853. Prof. Rhet. and Log., U. N. C., 1833. Chief Justice Supreme Court, Fla., 1851–'53. Died 1857.
ANDERSON, WILLIAM EDWARD, Hillsboro: A. B., 1825; A. M., 1829. Teacher. Merchant. Banker. Born 1805, died 1852.
ANDERSON, WILLIAM E., Wilmington: A. B., 1854. Pres. Citizens' Nat. Bank, Raleigh.
ANDERSON, WILLIAM J., Fayetteville: 1822–'26. A. M. Merchant. Died 1852.
ANDRES, EDWIN F., Bladen Co.: 1839–'41. Dead.
ANDREWS, CLINTON MILTON, Greensboro: 1850–'51. Teacher. Lt. Col. C. S. A. Born 1829, killed at Nottoway C. H., 1864.
ANDREWS, JOHN BARR, Greensboro: A. B., 1854. Teacher. Capt. C. S. A. Born 1833, killed at Richmond, 1863.
ANDREWS, SILAS MILTON, Rowan Co.: A. B., 1826; A. M., 1831. Tutor, 1827. Minister. Dead. Doylestown, Pa.
ANDREWS, SAMUEL JAY, Greensboro: 1858–'62. Born 1839. Dead.
ANDREWS, MILTON VOLNEY, Orange Co.: 1869.
ANDREWS, WILLIAM JOHNSTON, Raleigh: 1887–. Born 1871.
ANGIER, JOHN CICERO, Durham: 1876–'79. Merchant. Born 1857.
ANTHONY, JAMES G., Halifax Co.: 1853–'56. C. S. A. Dead.
ANTHONY, JOHN, Scotland Neck: A. B., 1857. Lawyer. Corp. C. S. A. Born 1836, killed at Malvern Hill, 1862.
ANTHONY, JOHN ALSTON, King's Mountain: 1881–'82.
ANTHONY, WILLIAM, 1822.
ARGO, THOMAS MONROE, Wetumpka, Ala.: A. B., 1863. Lieut. C. S. A. LL. B., 1866. Lawyer. Solicitor 4th Dist. Raleigh.
ARMFIELD, EUGENE MOREHEAD, Guilford Co.: A. B., 1888. Born 1869. Banker. High Point.
ARMFIELD H., Guilford Co.: 1826. Dead.
ARMSTEAD, RICHARD, Plymouth: A. B., 1804. Dead.
ARMSTEAD, ROBERT, Plymouth: 1815. Dead.
ARMSTEAD, STARK, Bertie Co.: 1834–'35. Born 1819, died 1843.
ARMSTEAD, THOMAS S., Martin Co.: 1823. Merchant. Died 1871.
ARMSTEAD, THOMAS STARK, Plymouth: A. B., 1862; A. M., 1868. Lieut. C. S. A. Lawyer and Journalist.
ARMSTEAD, WILLIAM J., Plymouth: 1815. Dead.
ARMSTRONG, EDWARD H., Wilmington: 1858–'61. Capt. C. S. A. Dead.

ARMSTRONG, EGBERT M., Somerville, Tenn.: 1858-'59. C. S. A. Killed in action, 1861.
ARMSTRONG, JAMES WATSON, Orange Co.: A. B., 1827. Dead.
ARMSTRONG, MARTIN W., Germantown: 1814. Dead.
ARMSTRONG, THOMAS LAPSLEY, Orange Co.: A. B., 1832. Tutor, 1833-'34.
ARMSTRONG, THOMAS T., Germantown: 1828.
ARNOLD, HUGH M., Newnan, Ga.: 1860-'62.
ARNOLD, SAMUEL JAMES, Newnan, Ga.: 1860-'61. Planter. Born 1841.
ARRINGTON, ARCHIBALD H., Montgomery, Ala.: 1859-'60. C. S. A. Born 1843, killed at Malvern Hill, 1862.
ARRINGTON, ARCHIBALD HUNTER, Hilliardston: 1876-'79. Rocky Mt.
ARRINGTON, ARTHUR, Louisburg: A. B., 1878. Planter.
ARRINGTON, GEORGE W., Nash Co.: 1852-'53. Teacher.
ARRINGTON, GEORGE WIMBERLEY, Hilliardston: 1882-'84. Died 1885.
ARRINGTON, JAMES N., Nash Co.: 1851-'53. Dead.
ARRINGTON, RICHARD T., Warrenton: A. B., 1853.
ARRINGTON, THOMAS C., Nash Co.: 1838-'39. Dead.
ARRINGTON, THOMAS MANN, Nash Co.: A. B., 1849. Lt. Col. C. S. A. Gen. Assem., Ala. Judge Montgomery City Court. Montgomery, Ala.
ASHE, JOHN B., Tenn.: 1831.
ASHE, RICHARD JAMES, Hillsboro: A. B., 1842. Capt. C. S. A. Law. Merchant. Born 1821. Bakersfield, Cal.
ASHE, SAMUEL P., Halifax Co.: 1806. Gen. Assem. Dead.
ASHE, SAMUEL S., Galveston, Texas: 1855-'57. Gen. Assem. Houston, Texas.
ASHE, THOMAS SAMUEL, Perry Co, Ala.: A. B., 1832; A. M., 1838; LL. D., 1878. Gen. Assem., N. C. Mem. Confed. Cong., 1861-'64. C. S. Sen., 1864. M. C., 1872-'76. Judge Supreme Court, 1878-'87. Died 1887.
ASHE, WILLIAM WILLARD, Raleigh: 1888-'89.
ASHLEY, CHESTER G., Little Rock, Ark.: 1864-'65.
ASHURST, JOHN MILTON, Eatonton, Ga.: 1834-'35. Lawyer. Sol. Gen., Ga. Born 1817, died 1852.
ASKEW, ABNER, H., Hertford Co.: A. B., 1866. Physician. Winton.
ASKEW, ANDREW JACKSON, Bertie Co.: 1837-'38. Physician. Dead.
ASKEW, CHARLES THOMPSON, Raleigh: 1875-'78.
ASKEW, DAVID OUTLAW, Bertie Co: 1815. Dead.
ASKEW, GEORGE WASHINGTON, Columbus, Miss.: A. B., 1860. Capt. C. S. A. Manufacturer. Born 1838. Stokesville, Miss.
ATKINS, BENJAMIN FRANKLIN, Cumberland Co.: A. B., 1841. Lawyer. Dead.
ATKINSON, EDWARD RUFFIN, Edgecombe Co.: 1860-'61. C. S. A. Born 1843. Killed at Charlottesville, 1863.
ATKINSON, JOHN WILDER, Wilmington: 1884-'86. Richmond, Va.
ATKINSON, WADE HAMPTON, Johnston Co.: 1884-'85. M. D. Georgetown Coll., 1889.
ATTMORE, ISAAC TAYLOR, New Berne: A. B., 1860. C. S. A. Born 1838. Killed at Spottsylvania, 1864.

ATWATER, ALFRED SIDNEY, Chatham Co.: 1881–'82. Physician.
AUSTIN, CHARLES J., Tarboro: A. B., 1865. Merchant.
AUSTIN, EDWARD, 1821.
AUSTIN, HENRY WILSON, Monroe: 1879–'80.
AUSTIN, ROBERT H., Tarboro: 1826–'30. Merchant.
AUSTIN, WILLIAM H., Tarboro: 1857–'59. C. S. A. Killed in battle.
AVENT, THOMAS W., Nash Co.: 1833–'34. Planter. Hilliardston.
AVERITT, JAMES BATTLE, Onslow Co.: 1850–'52. Episcopal Minister. Marlborough, Md.
AVERITT, JAMES LEONIDAS, Miccosukie, Fla.: A. B., 1856. C. S. A. Born 1834, died 1881. Madison Co., Miss.
AVERITT, JESSE, Miccosukie, Fla.: 1851–'53. Sergeant C. S. A. Born 1831. Killed at Wilderness, 1864.
AVERITT, JOHN A., Onslow Co.: 1847–'48. Capt. C. S. A. Killed in battle.
AVERY, ALPHONZO CALHOUN, Morganton: A. B., 1857. Capt. C. S. A. State Sen., 1866–'70. Judge Sup. Ct., 1878–'88. Judge Supreme Ct., 1888–.
AVERY, CLARKE MOULTON, Morganton: A. B., 1839. Colonel C. S. A. Killed in battle, 1864.
AVERY, ISAAC ERWIN, Morganton: 1847–'48. Colonel C. S. A. Killed in action, 1863.
AVERY, JOHN MOREHEAD, Morganton: A. B., 1881. Austin, Texas.
AVERY, THOMAS L., Morganton: A. B., 1841. Dead.
AVERY, WILLIAM WAIGHTSTILL, Morganton: A. B., 1837; A. M., 1850. Lawyer. Mem. Gen. Assem. Speaker State Sen. C. S. Sen. Colonel C. S. A. Killed at Morganton, 1864.
AVERY, WILLOUGHBY F., Morganton: 1860–'61. Capt. C. S. A. Dead.
AYCOCK, ALBERT ELIJAH, Wedgefield, S. C.: 1879–'80.
AYCOCK, CHARLES BRANTLEY, Wayne Co.: Ph. B., 1879. Lawyer. Pres. Elector, 1888. Goldsboro.
BACKHOUSE, BENJAMIN W., New Berne: 1830–'33. Dead.
BACKHOUSE, JOHN ALLEN, New Berne: A. B., 1830; A. M., 1838. Tutor 1830–'31. Minister. Dead.
BACOT, PETER B., Darlington District, S. C.: A. B., 1859. C. S. A. Physician. Mars Bluff.
BACOT, TOURS L., Darlington District, S. C.: 1857–'59. C. S. A. Died 1882.
BADGER, GEORGE EDMUND, Raleigh: 1855–'56. Physician.
BADGER, RICHARD COGSDELL, Raleigh: A. B., 1859. Major C. S. A. U. S. Dist. Att'y, 1873–'77. Gen. Assem. Member Convention, 1875. Born 1839, died 1882.
BADGER, THOMAS, Raleigh: 1859–'62. Ord. Sergeant C. S. A.
BADGETT, THOMAS JEFFERSON, Caswell Co.: A. B., 1859. Dead.
BADHAM, WILLIAM, Edenton: A. B., 1854. Lawyer. Capt. C. S. A. Dead.
BAGLEY, WILLIAM, Williamston: 1843–'45. Dead.
BAHNSON, GEORGE WILLIAM, Farmington, Davie Co.: 1887–'88.
BAILEY, JOHN LANCASTER, Pasquotank Co.: 1815–1819. Mem. Conv., 1835. Judge Super. Ct., 1836–'64. Died 1877.
BAILEY, THOMAS B., Hillsboro: 1845–'48. Teacher. Dead.
BAILEY, WILLIAM, Monticello, Fla.: 1851. Captain C. S. A. Killed in battle.

BAILEY, WILLIAM EDWARD, Charleston, S. C.: A. B., 1813. Professor Anc. Lang., Charleston Coll. Dead.
BAIRD, BENJAMIN R., Person Co.: 1832.
BAIRD, WILLIAM W., Person Co.: A. B., 1860. Lieutenant C. S. A. Dead. Macon, Miss.
BAKER, DANIEL BELLUNE, Brunswick Co.: A. B., 1824. Judge Super. Ct., Fla. Died 1870.
BAKER, ISAAC, Brunswick Co.: A. B., 1825. M. D. Judge Super. Ct., Ark. Born 1804. Dead. Little Rock.
BAKER, JAMES SMITH, Jackson Co., Fla.: A. B., 1858. Gen. Assem., 1864.
BAKER, JOHN A., Louisburg: 1860–'61. Sergeant C. S. A. Planter.
BAKER, JOHN BURGESS, Gates Co.: 1802. Physician. H. of Com. State Sen. Born 1785, died 1838.
BAKER, JOSEPH HENRY, Edgecombe Co.: 1826.
BAKER, JOSEPH HENRY, Tarboro: 1848–'51. Sergeant C. S. A. Mem. Conv., 1868. Gen. Assem. Physician. Born 1831.
BAKER, JOSEPH HENRY, Tarboro: A. B., 1887.
BAKER, JULIAN MEREDITH, Tarboro: B. S., 1879. Physician.
BAKER, MARMADUKE, Gates Co.: 1798. Dead.
BAKER, MARMADUKE, Ala.: 1841.
BAKER, SIMMONS JONES, Martin Co.: 1821–'25. M. D. Edinburgh. State Sen. Born 1775, died 1853.
BAKER, THOMAS ATKINSON, Tarboro: 1883–'85. Alabama.
BAKER, WILLIAM, Gates Co.: 1798. Dead.
BAKER, WILLIAM SPARKMAN, Edgecombe Co.: 1826–'30. Physician. Planter. Banker. Gen. Assem. Born 1809, died 1861.
BALDWIN, JOHN J., Chatham Co.: 1853–'54. Dead.
BALDWIN, LUCIAN F., Chatham Co.: 1858–'60.
BALDWIN, MELVILLE TRIAM, Siam, Chatham Co.: 1853–'54.
BALDWIN, WILLIAM G., Whiteville, Columbus Co.: 1858–'60.
BALL, McCORD WRIGHT, Greensboro: 1887–.
BALLANFANT, JOHN, Culleoka, Tenn.: A. B., 1844. Gen. Assem. Farmer.
BALLANTINE, JAMES ERASTUS, Varina, Wake Co.: 1884–'85.
BALLARD, JOHN WILLIAM, Raleigh: A. B., 1859. Captain C. S. A. Killed at Corinth.
BALLARD, ROBERT E., Louisburg: 1857–'58. Lieutenant C. S. A. Planter. Author. Warren Co.
BANKS, ANDREW JACKSON RAYNER, Wake Co.: 1869.
BANKS, GEORGE WASHINGTON, Wake Co.: 1869.
BANKS, JOHN TROUP, Columbus, Ga.: A. B., 1849. Dead.
BARBEE, ALGERNON SYDNEY, Chapel Hill: A. B., 1860. Born 1840. Lieutenant C. S. A. Merchant.
BARBEE, ALLEN JONES, Hillsboro: 1801. Dead.
BARBEE, ALLEN JONES, Orange Co.: A. B., 1825. Physician. Dead.
BARBEE, CHESLEY PAGE PATTERSON, Madison Co., Tenn.: A. B., 1843. Dead.
BARBEE, WILLIAM FRANKLIN, Haywood Co., Tenn.: A. B., 1844. Dead.

BARBEE, WILLIS, Chapel Hill: 1818. Planter. Physician. Born 1802, died 1869.
BARDEN, JEFFERSON DAVIS, Wilson: 1884–'86. Lawyer.
BARKER, JOHN ALEXANDER, Whiteville, Columbus Co.: 1884–'85. Durham Co.
BARKER, JOHN W., Halifax C. H., Va.: 1808. Dead.
BARKSDALE, EDWARD R., Marshall Co., Miss.: 1854–'55.
BARKSDALE, JOHN NASH, Rutherford Co., Tenn.: A. B., 1839. Lawyer. Born 1819, died 1844.
BARLOW, JULIUS SHIRLEY, Tarboro: A. B., 1868. C. S. A. Died 1871.
BARLOW, THADDEUS BATES, Tarboro: 1875–'77.
BARNES, ALLEN, N. C.: 1801. Dead.
BARNES, BENJAMIN BLOUNT, Wilson: A.B., 1857. Born 1838. Planter. Memphis, Tenn.
BARNES, CALVIN, Wilson Co.: A. B., 1861. Born 1839. Captain C. S. A. Farmer. Wilson.
BARNES, DAVID ALEXANDER, Northampton Co.: A. B., 1840. Born 1819. Gen. Assem. Mem. Conv., 1861. Judge Super. Ct., 1865–'68. Lawyer. Murfreesboro.
BARNES, EDWIN, Wilson Co.: 1858–'59. Physician. Surgeon C. S. A. Born 1839, died 1882.
BARNES, GEORGE BADGER, Northampton Co.: A. B., 1859. Born 1839. Q. M., C. S. A. Lawyer. Com. Merchant. Norfolk, Va.
BARNES, JESSE SHARP, Stantonsburg, Wilson Co.: A. B. 1858. Lawyer. Captain C. S. A. Born 1833. Killed at Seven Pines, 1862.
BARNES, JOHN PATTERSON, Suggville, Ala.: 1841–'42. Physician. Born 1826, died 1875. Mobile, Ala.
BARNES, WILLIAM DEANS, Hertford Co.: A. B., 1852. Born 1830. Lawyer. Planter. Lieutenant Col. C. S. A. Gen. Assem. of Fla. Speaker Fla. Sen., 1879. Comptroller, 1881. Marianna, Fla.
BARNETT, WILLIAM ELLIS, Crawford, Ala.: A. B., 1845. Lawyer. Born 1824, died 1860. Glennville, Ala.
BARR, ABSALOM KNOX, Rowan Co.: A. B., 1827. Minister. Born 1806, died 1846.
BARRETT, ALEXANDER, Carthage, Moore Co.: A. B., 1860. Lieutenant C. S. A.
BARRETT, DAVID S., Carthage, Moore Co.: 1859–'61. Captain C. S. A.
BARRETT, JAMES, Augusta, Ga.: 1860–'62. Born 1842. Lieutenant C. S. A.
BARRETT, JAMES FRANCIS, Mooresville, Iredell Co.: 1883–'84. Statesville.
BARRETT, JAMES FRANKLIN, Franklinton: 1883–'84.
BARRETT, JOHN T., Pitt Co.: 1855–'56.
BARRETT, ROBERT G., Carthage, Moore Co.: 1854–'56. A. M. Minister.
BARRINGER, DANIEL MOREAU, Cabarrus Co.: A. B., 1826. Gen. Assem. Mem. Conv. 1835. M. C. 1843–'49. Min. to Spain, 1849–'53. Born 1806, died 1873.
BARRINGER, RUFUS, Cabarrus Co.: A. B., 1842. Born 1821. Lawyer. Gen. Assem. Brig. Gen. C. S. A. Charlotte.

BARRINGER, VICTOR CLAY, Cabarrus Co.: A. B., 1848. Born 1827. Comr. to revise statutes of U. S. Judge Internat. Ct., Alexandria, Egypt.
BARRINGER, WILLIAM, Concord, Cabarrus Co.: 1833–'34. Meth. Minister. Born 1816, died 1873.
BARROW, CHARLES HENRY, Edgecombe Co.: A. B., 1861. Born 1839. Captain C. S. A. Physician. Planter. Whitaker's.
BARROW, FREDERICK PROBY, Jackson, Northampton, Co.: 1875–'77.
BARROW, WILLIAM L., Northampton Co.: 1837–'38. Physician. Died 1883.
BARROW, WILLIAM M., Edenton: 1839–'40.
BARRY, JOHN D., Wilmington: 1856–'59. Dead.
BARTEE, JAMES R., Columbus, Miss.: 1859–'61. Dead.
BARTLETT, LEONARD W., Sumpter, S. C.: 1859–'61. Captain C. S. A. Killed in battle.
BASKERVILLE, GEORGE, Orange Co.: 1812. Dead.
BASKERVILLE, GEORGE THOMAS, Mecklenburg Co., Va.: A. B., 1848. Captain C. S. A. Killed in battle.
BASKERVILLE, WILLIAM R., Boydton, Va.: 1813. Dead.
BASON, GEORGE F., Alamance Co.: 1859–'60. C. S. A. Lawyer. Dallas.
BASON, JOSEPH H., Alamance Co.: 1858–'60. Sergeant C. S. A. Born 1840. Killed in battle, 1861.
BASS, EDWARD F., Columbia, Tex.: 1859–'61. Dead.
BASS, GEORGE P., Columbia, Tex.: 1859–'60.
BASS, JOHN H., Macon, Ga.: 1858–'60.
BATCHELOR, FRANK HOWARD, Raleigh: 1887–.
BATCHELOR, KEMP BATTLE, Raleigh: 1887. M. D. Univ. of Md., 1889.
BATCHELOR, JOSEPH JOHN BRANCH, Halifax Co.: A. B., 1845. Att'y Gen. Raleigh.
BATCHELOR, OLIVER DOUGLAS, Nashville, Nash Co.: A. B., 1888. Born 1868. Lawyer.
BATCHELOR, WILLIAM PLUMMER, Raleigh: 1867–'68. Chief Clerk to Sect'y of State.
BATE, JAMES HENRY, Bertie Co.: A. B., 1836. Minister. Born 1815, died 1848.
BATTLE, ALFRED, Edgecombe Co.: 1806. Dead.
BATTLE, BURWELL, Edgecombe Co.: 1806. Dead.
BATTLE, CHRISTOPHER COLUMBUS, Edgecombe Co.: A. B., 1835. Lawyer. U. S. A., Mexican War. Born 1814, died 1859.
BATTLE, CULLEN, Edgecombe Co.: 1802. M. D. Univ. of Pa. Planter. Born 1785, died 1879. Eufala, Ala.
BATTLE, DOSSEY, Nash Co.: 1858–'61. Lt. C. S. A. Lawyer. Journalist. Tarboro.
BATTLE, ELISHA, Edgecombe Co.: Dead.
BATTLE, GASTON, Rocky Mount: 1886–. Born 1871.
BATTLE, GEORGE GORDON, Rocky Mount: 1881–'82.
BATTLE, HENRY L., Edgecombe Co.: 1802. Dead.
BATTLE, HENRY L., Edgecombe Co.: 1851–'52. C. S. A. Killed in battle.
BATTLE, HENRY LAWRENCE, Rocky Mount: 1878–'81.

BATTLE, HERBERT BEMERTON, Chapel Hill: Ph. B., 1881; Ph. D., 1887. Born 1862. Director State Exp. Station, 1887-. Raleigh.

BATTLE, ISAAC L., Edgecombe Co.: 1834-'35. Born 1816, died 1843. Marianna, Fla.

BATTLE, JACOB, Rocky Mount: 1866-'68. Born 1852. A. M. Univ. of Va. Lawyer.

BATTLE, JAMES P., Edgecombe Co.: 1847-'51. Physician. Dead.

BATTLE, JAMES SMITH, Edgecombe Co.: 1802. Planter. Born 1786, died 1854.

BATTLE, JAMES SMITH, Tarboro: 1863-'67. C. S. A. State Sen., 1881-'83. Raleigh.

BATTLE, JOEL, Edgecombe Co.: 1799. Dead.

BATTLE, JOEL DOSSEY, Chapel Hill: A. B., 1847; A. M., 1852. Physician. Died 1858.

BATTLE, JOHN B., Shelby Co., Tenn.: 1856-'57. Dead.

BATTLE, JUNIUS CULLEN, Chapel Hill: A. B., 1860. Corp. C. S. A. Born 1841. Killed at South Mountain, 1862.

BATTLE, KEMP PLUMMER, Chapel Hill: A. B., 1849; A. M., 1852. LL. D. Born 1831. Tutor Math., 1850-'54. Lawyer. Member Conven., 1861. Pres. Chatham R. R. State Treasurer. Pres. State Agric. Soc. Author. Pres. U. N. C., 1875-.

BATTLE, KEMP PLUMMER, Raleigh: A. B., 1879. M. D. Univ. of Va. and Bellevue Med. Coll.

BATTLE, LEWIS JUNIUS, Raleigh: Ph. B., 1886. U. S. Geol. Surv. Washington, D. C.

BATTLE, MARMADUKE, Tarboro: 1881-'83.

BATTLE, RICHARD HENRY, Edgecombe Co.: A. B., 1828. Lawyer. Born 1807, died 1885.

BATTLE, RICHARD HENRY, Chapel Hill: A. B., 1854. Tutor Greek, 1854-'58. Lawyer. Capt. C. S. A. Chm'n State Dem. Ex. Com., 1884-'88. Raleigh.

BATTLE, THOMAS HALL, Chapel Hill: A. B., 1880. Lawyer. Rocky Mount.

BATTLE, TURNER WESTRAY, Edgecombe Co.: A. B., 1846; A. M., 1849. Capt. C. S. A. Planter. Rocky Mount.

BATTLE, TURNER WESTRAY, Rocky Mount: 1879-'81. Com. Merchant. Norfolk, Va.

BATTLE, WESLEY LEWIS, Chapel Hill: 1859-'62. Lt. C. S. A. Born 1843. Killed at Gettysburg, 1863.

BATTLE, WILLIAM HORN, Edgecombe Co.: A. B., 1820; LL. D. Lawyer. H. of Com., 1833-'35. Reporter to Supreme Ct., 1834-'40. Judge Superior Ct., 1840-'52. Judge Supreme Ct., 1852-'68. Prof. Law U. N. C. 25 years. Twice Comr. to revise N. C. Statutes. Born 1802, died 1879.

BATTLE, WILLIAM HORN, Chapel Hill: A. B., 1853. Born 1833. M. D. Univ. of Pa. Surg. C. S. A. Lilesville.

BATTLE, WILLIAM JAMES, Chapel Hill: A. B., 1888; A.M., 1889. Born 1870.

BATTLE, WILLIAM SMITH, Edgecombe Co.: A. B., 1844. Mem. Conven., 1861. Planter. Tarboro.

BATTLE, WILLIAM SMITH, Edgecombe Co.: 1866–'67. Dead.
BATTLE, WILLIAM SMITH, Warrenton: 1886–'88. Wilmington.
BAXTER, GEORGE A., Richmond, Va.: 1851–'52. Capt. C. S. A. Killed in battle.
BEALL, FRANK HARPER, Linwood, Davidson Co: 1888–.
BEALL, JOHN M., Salisbury: 1883–'84.
BEALL, ROBERT LAMAR, Davidson Co.: A. B., 1852. Physician. Lenoir.
BEALL, ZEPHANIAH, Ga.: 1821–'22. Dead.
BEAMAN, JOHN ROBINSON, Clinton, Sampson Co.: 1877–'79.
BEAMER, PETER ROBERT, Dobson, Surry Co.: 1884–'85. Teacher.
BEARD, JOHN L., Rowan Co.: 1814. Dead.
BEARD, WILLIAM H., North Carolina.
BEASLEY, JAMES EDWARD, Plymouth: A. B., 1859. Born 1839. Lieut. C. S. A. Gen. Ins. Agt. Memphis, Tenn.
BEASLEY, JOSEPH H., Plymouth: 1835–'36. Talladega, Ala.
BEASLEY, WILLIAM FESSENDEN, Tarboro: 1865–'66. Born 1845. C. S. A. Oxford.
BEATTY, DOUGLAS PEARSON, Mocksville: 1848–'50. Physician.
BEATTY, HENRY F., Bladen Co.: 1809. Dead.
BEATTY, WILLIAM H., Hillsboro: 1840–'42. Dead.
BECK, THOMAS K., Cahawba, Ala.: 1825. Dead.
BECKTON, FREDERICK E., Jones Co.: 1804. Dead.
BECKWITH, JAMES FABIUS, Chatham Co.: 1878–'79.
BECKWITH, SIDNEY THOMAS, Lake Landing, Hyde Co.: 1882–'83. LL. B., 1885. Lawyer. Monroe.
BEENE, BENJAMIN YANCEY, Cahawba, Ala.: A. B., 1849. Lawyer. Born 1826, died 1856. Selma.
BEIN, HUGH HAGART, New Orleans, La.: A. B., 1859; LL. B. Adjt. Gen. C. S. A. Dead. Little Rock, Ark.
BELL, DAVID, Enfield: 1876–'78. Lawyer. Gen. Assem.
BELL, EDWARD STARKIE J., Bladen Springs, Ala.: A. B., 1858. Lieut. C. S. A. Killed in battle.
BELL, JAMES FRANKLIN, Statesville: 1852. Lawyer. Journalist. Died 1858.
BELL, JOHN FRANKLIN, Statesville: A. B., 1852. Sergt. C. S. A. Killed in battle.
BELL, JOSEPH MASTERS, Jackson, Ark.: A. B., 1854. Jacksonport, Ark.
BELL, LUTHER RICE, Oxford: A. B., 1861. C. S. A. Killed in battle.
BELL, ROBERT, Louisburg: 1801. Dead.
BELL, SAMUEL SLADE, New Berne: A. B., 1823. Lawyer. Born 1804. Dead.
BELL, WILLIAM ALEXANDER, Eutaw, Ala.: A. B., 1842. Born 1825, died 1850.
BELLAMY, BENJAMIN ALEXANDER, Marianna, Fla.: A. B., 1855. Born 1833. C. S. A. Carthage, Tex.
BELLAMY, CHARLES EDWARD, Marianna, Fla.: A. B., 1851. M. D. Univ. of Pa., 1855. Surg. C. S. A. Born 1832. Killed in battle July 27, 1864. Bolivar Co., Miss.

BELLAMY, EDWARD C., Nash Co.: 1818. Physician. Dead.
BELLAMY, JOHN DILLARD, Wilmington: 1886-.
BELLAMY, JOSEPH CLINCH, Edgecombe Co.: A. B., 1861. Born 1840. Sergt. C. S. A. Planter. Whitaker's.
BELLAMY, MARSDEN, Wilmington: 1858-'61. Born 1843. Paymaster C. S. A. Lawyer.
BELLAMY, RICHARD BLOUNT, Marianna, Fla.: A. B., 1855. Born 1833. Surg. C. S. A. Campbellton, Fla.
BELLAMY, RUSSELL, Wilmington: 1887-.
BELLAMY, SPIER COFFIELD, Enfield: 1878-'80. Planter.
BELLAMY, WILLIAM CROOM, Marianna, Fla.: 1847-'51. Born 1830. Surg. C. S. A. Physician. Atlanta, Ga.
BELLAMY, WILLIAM JAMES HARRISS, Wilmington: 1860-'63. Born 1844. C. S. A. M. D. Univ. of N. Y., 1868. Pres. New Hanover Med. Assoc.
BELSHER, THADDEUS CONSTANTINE, Pickensville, Ala.: A. B., 1857. A. M. Born 1832. C. S. A. Founder Univ. of Columbus, Miss. Pres. Carrollton Coll. Carrollton, Miss.
BELT, THOMAS WRIGHT, Iredell Co.: A. B., 1827. Physician. Planter. Died 1860.
BELTON, HENRY J. G., Salisbury: 1836.
BENBURY, JAMES E., Sunbury, Gates Co.: 1858-'62. Died 1862.
BENBURY, JOHN AVERY, Edenton: 1843-'44. A. B., Princeton. Gen. Assem. Capt. C. S. A. Born 1827. Killed at Malvern Hill, 1862.
BENBURY, JOSEPH, New Orleans, La.: 1857.
BENBURY, LEMUEL CREECY, Edenton: A. B., 1858. Capt. C. S. A. Gen. Assem. Dead.
BENJAMIN, JOSEPH, New Orleans, La.: A. B., 1847. Dead.
BENNEHAN, THOMAS DAVIS, Orange Co.: A. B., 1801. Planter. Born 1781, died 1847.
BENNERS, AUGUSTUS, New Berne: A. B., 1837. Lawyer. Gen. Assem. of Ala. Died 1886.
BENNETT, CRAWFORD DUNLAP, Norwood, Stanley Co.: 1888-.
BENNETT, JOHN TYLER, Norwood, Stanley Co.: 1886-.
BENNETT, MARK, Town Creek, Edgecombe Co.: 1851. Born 1833, died 1851.
BENSON, JAMES WILLIAM, Beasley Hill, Johnston Co.: 1885-'86.
BENTON, JOHN HOGAN, Monroe: 1878-'79.
BENTON, THOMAS HART, Orange Co.: 1799. Gen. Assem. of Tenn. Col. U. S. A., war of 1812. U. S. Sen. from Mo., 1820-'50. M. C., 1852-'54. Author of "Thirty Years View," and "Abridgment of Debates in Congress." Born 1782, died April 10th, 1858.
BERRY, CICERO N., Hillsboro: 1850-'52.
BERRY, GEE WOOD, Marion District, S. C.: A. B., 1847.
BETHELL, GEORGE WASHINGTON, Danville, Va.: 1885-'86.
BETHELL, PINKNEY C., Caswell Co.: 1835-'36. Dead.
BETHELL, WILLIAM D., Rockingham Co.: 1831-'33. Dead. Ruffin.
BETTENCOURT, WILLIAM H., Wilmington: 1851-'52. Merchant. Born 1834, died 1865.

BETTNER, GEORGE SHONNARD, New Berne: A. B., 1823. Tutor U. N. C. 1826. Physician. Born 1801, died 1860. New York.
BETTS, ALEXANDER DAVIS, Harnett Co.: A. B., 1855. Born 1832. Meth. Minister. Chaplain C. S. A. Died May, 1889. Swan Quarter.
BETTS, WILLIAM ARCHIBALD, Greensboro: Ph. B., 1880. Meth. Minister. S. C.
BIDDLE, SAMUEL SIMPSON, Craven Co.: A. B., 1832. Planter. Gen. Assem. Born 1811, died 1873.
BIGGS, WILLIAM, Williamston: 1858–'61. Capt. C. S. A. Lawyer. Journalist. Born 1843. Dead.
BILLINGSLEY, JOHN T., Marion, Ala.: 1858–'59.
BINGHAM, JOHN ARCHIBALD, Hillsboro: 1831–'35. A. B.; A. M. Minister. Prof. Caldwell Inst. Born 1815, died Oct. 18, 1855.
BINGHAM, ROBERT, Orange Co.: A. B., 1857. A. M. Born 1838. Capt. C. S. A. Prin. Bingham School, 1873–.
BINGHAM, ROBERT WORTH, Bingham School: 1888–. Born 1871.
BINGHAM, WILLIAM, Orange Co.: A. B., 1856. Col. C. S. A. Prin. Bingham School, 1865–'73. Author Latin and Eng. Text-books. Born 1835, died Feb. 18, 1873.
BINGHAM, WILLIAM JAMES, Hillsboro: A. B., 1825. Prin. Bingham School, 1826–'63. Born 1802, died Feb. 19, 1866.
BISHOP, GEORGE, Bertie Co.: 1859–'60. Planter.
BITTING, JOHN HENRY, Germantown: A. B., 1858. Dead.
BITTING, JOSEPH W., Stokes Co.: 1816.
BITTING, SAMUEL T., Mount Airy: 1869.
BIZZELL, ROBERT MOSELY, Johnston Co.: 1878–'79. Harper's.
BLACK, ARCHIBALD RAY, Moore Co.: A. B., 1853. Teacher. Burgaw.
BLACKLEDGE, BENJAMIN FRANKLIN, New Berne: A. B., 1821. Physician. Dead.
BLACKLEDGE, RICHARD B., New Berne: 1812. Dead.
BLACKLEDGE, THOMAS WHARTON, New Berne: A. B., 1813. Dead.
BLACKLEDGE, WILLIAM SALTER, New Berne: A. B., 1813. Gen. Assem. M. C. Dead.
BLACKMAN, WILLIAM S., Sampson Co.: 1805. Gen. Assem. Dead.
BLACKMER, WALTER STEELE, Salisbury: 1876–'78.
BLACKMON, CULLEN A., Wayne Co.: 1829–'30. Dead.
BLACKMON, CULLEN A., De Soto, Miss.: 1850–'54.
BLACKWELL, JAMES WASHINGTON, Durham: 1876–'78.
BLACKWOOD, CHARLES ALEXANDER, Chapel Hill: 1886–'88. Petersburg, Va.
BLAIN, JAMES M., Fairfield Dist., S. C.: 1858–'60.
BLAIR, BURWELL, Louisburg: 1866–'68. Merchant.
BLAIR, FRANCIS PRESTON, Washington, D. C.: 1839–'40. A. B. Princeton, 1841. Gen. Assem., Mo., 1852–'54. M. C. from Mo., 1856–'60. Maj. Gen. U. S. A., 1862. Collector, St. Louis, 1866. U. S. Sen., 1870–'73. Born 1821, died 1875.
BLAKE, JOEL CLIFTON, Miccosukie, Fla.: A. B., 1850. Planter. Capt. C. S. A. Born 1831. Killed at Gettysburg, 1863.

BLAKE, SAMUEL RICHARDSON, Fayetteville: A. B., 1834. Tutor U. N. C., 1834–'35. Dead.
BLAKE, SAMUEL RICHARDSON, Miccosukie, Fla.: A. B., 1850.
BLAKE, WILLIAM B., Fayetteville: 1847–'49.
BLAKE, WILLIAM KENNEDY, Fayetteville: A. B., 1846. Born 1824. Prof. Female Colleges at Greensboro and Fayetteville, N. C., and Spartanburg, S. C. Lawyer. Gen. Assem., S. C. Spartanburg, S. C.
BLAKELEY, JOHNSTON, Chatham Co.: 1797. Capt. U. S. N., War 1812. Captured "Reindeer" 1814. Rec'd Gold Medal from Congress. Captured "Atalanta." Lost at sea on the "Wasp," 1814.
BLANCHARD, JAMES D., Aberdeen, Miss.: 1859–'61.
BLAND, PETER R., Va.: 1817. Dead.
BLEDSOE, EDWARD M., Raleigh: 1867–'68. Planter.
BLEDSOE, WILLIAM H., Raleigh: 1863–'67. Lawyer.
BLEWITT, THOMAS G., S. C.: 1810. Dead.
BLOCKER, CHARLES H., Fayetteville: 1860–'61.
BLOCKER, OCTAVIUS H., Fayetteville: 1860–'61. Capt. C. S. A. Land Agent. Bladen Co.
BLOUNT, BENJAMIN J., Nashville: 1855–'57. Lieut. C. S. A. Killed in battle.
BLOUNT, FREDERICK SWANN, New Berne: 1822–'25. Lawyer. Born 1807. Mobile, Ala.
BLOUNT, JOHN GRAY, Washington: 1837–'39. Born 1819, died 1842.
BLOUNT, JOHN GRAY, Washington: 1887–.
BLOUNT, RICHARD H. L., Woodville, Perquimans Co.: 1849–'50. Dead.
BLOUNT, SAMUEL MASTERS, Washington: 1886–.
BLOUNT, WILLIAM AUGUSTUS, Washington: A. B., 1844. Born 1823. Maj. C. S. A. Planter.
BLUE, LUTHER, Richmond Co.: 1851–'52. Lawyer. Capt. C. S. A. Miss.
BLUME, BENJAMIN BYNUM, Stokes Co.: A. B., 1824; A. M., 1831. Dead.
BOBBITT, JAMES HENRY, Raleigh: 1881–'84.
BOBBITT, JOHN B., Franklin Co.: A. B., 1809. Dead.
BOBBIT, RUFUS LEE, Granville Co.: 1876–'78. Oxford.
BOBBITT, SIDNEY MANGUM, Granville Co.: 1880–'82. Franklinton.
BODDIE, NICHOLAS W., Nash Co.: 1843–'44. Gen. Assem. Nashville.
BOGGAN, WILLIAM KENDALL, Wadesboro: 1883–'85.
BOND, CHARLES, Windsor: 1875–'77. Bapt. Minister.
BOND, HENRY, Enfield: 1864–'65.
BOND, HENRY F., Kinston: 1833–'34. Dead.
BOND, HENRY J., Jefferson Co., Fla.: 1858–'59.
BOND, JAMES, Brownsville, Tenn.: 1858–'59.
BOND, LEWIS, Bertie Co.: 1847–'51. Dead.
BOND, LEWIS, Brownsville, Tenn.: A. B., 1860. Capt. C. S. A. Lawyer. Gen. Assem. Speaker H. of R., 1875. Born 1839, died Oct. 3d, 1878.
BOND, ROBERT C., Raleigh: 1822. Physician. Dead.
BOND, THOMAS, Bertie Co.: A. B., 1824. Dead.
BOND, WILLIAM PUGH, Bertie Co.: A. B., 1834. Dead.
BOND, WILLIAM ROBERT, Halifax Co.: A. B., 1861. Lt. C. S. A. Scotland Neck.

BONNER, GEORGE MILES, Washington: 1842–'44. Lawyer. Col. C. S. A. Born 1822, died Sept. 14, 1868.
BONNER, ROBERT TRIPP, Beaufort Co.: 1877–'79.
BONNER, THOMAS PASTEUR, Washington: A. B., 1859. Surg. C. S. A. Dead. Aurora.
BONNER, WILLIAM, Fayetteville, Tenn.: A. B., 1858.
BOOKER, JOHN, Farmville, Va.: 1815. Dead.
BOOKER, WILLIAM P., Farmville, Va.: 1815. Dead.
BOON, WILLIAM AUGUSTUS, Johnston Co.: A. B., 1814. Dead.
BOONE, ROBERT BAXTER, Roxboro: 1880–'81. Lawyer. Durham.
BOOTH, EDWIN GREENHILL, Nottoway, Va.: A. B., 1828.
BOOTH, GREEN H., Sussex C. H., Va.: 1811. Dead.
BOOTH, ROBERT HENRY, Nottoway, Va.: A. B., 1824. Dead.
BOOZER, ALBERT M., Lexington C. H., S. C.: A. B., 1864.
BORDEN, EDWIN BROWNRIGG, Goldsboro: 1885–'87.
BORDEN, FRANK KORNEGAY, Goldsboro: 1877–'78. Planter.
BORDEN, JOHN BECK, Wilcox Co., Ala.: A. B., 1844. Dead.
BORDEN, JOHN LEMUEL, Goldsboro: Ph. B., 1884. Merchant.
BORDEN, WALTER EUGENE, Goldsboro: 1885–'87. Wilmington.
BORDEN, WILLIAM HENRY HARRISON, Goldsboro: A. B., 1860. Lieut. C. S. A. Manufacturer.
BOURNE, LOUIS MILTON, Tarboro: A. B., 1887.
BOWERS, PATRICK H., Somerville, Tenn.: 1860–'61. Merchant. Born 1844, died Oct. 6th, 1878.
BOWERS, SOUTHERLAND, Fayetteville, Tenn.: 1851–'52.
BOWIE, ALLEN T., Lake St. Joseph, La.: 1858–'61.
BOWIE, JOHN R., Lake St. Joseph, La.: A. B., 1860. Sergt. C. S. A.
BOWIE, THOMAS C., Lake St. Joseph, La.: 1858–'61.
BOWMAN, JAMES, Stokes Co.: A. B., 1822. Dead.
BOWMAN, JOHN G., Germanton, Stokes Co.: 1823–'27. Dead.
BOYCE, JESSE THOMPSON, Clarksville, Tex.: A. B., 1859. C. S. A. Killed in battle.
BOYD, CHARLES, 1822. Dead.
BOYD, JAMES L., Warren Co.: 1826. Dead.
BOYD, JAMES MCCLURE, Camden, Wilcox Co., Ala.: A. B., 1843. Physician. Boiling Springs, Ala.
BOYD, R. WARREN, Chester Dist., S. C.: 1859–'60.
BOYDEN, NATHANIEL ALEXANDER, Salisbury: A. B., 1855. Lawyer.
BOYKIN, DAVID STEVENS, Clinton: 1878–'80.
BOYLAN, ALEXANDER MCCULLOCH, Raleigh: A. B., 1823. Dead.
BOYLAN, JAMES, Raleigh: 1837–'41. Dead.
BOYLAN, JOHN H., Raleigh: 1840–'44.
BOYLAN, JOHN S., Raleigh: 1856–'59. C. S. A. Dead.
BOYLAN, WELDON E., Somerville, Tenn.: 1852–'54. Dead.
BOYLAN, WILLIAM POLK, Raleigh: A. B., 1825. Dead.
BOZEMAN, JAMES FRANCIS, Clark Co., Ark.: 1854–'56. Planter. Born 1836, died 1883. Fort Griffin, Texas.

BOZMAN, JOSEPH LA FAYETTE, Eutaw, Ala.: 1844–'47. Col. C. S. A. Planter. Born 1831, died 1880. Tuscaloosa.
BRACKIN, JULIUS C. S., Caswell Co.: 1830–'34. Dead.
BRADFORD, EDWARD, Tallahassee, Fla.: A. B., 1854. C. S. A. Merchant. Born 1833, died 1870.
BRADFORD, JOHN, Coosa Co., Ala.: 1857–'60. C. S. A. Killed at Seven Pines, 1862.
BRADFORD, JOHN R., Tallahassee, Fla.: 1850–'51. Born 1834.
BRADFORD, RICHARD, Tallahassee, Fla.: A. B., 1854. Lawyer. C. S. A. Born 1836. Killed at Santa Rosa Island, Oct. 9, 1861.
BRADHAM, CALEB DAVIS, Chinquapin, Duplin Co.: 1886–'88.
BRADLEY, ALFRED OWEN, Wilmington: 1838–'41. Physician. Born 1821, died 1871.
BRADLEY, ISAAC W., Sumpter Dist., S. C.: 1859–'60.
BRADLEY, JOHN FRANCIS, Gastonia, Gaston Co.: 1886–'87.
BRADLEY, ORVILLE T. C., Tenn: 1814. Dead.
BRADLEY, PHILIP E., Wilmington: 1836–'38. Born 1818, died 1849.
BRADLEY, RICHARD, Wilmington: 1863–'64. C. S. A. Merchant. Born 1842, died 1879.
BRADLEY, SIMON BOLIVAR, Tarboro: 1853–'54. Born 1836. Planter.
BRADSHAW, MICHAEL, Asheboro: 1882–'83. Lawyer. Journalist.
BRADY, JOHN EVERETT, Davidson College: A. B., 1881. Ph. D. Prof. Smith Coll. Northampton, Mass.
BRADY, KINCHEN J., Tarboro: 1858–'59.
BRAGAW, STEPHEN CAMBRELENG, Washington: 1886–.
BRAGG, BRAXTON, Mobile, Ala: 1863–'64. C. S. A. Lawyer. City Atty.
BRAGG, JOHN, Warrenton: A. B., 1824; A. M., 1828. Gen. Assem., Ala. Judge Superior Ct., Ala., 1842. M. C., 1851. Member Conv., 1861. Died 1878.
BRAGG, JOHN, Raleigh: A. B., 1861. Telegraphy. Charlotte.
BRAGG, THOMAS, Warrenton: 1822. Gen. Assem. Governor, 1855–'59. U. S. Sen., 1859–'61. Atty. Gen. Confed. States, 1862–'63. Died 1872.
BRAGG, WILLIAM, Jackson: 1843–'44. Planter. Ala.
BRANCH, ALPHEUS PAUL, Wilson: 1888–.
BRANCH, EDWARD T., Halifax Co: 1867–'68. Lawyer.
BRANCH, HENRY, Enfield: 1833–'35. Dead.
BRANCH, JOHN, Halifax Co.: A. B., 1801. Gen. Assem. Speaker Senate, 1816–'17. Governor, 1817–'20. U. S. Sen., 1823–'29. Secretary Navy, 1829–'31. Mem. Conv., 1835. Gov. Fla. Ter., 1844–'45. Died 1863.
BRANCH, JOHN R., Halifax Co.: 1835–'36. Dead.
BRANCH, JOSEPH, Halifax Co.: 1806. Dead.
BRANCH, JOSEPH, Enfield: 1833–'35. Atty. Gen., Fla., 1845–'48. Dead.
BRANCH, JOSEPH HENRY, Tallahassee, Fla., 1861–'62. C. S. A. Born 1844. Killed in battle Aug. 13, 1864.
BRANCH, LAWRENCE O'BRIEN, Halifax Co.: 1835–'36. A. B. Princeton. Lawyer. Gen. Assem. Pres. Elector, 1852. M. C., 1855–'61. Brig. Gen. C. S. A. Killed at Sharpsburg, 1862.
BRANCH, WILLIAM A. B., Raleigh: 1863–'64. C. S. A. Lawyer. Washington.

BRANCH, WILLIAM H., Enfield: 1839–'40. Merchant.
BRASWELL, ABRAM H., Rockingham Co.: 1836–'39.
BRASWELL, ARCHIBALD, Whitaker's: B. S., 1888. Planter.
BRASWELL, JAMES CRAIG, Battleboro, Edgecombe Co.: 1887–.
BRASWELL, MACK CLAUDE, Battleboro, Edgecombe Co.: 1878–'80. Rocky Mount.
BRAXTON, ELIAS DAVID, Pitt Co.: 1882–'83. Lassiter's Mills.
BREARLEY, HENRY MARTYN, Darlington Dist., S. C.: A. B., 1855. Minister. Chaplain C. S. A. Maxton.
BREHON, JAMES G., Warrenton: 1820. Physician. Dead.
BREEDEN, DARIUS MEEKIN, Bennettsville, S. C.: 1879–'80. Lawyer.
BRENT, JOHN C., Rockingham Co.: 1855–'56. Dead.
BRETT, GEORGE AUGUSTUS, Hertford Co.: A. B., 1852. Born 1831. C. S. A. Planter. Como.
BREVARD, ALEXANDER FRANKLIN, Lincoln Co.: A. B., 1846. Iron Station.
BREVARD, EPHRAIM JOSEPH, Lincoln Co.: A. B., 1849. Dead.
BRICKELL, STERLING H., Halifax Co.: A. B., 1860. Capt. C. S. A. Killed in battle.
BRIDGERS, GEORGE JONES, Wilmington: 1886–'88.
BRIDGERS, JAMES KELLY, Northampton Co.: 1879–'80. Dead. Nashville.
BRIDGERS, JOHN LUTHER, Edgecombe Co.: A. B., 1843. Lawyer. Comr. to Confed. Govt. at Montgomery, 1861. Col. C. S. A. Planter. Born 1821, died 1884.
BRIDGERS, ROBERT RUFUS, Edgecombe Co.: A. B., 1841. Gen. Assem. Mem. Confed. Congress. Col. C. S. A. Pres. W. & W. R. R. Born 1819, died 1888.
BRIGGS, ROSCOE GILES, Chocowinity, Beaufort Co.: 1876–'77. Wilson.
BRIGHT, WILLIAM RANSOM, Beaufort Co.: 1885. Chocowinity.
BRINSON, SAMUEL MITCHELL, New Berne: A. B., 1858. Lawyer. Born 1836, died 1860.
BRITT, JAMES P., Edenton: 1860–'61.
BRITT, GEORGE WILLIAM, Clinton: 1875–'76.
BRITTON, ANDREW JACKSON, Jackson: 1867. Lawyer.
BRITTON, CHARLES WESLEY, Jackson: 1881–'82.
BROADFOOT, CHARLES W., Fayetteville: 1859–'60. Col. C. S. A. Gen. Assem., 1870–'72. Lawyer.
BROADNAX, ALEXANDER, Laurenceville, Va.: 1815. Dead.
BROADNAX, JOHN WILSON, Rockingham Co.: A. B., 1841. Maj. C. S. A.
BRODDIE, EDMUND, Franklin Co.: 1797. A. B. Dead.
BRODIE, EDMUND GHOLSON, Granville Co.: A. B., 1861. Born 1841. C. S. A. Henderson.
BRODNAX, WILLIAM F., Rockingham Co.: 1844–'46. Dead.
BRODNAX, WILLIAM FREDERICK, Leaksville, Rockingham Co.: 1882–'83.
BROOKES, CHARLES BLACKWELL, Stokes Co.: 1845–'48. Salem.
BROOKES, DANIEL IVERSON, Forsyth Co.: A. B., 1854. Born 1832, died 1856.

BROOKES, GEORGE W., Stokes Co.: 1846–'47. Pelahatchee, Miss.
BROOKS, IVERSON LEE, Caswell Co.: A. B., 1819. Minister. Dead.
BROOKS, JAMES COSTIN, Elizabeth City: 1888–.
BROOKS, JOHN Z., Johnson's Mills, Pitt Co.: 1883–'84.
BROOKS, THOMAS COOK, Woodsdale, Person Co.: Ph. B., 1880. Lawyer.
BROOKS, WILLIAM COSTIN, Elizabeth City: 1869.
BROOKS, WILLIAM M., Chatham Co.: A. B., 1860. C. S. A.
BROTHERS, JOHN EDWARD, Elizabeth City: 1882–'83. Newbegun Creek.
BROWN, AARON VAIL, Laurenceville, Va.: A. B., 1814. LL. D. Gen. Assem., Tenn. M. C., 1839–'45. Gov. Tenn., 1845–'49. Postmaster General, 1857–'59. Born 1797, died 1859. Tenn.
BROWN, ASHBEL GREEN, Granville Co.: A. B., 1843; A. M., 1846. Associate Prof. Greek U. N. C., 1844–'56. Born 1821. Dead. California.
BROWN, BEDFORD, Caswell Co.: 1813. H. of Com., 1815, '17, '23. Speaker Senate, 1829. U. S. Sen., 1829–'41. Mem. Conventions, 1861 and 1865. Born 1795, died 1870.
BROWN, BENJAMIN WARREN, Pitt Co.: 1856–'57. Planter. Born 1835, died 1885. Lassiter's Mills.
BROWN, FRANK WARREN, Greenville: 1879–'80. Physician.
BROWN, FREDERICK W., Caswell Co.: 1839–'40. Lassiter's Mills.
BROWN, HENRY I., Lynchburg, Va.: 1823. Dead.
BROWN, HUGH THOMAS, Wilkesboro: A. B., 1858. Capt. C. S. A. Killed in battle.
BROWN, JAMES W., Caswell Co.: 1808. Dead.
BROWN, JOHN BRIGHT, Bladen Co.: A. B., 1808. Dead.
BROWN, JOHN E., Caswell Co., 1820. Dead.
BROWN, JOHN L., Caswell Co., 1820.
BROWN, JOHN M., Iberville Parish, La.: 1857–'59.
BROWN, JOHN POTTS, Wilmington: A. B., 1829. Merchant. Dead.
BROWN, JOSEPH ADDISON CLARKE, Davidson Co.: A. B., 1858. M. D. Jefferson Med. Coll. Born 1841. C. S. A. Planter. Sedalia, Mo.
BROWN, LEONIDAS G., Salisbury: 1845–'46. Dead.
BROWN, LIVINGSTON, Caswell Co.: 1835–'36.
BROWN, OWEN N., Fayetteville: 1852–'54. Maj. C. S. A. Killed in battle.
BROWN, S. P., Portsmouth, Va.: 1841.
BROWN, SAMUEL T., Lynchburg, Va.: 1832.
BROWN, SYLVESTER T., Carteret Co.: 1841–'42.
BROWN, THOMAS, Bladen Co.: A. B., 1804. A. M. Dead.
BROWN, THOMAS H., New Berne: 1831–'35. Physician. Died 1884.
BROWN, WILLIAM, Brunswick Co., Va.: 1809. Dead.
BROWN, WILLIAM A., Grenada, Miss.: 1859–'61. Capt. C. S. A.
BROWN, WILLIAM FREDERICK, Caswell Co.: A. B., 1839. Dead.
BROWN, WILLIAM KING, Robeson Co.: 1879–'82. Teacher. Birmingham, Ala.
BROWN, ZENO H., Greenville: 1879–'80. Physician. Lassiter's Mills.
BROWNE, JACOB FAULCON, Warrenton: 1846–'47. Dead.
BROWNE, RIDLEY, Warren Co.: 1845–'46. Physician.
BROWNRIGG, HENRY, Edgecombe Co.: 1809. Dead.

BROWNRIGG, RICHARD THOMAS, Edenton: 1808. Gen. Assem., 1816–'22. Planter. Fisheries. Born 1793, died 1846. Columbus, Miss.
BROYLES, THOMAS TALIAFERRO, Anderson C. H., S. C.: A. B., 1863.
BRUCE, A., South Boston, Va.: 1825.
BRUCE, CHARLES, Guilford Co.: 1797. Dead.
BRUCE, CHARLES, Halifax C. H., Va.: A. B., 1845.
BRUCE, CHARLES, Halifax Co., Va.: A. B., 1860. Capt. C. S. A. Killed in battle.
BRUCE, JAMES, Halifax Co., Va.: A. B., 1856. Died 1858.
BRUCE, JAMES COLE, Halifax C. H., Va.: A. B., 1825. Gen. Assem. Dead.
BRUCE, JOHN, Hillsboro: 1814. Dead.
BRUCE, WILKINS, Halifax Co., Va.: A. B., 1858. C. S. A. Milton, N. C.
BRUCE, WILLIAM BALLARD, Halifax Co., Va.: A. B., 1856.
BRUTON, JOHN FLETCHER, Greensboro: 1884–'85. Lawyer.
BRYAN, CARNEY J., Washington: 1859–'61. C. S. A. Died Aug. 23, 1883.
BRYAN, CHARLES SHEPARD, Raleigh: A. B., 1852. Born 1832. Lawyer. Gen. Assem., Mo., 1874–'75 and 1878–'79. Cassville, Mo.
BRYAN, ELIAS HENRY, Haywood, Chatham Co.: A. B., 1865. Planter. Born 1844, died May 14, 1887.
BRYAN, FELIX, Lenoir Co.: 1813.
BRYAN, FRANCIS THEODORE, Raleigh: A. B., 1842; A. M., 1845. Born 1823. Topog. Engineer. Aid to Gen. Wool. U. S. A. Mexican War. St. Louis, Mo.
BRYAN, FREDERICK CHARLES, New Berne: 1881–'83. Chief Clerk, Seaboard R. R. Portsmouth, Va.
BRYAN, FREDERICK R., Raleigh: 1861–'62. Born 1846, died 1863.
BRYAN, GEORGE PETTIGREW, Raleigh: A. B., 1860. Tutor U. N. C., 1860–'62. Capt. C. S. A. Born 1841. Killed at Charles City Road, Va., 1864.
BRYAN, HENRY H., New Orleans, La.: 1860–'61.
BRYAN, HENRY RAVENSCROFT, Raleigh: A. B., 1856. Lawyer and Planter. Pres. Elector, 1880. New Berne.
BRYAN, HENRY RAVENSCROFT, New Berne: 1886–'87. Charlotte.
BRYAN, JAMES ALEXANDER, Spartanburg, S. C.: B. S., 1885. Presb. Minister.
BRYAN, JAMES PETTIGREW, Raleigh: A. B., 1849. Physician. Born 1829, died 1887. Kinston.
BRYAN, JAMES WEST, New Berne: A. B., 1824. Lawyer. Gen. Assem. Mem. Conv., 1835. Born 1805, died 1864.
BRYAN, JESSE G., Washington: 1837–'39. Physician. Dead.
BRYAN, JOHN, Sampson Co.: 1796. Dead.
BRYAN, JOHN A., Sampson Co.: 1841. Born 1830. Physician. Gen. Assem. Kenansville.
BRYAN, JOHN HERRITAGE, New Berne: A. B., 1815; A. M., 1820. Lawyer. State Sen., 1823–'25. M. C., 1825–'29. Born 1798, died 1870.
BRYAN, JOHN HERRITAGE, Raleigh: A. B., 1844; A. M., 1847. Born 1825. Lawyer. Campinas, San Paulo, Brazil.
BRYAN, JOSEPH B., Fayetteville: 1841–'42. Dead.

BRYAN, JOSEPH BONNER, Washington: A. B., 1851. Lieut. C. S. A. Merchant. Aurora.
BRYAN, JOSIAH E., Fayetteville: 1841. C. S. A. Killed in battle.
BRYAN, NEEDHAM G., Wayne Co.: 1814. Dead.
BRYAN, ROBERT K., Fayetteville: 1843–'45. Hickory.
BRYAN, ROBERT THOMAS, Kenansville: A. B., 1882. Bapt. Minister. Missionary to China.
BRYAN, SHEPARD, New Berne: 1887–.
BRYAN, WILLIAM SHEPARD, Raleigh: A. B., 1846; A. M., 1850. Born 1827. Lawyer. Associate Justice Supreme Ct., Md. Baltimore, Md.
BRYANT, VICTOR SILAS, Pineville, Mecklenburg Co.: 1884–'88. Teacher. Huntley.
BUCHANAN, A. H., Anson Co.: 1840–'41.
BUCHANAN, JOHN BLUE, Richmond Co.: A. B., 1858. Dead.
BUCHANAN, PLEASANT, Ala.: 1831–'32. Died 1846.
BUCHANAN, WILLIAM, Laurinburg: 1866. Brandon, Miss.
BUCK, DEWITT CLINTON, Lexington, Miss.: A. B., 1861. C. S. A. Killed in battle.
BUIE, DODDRIDGE WHITFIELD, Robeson Co.: 1881. Journalist. Died 1884. Red Banks.
BUIE, MALCOLM, Moore Co.: 1809. Dead.
BUIE, NEILL, Moore Co.: 1809. Dead.
BUIE, WILLIAM DOUGLAS, Clarkton, Bladen Co.: 1888–.
BULLOCK, ALFRED, Williamsboro, Granville Co.: 1856–'59. Dead.
BULLOCK, BENJAMIN FRANKLIN, Granville Co.: 1868. Gen. Assem. Franklin Co.
BULLOCK, DAVID W., Edgecombe Co.: 1838–'39. Born 1819. Planter. Battleboro.
BULLOCK, ERASMUS D., Granville Co.: 1828–'29. Dead.
BULLOCK, GEORGE BUNN, Warren Co.: A. B., 1861. Capt. C. S. A.
BULLOCK, JAMES M., Granville Co.: 1831–'32. Dead.
BULLOCK, JAMES MADISON, Greene Co., Ala.: A. B., 1853. Born 1835. Lawyer. Lieut. C. S. A. Gen. Assem. Planter. Eutaw, Ala.
BULLOCK, JOHN HENRY M., Person Co.: A. B., 1854. Capt. C. S. A.
BULLOCK, LEONARD H., Warrenton: 1821. Dead.
BULLOCK, RICHARD, Granville Co.: 1821. Dead.
BULLOCK, RICHARD A., Williamsboro, Granville Co.: A. B., 1860. Sergt. C. S. A.
BULLOCK, RICHARD H., Warren Co.: 1824. Dead.
BULLOCK, WALTER A., Grenada, Miss.: 1839–'40. Dead.
BULLOCK, WILLIAM C., Granville Co.: 1847–'48. Dead.
BULLOCK, WILLIAM H., Granville Co.: 1812. Dead.
BUNCH, JOSEPH M., Rutledge, Tenn.: 1840–'43. Dead.
BUNKER, ALBERT LEMUEL, Mt. Airy: 1879–'80. Lawyer.
BUNN, ELIAS, Nash Co.: 1859–'61. Lieut. C. S. A. Killed in battle.
BUNN, WILLIAM B., Nash Co.: 1836–'37. Dead.
BUNN, WILLIAM HENRY, Nash Co.: A. B., 1854. Lawyer. Capt. C. S. A. Killed in battle.

BUNTING, THOMAS, Sampson Co.: 1822. Physician. Dead.
BUNTING, THOMAS OWEN, Sampson Co.: 1861–'62. Born 1845. C. S. A. Merchant. Wilmington.
BURCH, C. H., Chapel Hill: 1888–.
BURCH, WILLIAM W., Surry Co.: 1831–'32. Dead.
BURGESS, ABRIDGETON S. H., Jerusalem, Va.: 1805–'09. Physician. Dead.
BURGESS, THOMAS, Halifax Co.: 1802. Lawyer. Dead.
BURGWYN, GEORGE P., Northampton Co.: 1863–'64. C. S. A. Planter. Jackson.
BURGWYN, HAZELL WITHERSPOON, Hillsboro: A. B., 1838. Physician. Maj. C. S. A. Planter.
BURGYWN, HENRY KING, Northampton Co.: 1857–'59. A. B. Va. Mil. Inst., 1861. Col. C. S. A. Killed at Gettysburg, 1863.
BURGYWN, JOHN COLLINSON, New Berne: 1834–'35. Planter. Born 1782, died 1845.
BURGYWN, HILL, Wilmington: 1840–'41. Born 1825. Lawyer. Pittsburg, Pa.
BURGWYN, THOMAS POLLOCK, Craven Co.: 1830–'34. Planter.
BURGWYN, WILLIAM HYSLOP SUMNER, Northampton Co.: A. B., 1868; A. M. LL.B., Harvard. Born 1846. Capt. C. S. A. Author Md. Digest. Lawyer and Banker. Henderson, N. C.
BURKE, JAMES M., Wilcox Co., Ala.: 1836–'39. Died 1841.
BURKE, THOMAS JEFFERSON, Barbour Co., Ala.: 1858–'60.
BURKHEAD, JOHN WATSON, Randolph Co.: 1878–'79.
BURNETT, JOSEPH HALSEY, Rocky Mt.: 1883–'84.
BURNEY, JOHN RICHARD, Warren Co.: A. B., 1856. Dead.
BURNEY, PHILO HENDERSON, Davidson College: 1880–'81.
BURNEY, ROBERT S., New Berne: 1838–'39. Born 1818, died 1866.
BURROUGHS, JOHN WILLIAM, Cary, Wake Co.: 1888–.
BURT, CHARLES W., Raleigh: 1876–'77.
BURTON, ALFRED M., Granville Co.: 1802. Dead.
BURTON, ANDREW JOYNER, Halifax Co.: 1863–'66. Adj. C. S. A. Lawyer. Gen. Assem. Weldon.
BURTON, AUGUSTUS, Granville Co.: 1809. Dead.
BURTON, AUGUSTUS H., Lincolnton: 1848–'49. Lawyer.
BURTON, FRANCIS NASH WILLIAMS, Granville Co.: A. B., 1799. Dead.
BURTON, HARDY M., Murfreesboro, Tenn.: 1833–'35. Dead.
BURTON, HENRY L., Tenn.: 1854–'56. Physician. Died 1873. La Grange.
BURTON, HENRY W., Lincoln Co.: 1837–'39. Lincolnton.
BURTON, HORACE A., Granville Co.: 1809. Dead.
BURTON, HUTCHINS, Granville Co.: 1797. Dead.
BURTON, HUTCHINS G., Halifax Co.: 1795. Gov. N. C., 1824–'27. Died 1836.
BURTON, HUTCHINS GOODLOE, Bel Green, Ala.: 1848–'51. C. S. A. Born 1831. Killed at Chattanooga, June 22, 1862.
BURTON, JOHN F., Lincoln Co.: 1830–'31. Dead.
BURTON, JOHN M., Granville Co.: 1813. Dead.

BURTON, JOHN WAR, Granville Co.: 1813. Dead.
BURTON, JOHN W., Halifax Co.: 1844–'45. Born 1826, died 1845.
BURTON, JOHN WILLIAMS, Granville Co.: 1813. Dead.
BURTON, PETER GARLAND, Mecklenburg Co., Va.: A. B., 1845. Dead.
BURTON, ROBERT, Granville Co.: 1797. Dead.
BURTON, ROBERT, Lincoln Co.: A. B., 1841.
BURTON, ROBERT A., Halifax Co.: 1832–'33. Dead.
BURTON, ROBERT H., Granville Co.: 1796. Lawyer. Judge Superior Ct. Dead.
BURTON, ROBERT M., Chapel Hill: 1817. Dead.
BURTON, THOMAS BURKE, Halifax Co.: A. B., 1852. C. S. A. Dead.
BURTON, WILLIAM B., Lincoln Co.: 1837–'39.
BURWELL, BLAIR, Louisburg: 1865–'67. Born 1847. Merchant. Surveyor. Colorado.
BURWELL, HENRY JORDAN, Granville Co.: 1880–'82. Williamsboro.
BURWELL, ROBERT TURNBULL, Raleigh: Ph. B., 1887.
BURWELL, WILLIAM ARMISTEAD, Manson, Warren Co.: 1882–'84. Merchant and Planter.
BURWELL, WILLIAM HENRY, Warren Co.: A. B., 1856. C. S. A. Teacher. Manson.
BURY, S. WALLACE, Florence, Ga.: 1860–'61.
BUSBEE, CHARLES MANLY, Raleigh: 1865–'68. Lawyer.
BUSBEE, FABIUS HAYWOOD, Raleigh: A. B., 1868; A. M. Lieut. C. S. A. U. S. Dist. Atty. Lawyer.
BUSBEE, PERRIN, Wake Co.: A. B., 1837. Lawyer. Reporter Supreme Ct. Dead.
BUSBEE, PERRIN, Raleigh: 1888–.
BUSBEE, QUENTIN DURWARD, Wake Co.: 1841–'42. Lawyer. Dead.
BUSH, LEWIS B., Wayne Co.: 1812. Dead.
BUSTIN, JAMES GRANT, Halifax Co.: A. B., 1859. Sergt. C. S. A. Killed at Pine Mt., Ga.
BUTLER, GEORGE EDWIN, Huntley, Sampson Co.: 1887–.
BUTLER, LEWIS P., Tulip, Ark.: 1860–'61.
BUTLER, MARION, Clinton: A. B., 1885. Journalist.
BUTLER, PIERCE M., Edgefield, S. C.: A. B., 1860. Lt. C. S. A.
BUTLER, WILLIAM EDWARD, Jackson, Tenn.: A. B., 1861. Planter. Miflin, Tenn.
BUTTS, JAMES ELDRIDGE, Columbus, Ga.: A. B., 1861. Lt. C. S. A. Killed in battle.
BUTTS, WILLIS B., Columbus, Ga.: 1858–'59.
BUXTON, JARVIS, Fayetteville: A. B., 1839; D. D. Episc. Minister. Asheville.
BUXTON, RALPH POTTS, Fayetteville: A. B., 1845. Born 1826. Mem. Conventions 1861 and 1875. Solic. 6th Dist., 1863. Judge Super. Ct., 1866.
BYERLY, JOSEPH, Lexington: 1850–'51. Died 1855.
BYERS, WASHINGTON, Iredell Co.: 1846–'47. Dead.
BYNUM, EDWARD TURNER, Tarboro: 1875–'77. Died April 3, 1889.
BYNUM, ERNEST TAYLOR, Chatham Co.: 1887–'88.

BYNUM, GEORGE C., Chatham Co.: 1860–'61.
BYNUM, JEPTHA A., Northampton Co.: 1817. Dead.
BYNUM, JOHN BOWEN, Northampton Co.: A. B., 1848. Dead.
BYNUM, JOHN GRAY, Stokes Co.: A. B., 1833; A. M., 1836. Gen. Assem. Died 1857.
BYNUM, OLIVER CLEGG, Pittsboro: A. B., 1886. Lawyer.
BYNUM, WILLIAM ROBERT, Tarboro: 1877–'78.
BYNUM, WILLIE, Winston: 1882–'83. Texas.
BYRD, THOMPSON, Caswell Co.: A. B., 1827; A. M., 1831. Tutor. Minister.
CABELL, BENJAMIN WILLIAM SHERIDAN, Danville, Va.: 1882–'84.
CAFFEY, HUGH WASHINGTON, Montgomery, Ala.: 1863–'64. C. S. A. Planter. Died 1879.
CAIN, JAMES, Orange Co.: 1803. Dead.
CAIN, JAMES FREDERICK, Orange Co.: A. B., 1850. Physician.
CAIN, ROBERT LEE, Mocksville: 1878–'80.
CAIN, WILLIAM, Orange Co.: 1800. Dead.
CAIN, WILLIAM, Orange Co.: 1839–'41. Physician. Dead.
CALDCLEUGH, ALEXANDER BLACKSTONE, Lexington: 1847–'48. M. D. Univ. of Pa. St. Charles, Ark.
CALDWELL, ARCHIBALD HENDERSON, Salisbury: A. B., 1841. Lawyer. Gen. Assem. Clerk and Master in Equity. Born 1821, died 1861.
CALDWELL, ARCHIBALD HENDERSON, Salisbury: 1888–.
CALDWELL, DAVID FRANKLIN, Iredell Co.: 1813. H. of Com., 1816. Speaker Senate 1829. Judge Superior Ct., 1844–'59. Born 1791, died 1867.
CALDWELL, DAVID THOMAS, Mecklenburg Co.: A. B., 1819. Physician. Dead.
CALDWELL, JAMES AUGUSTUS, Morganton: A. B., 1842. Planter. Gen. Assem. Born 1820, died 1876.
CALDWELL, JOSEPH P., New York: 1819. Dead.
CALDWELL, JULIUS ALEXANDER, Salisbury: A. B., 1850. Physician.
CALDWELL, RICHARD ALEXANDER, Salisbury: A. B., 1848. Lawyer. Mem. Conv. 1861. Born 1830. Dead.
CALDWELL, ROBERT ERNEST, Greensboro: A. B., 1879. Minister.
CALDWELL, SAMUEL PINCKNEY, Charlotte: A. B., 1856. C. S. A. Dead.
CALDWELL, TOD ROBINSON, Morganton: A. B., 1840. H. of Com. and State Senator. Mem. Conv. 1865. Lieut. Gov. 1868–'70. Gov. 1870–'74. Born 1818, died 1874.
CALER, VANCE MONROE, West Mills, Macon Co.: 1883–'84.
CALL, WILLIAM H., Mocksville: 1861–'62. Minister.
CALLAWAY, ABNER SYDENHAM, Wilkesboro: A. B., 1859. Dead.
CALVERT, SAMUEL JAMES, Jackson: A. B., 1845; A. M., 1848. Dead.
CAMERON, JOHN, Hillsboro: 1830–'31.
CAMERON, JOHN ADAMS, Va.: A. B., 1806; A. M., 1809. H. of Com. Maj. U. S. A. War of 1812. Consul to Vera Cruz, 1829. Judge U. S. Dist. Ct., Fla., 1831. Born 1788, died 1837.
CAMERON, JOHN ATKINS, Harnett Co.: A. B., 1862; A. M., 1866. Sergt. C. S. A.
CAMERON, JOHN D., Fayetteville: 1839–'41. Journalist. Asheville.

CAMERON, JOHN WILDER, Fayetteville: A. B., 1848.
CAMERON, JOHN WORTHY, Moore Co.: A. B., 1840. Lawyer. Journalist. Dead.
CAMERON, PAUL CARRINGTON, Orange Co.: 1824–'25. State Senator. Planter. Hillsboro.
CAMERON, WILLIAM, Va.: 1805. Physician. Dead.
CAMPBELL, DUNCAN GREEN, Orange Co.: A. B., 1807. Dead.
CAMPBELL, GREEN H., N. C.: 1807. Dead.
CAMPBELL, JAMES, Cumberland Co.: A. B., 1855. Minister.
CAMPBELL, JAMES G., Brunswick: 1825–'29. Born 1809. Dead.
CAMPBELL, JAMES G., Opelousas, La.: 1855–'56. Red River, La.
CAMPBELL, JAMES WILLIAMSON, Marengo Co., Ala.: A. B., 1842. Lawyer. Born 1820, died 1844.
CAMPBELL, JOHN, Fayetteville: 1852. Minister.
CAMPBELL, JOHN K., Raleigh: 1825. A. B. S. C. Coll. U. S. Atty., Fla. Died 1833.
CAMPBELL, JOHN XAVIER, Marengo Co., Ala.: A. B., 1848. Lawyer. Capt. C. S. A. Born 1827. Dead.
CAMPBELL, REUBEN, Statesville: 1887–.
CAMPBELL, ROBERT, Cumberland Co.: A. B., 1808. Dead.
CAMPBELL, ROBERT MCGREGOR, Marengo Co., Ala.: A. B., 1842. Capt. C. S. A. Born 1822. Dead.
CAMPBELL, WILLIAM C., Cumberland Co.: 1802. Dead.
CAMPBELL, WILLIAM S., Brunswick Co.: 1829. Civil Engineer. Born 1806, died 1857.
CAMPBELL, WILLIAM S., Opelousas, La.: 1854–'57.
CANNADAY, SAMUEL HILMON, Wilton, Granville Co.: 1884–'85.
CANNON, HENRY JORDAN, Raleigh: A. B., 1831. Lawyer. Planter. Born 1811, died 1862. Memphis, Tenn.
CANNON, JOSEPH S., Perquimans Co.: 1848–'49. Dead.
CANNON, ROBERT H., Northampton Co.: 1840–'41. Physician. Dead.
CANNON, ROBERT JOHN, Somerville, Tenn.: A. B., 1857. Dead.
CANNON, WILLIAM JAMES, Jackson: 1842–'43. Born 1827. Physician. Surgeon C. S. A. Somerville, Tenn.
CANSLER, ALEXANDER JACOB, Lincolnton: A. B., 1847.
CAPEHART, BALDY ASHBURNE, Murfreesboro: A. B., 1853. Planter. Kittrell.
CAPEHART, THOMAS, Bertie Co.: 1858–'60. Lieut. C. S. A. Planter. Kittrell.
CAPEL, AARON WILLIAM ELIJAH, Richmond Co.: 1875–'77. Capel's Mills.
CARNEY, THOMAS, 1820.
CARPENTER, JOHN DANIEL, Mill Springs, Polk Co.: 1880–'81.
CARR, ALBERT G., Chapel Hill: A. B., 1867. Physician. Durham.
CARR, ELIAS, Sparta, Edgecombe Co.: 1855–'57. Born 1839. C. S. A. Planter. Old Sparta.
CARR, JONAS JOHNSTON, Oxford: 1877–'78.
CARR, JULIAN SHAKESPEARE, Chapel Hill: 1862–'64. Manufacturer. Banker. Durham.

CARR, LEWIS F., Sampson Co.: 1842–'43. Lawyer. Born 1822. Dead.
CARR, MATTHEW H., Lenoir Co.: 1857–'59. Physician. Lumberman. Craven Co.
CARR, TITUS WILLIAM, Pitt Co.: A. B., 1863. Born 1841. Lieut. C. S. A. Planter and Merchant. Snow Hill, Greene Co.
CARR, ROBERT LEE, Chapel Hill: 1869. Merchant.
CARR, WILLIAM MERCER GREEN, Chapel Hill: 1857–'59. Died 1860.
CARRAWAY, DAVIS STEPHEN, New Berne: 1885–'86. Druggist.
CARRIGAN, ALFRED HOLT, Alamance Co.: A. B., 1850. Born 1828. Planter. Gen. Assem. Ark. Mem. Conv. 1861. Lieut. Col. C. S. A. Washington, Ark.
CARRIGAN, ROBERT ADAMS, Alamance Co.: A. B., 1855. Lawyer. Planter. Capt. C. S. A. Born 1835, died 1877.
CARRIGAN, WILLIAM MICHAEL, Alamance Co.: A. B., 1852. Planter. Lieut. C. S. A. Born 1834. Killed in battle 1864.
CARRINGTON, ISAAC C., Va.: 1826.
CARRINGTON, ISAAC H. C., Charlotte Co., Va.: 1842–'44.
CARRINGTON, PAUL S., Smithville, Va.: 1813. Dead.
CARRINGTON, TUCKER, Va.: 1815. Dead.
CARRINGTON, WILLIAM, Va.: 1822.
CARRINGTON, WILLIAM A., Smithville, Va.: 1812. Dead.
CARROLL, JOHN LEMUEL, Kenansville: A. B., 1863; A. M. D. D. Minister. Asheville.
CARROLL, WILLIAM HOUSTON, Magnolia, Duplin Co.: A. B., 1886. Lawyer and Teacher. Burlington.
CARROW, SAMUEL TOPPING, Beaufort: 1882–'83.
CARSON, HENRY CLAY, Sparta, Alleghany Co.: 1888–.
CARSON, HUGH, Lexington: 1804. Dead.
CARSON, JAMES P., Charleston, S. C.: 1863–'64.
CARSON, JOSEPH L., Rutherfordton: 1866–'67.
CARSON, ROBERT, Iredell Co.: 1818. Physician. Dead.
CARTER, ARCHIBALD GRAYSON, Caswell Co.: A. B., 1820. Lawyer. Planter. Born 1801, died 1887. Mocksville.
CARTER, DAVID MILLER, Hyde Co.: A. B., 1851. Lawyer. Planter. Gen. Assem. Col. C. S. A. Born 1830, died 1879.
CARTER, EUGENE DOUGLAS, Asheville: 1875–'76.
CARTER, FRANCIS MARION, Carter Co., Mo.: A. B., 1862. Columbia, Mo.
CARTER, JESSE, Milton, Caswell Co.: A. B., 1825. M. D. Phila. Med. Coll. Born 1807. Dead. Mobile, Ala.
CARTER, MELVILLE E., Madison Co.: Capt. C. S. A. Gen. Assem. Lawyer. Born 1843. Asheville.
CARTER, ROBERT EDWARD, Fairfield, Hyde Co.: 1886–'88.
CARTER, WILLIAM BROWN, Caswell Co.: A. B., 1834. Born 1814. Lawyer and Planter. Dead. Stokes Co.
CARTER, WILLIAM FRANKLIN, Mocksville: A. B., 1846. Dead.
CARTHY, THOMAS, 1820.
CASWELL, RICHARD W., Lenoir Co.: 1799. Dead.
CATES, ADDISON, Chapel Hill: 1869.

CATES, CALEB GILMER, Rock Spring, Orange Co.: Ph. B., 1889.
CATES, HENRY B., Shreveport, La.: 1858–'59.
CATES, HUDSON, Chapel Hill: 1869.
CAVE, BELFIELD WILLIAM, Chapel Hill: A. B., 1848; A. M., 1852. Lawyer. Born 1826, died 1856. Thomasville, Ga.
CHADWICK, EDWIN, Beaufort: 1882–'83.
CHALMERS, CHARLES, Fayetteville: 1826. Dead.
CHALMERS, DAVID, Va.: 1821. Dead.
CHALMERS, JAMES, Va.: 1847–'48. C. S. A. Killed in battle.
CHALMERS, JAMES R., Va.: 1817. Dead.
CHALMERS, JOHN A., Chapel Hill, 1829–'31. Physician. Dead.
CHALMERS, JOHN G., Va., 1821. Physician. Dead.
CHALMERS, JOSEPH W., Halifax Co., Va.: 1861–'62. New's Ferry, Va.
CHALMERS, WILLIAM M., Halifax Co., Va.: 1861–'63. Ex-Pres. Columbus Coll. Varden, Miss.
CHAMBERS, EDWARD COKE, Montgomery Co.: A. B., 1850; A. M. Born 1831. Gen. Assem., Tenn. Teacher. Thornton, Texas.
CHAMBERS, EDWARD R., Lunenburg C. H., Va.: 1813. Dead.
CHAMBERS, HENRY, Salisbury: 1804–'06. Physician. Dead.
CHAMBERS, JOHN SAMUEL, Montgomery Co.: A. B., 1854. Lt. C. S. A. Born 1832. Killed in battle 1862. Ark.
CHAMBERS, MAXWELL, Salisbury: A. B., 1809. Physician. Dead.
CHAMBERS, ROBERT AZARIAH, Pekin, Montgomery Co.: A.B., 1853. M.D. Univ. of N. Y. Born 1833, died 1866.
CHAMBERS, SAMUEL D., Person Co., 1838–'40.
CHAMBLISS, WALTER B., Hicksford, Va.: 1862–'64. Dead.
CHANDLER, WILLIAM G., Buncombe Co.: 1854–'55. Lawyer.
CHAPMAN, LAWRIE JOHN, Craven Co.: 1878–'79. Lawyer. Maple Cypress.
CHAPMAN, SAMUEL EDWARD, New Berne: A. B., 1826. M. D. Univ. N. Y. Born 1807, died 1862.
CHAPMAN, SIMEON J., Cheraw, S. C.: 1834–'35. Died 1861.
CHAPMAN, WILLIAM SMITH, Chapel Hill: A. B., 1823; A. M., 1826. Judge, Ala. Dead.
CHARLES, THOMAS M., Wake Co.: 1822. Dead.
CHATHAM, PAUL, Elkin, Surry Co.: 1887–'88.
CHAUNCEY, SAMUEL JACKSON, Flemington, Columbus Co.: 1880–'83.
CHEEK, BENJAMIN A., Warren Co.: 1855–'57. Physician. C. S. A.
CHERRY, GEORGE OUTLAW, Bertie Co.: 1858–'60. C. S. A. Druggist. Dead. Texas.
CHERRY, JAMES J., Bertie Co.: 1858–'60. Capt. C. S. A. Killed at Chancellorsville, 1863.
CHERRY, JESSE GLASGOW, Greenville: 1875–'76.
CHERRY, JOSEPH B., Bertie Co.: 1836–'37. Gen. Assem. Dead.
CHERRY, JOSEPH D., Bertie Co.: 1858–'60. C. S. A. Killed in battle.
CHERRY, TILMAN BROWN, Greenville: 1881–'83. Lawyer. Lassiter's Mills.
CHERRY, WILLIAM, Bertie Co.: A. B., 1800. Dead.

CHERRY, WILLIAM A., Greenville: 1856–'59. Lieut. C. S. A. Gen. Assem. Dead.
CHILDRESS, JOHN W., Murfreesboro, Tenn.: 1822. Lawyer. Gen. Assem. Dead.
CHILTON, EDWARD J., Brownsville, Tenn.: 1859–'60. C. S. A. Killed at Yorktown, 1861.
CHILTON, LEVIN P., Va.: 1817. Dead.
CHISHOLM, SEABORN W., Polk Co., Ga.: 1860–'61. C. S. A. Killed in battle.
CHRISTIAN, ROBERT WALL, Mt. Gilead, Montgomery Co.: 1887–'88.
CHRISTIE, MARK A., Edgefield, S. C.: 1859–'60.
CHRISTMAS, THOMAS HILLIARD, Bolivar, Miss.: A. B., 1857. Physician.
CHUNN, A. B., Buncombe Co.: 1832–'33. Gen. Assem. Asheville.
CHURCH, WILLIAM L., Ga.: 1860–'61. Capt. C. S. A.
CLAIBORNE, BENJAMIN WATKINS LEIGH, Tipton, Tenn.: A. B., 1851. Dead.
CLAIBORNE, FELIX GRUNDY, Danville, Va.: 1859. Dead.
CLAIBORNE, JAMES L., Va.: 1846–'47. Dead.
CLAIBORNE, RICHARD HENRY, Va.: A. B., 1840; A. M., 1843. Dead.
CLAIBORNE, THOMAS D., Danville, Va.: 1855–'56. Lieut. Col. C. S. A. Born 1845. Killed at Nottoway C. H., Va., 1864.
CLANCY, JOHN DUNHAM, Hillsboro: A. B., 1825. Dead.
CLANTON, DUDLEY, Halifax Co.: A. B., 1847. Dead.
CLANTON, JESSE R., Halifax Co.: 1846–'47. Dead.
CLANTON, WILLIAM, Warrenton: 1851–'53.
CLARK, AMBROSE, Apple Grove, Ashe Co.: 1887.
CLARK, COLIN M., Halifax Co.: 1822. Dead.
CLARK, DAVID C., Bertie Co.: 1850–'53. Physician. Planter. Capt. C. S. A. Gen. Assem. Died 1886.
CLARK, DAVID H., Va.: 1814. Dead.
CLARK, FRANCIS MOORE, Middletown, Hyde Co.: 1888–.
CLARK, GEORGE, Bertie Co.: 1796. Born 1779, died 1798.
CLARK, GEORGE MCINTOSH, Montgomery Co.: 1860–'61. Maj. C. S. A. Born 1838. Killed in battle, 1863.
CLARK, HENRY SELBY, Beaufort Co.: A. B., 1828. Lawyer. M. C., 1845–'47. Born 1809, died 1869.
CLARK, HENRY TOOLE, Tarboro: A. B., 1826; A. M., 1832. Planter. State Senator 12 years. Speaker Senate 1858–'61. Gov. N. C. 1861–'62. Born 1808, died 1874.
CLARK, ISAAC W., Coffeeville, Upshur Co., Tex.: 1858–'61.
CLARK, JAMES F., Beaufort Co.: 1859–'60. C. S. A. New Berne.
CLARK, KENNETH M., Bertie Co.: 1845–'46. Dead.
CLARK, NEVIN DANIEL JOSEPHUS, Montgomery Co.: A. B., 1858. Born 1830. Teacher. Clark's Mills, Moore Co.
CLARK, PLEASANT B., Harrison Co., Texas: 1857–'61. Jefferson, Texas.
CLARK, ROBERT SPENCER, Upshur Co., Texas: A. B., 1861.
CLARK, SAMUEL JOHNSON, Bertie Co.: 1845–'47. Dead.
CLARK, THOMAS CHRISTOPHER, Stone, Ala.: A. B., 1856. Born 1833. Planter. C. S. A.

CLARK, WALTER MCK., Halifax Co.: A. B., 1864; A. M., 1867. Born 1846. Lt. Col. C. S. A. Judge Superior Ct. Raleigh.
CLARK, WILLIAM MCKENZIE, Martin Co.: A. B., 1801. Dead.
CLARKE, WILLIAM JOHN, Raleigh: A. B., 1841; A. M., 1844. Captain U. S. A. Mex. War. State Comptroller. Col. C. S. A. Judge Superior Ct. Died 1886. New Berne.
CLARKE, WILLIAM WHIPPLE, Fine's Creek, Haywood Co.: 1882–'83.
CLARKSON, HERIOT, Charlotte: 1883–'84. Lawyer.
CLEGG, MONTRAVILLE D., Chatham Co.: 1860–'61. C. S. A. Killed in battle.
CLEGG, THOMAS DAVID, Silk Hope, Chatham Co.: 1884–'85. Texas.
CLEMENT, HENRY LAWRENCE, Mocksville, Davie Co.: A.B., 1843. Lawyer. Born 1821, died 1844.
CLEMENT, HERBERT, Mocksville, Davie Co.: A. B., 1889.
CLEMENT, RALPH ALEXANDER, Franklin, Va.: 1837–'40. Dead.
CLEMENT, SAMUEL WILSON, Granville Co.: A. B., 1858.
CLEMENT, WILEY ADAM, Mocksville, Davie Co.: 1859–'60. Born 1840. Capt. C. S. A. Lawyer.
CLEMENTS, GEORGE R., Williamston: 1844–'45. Planter. Warrenton.
CLEMENTS, WILLIAM H., Williamston: 1844–'45. Dead.
CLIFTON, L. BERRIE, Franklin Co.: 1860–'61. Merchant. Died 1888. Louisburg.
CLIFTON, LUNSFORD CLAIBORNE, Cedar Shoals, S. C.: 1876–'79. Lancaster C. H., S. C.
CLINCH, DUNCAN LAMONT, Ga.: A. B., 1847. U. S. A.
CLINCH, JOHN HOUSTON MCINTOSH, St. Mary's, Ga.: A. B., 1844.
CLINE, EDWARD BOST, Hickory: A. B., 1886.
CLINE, FRANK LEE, Hickory: 1877–'78.
CLINE, GEORGE WILBUR, Hickory: 1887–.
CLINE, WILLIAM PINKNEY, Newton: Ph. B., 1878.
CLINGMAN, THOMAS LANIER, Surry Co.: A. B., 1832. LL.D. Lawyer. Gen. Assem. M. C. U. S. Senator. Brig. Gen. C. S. A. Asheville.
CLINTON, RICHARD SPAIGHT, Cahaba, Ala.: A. B., 1825. Judge Probate Ct., Ala. Dead.
CLOMAN, SAMUEL F., Williamston: 1851–'53.
CLOPTON, ABNER WENTWORTH, Va.: A. B., 1809; A. M., 1812. Tutor 1809. M.D. Baptist Minister. Dead.
CLOPTON, ROBERT A., Va.: 1816. Dead.
CLOSS, JUNIUS T., Orange Co.: 1853–'54. Dead.
CLOSS, THOMAS O., Orange Co.: 1853–'56. Capt. C. S. A. Killed in battle.
COBB, CHARLES COTESWORTH, Lincolnton: Ph. B., 1880. Dallas, Texas.
COBB, COLLIER, Chapel Hill: 1880–'81. Teacher. Cambridge, Mass.
COBB, FREDERICK HENRY, Kinston: A. B., 1853. Accountant. Montgomery, Ala.
COBB, JESSE, Lenoir Co.: 1799. Dead.
COBB, JOHN PROBERT, Wayne Co.: A. B., 1854. Lieut. Col. C. S. A. Goldsboro.

Cobb, Needham Bryan, Wayne Co.: A. B., 1854; A. M. Born 1836. Baptist Minister. Chaplain C. S. A. Pres. N. C. Bapt. Conv., 1879-'81.
Cobb, Needham Tyndall, Chapel Hill: 1882-'83. Asheville.
Cobbs, Edward H., Prince Edward Co., Va.: 1860-'61.
Coble, Albert Lucien, Alamance Co.: A. B., 1880. Assoc. Prof. Math. 1883-'85. Lawyer. Statesville.
Coble, John Hanner, Guilford Co.: A. B., 1857. A. M., Princeton. Minister. Born 1829, died 1888. Laurinburg.
Cochran, Addison, N. C.: 1820. Dead.
Cochran, Alfred Wellborn, Glennville, Ala.: 1867-'68. New York City.
Cochran, Joseph L., Mecklenburg Co.: 1840-'41. Physician. Dead.
Cockrell, Samuel William, Greene Co., Ala.: A. B., 1845. Died 1876.
Cody, James Adolphus, Columbus, Ga.: 1858-'59. Inspector C. S. A. Atlanta, Ga.
Coffin, James Park, Knoxville, Tenn.: A. B., 1859. Born 1838. Capt. C. S. A. Clerk of Circuit Ct. 1873-'86. Powhatan, Ark.
Coffin, Rufus Lawrence, Pontotoc, Miss.: A. B., 1861. Born 1841. C. S. A. Merchant. Memphis, Tenn.
Coggin, Joseph B., Orange Co.: 1860-'61. Lieut. C. S. A. Killed in battle.
Cohoon, Thomas P., Elizabeth City: 1852-'53. Physician. Dead.
Coit, John T., Cheraw, S. C.: 1844-'45. Dead.
Coit, Julius T., Cheraw, S. C., 1853-'54. Dead.
Cole, Alexander T., Richmond Co.: A. B., 1860. Capt. C. S. A.
Cole, Hugh L., New Berne: 1855-'56. A. M., A. B. and A. M., Princeton. Maj. C. S. A. Lawyer. Assist. Corporation Counsel, New York City, 1875-'80. New York.
Cole, John Wyatt, Richmond Co.: A. B., 1859. Lieut. C. S. A.
Cole, Robert William, Greensboro: A. B., 1859. Lieut. C. S. A. Texas.
Cole, Stephen W., Andrew's Chapel, Tenn.: 1859-'60.
Coleman, Bestor, Eutaw, Ala.: 1855-'57. C. S. A. Planter. Born 1837, died 1868.
Coleman, Daniel Perrin Bestor, Ala.: 1846-'47. Planter. Born 1827, died 1857.
Coleman, Daniel R., Concord: A. B., 1860. C. S. A.
Coleman, David, Buncombe Co.: A. B., 1842. U. S. N. Col. C. S. A. Dead.
Coleman, George S., Asheville: 1838-'39. Physician. Gonzales, Tex.
Coleman, Henry Embry, Halifax C. H., Va.: A. B., 1824. Dead.
Coleman, Henry Embry, Halifax C. H., Va.: 1862-'63. Dead.
Coleman, James W., Church Hill, Miss.: 1854-'55. Lieut. C. S. A. Died March, 1886. Fayette, Miss.
Coleman, John, Halifax C. H., Va.: 1815. Dead.
Coleman, John, Anson Co.: A. B., 1808. Physician. Dead.
Coleman, John Clark, Halifax Co., Va.: A. B., 1847. Dead.
Coleman, John H., Buncombe Co.: 1842-'43. Dead.

COLEMAN, NATHANIEL RAGSDALE, Halifax Co., Va. 1861–'62. New's Ferry, Va.
COLEMAN, NEWTON, Buncombe Co.: 1844–'45. Dead.
COLEMAN, THADDEUS C., Buncombe Co.: 1856–'57. C. S. A. Asheville.
COLEMAN, THOMAS G., Halifax C. H., Va.: 1815. Dead.
COLEMAN, WILLIAM MACON, Concord: A. B., 1858. Atty. Gen.
COLES, ROBERT, Va.: 1817. Dead.
COLLIER, EDWARD, Chapel Hill: 1799. Dead.
COLLIER, JOSEPH T., Wayne Co.: 1823. Dead.
COLLINS, BENJAMIN MOSELY, Warren Co.: A. B., 1861. Capt. C. S. A. Lawyer. Planter. Gen. Assem. Ridgeway.
COLLINS, GEORGE WILLIAM KENT, Hillsboro: 1886–'88.
COLLINS, PLATO, Kinston: 1887–.
COLTON, JAMES HOOPER, Cumberland Co.: A. B., 1855. Minister.
COMAN, MATT J., Wake Co.: 1821. Born 1806, died 1849.
COMAR, NATHANIEL, Caswell Co.: 1824–'25. Dead.
CONNER, CHARLES, Lincolnton: 1812. Dead.
CONNER, HENRY, Bladen Springs, Ala.: 1857–'58. C. S. A. Merchant. Born 1837, died 1878.
CONNER, HENRY W., Beattie's Ford, Lincoln Co.: 1866–'67. Dead.
CONNER, JAMES F., Lincolnton: 1825. Dead.
CONNER, JOHN, Nixonton, Pasquotank Co.: 1805. Dead.
CONNER, SAMUEL Z., Lincolnton: 1825. Physician. Dead.
CONNOR, GEORGE WHITFIELD, Wilson: 1888–.
CONRAD, JAMES MADISON, Midway, Davidson Co.: 1881–'83. Physician.
CONRAD, JOHN C., Conrad's, Yadkin Co.: 1857–'59. Born 1840. Planter.
COOK, CHARLES ALSTON, Warren Co.: 1866–'68. A. M. Princeton, 1870. Born 1848. Solic. Warren Co. Warrenton.
COOK, JOHN THOMAS, Warrenton: A. B., 1859. Sergt. Maj. C. S. A. Killed at Chancellorsville, 1863.
COOPER, ELI McF., Sumpter Dist., S. C.: 1859–'60.
COOPER, GEORGE V., Hertford Co.: 1865–'66.
COOPER, ROBERT ENGLISH, Sumpter Dist., S. C.: A. B., 1860. Chaplain C. S. A. Dead. Hillsboro, Tex.
COOPER, ROBERT LEE, Murphy, Cherokee Co.: 1885–'87. Lawyer.
COOPER, THOMAS ERVIN, Jackson, Miss.: 1860–'61.
COOPER, THOMAS L., Hertford Co.: 1852.
COOPER, THOMAS WATSON, Bertie Co.: A. B., 1860. Lieut. C. S. A. Killed at Gettysburg, 1863.
COPELAND, ROBERT ERNEST, Wilson: 1885–'86.
COPELAND, VIRGINIUS, Jackson: 1860–'61. Lieut. Col. C. S. A. Killed in battle.
CORBETT, JOHN ARCHIBALD, New Hanover Co.: A. B., 1849. Born 1824. Gen. Assem. Planter. Delta, Sampson Co.
CORNELIUS, WILLIAM HENRY, Statesville: 1884–'85.
CORPENING, LINWOOD ELISHA, Lenoir: 1888–.
CORPENING, MARTIN LUTHER, Lenoir: 1879–'80. Physician.
COSTIN, ANDREW JACKSON, Wilmington: A. B., 1859. Dead.

COSTNER, ROBERT EDWIN, Lincolnton: 1884–'86.
COTTEN, JOHN W., Raleigh: 1861–'63. C. S. A. Col. N. C. S. G. Tarboro.
COTTEN, JOSEPH C., Scotland Neck, Halifax Co.: 1863–'64. C. S. A.
COUNCIL, ALEXANDER MCALISTER, Bladen Co.: 1877–'78. Prospect Hill, Caswell Co.
COURTS, DANIEL WILLIAM, Surry Co.: A. B., 1823; A. M., 1832. Lawyer. Gen. Assem. Treasurer N. C., 1850–'63. Born 1802, died 1884.
COURTS, GEORGE A., Raleigh: 1854–'55. Dead.
COURTS, WILLIAM JAMES, Raleigh: 1852–'54. Physician.
COVINGTON, BENJAMIN W., Richmond Co.: 1830–'33. Dead.
COVINGTON, CHARLES COLEMAN, Wilmington: 1875–'78.
COVINGTON, EDMUND DEBERRY, Richmond Co.: A. B., 1844. Dead.
COVINGTON, EDMUND DEBERRY, Summerville, Harnett Co.: 1863–'64.
COVINGTON, FRANK LEAK, Wilmington: 1887–.
COVINGTON, HARRISON WALL, Richmond Co.: A. B., 1834. Dead.
COVINGTON, JAMES M., Richmond Co.: 1836–'37. Dead.
COVINGTON, JAMES M., Richmond Co.: 1858–'61. Physician. Dead.
COVINGTON, JOHN MALLOY, Laurinburg: 1888–.
COVINGTON, STEPHEN W., Richmond Co.: 1836–'37. Dead.
COVINGTON, THOMAS AREY, Richmond Co.: A. B., 1843. Dead.
COVINGTON, THOMAS T., Laurinburg: 1878–'79.
COWAN, DAVID STONE, Wilmington: 1850–'51.
COWAN, DAVID STONE, Columbus Co.: 1879–'81.
COWAN, JOHN, Wilmington: A. B., 1844. Born 1823, died 1861.
COWAN, JOHN, Wilmington: 1859–'60.
COWAN, ROBERT H., Wilmington: A. B., 1821. Lawyer. Born 1801, died 1845.
COWAN, ROBERT H., Wilmington: A. B., 1844. Lawyer. Col. C. S. A. R. R. Comr. Born 1824, died 1872.
COWAN, THOMAS, Wilmington: 1821. Dead.
COWAN, THOMAS, Wilmington: A. B., 1858. Lawyer. Lieut. C. S. A. Born 1839. Killed in battle, 1862.
COWAN, THOMAS, Wilmington: A. B., 1858. Capt. C. S. A. Killed in battle.
COWAN, WILLIAM, Wilmington: 1819. Dead.
COWAN, WILLIAM DICK, Wilmington: A. B., 1843. Physician. Born 1821, died 1859.
COWAN, WILLIAM JAMES, Wilmington: A. B., 1808. Dead.
COWPER, GEORGE V., Hertford Co.: 1863–'64. Lawyer. Winton.
COWPER, ROSWELL, Hertford Co.: 1845–'46.
COWPER, THOMAS L., Hertford Co.: 1852–'53. Died 1853.
COX, BERIAH THADDEUS, Coxville, Pitt Co.: 1884–'86.
COX, CADER GREGORY, Onslow Co.: A. B., 1858. Physician. Surg. C. S. A. Died 1877.
COX, CHARLES GREGORY, Richlands, Onslow Co.: 1879–'80.
COX, JOHN DAVID, Coxville, Pitt Co.: 1882–'85.
COX, JOSEPH BROWN, Tryon City, Polk Co.: 1885–'86.
COX, PIERRE BAYARD, Raleigh: A. B., 1886.

Cox, Thomas, Greenville: 1879–'80. Died 1882.
Cox, Thomas Alexander, Hertford, Perquimans Co.: 1886–'88.
Cox, William Gaston, Hertford, Perquimans Co.: 1888–.
Cox, William R., Miss.: 1810. Dead.
Cozart, William M., Columbus, Miss.: 1855–'58. Born 1838, died 1860.
Craddock, Charles James Fox, Va.: A. B., 1838. Physician. Dead.
Craig, Andrew M., Orange Co.: 1822. Minister. Dead.
Craig, Andrew Murdock, Alamance Co.: 1866–'67.
Craig, Braxton, Chapel Hill: 1880–'83. Planter. Windsor.
Craig, James Alexander, Lincoln Co.: A. B., 1816. Physician. Born 1790, died 1849.
Craig, James Francis, Chapel Hill: 1852–'53. Born 1832. Minister Friend's Society.
Craig, Locke, Windsor, Bertie Co.: A. B., 1880. Lawyer. Asheville.
Craig, William Harrison, Chapel Hill: A. B., 1868. Born 1841. C. S. A. Merchant and Teacher. Kenyon, Ark.
Craige, Burton Francis, Salisbury: A. B., 1829; A. M., 1847. Lawyer. Gen. Assem. M. C., 1853–'61. Mem. Conv., 1861. Mem. Confed. Congress. Born 1811, died 1875.
Craige, Kerr, Salisbury 1859–'61. Born 1843. Capt. C. S. A. Lawyer. Gen. Assem. Collector Internal Revenue.
Craighead, George, Va.: 1815. Physician. Dead.
Crawford, John C., Wayne Co.: 1852–'53. Dead.
Crawford, William Dunlap, Rowan Co.: A. B., 1799. Dead.
Crawford, William Dunlap, Cabarrus Co.: A. B., 1827. Lawyer. Gen. Assem. Born 1806, died 1844. Salisbury.
Creecy, Richard Benbury, Edenton: A. B., 1835. Lawyer and Journalist. Col. C. S. A. Elizabeth City.
Creswell, John D., Greenwood, S. C.: 1858–'59.
Crenshaw, William Martin, Wake Forest: A. B., 1833; A. M., 1836. Physician. Dead.
Crichton, James Edward, Lawrenceville, Va.: A. B., 1836. Physician. Dead.
Crocker, James Thaddeus, Northampton Co.: 1867–'68. Born 1845. Lieut. C. S. A. Lawyer. Journalist. Ashboro.
Cromartie, Neill, Gravel Hill, Bladen Co.: 1884.
Cromwell, Berrien, Sumpter, Ala.: 1847–'48. Lieut. C. S. A. Died 1863.
Croom, Bryan S., Lenoir Co.: A. B., 1821; A. M., 1824.
Croom, Cicero Stephen, New York City: A. B., 1859. Maj. C. S. A. Lawyer. City Atty. Mobile, Ala., 1875–'77. Born 1839, died 1884.
Croom, Isaac, Lenoir Co.: A. B., 1815; A. M. Dead.
Croom, Hardy Bryan, Lenoir Co.: A. B., 1817; A. M., 1820. Dead.
Croom, James R., Lenoir Co.: 1813. Dead.
Croom, Richard S., Lenoir Co.: A. B., 1826. Physician. Dead.
Croom, Thomas Holliday, Ala.: 1839–'40. Born 1821, died 1858. New Berne, Ala.
Croom, Willie B., Lenoir Co.: 1804. Dead.
Croom, Willie J., Lenoir Co.: 1814. Dead.

CROSS, WILLIAM W., Thibodeaux, La.: 1858–'59. Physician. Surg. C. S. A. Planter. Died 1875.
CROWDER, JOSEPH, Raleigh: 1869.
CROWELL, GEORGE HENRY, Bilesville, Stanly Co.: 1887-.
CROWELL, JAMES LEE, Bilesville, Stanly Co.: 1885–'88. Lawyer. Concord.
CRUMP, JOHN PAUL, Danville, Va.: 1884–'85.
CRUMP, THOMAS STEELE, Stanly Co.: A. B., 1856. Dead.
CRUMPLER, THOMAS NEWTON, Rockford, Surry Co.: 1850–'52. Maj. C. S. A. Killed in battle.
CUNINGGIM, JESSE LEE, Chapel Hill: 1887-.
CUNNINGHAM, ALEXANDER, Person Co.: A. B., 1849. Dead. Danville, Va.
CUNNINGHAM, JOHN, Gallaway, Tenn.: 1877–'78. Merchant.
CUNNINGHAM, JOHN SOMERVILLE, Cunningham's, Person Co.: 1878–'79.
CUNNINGHAM, JOHN WILSON, Person Co.: A. B., 1840. Died 1887.
CUNNINGHAM, ROBERT B., Person Co.: 1834–'35.
CURRIE, DANIEL BROWN, Robeson Co.: A. B., 1840. Physician. Dead.
CURRIE, DANIEL JOHNSON, Stewart's, Richmond Co.: A. B., 1889.
CURRIE, GEORGE HENDON, Clarkton, Bladen Co.: 1887-.
CURRIE, JOHN DUNCAN, Bladen Co.: A. B., 1861. Lieut. C. S. A. Gen. Assem. Merchant. Clarkton, Bladen Co.
CURRIE, NEILL ALEXANDER, Clarkton, Bladen Co.: 1887-.
CURRIE, SHELBY SWAIN, Caswell Co.: A. B., 1840. Physician.
CURRIE, THOMAS A., Haywood Co., Tenn.: 1850–'52.
CURRIE, WILLIAM M., N. C.: 1819. Dead.
CURTIS, ASHLEY M., Hillsboro: 1862–'63. Dead.
CURTIS, WALTER MAKEPEACE, Franklinville, Randolph Co.: Ph. B., 1889.
CUTCHIN, JOHN A., Edgecombe Co.: 1860–'61. Merchant. Died 1866.
CUTHBERT, GREEN MOSELY, New Berne: A. B., 1838. Dead.
CUTLAR, DUBRUTZ, Wilmington: A. B., 1853. Born 1832. Lawyer. C. S. A.
CUTLAR, FREDERICK JOHN, Wilmington: A. B., 1821. Physician. Born 1801, died 1876.
DAIL, WILLIAM JACKSON BEAUREGARD, Snow Hill, Greene Co.: B. S., 1888. Teacher.
DALRYMPLE, PALMER, Jonesboro, Moore Co.: 1887-.
DALTON, DAVID NICHOLAS, Dalton, Stokes Co.: 1878–'79. Born 1859. Winston.
DALTON, PLEASANT HUNTER, Rockingham Co.: A. B., 1844. Born 1821. Presb. Minister. High Point.
DANCY, DAVID, Tarboro: 1808. M. D. Phila. Med. Coll. Born 1798, died 1826.
DANCY, EDWIN C., Tarboro: 1826. Born 1811. Physician. Planter. Ala.
DANCY, FRANCIS LITTLE, Tarboro: A. B., 1801. Lawyer and Planter. Born 1776, died 1848.
DANCY, FRANK BATTLE, Tarboro: A. B., 1881. Born 1860. Chemist. Raleigh.
DANCY, JOHN SESSUMS, Tarboro: A. B., 1841. Gen. Assem. Maj. C. S. A. Planter. Born 1821, died 1888.

DANCY, JOHN W., Northampton Co.: 1808. Dead.
DANCY, LEONIDAS LAFAYETTE, Tarboro: A. B., 1841. Born 1820. Physician. Planter.
DANCY, WILLIAM FRANCIS, Tarboro: A. B., 1841. Lawyer. Planter. Gen. Assem. Born 1818, died 1860.
DANDRIDGE, CHARLES F., Va.: 1830–'31.
DANIEL, CHESLEY, Halifax Co.: A. B., 1803; A. M. Gen. Assem.
DANIEL, CHESLEY B., Granville Co.: 1832–'33. Minister. Dead.
DANIEL, HENRY RIVES, Bladen Co.: A. B., 1859. Lieut. C. S. A. Died in service.
DANIEL, ISHAM, Oxford: 1869.
DANIEL, JOHN NAPOLEON, Halifax Co.: A. B., 1846. Lawyer. Died 1852.
DANIEL, JOHN RIVES JONES, Halifax Co.: A. B., 1821; A. M., 1834. Lawyer. Gen. Assem. Atty. Gen., 1834–'41. M. C., 1841–'51. Died 1868.
DANIEL, JOSEPH J., Halifax Co.: 1801. Gen. Assem. Judge Superior Ct., 1816–'32. Judge Supreme Ct., 1832–'48. Mem. Conv., 1835. Died 1848.
DANIEL, NATHANAEL, Halifax Co.: A. B., 1816. Dead.
DANIEL, S. VENABLE, Granville Co.: A. B., 1860. Lieut. C. S. A.
DANIEL, WILLIAM ALEXANDER, Halifax Co.: A. B., 1846. Gen. Assem. 1866–'67. Weldon.
DANIELS, FRANK ARTHUR, Wilson: 1878–'79. Lawyer.
DANIELS, JOHN L., 1821.
DANIELS, JOSEPHUS, Wilson: 1884–'85. Lawyer. Journalist. Raleigh.
DARDEN, WILLIAM EDWARD, Kinston: 1888–.
DARNALL, HARRY JOHNSTON, Durham: 1886–'88.
DAUGHTRY, LEMUEL GOODMAN, Gatesville: 1851–'52. Died 1852.
DAUGHTRY, W. MILLS, Gatesville: 1851–'52. Planter.
DAVIDSON, ALLEN TURNER, Asheville: Ph. B., 1882. Died 1888.
DAVIDSON, GEORGE FRANKLIN, Mt. Mourne, Iredell Co.: A. B., 1823; A. M., 1826. Lawyer. Gen. Assem. Born 1805. Dead.
DAVIDSON, SAMUEL MCCABE, Charlotte: 1867–'68. Catawba.
DAVIDSON, THOMAS BENJAMIN, Mansfield, La.: A. B., 1861. C. S. A. Killed at New Hope Church, Ga., 1864.
DAVIDSON, WILLIAM A. F., Charlotte: 1828.
DAVIE, ALLEN JONES, Halifax Co.: 1795. Dead.
DAVIE, AMBROSE, Montgomery Co., Tenn.: A. B., 1858. Born 1838, died 1861.
DAVIE, DAVID ASHBURNE, Montgomery Co., Tenn: 1858–'59. Planter. Born 1838, died 1863.
DAVIE, GABRIEL JONES, Montgomery Co., Tenn.: A. B., 1857. Born 1836. Capt. C. S. A. Planter. Teacher. Millwood, Collin Co., Texas.
DAVIES, ALLEN, Orange Co.: A. B., 1861.
DAVIES, JOHN LEROY, S. C.: A. B., 1822. Minister. Dead.
DAVIES, J. WILLIAM, Chapel Hill: A. B., 1868.
DAVIES, ROBERT LEON, Chapel Hill: 1881–'82.
DAVIES, WILLIAM BEAUFORD, S. C.: A. B., 1822. Minister.
DAVIES, WILLIAM W. M., Augusta, Ga.: 1861–'62.

DAVIES, WILLIAM WATKINS, Drapersville, Va.: 1887–.
DAVIS, ALLEN, Orange Co.: 1853–'55. Teacher. Born 1825, died 1867.
DAVIS, BAXTER, Boydton, Va.: 1817. Dead.
DAVIS, BERTRAM SWIFT, Chapel Hill: 1883–'84.
DAVIS, EDWARD H., Elizabeth City: 1854–'59. Lt. C. S. A. Planter.
DAVIS, EDWARD HENRY, Louisburg: 1883–'84. Lawyer. Smithfield.
DAVIS, FREDERICK, Elizabeth City: 1875–'77.
DAVIS, GEORGE R., Wilmington: A. B., 1838. LL. D. Lawyer. Conf. Senator. Atty. Gen. Conf. States.
DAVIS, GOODERUM, Fayetteville: A. B., 1817. Physician. Dead.
DAVIS, ELNATHAN HAYNE, Iredell Co.: A. B., 1854. Capt. C. S. A. Planter. Statesville.
DAVIS, HAYNE, Statesville: A. B., 1888. Lawyer.
DAVIS, HUGH LEVIN, Louisburg: 1877.
DAVIS, JAMES E. B., Pikeville, Wayne Co.: Ph. B., 1889.
DAVIS, JEREMIAH L., Norfolk, Va.: LL. B., 1849. Lawyer.
DAVIS, JOHN, Boydton, Va.: 1807. Dead.
DAVIS, JOHN, N. C.: 1825.
DAVIS, JOHN Z., Orange Co.: 1835. Physician. Dead.
DAVIS, JOSEPH J., Franklin Co.: 1847–'50. LL. B., 1850; LL. D., 1887. M. C. Judge Supreme Court. Raleigh.
DAVIS, MATTHEW S., Warren Co.: A. B., 1855. Teacher. Louisburg.
DAVIS, PLUMMER A., Franklin Co.: 1865–'66. Planter. Register of Deeds. Louisburg.
DAVIS, RICHARD BRYANT, Wayne Co.: 1881–'84.
DAVIS, RICHARD F., Antauga Co., Ala.: 1858–'59.
DAVIS, ROBERT HENRY, Louisburg: 1875–'77.
DAVIS, ROBERT MAYO, Tarboro: 1888–.
DAVIS, SAMUEL C., Huntsville, Yadkin Co.: A. B., 1860. Lieut. C. S. A.
DAVIS, STEPHEN, Warren Co.: A. B., 1807. Physician. Dead.
DAVIS, THOMAS, Franklin Co.: 1856–'58. C. S. A. Dead.
DAVIS, THOMAS ATKINSON, Wilson: 1884–'85.
DAVIS, THOMAS H., Union Co.: 1864–'65.
DAVIS, THOMAS FREDERICK, Wilmington: A. B., 1822; D. D. Bishop of S. C. Dead.
DAVIS, THOMAS FREDERICK, Salisbury: A. B., 1845. Minister. Dead.
DAVIS, THOMAS J., Wilmington: 1803. Dead.
DAVIS, THOMAS WHITNALL, Louisburg: A. B., 1860. Lieut. C. S. A.
DAVIS, TIMOTHY W., Macon Co., Ala.: 1860. C. S. A. Died 1866.
DAVIS, WELDON EDWARDS, Warren Co.: A. B., 1861. Capt. C. S. A. Killed at Kelly's Ford, 1863.
DAVIS, WILLIAM HITH, Elizabeth City: 1845–'47. Planter. Dead.
DAVIS, WILLIAM W., New Hanover Co.: 1834–'35. Physician.
DAVIS, ZACHARIAH JOHN, Orange Co.: 1835–'36. Physician.
DAY, THOMAS ARCHIBALD, Durham: 1876–'77. Born 1856, died 1880.
DAY, WILLIAM HENRY, Halifax Co.: 1860–'61. Capt. C. S. A. Gen. Assem. Lawyer. Weldon.
DAYWALT, GEORGE WASHINGTON, Concord: 1881–'82.

DEANS, WILEY BEAUREGARD, Taylor, Wilson Co.: 1885–'87.
DEBERNIERE, JOHN MALLETT, Fayetteville: A. B., 1849. Lawyer. Died 1851.
DEBERRY, JUNIUS BYNUM, Northampton Co.: A. B., 1857. Born 1834. Capt. C. S. A. Teacher. Minister. Currituck C. H.
DEBOW, ARCHIBALD MURPHY, New Orleans, La.: 1824. Journalist. Author. Dead.
DEJARNETTE, REUBEN R., Eatonton, Ga.: 1859–'61. C. S. A. Killed in battle.
DEJEAN, ALEXANDRE, St. Landry Parish, La.: 1859–'61.
DELK, JAMES ALLISON, Clarksville, Va.: A. B., 1841. LL. D. Prof. Thomasville Fem. College. Minister. Thomasville.
DENNIS, JOHN MULDROW, Bishopville, S. C.: A. B., 1852; A. M. Lieut. C. S. A. Teacher. Red Hill, Ga.
DENNIS, THOMAS COLGATE, Bishopville, S. C.: A. B., 1854. Physician. Surgeon C. S. A. Charlotte Co., Va.
DEROSSET, ARMAND JOHN, Wilmington: A. B., 1824. Physician. Born 1807.
DE ROSSET, LOUIS HENRY, Wilmington: 1857–'58. Born 1840, died 1875.
DE ROSSET, MOSES JOHN, Wilmington: A. B., 1816. Physician. Born 1796, died 1826.
DE ROSSET, THOMAS CHILDS, Wilmington: 1865–'66. Born 1845, died 1878.
DE ROSSET, WILLIAM LORD, Wilmington: 1837.
DE ROSSET, WILLIAM LORD, Wilmington: 1850–'52. Born 1832. Lt. Col. C. S. A.
DE VANE, MATTHEW BAILEY, Clinton: 1888–.
DEWEY, CHARLES FRANCIS, Raleigh: A. B., 1844. Physician. Dead.
DEWEY, THOMAS WEBER, Raleigh: A. B., 1847. Banker. Dead.
DEWS, THOMAS, Lincolnton: A. B., 1824. Dead.
DIBRELL, ANTHONY, Lynchburg, Va.: 1823. Minister.
DICK, JOHN MCCLINTOCK, Greensboro: 1879–'83.
DICK, JOHN W., Guilford Co.: 1813. Dead.
DICK, ROBERT PAINE, Greensboro: A. B., 1843; A. M., 1847; LL. D. Born 1823. Lawyer. U. S. Dist. Atty. Mem. Conv., 1861. State Senator. Mem. Conv., 1865. Judge Supreme Ct., 1868–'72. Judge U. S. Dist. Ct., 1872–.
DICK, SAMUEL WEIR, Greensboro: 1882–'83.
DICK, WILLIAM ALEXANDER, Greensboro: A. B., 1849. Physician. Dead. Lumberton.
DICKIE, DAVID, Orange Co.: 1834–'36. Minister. Dead.
DICKSON, JAMES HENDERSON, Wilmington: A. B., 1823. M. D. Columbia Coll. Pres. State Med. Soc. 1854. Born 1807, died 1862.
DICKSON, LOUIS, Duplin Co.: 1796. Dead.
DICKSON, ROBERT DUNCAN, Wilmington: A. B., 1841. Physician. Dead.
DICKSON, WILLIAM, Burke Co.: 1795. Dead.
DILLARD, JAMES WASHINGTON, Hertford Co.: 1843–'44. Planter and Com. Merchant. Born 1826. Dead. Norfolk, Va.

DILLARD, JOHN H., Rockingham Co.: 1837–'39. LL. D. Judge Supreme Court. Greensboro.

DILLARD, JOHN HENRY, Leaksville, Rockingham Co.: 1877–'78. Greensboro.

DILLARD, RICHARD, Edenton: 1875–'77. Physician.

DISMUKES, JAMES W., Wadesboro: 1825. Dead.

DISMUKES, JOHN LYNCH, Nashville, Tenn.: A. B., 1852. M. D. Univ. Penn. Born 1830. Surgeon C. S. A. Author. Pres. Ky. Med. Assoc. Mayfield, Ky.

DISMUKES, THOMAS TERRELL, Nashville, Tenn.: A. B., 1853. Physician. Surgeon C. S. A. Born 1832, died 1874.

DIXON, AMZI CLARENCE, Shelby: 1877–'78. Bapt. Minister.

DIXON, FRANK, Shelby: A. B., 1886. Bapt. Minister.

DIXON, GEORGE FAUCETTE, Alamance Co.: A. B., 1859. Born 1833. C. S. A. Planter. Wittsburg, Ark.

DIXON, JOHN HOWIE, Query, Mecklenburg Co.: 1876–'77. Minister.

DIXON, HENDERSON MCCAMIE, Query, Mecklenburg Co.: 1884–'85. Minister.

DIXON, JOSEPH, Fountain Hill: Greene Co.: 1882–'84.

DOAK, DANIEL GILLESPIE, Guilford Co.: A. B., 1832. Minister. Died 1860.

DOBBIN, JAMES COCHRAN, Fayetteville: A. B., 1832. Lawyer. Gen. Assem. Speaker H. of C. M. C., 1845–'47. Secretary of the Navy, 1853–'57. Born 1814, died 1857.

DOBBIN, JAMES COCHRAN, Fayetteville: 1858–'59. Lawyer. Born 1839, died 1869.

DOBBIN, JOHN HOLMES, Fayetteville: A. B., 1861. C. S. A. Born 1841. Died in service, 1865.

DOBSON, JOHN HAMLIN, Rockford, Surry Co.: 1875–'77. Mt. Airy.

DOCKERY, CLAUDIUS, Mangum, Richmond Co.: Ph. B., 1887. Tutor Latin, 1887–'88. Lawyer.

DOCKERY, OLIVER HART, Richmond Co.: Ph. B., 1848. Gen. Assem. Lieut. Col. C. S. A. Mem. Conv., 1865. M. C. Planter. Mangum.

DODSON, CHARLES RUSSELL, Milton, Caswell Co.: A. B., 1835. Physician.

DOLES, ROBERT M., Jerusalem, Va.: 1839–'40. Dead.

DONALDSON, ROBERT, Cumberland Co.: A. B., 1818. Lawyer. Dead.

DONELSON, ANDREW JACKSON, Jefferson, Tenn.: 1833–'35. Dead.

DONELSON, JOHN E., Bainbridge, Ga.: 1863–'64. Lawyer.

DONELSON, SAMUEL, Hendersonville, Tenn.: 1860–'61. Lieut. C. S. A. Cl'k Davidson Co. Ct. Door-keeper U. S. H. of R., 1883–'87. Washington, D. C.

DONNELL, JOHN ROBERT, New Berne: A. B., 1807. State Solicitor, 1815. Judge Superior Ct., 1819–'36. Born 1791, died 1864.

DONNELL, RICHARD SPAIGHT, Craven Co.: A. B., 1839. Gen. Assem. M. C., 1847–'49. Speaker H. of C., 1864. Mem. Conv., 1865. Born 1820, died 1867.

DONNELL, WASHINGTON, Guilford Co.: A. B., 1825. Physician. Dead.

DONOHO, CHARLES DIXON, Milton, Caswell Co.: A. B., 1820; A. M., 1826. Dead.

DONOHO, RICHARD A., Milton, Caswell Co.: 1834–'36.
DONOHO, SAUNDERS, Milton, Caswell Co.: 1804. Maj. U. S. A. Dead.
DONOHO, THOMAS A., Milton, Caswell Co.: 1845–'46.
DORLAND, CHARLES JOHNSON, Concord: 1869–'70.
DORLAND, WILLIAM GARDINER, Concord: 1869–'70.
DORSEY, LAWRENCE A., Wilmington: 1795. Dead.
DORTCH, WALTER ROSS, Camden, Ala.: 1865–'66. Lawyer. Gadsden, Ala.
DORTCH, WILLIAM BASKERVILL, La Grange, Tenn.: A. B., 1849. Lawyer. C. S. A. Gen. Assem., 1853 and 1855–'56. Born Aug. 10, 1828, died March 10, 1882. Somerville, Tenn.
DORTCH, WILLIAM THEOPHILUS, Goldsboro: 1881–'85. Lawyer.
DOSS, HENRY WILEY, Pickensville, Ala.: 1852–'54. Maj. C. S. A. Physician. Died 1887.
DOUB, PETER F., Chapel Hill: 1854–'55.
DOUGHTON, RUFUS ALEXANDER, Alleghany Co.: 1879–'80. Lawyer. Gen. Assem., 1889. Sparta.
DOUGLAS, T. J. H., S. C.: 1859–'60.
DOUGLAS, WILLIAM, Wetumpka, Ala.: 1858–'59. Dead.
DOUGLAS, WILLIAM W., St. Augustine, Fla.: 1840.
DOUGLASS, JAMES T., S. C.: 1858–'60.
DOWD, CLEMENT, Carthage, Moore Co.: A. B., 1856. Lawyer. M. C.
DOWD, CORNELIUS FURMAN, Wake Co.: A. B., 1861. Physician.
DOWD, JOSEPH CAREY, Tarboro: 1876–'77. Planter.
DOWD, WILLIAM CAREY, Wake Co.: A. B., 1858.
DOWNEY, JAMES WEBB, Granville Co.: A. B., 1843. Dead.
DOWNEY, JOHN ALEXANDER, Granville Co.: A. B., 1836. Physician. Dead.
DOXEY, SAMUEL, Sumner Co., Tenn.: 1856–'58.
DRAKE, EDWIN L., Fayetteville, Tenn.: A. B., 1860. Lieut. Col. C. S. A. Physician. Journalist. Winchester, Tenn.
DRAKE, JOHN R., Nashville, Tenn.: 1846–'48. Physician.
DRAKE, NICHOLAS JOHN, Nash Co.: A. B., 1821. Physician. Gen Assem. Dead.
DRAKE, WILLIAM GREEN, Uchee, Ala.: A. B., 1856. Physician. Surgeon C. S. A.
DRAUGHON, JAMES WELLS, Edgecombe Co.: 1860–'61. Lieut. C. S. A. Planter. Born 1840, died 1884.
DREW, FRANK, Jacksonville, Fla.: LL. B., 1888.
DRISDALE, WILLIAM EDWARD, Franklin Co., Ala.: A. B., 1852. Born 1831. C. S. A. Planter. La Grange, Texas.
DROMGOOLE, EDWARD, Lawrenceville, Va.: A. B., 1845. Dead.
DROMGOOLE, GEORGE C., Lawrenceville, Va.: Gen. Assem. Speaker Senate. M. C. Dead.
DROMGOOLE, PETER, Lawrenceville, Va.: 1830–'32. Dead.
DUBOSE, ROBERT M., Wilkes Co., Ga.: 1859–'60.
DUDLEY, EDWARD B., Wilmington: 1837–'38. Born 1820, died 1840.
DUDLEY, WILLIAM HENRY HAYWOOD, Raleigh: A. B., 1840. Dead.
DUGGER, JOHN EDWARD, Warrenton: A. B., 1857. Capt. C. S. A. Teacher. Died 1887.

DUGGER, MACON TUCKER, Warrenton: A. B., 1858. Dead.
DUGGER, SHEPHERD MONROE, Watauga Co.: 1880–'81. Lawyer and Teacher. Banner's Elk, Watauga Co.
DUKE, GREEN, Warren Co.: 1799. Dead.
DUKE, LEWIS B., Warren Co.: 1803. Dead.
DUKE, WILLIAM JAMES, Pontotoc, Miss.: A. B., 1846. Dead.
DULANY, THOMAS WASHINGTON, Onslow Co.: A. B., 1829. Dead.
DULS, CHARLES HENRY, Charlotte: 1887. Lawyer.
DUNBIBIN, JUNIUS CHATHAM, Wilmington: 1825–'28. Physician. Born 1809, died 1833.
DUNCAN, JOHN, Matagorda, Texas: A. B., 1859.
DUNHAM, JOHN WHITTIER, Pitt Co.: 1866–'67. Maj. C. S. A. Gen. Assem. State Senator. Lawyer. Died 1889. Wilmington.
DUNLAP, JOSEPH INGRAM, Cedar Hill, Anson Co.: 1876–'77. Wadesboro.
DUNLAP, ROBERT W., Lancaster, S. C.: 1832–'35.
DUNN, FRANCIS CLYDE, Kinston: 1888–.
DUNN, WILLIAM A., Wake Co.: 1857–'58.
DUNN, WILLIAM BELL, Raleigh: A. B., 1826; A. M., 1836. Physician. Dead.
DUNSTON, WALTER SEATON, Creswell, Washington Co.: Ph. B., 1886.
DUPRÉ, ALCÉE, St. Landry Parish, La.: 1859–'60.
DUPRÉ, OVIDE, St. Martin Parish, La.: A. B., 1862. Lawyer. New York City.
DUPREE, JEPTHA, Northampton Co.: 1802. Dead.
DUPREE, JOSEPH S., Pitt Co.: 1867–68.
DURHAM, JACKSON, Orange Co.: 1869.
DUSENBERY, EDWIN LAFAYETTE, Lexington: A. B., 1845. Physician. C. S. A. Born 1824. Killed in battle, 1862.
DUSENBERY, HENRY MCRORIE, Lexington: A. B., 1849. Born 1829, died 1862.
DUSENBERY, JAMES LAURENCE, Lexington: A. B., 1842. Born 1821. Surgeon C. S. A. Physician.
DUSENBERY, WILLIAM BREVARD, Lexington: A. B., 1853. Born 1834, died 1861.
DUSKIN, GEORGE MICHAEL, Chapel Hill: A. B., 1857. Born 1836. Lawyer. Gen. Assem. Ala. U. S. Dist. Atty. Ala. Greensboro, Ala.
DUVAL, HARVIE SHEFFIELD, Tallahassee, Fla.: 1851–'52. Born 1830. Civil Engineer. C. S. A. Chattahoochee, Fla.
EAGLES, JOSEPH, Wilmington: 1807. Dead.
EAGLES, RICHARD A. B., Wilmington: 1795. First Pres. Philanthropic Society. Dead.
EARL, JOHN CARTER, Chapel Hill: 1869–'70.
EARL, LOUIS MINTER, Chapel Hill: 1869–'70.
EASON, ROBERT RANSOM, Selma: 1887–.
EASTERLING, EDWARD C., Georgetown, S. C.: 1858–'61.
EASTIN, JOHN D., Maury Co., Tenn.: 1838–'39.
EATON, EDWIN J. B., Warrenton: 1824. Dead.
EATON, JAMES W., Williamsboro: 1835–'36. Born 1815, died 1855.

EATON, JOHN SOMERVILLE, Granville Co.: 1819. Born 1800, died 1854.
EATON, JOHN H., Halifax Co.: 1803. A. M., 1825. U. S. S. Tenn., 1818–'29. Gov. Fla. Ter., 1834. U. S. Sec. War, 1829–'31. Min. to Spain, 1836–'40. Author. Died 1856.
EATON, LAFAYETTE BROWN, Warrenton: 1878–'81. Washington.
EATON, OSCAR BENJAMIN, Mocksville: 1881–'83.
EATON, WILLIAM, Warrenton: A. B., 1829. Atty. Gen. N. C., 1851–'52. Gen. Assem. Conv. 1868. Dead.
EATON, THOMAS, Warren Co.: 1820. Dead.
ECCLES, JOHN, Fayetteville: 1837–'38. Dead.
EDGERTON, CHARLES NEWTON, Goldsboro: 1887–.
EDMONDSON, ANDREW KINKAMAN, Fayetteville, Tenn.: A. B., 1861.
EDMONDSON, WILLIAM ELAM, Morganton: 1884–'86. Meth. Minister.
EDMUNDS, AUGUSTUS T., Halifax Co.: 1836–'37. Dead.
EDMUNDS, BENJAMIN C., Halifax Co.: 1834–'35. Dead.
EDMUNDS, JOHN T., Lawrenceville, Va.: 1816. Dead.
EDMUNDS, LITTLETON, Va.: 1834–'35.
EDMUNDS, WILLIAM H., Lawrenceville, Va.: 1833–'34. Dead.
EDMUNDSON, THOMAS, Goldsboro: 1876–'78. Manufacturer.
EDWARDS, ARTHUR JOSEPH, Elk Creek: 1888–.
EDWARDS, CHARLES, Person Co.: 1821.
EDWARDS, DAVID H., Green Co.: 1862–'63. Ark.
EDWARDS, GEORGE WALTER, Elk Creek: 1885–'88.
EDWARDS, JAMES L., Anson Co.: 1864–'65.
EDWARDS, JOHN HENRY, Person Co.: A. B., 1830; M. D. Dead.
EDWARDS, JOHN R., Norfolk, Va.: 1860–'61.
EDWARDS, LEONIDAS COMPTON, Person Co.: A. B., 1844. Lawyer. Col. C. S. A. Gen. Assem. Oxford.
EDWARDS, LUTHER BELL, Henderson: A. B., 1888. Teacher. Winston.
EGERTON, BENJAMIN IREDELL, Macon: 1877–'79.
EGERTON, MONTRAVILLE WALKER, Hendersonville: 1885–'88. Born 1867. Lawyer.
EHRINGHAUS, JOHN C. B., Elizabeth City: 1832–'33. Lawyer. Gen. Assem. Died 1853.
ELLER, ADOLPHUS HILL, Ashe Co.: A. B., 1885. Lawyer. Winston.
ELLERBEE, JOHN CRAWFORD, S. C.: A. B., 1823. Dead.
ELLERBEE, JOHN G., S. C.: 1822.
ELLERBEE, WILLIAM, S. C.: 1818.
ELLINGTON, DAVID S., Wentworth: 1858–'60.
ELLIOTT, ALEXANDER, Cumberland Co.: 1816. Dead.
ELLIOTT, BENJAMIN R., Ashboro: 1854–'56.
ELLIOTT, EDMUND, 1819.
ELLIOTT, HENRY BRANSON, Randolph Co.: A. B., 1826.
ELLIOTT, JOHN, Cumberland Co.: A. B., 1822.
ELLIOTT, JOHN B., Wayne Co.: 1850–'52.
ELLIOTT, JOHN G., Sampson Co.: 1816. Dead.
ELLIOTT, JOHN S., Cumberland Co.: 1826.
ELLIOTT, WARREN G., Elizabeth City: 1864–'65. Lawyer. Norfolk, Va.

ELLIS, ANDREW JACKSON, Garysburg: 1855–'56. M. D. Capt. C. S. A.
ELLIS, JOHN, Rowan Co.: 1804. Dead.
ELLIS, JOHN CALHOUN, Whiteville: 1879–'80.
ELLIS, JOHN WHITE, Davidson Co.: A. B., 1841. Judge Superior Ct. N. C. Gov. N. C., 1859–'61. Died 1861.
ELLIS, PEARSON, Whiteville: 1879–'80.
ELY, JOHN RANDOLPH, Marianna, Fla.: 1857–'58. Adjt. Gen. C. S. A. Merchant.
EMERSON, ISAAC C., Chapel Hill: 1869–'70.
EMERY, THOMAS R., New Berne: 1855–'56. Minister.
ENGELHARD, EDWARD BENSON, Wilmington: 1875–'78. Raleigh.
ENGELHARD, JOHN COTTON, Raleigh: 1884–'86. Durham.
ENGELHARD, JOSEPH ADOLPHUS, Jackson, Miss.: A. B., 1854. Lawyer. Maj. C. S. A. Journalist. Sec. State N. C., 1877–'79. Born 1832, died 1879.
ENGLISH, JOHN LUCIUS, California Creek: 1882–'84. Lawyer.
ENNETT, WILLIAM T., Onslow Co.: 1859–'61. Maj. C. S. A. Physician. Pres. N. C. Med. Society. Wilmington.
EPPS, HENRY W., Sussex C. H., Va.: 1815. Dead.
EPPS, JOHN T., Nottoway C. H., Va.: 1814. M.C. Dead.
ERVIN, WILLIAM CARSON, Lenoir Co.: 1879–'80. Lawyer.
ERWIN, JOHN BRATTON, Yorkville, S. C.: A. B., 1856.
ERWIN, JOHN SIMIANER, Burke Co.: A. B., 1841. Physician.
ERWIN, JOSEPH EARNEST, Morganton: 1884–'86.
ERWIN, SAMUEL JETHRO, Lincolnton: A. B., 1847. Supt. Pub. Schools, Jackson Co., Fla. Greenwood, Fla.
ERWIN, SIDNEY BULOW, Burke Co.: 1841–'42. Dead.
ERWIN, WILLIAM EDWARD, Hendersonville: 1877–'78.
ESKRIDGE, THOMAS JOSEPH, Shelby: B. S., 1888. Teacher. Mountain City, Tenn.
ESTES, GEORGE HENSON, Columbus, Ga.: 1866–'67. Merchant. Talbotton, Ga.
ESTES, JOEL H., Haywood Co., Tenn.: 1858–'59.
EURE, MILLS CLARENCE, Gates Co.: 1878–'79.
EURE, MILLS LEE, Gates Co.: A. B., 1859. Lawyer. Judge N. C. Superior Ct. Com. Merch. Norfolk, Va.
EURE, MILLS ROBERTS, Norfolk, Va.: A. B., 1889. Born 1868.
EURE, STEPHEN EDWARD, Nash Co.: 1881–'82.
EVANS, DAVID, Edgecombe Co.: 1796. Dead.
EVANS, GEORGE NAPOLEON, Edgecombe Co.: 1832–'33. Planter. Dead.
EVANS, JAMES HAMILTON, Marion, S. C.: A. B., 1857.
EVANS, JONATHAN, Cumberland Co.: 1854–'56. Fayetteville.
EVANS, JOSEPH WASHINGTON, Cumberland Co. A. B., 1838.
EVANS, PETER G., Chatham Co.: 1843–'44. Planter. Col. C. S. A. Born 1822. Killed at Upperville, Va., 1863.
EVANS, RICHARD, Pitt Co.: A. B., 1824. Dead.
EVANS, THOMAS ADDIS EMMETT, Fayetteville: A. B., 1851. Dead.
EVANS, THOMAS CLANY, Milton: 1856–'58. Reidsville.
EVANS, WILLIAM A., Cumberland Co.: 1846–'48.

Eve, Francis Edgeworth, Augusta, Ga.: 1861–'62. Born 1844. Capt. C. S. A. Lawyer. Planter.
Everett, Charles E., Smithville (now Southport): 1838–'39.
Everett, James Abington, Shongalo, Miss.: A. B., 1861. Planter. Lumberman. Ft. Valley, Ga.
Everett, Thomas Calvin, Laurinburg: 1888–.
Everett, William Isaac, Rockingham: 1859–'60. Q. M. C. S. A. Civil Eng. Merchant. Born 1835.
Everett, William Nash, Rockingham: 1882–'84. Com. Merch. Norfolk, Va.
Ewell, Alexander, Brentsville, Va.: 1821. Dead.
Ewell, Edgar, Williamston: 1876–'78. M. D. Died 1885. Pekin, Montgomery Co.
Ewing, James William, Montgomery Co.: A. B., 1855. Born 1833. Physician. C. S. A.
Ewing, Joseph Preston, Pekin: 1882–'83.
Exum, James H., Goldsboro: 1858–'61. Capt. C. S. A. Gen. Assem.
Ezzell, Robert Frederick, Poortith. 1884–'87.
Faddis, Thomas J., Hillsboro: A. B., 1813. M. D. Dead.
Fain, John H. D., Warren Co.: A. B., 1860. Capt. C. S. A. Killed in battle, 1865.
Fairley, Archibald, Richmond Co.: A. B., 1813; A. M., 1827. M. D. Dead.
Fairley, John Laurin, Richmond Co.: A. B., 1827. Gen. Assem. Dead.
Faison, Edward Livingston, Sampson Co.: A. B., 1854. C. S. A. Planter. Born 1830.
Faison, Elias J., Duplin Co.: 1846–'48. Planter. Faison.
Faison, Frank S., Northampton Co.: 1863–'64. Capt. C. S. A. Garysburg.
Faison, Henry Elias John, Duplin Co.: A. B., 1880. Lawyer. Pres. Elector, 1888. Clinton.
Faison, Henry W., Duplin Co.: A. B., 1842. Physician. Dead.
Faison, James Hicks, Duplin Co.: A. B., 1878. Died 1887.
Faison, John Miller, Duplin Co.: 1877–'78. A. B. Davidson College. M. D. Univ. of Va. Faison.
Faison, Julian P., Sampson Co.: 1842–'43. Harrell's Store.
Faison, Peter Ballard, La Grange, Tenn.: A. B., 1858. Texas.
Faison, Solomon James, Sampson Co.: A. B., 1846. Lawyer. Teacher. Planter. Mem. Conv., 1875. Born 1825, died 1880.
Faison, William Alexander, Sampson Co.: A. B., 1846. Planter. Born 1821. Warsaw, Duplin Co.
Falconer, James T., Granville Co.: 1811. Dead.
Farabee, Benjamin F., Shelby Co., Tenn.: 1857–'58. Dead.
Farmer, James Arthur, Wilson: 1886–'87. Lawyer.
Farmer, Joshua Barnes, Wilson: 1883–'84.
Farmer, William Moses, Wilson: 1883–'84.
Farrar, Joseph William, Chatham Co.: 1878–'79.
Farrior, James, Duplin Co.: A. B., 1814. Physician. Dead.
Farrow, George Ferdinand, White Haven, Tenn.: 1860–'61. Born 1841. C. S. A. Planter. Gen. Assem. Memphis.

FARRELL, JOHN THOMAS, Bingham School: 1887-'88.
FAUCETT, ROBERT H., Orange Co.: 1832-'34. Dead.
FAULCON, ROBERT J. T., Halifax Co.: 1846-'47. Dead.
FEARING, ISAIAH, Elizabeth City: 1852-'53.
FEARING, WOODSON BRADFORD, Elizabeth City: 1875-'76. Physician.
FEARRINGTON, FRED., Belvoir: 1888-.
FEARRINGTON, JOSEPH PEYTON, Belvoir: 1884-'85.
FEARN, RICHARD LEE, Chatham, Va.: A. B., 1824; A. M., 1828. Physician. Dead.
FELTON, CLAUDIUS BELL, Beaufort: 1885-'87.
FELTS, JOHN, Ala.: 1820.
FENNELL, HARDY LUCIAN, Wilmington: 1882-'84.
FENNER, WILLIAM K., Franklin Co.: 1813. Physician. Dead.
FEREBEE, CORNELIUS MACKIE, Camden C. H.: 1880-'82. Lawyer.
FEREBEE, DENNIS DOZIER, Currituck Co.: A. B., 1839; A. M., 1847. Lawyer. Gen. Assem. Mem. Conven. 1861 and 1865. Col. C. S. A. Died 1884.
FEREBEE, EDWIN B., Camden C. H.: 1880-'81. Physician.
FEREBEE, JAMES W., Princess Anne C. H., Va.: 1857-'58. Capt. C. S. A. Died in Service at Princess Anne C. H., July 19, 1862.
FEREBEE, NELSON M., South Mills, Camden Co.: 1866-'67. A. M., 1882. Born 1849. Surg. U. S. N. Jamestown, Pacific Station, U. S. N.
FEREBEE, THOMAS COOPER, Camden Co.: A. B., 1853. Camden C. H.
FERGUSON, ANGUS M., Moore Co.: 1859-'60. Minister.
FERGUSON, HERBERT REEVES, Waynesville: 1888-.
FERGUSON, ISAAC REUBEN, Cuthbert, Ga.: A. B., 1859.
FERGUSON, WILLIAM D., Pickensville, Ala.: 1860-'61.
FERRAND, EUGENE, Cumberland Co.: 1849-'51. Dead.
FERRAND, HORACE, Columbia, La.: A. B.: 1860. C. S. A. Planter.
FERRAND, WILLIAM, Swansboro: 1835-'36. Dead.
FERRAND, WILLIAM PUGH, Onslow Co.: A. B., 1808. Gen. Assem. Physician. Dead.
FERRELL, LEONIDAS C., La Grange, Ga.: A. B., 1846. M. D. Univ. of Ga. Surg. C. S. A. Died in service, Aug. 19, 1867.
FETTER, CHARLES, Chapel Hill: A. B., 1868. Born 1845. C. S. A. Teacher. Pulaski City, Va.
FETTER, FREDERICK AUGUSTUS, Chapel Hill: A. B., 1859; A. M. Born 1838. Tutor U. N. C., 1858-'66. Lt. C. S. A. Teacher. Washington.
FETTER, HENRY, Chapel Hill: 1861-'62. Born 1843. C. S. A. Merchant. Statesville.
FETTER, WILLIAM MUHLENBERG, Chapel Hill: 1858-'61. Lt. C. S. A. Born 1841, died 1871.
FIELD, ALEXANDER, Boydton, Va.: 1810. Dead.
FIELD, ALEXANDER JONES, Ridgeway, Warren Co.: A. B., 1885.
FIELD, DRURY, Boydton, Va.: 1810. Dead.
FIELD, JAMES, Boydton, Va.: 1810. Physician. Dead.
FIELD, JOSEPH HARRIS, Columbus, Miss.: A. B., 1859. Born 1840. Adj. and Insp. Gen. C. S. A. Gen. Assem. Planter.

FIELDS, ALPHEUS, La Grange: 1882–'84.
FIELDS, WILLIAM CALLAHAN, Gap Civil, Ashe Co.: 1869–'70.
FINCH, EDWARD FRANKLIN, Lexington: 1884–'85. Lawyer.
FISHER, DAVID WHITE, Lowndesboro, Ala.: 1848–'50. Died 1850.
FISHER, HORATIO W., Hayneville, Ala.: 1849–'50. New Waverly, Tex.
FISHER, LORENZO C., Lowndes Co., Ala.: 1850–'51.
FITE, HENRY JULIUS, Mt. Holly, Gaston Co.: 1880–'81.
FITTS, JAMES H., Warrenton: 1851–'53. C. S. A. Killed in battle.
FITTS, JOHN, St. Stephens, Ala.: 1820. Dead.
FITTS, JOHN H., Warren Co.: 1823. Dead.
FITZGERALD, ADOLPHUS LEIGH, Rockingham Co.: A. B., 1862.
FIVEASHE, BENJAMIN, Edenton: 1818.
FLANNER, ANDREW JACKSON, Wilmington: A. B., 1857. C. S. A. Killed in battle.
FLANNER, BENNETT, Wilmington: 1857–'59. Dead.
FLANNIGAN, ROBERT ANDREW, Cabarrus Co.: 1877–'79. Mill Grove.
FLEMING, JOHN MARTIN, Wake Co.: A. B., 1859. Dep. Warden State Penitentiary. Raleigh.
FLEMING, JOHN MARTIN, Raleigh: 1887–.
FLEMING, WILLIAM JOHN, Mill Hill: 1886–'87. Died March, 1889.
FLEMING, WILLIAM WOODVILLE, McDowell Co.: 1863–'64. Born 1846. Maj. C. S. A. Lawyer. Gen. Assem. Washington, D. C.
FLETCHER, SAMUEL S., Elizabeth City: 1858–'61. Died 1861.
FLINN, ANDREW, S. C.: A. B., 1799; A. M., 1802. D. D. Minister. Dead.
FLOWERS, OLIVER BROOKS, Warren Co., Miss.: A. B., 1861.
FLOYD, ARCHIBALD ANDREWS, Boone, Watauga Co.: 1880–'83. Lawyer. Columbia, Tenn.
FLOYD, ROBERT PURNELL, Wilton, Granville Co.: 1869–'70.
FLYTHE, AUGUSTUS MOORE, Northampton Co.: A. B., 1859; A. M., 1866. Episc. Minister. Dead.
FOARD, FREDERICK C., Concord, Cabarrus Co.: 1859–'60. Lt. C. S. A.
FOARD, NOAH PARTEE, Concord, Cabarrus Co.: A. B., 1861. Surry Co.
FOGLE, JAMES O. A., Columbus, Ga.: A. B., 1860. C. S. A.
FONTAINE, EDMUND, Hanover C. H., Va.: 1817. Dead.
FOOTMAN, RICHARD M., Kington, S. C. 1860–'61. C. S. A. Killed in battle.
FORBES, ARCHIBALD A., Jackson, Miss.: 1854–'56.
FORBES, EDWARD MCCARTNEY, New Berne: 1828. Born 1811. Episcopal Minister. Beaufort.
FORBES, RICHARD NATHAN, New Berne: A. B., 1846. Lawyer. Died 1858.
FORBIS, JAMES WILEY, Greensboro: 1876–'78.
FORD, CHARLES HENRY, Duplin Co.: 1881–'83. Lawyer. Albertson.
FOREMAN, IVEY, Washington: 1881–'82.
FOREMAN, JOHN L., Pitt Co.: 1828–'29. Gen. Assem. 1835–'44. Planter. Merchant. Born 1808, died 1844.
FOREMAN, WILLIAM JOHN, Pitt Co.: A. B., 1858. C. S. A. Born 1857, died 1869.

FORNEY, DANIEL M., Lincoln Co.: 1804. Gen. Assem. Dead.
FORSYTHE, JAMES N., Stokes Co.: 1824.
FORT, ELIAS X., Halifax Co.: 1807. Dead.
FORT, HILLIARD, Enfield: 1839-'41.
FORT, JOHN, Halifax Co.: 1803. Dead.
FORT, WILLIAM B., Lenoir Co.: 1859-'61. Paymaster C. S. N. Planter. Pikeville, Wayne Co.
FOSCUE, HENRY CLAY, Pollocksville, Jones Co.: 1860-'61. C. S. A. Planter.
FOSCUE, JULIAN S., Jefferson, Tex.: 1858-'60. Dead.
FOSTER, ALEXIUS, S. C.: 1803. Dead.
FOSTER, ALFRED GAITHER, Lexington: A. B. 1844. Lawyer. Gen. Assem. Born 1826, died 1866.
FOSTER, ANDERSON E., Rowan Co.: 1822. Dead.
FOSTER, ANTHONY, Charleston, S. C.: A. B., 1800. Dead.
FOSTER, AUGUSTUS JOHN, Franklin Co.: A. B., 1835. Physician. Dead.
FOSTER, FENTON G., Wake Co.: 1855-'56. Dead.
FOSTER, JACOB F., De Soto, La.: 1858-'59. C. S. A. Killed at Chancellorsville, May 2, 1863. Shreveport, La.
FOSTER, JAMES LEE, Union Ridge, Hertford Co.: 1884-'85. McCrary's.
FOSTER, JOHN, Davie Co.: 1840-'41. Dead.
FOSTER, OMEGA HARDEN, Louisburg: 1852-'55. Merchant. Lt. C. S. A. Born 1835, died 1864.
FOSTER, WILBUR FISK, Glennville, Ala.: A. B. 1859. Lawyer. C. S. A. Gen. Assem. of Ala. Tuskegee, Ala.
FOUST, CHARLES GEORGE, Columbia Factory, Alamance Co.: Ph. B., 1888. Born 1863. Teacher.
FOUST, EDWIN MICHAEL, Columbia Factory, Alamance Co.: A. B., 1885. Editor. Kemp, Texas.
FOUST, ISAAC H., Randolph Co.: 1865-'66.
FOUST, JULIUS ISAAC, Graham: 1885-.
FOUST, THOMAS ROSWELL, Graham: 1888-.
FOUNTAINE, JOHN D., Va.: 1818. Dead.
FOX, WILLIAM W. G., Monticello, Miss.: 1840-'41. Died 1842.
FOXHALL, EDWIN D., Tarboro: 1855-'58. Capt. C. S. A. Planter.
FOXHALL, FRANCIS D., Edgecombe Co.: 1851-'54. Lt. C. S. A. Died in service, June, 1862.
FOY, DAVID HIRAM, New Hanover Co.: A. B., 1861. C. S. A. Born 1840, died 1862.
FRANCK, EDWARD LAFAYETTE, Richlands, Onslow Co.: 1876-'77.
FRANKLIN, JAMES, Surry Co.: 1813. Dead.
FRANKLIN, JESSE D., Early Grove, Miss.: 1859-'61. Dead.
FRANKLIN, SAMUEL R., Marshall Co., Miss.: 1858-'60. C. S. A. Killed in battle.
FREEAR, ROBERT, N. C.: 1821.
FREEMAN, GEORGE R., Raleigh: 1838-'39. Dead.
FREEMAN, JACOB R., N. C.: 1816. Dead.
FREELING, JOHN, N. C.: 1799.

FREEZE, JACOB ALEXANDER, Enochville: 1886. Died Oct., 1886.
FREMONT, FRANK MURRAY, Wilmington: B. S., 1877. Atlanta, Ga.
FRENCH, CHARLES E., Wilmington: 1866–'68. Born 1846. Merchant. Minneapolis, Minn.
FRENCH, JAMES MCDANIEL, Wilmington: 1862–'63. Born 1843. Merchant. Lumberton.
FRENCH, W. FOSTER, Lumberton, Robeson Co.: 1867–'68. Lawyer.
FRIERSON, ERVIN JAMES, Tenn.: A. B., 1824. Lawyer. Planter. Merchant. Born 1803, died 1849. Ashwood, Tenn.
FRIERSON, LUCIUS, Columbia, Tenn.: A. B., 1859. Born 1840. Banker.
FRIERSON, WILLIAM, Shelbyville, Tenn.: 1856–'58. Born 1839. Lawyer. Lieut. Col. C. S. A. Merchant.
FRIES, JOHN W., Salem: 1866–'68. Born 1846. Manufacturer.
FROST, SAMUEL MILTON, Mocksville, Davie Co.: A. B., 1852; D. D. Minister. Dead.
FULLER, BARTHOLOMEW, Fayetteville: A. B., 1851. Journalist. Banker. Dead. Durham.
FULLER, EDWIN WILEY, Louisburg: 1864–'65. Novelist. Poet. Merchant. Born 1847, died 1876.
FULLER, JESSE W., Fayetteville: 1857–'59. Dead.
FULLER, JOHN L., Leasburg: 1854–'55.
FULLER, ROBERT THOMAS, Caswell Co.: A. B., 1844. Lawyer. Judge Circuit Ct., Ark. Justice Supreme Ct., Ark. Princeton, Ark.
FULLER, RALZAMON WOODFORD, Lumberton: 1879–'80.
FULLER, THOMAS C., Fayetteville: 1849–'50. Col. C. S. A. Lawyer. Raleigh.
FULP, ELIAS, Stokes Co.: 1878–'79. Physician.
FULTON, ROBERT F., Fayetteville, Tenn.: A. B., 1862. C. S. A. Killed at Chickamauga.
FURGURSON, HENRY BEAUREGARD, Littleton, Halifax Co.: 1877–'80. Physician.
FURGURSON, MACMURRAY, Littleton, Halifax Co.: 1877–'82.
FUQUAY, ALDRICH PARTIN, Varina, Wake Co.: 1885–'87.
GAINES, EDMUND JAMES, Montgomery Co.: A. B., 1855. C. S. A. Gen. Assem. Born 1834, died 1866.
GAINES, JAMES LUTTRELL, Asheville: A. B., 1859. State Comptroller, Tenn. Nashville, Tenn.
GAINES, JOHN C., Montgomery Co.: 1858–'61. Capt. C. S. A. Born 1858. Killed at battle of Wilderness, 1864.
GAITHER, ALFRED M., Iredell Co.: 1813. Dead.
GALES, SEATON, Raleigh: A. B., 1848. Journalist. Maj. C. S. A. Died 1878.
GALLIER, JAMES, New Orleans, La.: 1845–'47. Architect and Builder. Died 1868.
GALLOWAY, ALEXANDER HENDERSON, Rockingham Co.: 1855–'57. Capt. C. S. A. Planter. Reidsville.
GALLOWAY, CHARLES WELCHER, Mt. Airy: 1875–'78. Dead.
GALLOWAY, GEORGE W., Smithville (now Southport): 1833–'35. Dead.

GALLOWAY, JAMES, N. C.: 1819.
GALLOWAY, JOHN MARION, Rockingham Co.: A. B., 1854. Col. C. S. A.
GALLOWAY, RAWLEY, Rockingham Co.: A. B., 1830. Dead.
GALLOWAY, ROBERT, Rockingham Co.: A. B., 1826. Dead.
GALLOWAY, ROBERT, Rockingham Co.: 1847–'48. Physician.
GALLOWAY, ROBERT M., S. C.: A. B., 1821. Dead.
GALLOWAY, THOMAS SPRAGGINS, Rockingham Co.: 1825. Dead.
GALLOWAY, THOMAS SPRAGGINS, Rockingham Co.: 1855–'58. Born 1840. Col. C. S. A. Lawyer. Somerville, Tenn.
GARDNER, HUGH WALKER, Wilmington: A. B., 1857. Lawyer. C. S. A. Killed in battle.
GARLAND, JOSIAH, Greene Co.: 1814. Dead.
GARLAND, THOMAS, Milton, Caswell Co.: 1845–'47. Dead.
GARLAND, WILLIAM H., Tenn.: 1838–'39.
GARLINGTON, JOHN, Laurens District, S. C.: 1859–'61. C. S. A. Killed in battle.
GARNETT, HENRY TURNER, King and Queen C. H., Va.: A. B., 1821. Dead.
GARNETT, JAMES T., 1821.
GARRETT, FRANKLIN, Monroe, La.: A. B., 1861. Born 1840. Capt. C. S. A. Lawyer.
GARRETT, THOMAS MILES, Hertford Co.: A. B., 1851. Lawyer. Col. C. S. A. Killed at Spottsylvania, May, 1864.
GARRETT, WILLIAM D., Nash Co.: 1838–'39.
GARRETT, WILLIAM RICHARD, Greene Co., Ala.: 1852–'54. Born 1838, died 1875.
GARRETT, WOODSON L., Greene Co., Ala.: A. B., 1860. Lieut. C. S. A. Born 1840, died 1870.
GARROTT, ISHAM W., Wake Co.: 1837–'40. Lawyer. Gen. Assem., Ala. Brig. Gen. C. S. A. Killed in battle.
GARROTT, MARTIN R., Bertie Co.: 1818.
GATLIN, ALFRED, New Berne: A. B., 1808; A. M., 1812. M. C., 1823–'25. Dead.
GATLIN, J. S., Lenoir Co.: 1824. Surg. U. S. A. Killed at Withlacoochee in Seminole War, 1836.
GATLIN, RICHARD C., Lenoir Co.: 1824. U. S. A. Maj. Gen. C. S. A. Dead.
GATLING, BARTHOLOMEW MOORE, Raleigh: 1888–.
GATLING, JAMES ROBERT, Gatesville: A. B., 1855. Died 1861.
GATLING, JOHN THOMAS, Gates Co.: A. B., 1859. Lawyer. Adj. C. S. A. Gen. Assem. Dead. Raleigh.
GATTIS, FRED NORWOOD, Belvoir, Chatham Co.: 1888–.
GATTIS, ROBERT LEE, Belvoir, Chatham Co.: 1884–'86.
GATTIS, SAMUEL MALLETT, Chapel Hill: Ph. B., 1884. Lawyer. Hillsboro.
GATTIS, THOMAS W., Orange Co.: 1853–'55. . Minister. Durham.
GATTIS, WILLIAM HENRY, Orange Co.: 1869–'70.
GAUSE, JOHN PETER, Brunswick Co.: A. B., 1828. Lawyer. Gen. Assem., 1829–'31.

GAY, CHARLES EDWARD, Columbus, Miss.: A. B., 1860. Lieut. C. S. A. Merchant. Starkville, Miss.

GAY, JOHN LENOIR, Oxford: 1831–'33. Episc. Minister. Prof. of English, Univ. of Ind., 1871–'72. Fayette, Mo.

GEE, ALBERT G., Halifax Co.: 1829–'32. Dead.

GEE, DRURY, Halifax Co.: 1803. Dead.

GEE, JOHN MASON, Halifax Co.: A. B., 1825. Dead.

GEORGE, FOURNEY, Columbus Co.: A. B., 1849. A. M. Lawyer. Lieut. Col. C. S. A. Gen. Assem. Mem. Conv., 1875. Dead.

GHOLSON, THOMAS, Lawrenceville, Va.: A. B., 1836. Dead.

GIBBS, HENRY SYLVESTER, Middleton, Hyde Co.: 1850–'53. Born 1831. Planter. Gen. Assem.

GIBSON, ISAAC G., Stokes Co.: 1827.

GIBSON, JOHN K., Richmond Co.: 1867–'68. Born 1845. Lawyer. Powhatan, Ark.

GIBSON, JOHN PHIFER, Concord: A. B., 1858.

GIBSON, TOBIAS, Houma, La.: 1856–'57.

GIBSON, WILLIAM HENRY, Concord: A. B., 1858. Lieut. C. S. A. Killed in battle.

GIBSON, WILLIAM NELSON, Germanton, Stokes Co.: A. B., 1824. Physician. Dead.

GIDNEY, CHARLES CHAUNCY, Shelby: 1884–'86.

GIDNEY, JOHN W., Shelby: 1866.

GIDNEY, SAMUEL ELEAZAR, Shelby: 1884–'86. Teacher. King's Mt.

GILBERT, WILLIE LEON, Mooresboro: 1886–'87.

GILCHRIST, ARCHIBALD, Richmond Co.: A. B., 1826. Dead.

GILCHRIST, JOHN, Robeson Co.: A. B., 1809; A. M., 1812. Gen. Assem. Dead.

GILCHRIST, WILLIAM, Moore Co.: 1809. Gen. Assem. of Tenn. Dead.

GILES, JOHN B., Salisbury: A. B., 1808. M. C. Dead.

GILES, MILO ALEXANDER, Salisbury: A. B., 1825. Physician. Dead.

GILL, BENJAMIN LLEWELLYN, Franklin Co.: A. B., 1859. Lt. C. S. A. Killed in battle.

GILL, EDWARD JAMES, Laurinburg: 1883–'85. Merch. Rockingham.

GILL, THOMAS JEFFRIES, Laurinburg: 1879–'80.

GILL, WILLIAM P., Franklin Co.: 1860–'61. Lt. C. S. A. Killed in battle.

GILLESPIE, DAVID, Duplin Co.: 1795. Dead.

GILLESPIE, JOSEPH, Duplin Co.: 1796. Dead.

GILLIAM, BRAXTON BRAGG, Bertie Co.: 1864–'65. Dead.

GILLIAM, DONNELL, Raleigh: 1877–'79. Lawyer. Pres. Elector, 1884. Tarboro.

GILLIAM, EDWARD WINSLOW, Fayetteville: A. B., 1855. Episc. Min. Baltimore, Md.

GILLIAM, HENRY AUGUSTUS, Tarboro: 1887–.

GILLIAM, JOHN BOND, Bertie Co.: A. B., 1855. C. S. A.

GILLIAM, ROBERT BALLARD, Oxford: A. B., 1823; A. M., 1826. Gen. Assem. Mem. Conv., 1835. Speaker H. of Com., 1848 and 1862. Judge Superior Ct., 1863–'65, and 1867–'68. M. C., 1870. Died 1870.

GILLIAM, THOMAS, Windsor: 1876–'77.
GILLIAM, THOMAS HOWELL, Gatesville: A. B., 1852. Dead.
GILMER, ELLISON LINDSAY, Greensboro: 1884–'86.
GILMER, JAMES C., Mt. Airy: A. B., 1864. Dead.
GILMER, JOHN ALEXANDER, Greensboro: A. B., 1858; A. M. Col. C. S. A. Judge Superior Ct.
GILMER, SAMUEL J., Charlotte: 1838–'39.
GILMORE, ALEXANDER, 1808. Dead.
GILMORE, JOHN, 1822. Dead.
GILMORE, JOHN TAYLOR, Noxubee Co.: Miss.: A. B., 1856. Surg. C. S. A. Born 1835, died 1875.
GILMOUR, WILLIAM, Halifax Co.: 1805. Dead.
GLASCOCK, WILLIAM F., Va.: 1816.
GLAZE, RICHARD HENRY, St. Landry Parish, La.: 1851–'52. C. S. A. Born 1833. Killed in service, 1863.
GLENN, EDWARD TRAVIS BRODNAX, Leaksville, Rockingham Co.: 1876–'77.
GLENN, JAMES A., Halifax Co., Va.: 1824–'25. Dead.
GLENN, JOHN W., Va.: 1812.
GLENN, JOHN W., Va.: 1834–'35.
GLOVER, WILLIAM, Elizabeth City: 1852–'55. Dead.
GLOVER, WILLIAM WATTS, Robeson Co.: A. B., 1855. Civ. Eng. Dead.
GODDARD, JULIUS GUSTAVUS, Williamston: 1882–'83.
GODFREY, FRANCIS MERRIMON, Elizabeth City: 1853–'54. Planter. Newbegun Creek.
GODFREY, FRANK MERRIMON, Newbegun Creek, Pasquotank Co.: 1882–'83.
GODFREY, WILLIAM ROBBINS, Cheraw, S. C.: 1858–'59. Born 1841. C. S. A. R. R. and Ins. Business.
GOGGIN, JOHN O. L., Va.: 1835–'36.
GOLDING, FRANCIS L., Germanton, Stokes Co.: 1849–'50. Dead.
GOODE, FLAVILLUS S., Thibodeaux, La.: 1848–'49. Born 1831. Gen. Assem. Pres. Elector, 1860. Capt. C. S. A. Atty. Gen. La. Judge Superior Ct., 1880.
GOODE, JOHN, Va.: 1799. Lawyer. Died 1874.
GOODE, THOMAS, Va.: 1807. Dead.
GOODLOE, DAVID SHORT, Canton, Miss.: A. B., 1858. Capt. C. S. A. Minister. Died 1872.
GOODLOE, WINTER HEVE, Canton, Miss.: A. B., 1858. C. S. A.
GOODMAN, ERASTUS GENAIR, Town Creek, Brunswick Co.: Ph. B., 1885.
GOODMAN, JOHN C., Gates Co.: A. B., 1858. Reynoldson.
GORDON, BENJAMIN W., Gates Co.: 1829–'31. Dead.
GORDON, GEORGE B., Gates Co.: 1839–'40. Dead.
GORDON, HENRY A., Person Co.: 1860–'61.
GORDON, JOSEPH H., Gates Co.: 1839–'40. Dead.
GORDON, RICHARD C., Hickman Co., Tenn: 1854–'56. Capt. C. S. A. Planter. Maury Co., Tenn.
GORDON, ROBERT, Richmond Co.: A. B., 1813. Dead.

GORHAM, EDWIN, Pitt Co.: 1817. Dead.
GORRELL, ALBERT BARROW, Winston: A. B., 1862. Born 1840. Col. N. C. S. G. Merchant.
GORRELL, JULIUS LA FAYETTE, Greensboro: A. B., 1850. Dead.
GORRELL, RALPH, Guilford Co.: A. B., 1825. Dead.
GOZA, GEORGE W., Carroll Parish, La.: 1857–'58.
GOZA, GEORGE W., Chicot, Ark.: B. S., 1859.
GOZA, SAMUEL DUPUY, Carroll Parish, La.: A. B., 1858.
GRADY, BENJAMIN FRANKLIN, Duplin Co.: A. B., 1857. Prof. Math. and Nat. Science, Austin Coll., Huntersville, Tex., 1859–'61. Sergt. C. S. A. Planter. Albertson's.
GRAHAM, ALBERT KIMBROUGH, Memphis, Tenn: A. B., 1854.
GRAHAM, ALEXANDER, Fayetteville: A. B., 1868; A. M. Supt. Public Schools. Charlotte.
GRAHAM, AUGUSTUS WASHINGTON, Hillsboro: A. B., 1868. Born 1849. C. S. A. Lawyer. Oxford.
GRAHAM, CHARLES CHAUNCEY, Lincoln Co.: A. B., 1840. Born 1819. Manufacturer. Banker. Com. Merchant. Memphis, Tenn.
GRAHAM, CHARLES MONTROSE, New Berne: 1853–'54. Lawyer. Capt. C. S. A. Born 1838, died 1869.
GRAHAM, CHAUNCEY WILLIAMS, Kenansville: A. B., 1841. Physician. Born 1819, died 1866.
GRAHAM, DANIEL, Anson Co.: A. B., 1812. Sec. State, Tenn. Dead.
GRAHAM, DANIEL McLEAN, Fayetteville: A. B., 1857. Physician. Surg. C. S. A. Duplin Roads.
GRAHAM, EDWARD, New Berne: 1851–'52. Born 1834, died 1860.
GRAHAM GEORGE FRANKLIN, Lincoln Co: A. B., 1815. Physician. Dead.
GRAHAM, GEORGE MORDECAI, Hillsboro, 1887–. Born 1871.
GRAHAM, GEORGE W., Hillsboro: A. B., 1868. Born 1847. C. S. A. M. D. Univ. of N. Y. Charlotte.
GRAHAM, HAMILTON CLAVERHOUSE, New Berne: A. B., 1861. Born 1840. Capt. C. S. A. Planter. Clerk of Circuit Ct. Selma, Ala.
GRAHAM, HENRY WILLIAM, Lincoln Co.: A. B., 1844; A. M., 1849. Physician. Dead.
GRAHAM, JAMES, Lincoln Co.: A. B., 1814. Lawyer. Gen. Assem. Born 1793, died 1851.
GRAHAM, JAMES AUGUSTUS, Hillsboro: A. B., 1860; A. M. Born 1841. Capt. C. S. A. Lawyer. Gen. Assem. Graham.
GRAHAM, JAMES F., Catawba Co.: 1846–'47.
GRAHAM, JOHN EDWARD, Richmond Co.: A. B., 1816. Dead.
GRAHAM, JOHN WASHINGTON, Hillsboro: A. B., 1857. Born 1838. Tutor Math. and Latin, U. N. C., 1857–'60. Maj. C. S. A. Lawyer. Gen. Assem. Mem. Conv., 1868.
GRAHAM, JOHN WOOTEN, Keyser, Moore Co.: 1885–.
GRAHAM, JOSEPH, Hillsboro: A. B., 1857. Physician. Capt. C. S. A. Charlotte.
GRAHAM, JOSEPH, Memphis, Tenn.: 1855–'56.

GRAHAM, JOSEPH MONTROSE, Catawba Co.: A. B., 1844. Dead.
GRAHAM, PAUL CAMERON, Hillsboro: 1887–. Born 1869.
GRAHAM, ROBERT DAVIDSON, Hillsboro: 1859–'61. A. B., 1868. Capt. C. S. A. Lawyer. Washington, D. C.
GRAHAM, STEPHEN, Duplin Co.: A. B., 1841. Gen. Assem. Planter. Kenansville.
GRAHAM, THOMAS, Cumberland Co.: A. B., 1823. Physician. Dead.
GRAHAM, THOMAS BAKER, Hillsboro, Miss.: A. B., 1855. Forest, Miss.
GRAHAM, WILLIAM ALEXANDER, Lincoln Co.: A. B., 1824; LL. D. Lawyer. Gen. Assem. Speaker H. of Com. M. C. U. S. Senator, 1841–'44 and 1866. Gov. N. C., 1845. Sec. Navy, 1850. C. S. Senator. Born 1804, died 1875. Hillsboro.
GRAHAM, WILLIAM ALEXANDER, Charlotte: 1882–'83. Physician.
GRAHAM, WILLIAM ALEXANDER, Hillsboro: 1856–'59. Born 1839. Assist. Adj. Gen. C. S. A. Planter. Gen. Assem. Lincolnton.
GRAHAM, WILLIAM H., Ga.: 1845–'47. Physician.
GRAINGER, CHARLES WILLIAMS, Goldsboro: 1887. Born 1868.
GRANBERY, JOSEPH LANGLEY, Macon, Tenn.: A. B., 1859. Born 1838. Capt. C. S. A.
GRANBURY, JOSIAH THOMAS, Perquimans Co.: 1821. Planter. Fishery owner. Gen. Assem. Born 1806, died 1862.
GRANDY, ALBERT SIDNEY, Oxford: A. B., 1882. Lawyer.
GRANDY, CHARLES TAYLOR, Shiloh, Camden Co.: Ph. B., 1886. Journalist. Raleigh.
GRANDY, LUTHER BELL, Oxford: Ph. B., 1886.
GRANDY, W. S., Camden Co.: 1842–'43.
GRANT, JAMES, Halifax Co.: A. B., 1831; A. M., 1836; LL. D., 1878. Born 1812. Gen. Assem., Iowa. Judge Superior Ct., 1846–'51. Speaker H. of Com., 1852. Davenport, Iowa.
GRANT, RICHARD SWEPSON, Norfolk, Va.: A. B., 1851. Born 1829, died 1858. Polk Co., Texas.
GRASTY, JOHN S., Danville, Va.: 1842–'43. Minister.
GRAVES, AUGUSTUS SIDNEY, Newton, Ga.: 1845–'48. Born 1827. Bremond, Texas.
GRAVES, BARZILLAI, Ga.: 1823. Dead.
GRAVES, BERNARD FRANKLIN, Mt. Airy: 1880–'83.
GRAVES, CALVIN, Caswell Co.: 1823. Lawyer. Gen. Assem. Speaker State Senate. Mem. Conven., 1835. Born 1804, died 1878.
GRAVES, ELIJAH, Granville Co.: 1809. Minister. Born 1791, died 1869.
GRAVES, GEORGE WASHINGTON, Caswell Co.: 1831–'32. Physician. Born 1809, died 1876.
GRAVES, HENRY, Granville Co.: 1811. Dead.
GRAVES, HENRY LEA, Caswell Co.: A. B., 1835. Born 1811. Minister. Washington, Texas.
GRAVES, JESSE D., Granville Co.: 1837–'38. Physician.
GRAVES, JOHN LEWIS, Caswell Co.: A. B., 1814. Physician. Born 1795, died 1870.
GRAVES, JOHN WILLIAMS, Caswell Co.: A. B., 1814. Planter. Gen. Assem. Born 1792, died 1846.

GRAVES, JOHN WILLIAMS, Caswell Co.: A. B., 1854. Lawyer. Capt. C. S. A. Born 1836, died 1872.

GRAVES, RALPH HENRY, Granville Co.: A. B., 1836; A. M., 1839. Tutor Math., U. N. C., 1837–'43. Prof. Math., Caldwell Inst. Born 1817, died 1876.

GRAVES, RALPH HENRY, Williamsboro, Granville Co.: 1867–'68. B. Sc., C. and M. E., Univ. of Va. Prof. Math., U. N. C., 1875–. Chapel Hill.

GRAVES, RICHARD STAMFORD, Orange Co.: 1832–'36. Dead.

GRAVES, STEPHEN PORTER, Mt. Airy: 1884–'87. Lawyer.

GRAY, JOHN BOVICE, Fredericksburg, Va.: 1863–64.

GRAY, ROBERT PERCY, Greensboro: 1880–'83. Sec. and Treas. North State Improvement Co.

GRAY, SAMUEL WILEY, Winston: 1860–'61. Capt. C. S. A. Born 1843. Killed at Gettysburg, 1863.

GRAY, WILLIAM HENRY, Northampton Co.: A. B., 1826.

GREEN, ALLEN J., S. C.: 1795. Dead.

GREEN, BENJAMIN THORPE, Granville Co.: A. B., 1853. Dead.

GREEN, BENJAMIN THORPE, Franklinton, Franklin Co.: 1887–.

GREEN, BERRYMAN, Danville, Va.: A. B., 1859. Col. C. S. A. Judge U. S. Circuit Ct.

GREEN, FREDERICK AUGUSTUS, Durham: 1887–. Born 1871.

GREEN, GEORGE, New Berne: 1876–'77. Gen. Assem.

GREEN, GEORGE ALEXANDER, Cool Spring, Iredell Co.: 1878–'79.

GREEN, HERBERT LINWOOD, Wilkesboro: 1883–'86.

GREEN, JAMES B., 1832–'33.

GREEN, JAMES COLQUHOUN, Danville, Va.: A. B., 1859. Surg. C. S. A. Physician.

GREEN, JAMES SEVERIN, Chapel Hill: 1841–'42. Born 1825. M. D. Univ. of Pa. Sewanee, Tenn.

GREEN, JAMES GABIE, Wilmington: 1838–'39. R. R. Business. Born 1821, died 1876.

GREEN, JAMES RANDOLPH, Durham: 1886–'87.

GREEN, JOHN A., Goldsboro: 1860–'61. Sergt. C. S. A. Killed in battle.

GREEN, JOHN CICERO, New Berne: 1876–'77.

GREEN, JOHN SOMERVILLE, Memphis, Tenn.: 1855–'58. C. S. A. Born 1839. Died in service, 1865.

GREEN, PLUMMER W., Warrenton: A. B., 1853. Dead.

GREEN, ROBERT G., Wilmington: 1809. Dead.

GREEN, ROBERT T., Granville Co.: 1853–'55.

GREEN, SOLOMON PLUMMER, Warrenton: A. B., 1856. Born 1835. Physician. Surg. C. S. A. Memphis, Tenn.

GREEN, STEPHEN SNEED, Chapel Hill: A. B., 1842. Born 1822, died 1846.

GREEN, THOMAS JEFFERSON, Va.: A. B., 1818; A. M., 1822. Died 1863.

GREEN, THOMAS J., Warren Co.: 1819. Gen. Assem. N. C., Fla., Cal., Tex. Brig. Gen. Texan Army. Mem. Texan Congress. Died 1863.

GREEN, WILLIAM, Warren Co.: A. B., 1808. Gen. Assem. Born 1786, died 1824.

GREEN, WILLIAM H., Livingston, Ala: 1858–'59. Lieut. C. S. A.

GREEN, WILLIAM MERCER, Wilmington: A. B., 1818; A. M., 1833; D. D.; L. L. D. Prof. U. N. C., 1838–'49. Bishop of Miss., 1849–'87. Chancellor Univ. of the South. Born 1798, died 1887. Sewanee, Tenn.

GREEN, WILLIAM SHAKESPEARE, Danville, Va.: A. B., 1840; A. M., 1843. Physician.

GREEN, WILLIAM WILLS, Goshen, Granville Co.: A. B., 1841. Physician.

GREEN, WILLIS LEWIS, Warrenton: A. B., 1855. Lawyer. C. S. A. Born 1837, died April 2, 1865.

GREENE, CANNON, Greenville: 1849–'51. Dead.

GREENE, THOMAS E., Warren Co.: 1815. Dead.

GREENLEE, EDWARD THOMAS, Marion, McDowell Co.: 1877–'81.

GREENLEE, ROBERT LEE, Greenlee, McDowell Co.: 1883–'85.

GREENING, ELDRIDGE S., S. C.: 1816.

GREENING, WADE HAMPTON, S. C.: 1816.

GREGORY, FRANCIS R., Granville Co.: 1857–'58. Sassafras Fork.

GREGORY, GEORGE HENRY, Washington: A. B., 1857. Capt. C. S. A. Lawyer. Gen. Assem.

GREGORY, HERBERT, Granville Co.: 1851–'52. Sassafras Fork.

GREGORY, SAMUEL BABCOCK, Crowell, Halifax Co.: 1887–'88.

GRETTER, JOHN BIRNEY, Greensboro: A. B., 1852. Dead.

GRIER, EBENEZER CLARKSON, Mecklenburg Co.: A. B., 1844. Dead. Macon, Ga.

GRIFFIN, HENRY W., Marksville, La.: 1853–'55. Born 1833. Big Bend, La.

GRIFFIN, JOHN D., Martin Co.: 1821. Dead.

GRIFFIN, MALACHI RUSSELL, Elizabeth City: 1875–'76. R. R. Agt.

GRIFFITH, ENOCH ALEXANDER, Winston: 1883–'84. Lawyer.

GRIFFITH, WALTER EVANS, Chapel Hill: 1887.

GRIGSBY, MADISON RUTH, Canton, Miss.: A. B., 1861.

GRIGSBY, RHYDON, Homer, La.: 1855–'57.

GRIMES, ALSTON, Washington: 1882–'83.

GRIMES, BRYAN, Washington: 1813. Dead.

GRIMES, BRYAN, Washington: A. B., 1848. Member Conven., 1861. Maj. Gen. C. S. A. Born Nov. 2, 1828, died 1880.

GRIMES, JOHN BRYAN, Washington: 1882–'85.

GRIMES, JOHN GRAY BLOUNT, Pitt Co.: A. B., 1854. Born 1834. Capt. C. S. A. Raleigh.

GRIMES, WALTER HANRAHAN, Raleigh: 1886–'87.

GRIMES, WILLIAM M., Washington: 1840–'41. Planter. Dead.

GRIMES, WILLIAM THOMAS, Hamilton, Martin Co.: 1884–'85.

GRISSOM, EUGENE, Raleigh: 1884–'88.

GRISSOM, ROBERT GILLIAM, Raleigh: B. S., 1887.

GRIST, FREDERICK, Beaufort Co.: 1825. Dead.

GROOVER, JAMES IRVING, Thomasville, Ga.: A. B., 1858.

GUION, ALEXANDER HENDERSON, New Berne: 1847–'49. Civil Eng. Born 1831, died 1856.

GUION, BENJAMIN SIMMON, New Berne: A. B., 1848. Civil Eng. Maj. C. S. A.

Guion, Bernard Bryan, Raleigh: 1849–'52. Born 1832. Capt. C. S. A. Battleboro.
Guion, Haywood Williams, New Berne: A. B., 1835; A. M., 1846. Lawyer. Author. Born 1814, died 1876.
Guion, John Osborne, Raleigh: A. B., 1847. Born 1826, died 1874.
Guion, Julius, Raleigh: A. B., 1851. Born 1830, died 1873.
Guirkin, Levi, Elizabeth City: 1887–'88.
Gulick, William McKee, Oxford: 1885–'87.
Gunn, William Pinckney, Caswell Co.: A. B., 1834. Dead.
Gunnels, William M., Laurens C. H., S. C.: 1859–'60. C. S. A. Killed in battle.
Gunter, John Doctor, Jonesboro, Moore Co.: 1877–'79.
Guthrie, Brooks Harris, Chatham Co.: 1866–'67. Born 1845. Pedlar's Hill, Chatham Co.
Guthrie, Walter Hugh, Chapel Hill: 1866–'68. Born 1850. Civ. Eng. Machinist. Boston, Mass.
Guthrie, William Anderson, Chapel Hill: A. B., 1864; A. M. C. S. A. Lawyer. Mem. Conven., 1871. Durham.
Guthrie, Winfield Scott, Chapel Hill: A. B., 1867. Born 1848. Machinist. Boston, Mass.
Guyer, Samuel Jacob, Bethany: 1887–'88.
Hackett, Richard Nathaniel, Wilkesboro: Ph. B., 1887. Lawyer.
Hackler, Thomas Jefferson, Dallas, Texas: 1883–'84. Lawyer.
Haden, Richard G., Fincastle, Va.: 1863–'64. Farmer. Gala, Va.
Hadley, James, Davidson Co., Tenn.: A. B., 1855.
Hadley, Jerome James, Gallatin, Tenn.: 1852–'55. Dead.
Hadley, John L., Fayetteville: 1806. Dead.
Hadley, John Livingston, Nashville, Tenn.: A. B., 1839. Physician. Farmer. Davidson Co., Tenn.
Hadley, Lucian Sanders, Wilson: 1887.
Hadley, Oscar Fitz-Allen, Sumpter, Ala.: A. B., 1858.
Hadley, Thomas Jefferson, Wilson: A. B., 1862; A. M., 1866. Born 1838. Capt. C. S. A. Lawyer. Merchant.
Hagood, Thomas Barrett, Barnwell C. H., S. C.: 1860–'61. Born 1841. C. S. A. Planter.
Haigh, Charles, Fayetteville: A. B., 1860. Sergt. Maj. C. S. A. Physician. Merchant.
Haigh, Charles Thomas, Fayetteville: 1882–'84. Physician. Chemist.
Haigh, Claude Hamilton, Fayetteville: 1887–'88.
Haigh, De Lagnel, Fayetteville: 1878–'81. Chemist.
Haigh, George Henry, Fayetteville: A. B., 1852. Capt. C. S. A.
Haigh, Thomas Devereux, Fayetteville: A. B., 1849. Physician.
Haigh, William Hooper, Fayetteville: A. B., 1842. Dead.
Hailey, Robert T., Richmond Co.: 1859–'60. Born 1835. Civil Eng. Planter. Marshall, Tex.
Hairston, George, Va.: A. B., 1832; A. M., 1850. Dead.
Hairston, George, Va.: 1838–'39. Dead.
Hairston, Nicholas P., Martinsville, Va.: 1810. Dead.

HAIRSTON, PETER, Rocky Mt., Va.: 1816. Dead.
HAIRSTON, PETER WILSON, Pittsylvania Co., Va.: A. B., 1837. Dead.
HAIRSTON, ROBERT, Va.: 1839–'40. Dead.
HAIRSTON, ROBERT ANDREW, Lowndes Co., Miss.: A. B., 1850.
HAIRSTON, WILLIAM LASH, Winston: 1880–'81.
HAIZLIP, JAMES DANIEL, Graham: 1881–'82. Lawyer.
HALE, EDWARD JOSEPH, Fayetteville: A. B., 1860. Maj. C. S. A. U. S. Consul, Manchester, Eng., 1885–'89.
HALE, PETER MALLETT, Fayetteville: A. B., 1849. Journalist. Raleigh. Died June 2, 1887.
HALE, ROBERT H., S. C.: 1818.
HALL, DAVID CLARK, Warren Co.: A. B., 1853. Lawyer.
HALL, EDWARD, Warrenton: A. B., 1815. Judge Superior Ct., 1840. Died 1877.
HALL, ELI WEST, Wilmington: A. B., 1847. Lawyer. Dead.
HALL, ELIAS, Iredell Co.: 1834–'35.
HALL, EZEKIEL, Wilmington: 1809. Physician. Dead.
HALL, ISAAC, A. B., 1823. Physician. Dead.
HALL, JAMES, N. C.: 1797. Dead.
HALL, JAMES DAVIDSON, Iredell Co.: A. B., 1828. Minister. Dead. Gaston Co.
HALL, JAMES GATLIN, Currituck: A. B., 1822; A. M., 1832. Dead.
HALL, JOHN, Warrenton: 1858–'60. C. S. A. Planter. Ridgeway.
HALL, JOHN HUBBARD, Fayetteville: 1877–'78. Meth. Minister.
HALL, JOHN NISBET, Iredell Co.: 1876–'78. Died 1878. Tipton Co., Tenn.
HALL, JOSHUA STANLEY, Fayetteville: 1881–'82.
HALL, ROBERT JAMES, Iredell Co.: A. B., 1824. Minister. Died 1877. Ohio.
HALL, ROBERT P., Warrenton: 1834–'35. Physician. Dead.
HALL, ROBERT SLOANE, Iredell Co.: A. B., 1814. Teacher. Dead. Indiana.
HALL, ROBERT TROY, Chapel Hill: A. B., 1844. Planter. Born 1823. Dead.
HALL, SAMUEL, Wilmington: 1837–'39. Chief Justice Supreme Ct. of Ga. Died 1887.
HALL, THOMAS CHAMBERS, Chapel Hill: A. B., 1847. M. D. Univ. of Pa. Born 1829, died 1860.
HALL, THOMAS G., Cumberland Co.: 1859–'60.
HALL, THOMAS H., Edgecombe Co.: 1799. M. C. Dead.
HALL, THOMAS PLEASANT, Iredell Co.: A. B., 1827.
HALL, WELDON E., Warrenton: 1830–'32. Dead.
HALL, WILLIAM ALEXANDER, Iredell Co.: A. B., 1822. Minister. Teacher. Born 1799, died 1877. Tipton Co., Tenn.
HALL, WILLIAM HUNT, Wilmington: A. B., 1855; A. M. Born 1833. M. D. Univ. of N. Y. Surg. C. S. A. New York City.
HALL, WILLIAM PLEASANT, Halifax Co.: A. B., 1803; A. M. Dead.
HALLIBURTON, DAVID C., Wake Co.: 1858–'59. Dead.

HALLIBURTON, JOHN WESLEY, Woodville, Tenn.: A. B., 1861.
HALLIDAY, ROBERT J., Fayetteville; 1834–'35. Dead.
HAMER, JOHN H., Marion, S. C.: 1854–'57.
HAMER, MISSOURI ROBERT, Little Rock, S. C.: A. B., 1884.
HAMILTON, WILLIAM, Edenton: 1802. Dead.
HAMLEN, HUBERT CHESLEY, Winston: 1888–.
HAMLETT, JAMES EDWARD, Va.: A. B., 1836. Dead.
HAMLIN, RICHARD FRANKLIN, Calloway Co., Ky.: A. B., 1859. Born 1834. C. S. A. Pres. Blandville College. Murray, Ky.
HAMLIN, WILLIAM A., 1825.
HAMMOND, WALTER MONROE, Archdale Ph. B., 1889.
HAMMOND, WILLIAM MAY, Wadesboro, Anson Co.: A. B., 1858. Capt. C. S. A.
HAMPTON, DAVID AMZI, Statesville: A. B., 1882.
HAMPTON, MANOAH B., Lawrence Co., Ala.: 1855–'58.
HANCOCK, WILLIAM J., New Berne: 1823. Merchant. Born 1807, died 1838.
HARALSON, ARCHIBALD, La.: 1808. Dead.
HARALSON, PAUL A., Caswell Co.: 1818.
HARDEMAN, THOMAS, Rutherford Co., Tenn.: A. B., 1821. Born 1800. Planter. Dead. Grenada, Miss.
HARDEMAN, THOMAS W. D., Matagorda Co., Texas: 1858–'61.
HARDEMAN, WILLIAM, Columbia, Tenn.: A. B., 1822. Merchant. Dead.
HARDIE, HENRY, Raleigh: A. B., 1850; A. M. Minister.
HARDIN, EDWARD JONES, Columbia, Tenn.: A. B., 1860. Asst. Adj. Gen. C. S. A. Merchant. Raleigh.
HARDIN, WILLIAM HILL, Rockingham Co.: A. B., 1820; A. M., 1828. Lawyer. Teacher. Fayetteville.
HARDING, JOHN, Nashville, Tenn.: 1850–'52. Born 1831. Planter.
HARDING, NEHEMIAH HENRY, Milton, Caswell Co.: 1824–'25. D. D. Dead.
HARDY, HENRY B., Bertie Co.: 1846–'47. LL. B., 1848. C. S. A. Lawyer. Jackson. Born 1826, died 1866.
HARE, JOHN L., Granville Co.: 1849–'50.
HARFORD, WILLIAM H., Georgia: 1821. U. S. A. Dead.
HARGET, FREDERICK WALTER, Richlands, Onslow Co.: 1876–'77.
HARGRAVE, ALFRED FRONTICE, Lexington: 1876–'78.
HARGRAVE, FRANKLIN GULLEN, Lexington: 1831–'34. Born 1814, died 1845.
HARGRAVE, JESSE, Lexington: A. B., 1857. Born 1838. Lawyer. Col. C. S. A. Planter. Laurel Hill, Richmond Co.
HARGRAVE, JESSE FRANKLIN, Lexington: 1851–'52. Merchant. Born 1833, died 1858.
HARGRAVE, JESSE HAMILTON, Lexington: 1833–'35. Born 1816, died 1879.
HARGRAVE, JOHN LINDSAY, Lexington: A. B., 1832. Lawyer. Mem. Conven., 1835. Born 1813, died 1841.

HARGRAVE, WILLIAM FREDERICK, Chapel Hill: 1865-'66. New York City.
HARGROVE, CHARLES BUDWOOD, Tarboro: 1886-'88.
HARGROVE, WILLIAM T., Granville Co.: 1826.
HARGROVE, WILLIAM T., Granville Co.: 1860-'62. C. S. A. Killed in battle.
HARKINS, GILES WELLINGTON, Tishemingo, Indian Ter.: 1882-'83.
HARPER, FRANCIS MARION, Kinston: Ph. B., 1888. Teacher. Raleigh.
HARPER, HOWELL P., Boydton, Va.: 1810. Dead.
HARPER, JAMES WARREN, Lenoir Co.: A. B., 1868. Lawyer. Died Jan. 29, 1883.
HARPER, JESSE, Randolph Co.: 1804. Dead.
HARRELL, HIRAM POWELL, Madison, Miss.: A. B., 1857. Lawyer.
HARRELL, JAMES JOSEPH, Lumberton, Robeson Co.: 1878-'81.
HARRINGTON, ALONZO LLEWELLYN, Ayden, Pitt Co.: 1885-'86.
HARRINGTON, CYRUS, Moore Co.: A. B., 1853. Minister. Mansfield, La.
HARRINGTON, JAMES AULD, Richmond Co.: A. B., 1808. Planter. Gen. Assem. S. C. Born 1790, died 1835. Marlboro, S. C.
HARRINGTON, PINCKNEY COTESWORTH, Meadville, Miss.: A. B., 1857.
HARRIS, ANDREW JACKSON, Oxford: A. B., 1884. Lawyer. Henderson.
HARRIS, BENJAMIN W., Halifax C. H., Va.: 1824. Dead.
HARRIS, CLINCH, Ala.: 1848-'51. Born 1832. C. S. A. Planter. Friar's Point, Miss.
HARRIS, EUGENE LEWIS, Granville Co.: Ph. B., 1881. Sec'y Y. M. C. A. Winston.
HARRIS, HENRY, Falkland, Pitt Co.: 1852-'55. C. S. A. Planter.
HARRIS, HUNTER LEE, Raleigh: B. S., 1889.
HARRIS, JAMES ROBERT, Rolesville, Wake Co.: 1886-'88. Asst. Chemist Exp. Station. Raleigh.
HARRIS, JOHN B. S., Mecklenburg Co.: 1821-'24. Physician. Dead.
HARRIS, JOHN S., Pitt Co.: 1867-'68. Lawyer.
HARRIS, JOHN T., Franklin Co.: 1859-'61. Dead.
HARRIS, JOHN WILLIAMS, Chatham Co.: A. B., 1861. Dead.
HARRIS, LIVINGSTON, Mecklenburg Co.: A. B., 1825. Dead.
HARRIS, NATHANIEL, Orange Co.: A. B., 1821; A. M., 1824. Minister. Dead.
HARRIS, NATHANIEL W., Salisbury: 1818.
HARRIS, PAUL B., Lancasterville, S. C.: 1859-'60. Dead.
HARRIS, RICHARD J., Warren Co.: 1851-'52.
HARRIS, ROBERT, Cabarrus Co.: 1795. Dead.
HARRIS, ROBERT B. P., Warren Co., Miss.: 1857-'58.
HARRIS, ROBERT THEODORE, Mackinley, Ala.: A. B., 1858. Capt. C. S. A. Lawyer. Born 1837, died 1872.
HARRIS, STEPHEN, Craven Co.: 1834-'36. Born 1816. Planter. Dead.
HARRIS, THOMAS BRANCH, Warrenton, Ala.: 1856-'58. Adjt. C. S. A. Born 1839, died 1869. Madison Station, Ala.
HARRIS, THOMAS WEST, Chatham Co.: A. B., 1859; A. M. M. D., Paris. Capt. C. S. A. Prof. Anat. and Mat. Med. U. N. C., 1878-'86. Born 1839, died 1888. Durham.

HARRIS, WILLIAM J., Wilmington, 1815. Physician. Dead.
HARRIS, WILLIAM SHAKESPEARE, Cabarrus Co.: 1835–'36. Dead.
HARRISON, ATLAS OCTAVIUS, Raleigh: A. B., 1841. Dead.
HARRISON, CARTER B., Franklin Co.: 1833–'36. Dead.
HARRISON, FREDERICK WILLIAM, Eastville, Va.: A. B., 1825; A. M., 1832. Physician. Dead.
HARRISON, JOHN ADAMS, Castalia: 1878–'81.
HARRISS, EDWIN ROBERT, Cabarrus Co.: A. B., 1828. Dead.
HARRISS, ELIAS SPENCER, Falkland, Pitt Co.: 1877–'78.
HARRISS, THOMAS WHITMEL, Halifax Co.: A. B., 1832.
HARRISS, WILLIAM WHITE, Wilmington: A. B., 1842; A. M., 1847. M. D. Univ. of N. Y. Surg. C. S. A.
HART, DAVID, Caswell Co.: 1809. Dead.
HART, FRANKLIN, Edgecombe Co.: 1839–'40. Physician. Dead.
HARTSFIELD, ALVA C., Wake Co.: 1861–'63. Dead.
HARVEY, ADDISON, Canton, Miss.: A. B., 1858. Capt. C. S. A. Leader Harvey's Scouts. Killed at Atlanta, Ga., 1865.
HARVEY, ALLEN, Tenn.: 1797. Dead.
HARVEY, CHARLES FELIX, Kinston: 1888–.
HARVEY, EDMUND B., Perquimans Co.: 1802. Dead.
HARVEY, HUBERT, Saline Co., Mo.: A. B., 1857. C. S. A. Died in service.
HARVEY, JOHN, Perquimans Co.: 1822.
HARWELL, ISHMAEL, Halifax Co.: 1807. Dead.
HARWELL, THOMAS, Sussex Co., Va.: 1815. Dead.
HARWOOD, S. PATTON, Robbinsville, Graham Co.: 1884–'85.
HASSELL, SYLVESTER, Williamston: A. B., 1862; A. M., 1866. Born 1842. Minister. Prin. Wilson Collegiate Institute. Wilson.
HATCH, ANTHONY, New Berne: 1818.
HATCH, CALVIN J., Craven Co.: 1821.
HATCH, DURANT, Jones Co.: A. B., 1806. Dead.
HATCH, GEORGE SEARS, New Berne: 1851–'52. Born 1830. St. Louis, Mo.
HATCH, LEMUEL, New Berne: A. B., 1815. Dead.
HATCHETT, JOHN, Caswell Co.: 1821. Dead.
HATTER, DAVID, N. C.: 1799. Dead.
HAUGHTON, JOHN HOOKER, Tyrrell Co.: A. B., 1832; A. M., 1840. Lawyer. Gen. Assem. Dead.
HAUGHTON, JOHN LAURENCE, Chatham Co.: A. B., 1861. Lt. C. S. A. Killed in battle.
HAUGHTON, JOHN R., Pittsboro: 1862–'63. C. S. A. Killed in battle.
HAUGHTON, JONATHAN HATCH, Chowan Co.: A. B., 1825; A. M., 1834. Gen. Assem. Dead.
HAUGHTON, MALACHI, Edenton: 1850–'53. Planter. Dead.
HAUGHTON, THOMAS GOELET, Edenton: A. B., 1834. Minister. Dead.
HAUGHTON, THOMAS HILL, Pittsboro: A. B., 1861. Born 1841. Capt. C. S. A. Charlotte.
HAUGHTON, TIPPOO SAIB, Edenton: 1844. Fla.
HAUSER, SAMUEL T., Stokes Co.: A. B., 1817. Dead.
HAVENS, LEROY C., Washington: 1861–'63. Died 1882.

HAWES, JESSE BOWDEN, Wilmington: A. B., 1884. Birmingham, Ala.
HAWES, JOHN ROBERT, New Hanover Co.: 1839–'40. Born 1823. M. D. Univ. of N. Y. Capt. C. S. A. Gen. Assem. Planter.
HAWKINS, ALEXANDER BOYD, Franklin Co.: A. B., 1845. Born 1825. Physician. Planter. Tallahassee, Fla.
HAWKINS, BENJAMIN FRANKLIN, Warren Co.: A. B., 1805. Dead.
HAWKINS, COLIN M., Warren Co.: 1864–'66. Pres. Gas Co. Raleigh.
HAWKINS, FRANK, Warren Co.: A. B., 1813. Physician. Dead.
HAWKINS, FRANK, Franklin Co.: 1833–'36. Born 1815. Planter. Gen. Assem. of Miss. Winona, Miss.
HAWKINS, GEORGE WASHINGTON, Warren Co.: A. B., 1813. Dead.
HAWKINS, JOHN DAVIS, Warren Co.: A. B., 1801. Dead.
HAWKINS, JOHN DAVIS, Franklin Co.: A. B., 1841. Born 1821. Cotton Factor. New Orleans, La.
HAWKINS, JOHN D., Winona, Miss.: 1854–'57. C. S. A. Merchant. Dead.
HAWKINS, JOHN H., Warren Co.: 1801. Gen. Assem. Dead.
HAWKINS, JOHN HENRY, Warren Co.: A. B., 1817. Physician. Dead.
HAWKINS, JOSEPH WARREN, Warren Co.: A. B., 1805; A. M., 1808. Physician. State Comptroller 1825–'27. Dead.
HAWKINS, MADISON, Franklin Co.: A. B., 1850. Merchant. Henderson.
HAWKINS, MICAJAH T., Warren Co.: 1803. M. C., 1831–'41. Dead.
HAWKINS, PETER B., Warren Co., 1835–'36. Physician.
HAWKINS, PHILEMON, Warren Co.: A. B., 1809. Dead.
HAWKINS, PHILEMON BENJAMIN, Louisburg: A. B., 1844. Born 1823. Gen. N. C. S. G. Gen. Assem. Planter.
HAWKINS, WILLIAM JOSEPH, Franklin Co.: 1837–'39. Born 1819. Physician. Ex.-Pres. R. & G. R. R. Raleigh.
HAWKS, BENJAMIN, N. C.: 1822. Dead.
HAWKS, CICERO STEPHENS, New Berne: A. B., 1830; A. M., 1834; D. D. Univ. of Mo., 1847; LL. D. Bishop of Mo., 1844–'68. Died 1868.
HAWKS, FRANCIS HALLIDAY, Washington: A. B., 1840. Lawyer. Planter. Born 1819, died 1866. New Berne, Ala.
HAWKS, FRANCIS LISTER, New Berne: A. B., 1815; A. M., 1824; D. D. Columbia Coll., 1832; LL. D., 1847. Reporter Supreme Ct., 1820–'26. Episc. Minister. Prof. Divinity Trinity Coll., Conn. V.-Pres. Amer. Ethnological Soc., 1855–'59. Pres. Am. Geographical and Statistical Soc., 1855–'61. Author. Born 1798, died 1866. New York.
HAWKS, SAMUEL, N. C.: 1820. Dead.
HAY, DAVID, Fayetteville: 1804. Lawyer. Dead.
HAY, PHILIP THORNHILL, Rockingham Co.: A. B., 1858.
HAYES, GEORGE WASHINGTON, Murphy: 1882–'83. Lawyer. Columbia, Tenn.
HAYES, WILLIAM J., Pittsboro: 1805. Dead.
HAYES, WILLIAM JAMES, Lincoln: A. B., 1842. Physician. Charlotte.
HAYLEY, LEONIDAS NAPOLEON BONAPARTE, Franklin Co., Ala.: A. B., 1857. Physician. Barton, Ala.
HAYLEY, WILLIAM HOLLIDAY, Franklin Co., Ala.: A. B., 1857. Physician. Dead.

HAYNES, ROBERT WALTER, Knoxville, Tenn.: A. B., 1862. Gen. Assem. Jackson, Tenn.
HAYS, JAMES MACKINTOSH, Oxford: 1880–'81. Physician.
HAYS, JOHN WILLIS, Oxford: 1880–'81. U. S. Geol. Survey. Washington, D. C.
HAYS, MIDDLETON, Jackson, Tenn.: 1860–'61.
HAYS, ROBERT B., Jackson, Tenn.: 1859–'60. C. S. A.
HAYWOOD, ADAM, Tarboro: 1795. Dead.
HAYWOOD, ALFRED, Raleigh: 1821. Dead.
HAYWOOD, BENJAMIN FRANKLIN, Raleigh: A. B., 1822. Lawyer. Born 1802, died 1824.
HAYWOOD, ERNEST, Raleigh: A. B., 1880.
HAYWOOD, E. BURKE, Raleigh: 1843–'46. A. M., 1868. Physician.
HAYWOOD, FABIUS JULIUS, Raleigh: A. B., 1822. Physician. Dead.
HAYWOOD, FABIUS JULIUS, Raleigh: A. B., 1861. Adj. C. S. A. Physician.
HAYWOOD, FRANCIS PHILEMON, Raleigh: 1825. Born 1810. C. S. A. Dead. Smithville.
HAYWOOD, GEORGE WASHINGTON, Raleigh: A. B., 1821. Physician. Dead.
HAYWOOD, HOWARD, Raleigh: 1877–'79.
HAYWOOD, JOHN A., Franklin Co.: 1802. Dead.
HAYWOOD, JOHN LEE, Raleigh: 1821. Physician. Born 1804, died 1837. Smithfield.
HAYWOOD, JOHN STEELE, Raleigh: A. B., 1820. Dead.
HAYWOOD, JOSEPH ALLEN, Raleigh: A. B., 1862. Born 1842. Lt. C. S. A. Planter.
HAYWOOD, RICHARD BENNEHAN, Raleigh: A. B., 1841. Physician. Surg. C. S. A. Pres. N. C. Med. Soc. Born 1819, died 1888.
HAYWOOD, RUFUS, Raleigh: 1821.
HAYWOOD, THOMAS, Raleigh: 1821.
HAYWOOD, THOMAS BURGESS, Raleigh: A. B., 1823. Dead.
HAYWOOD, THOMAS J., Nashville, Tenn.: 1812. Judge Supreme Ct., Tenn. Author. Dead.
HAYWOOD, WILLIAM DALLAS, Raleigh: 1825. Born 1810. Dead.
HAYWOOD, WILLIAM HENRY, Raleigh: A. B., 1819. Lawyer. Gen. Assem. Speaker H. of Com. U. S. Senator. Dead.
HAYWOOD, WILLIAM RUFUS, Raleigh: A. B., 1821. Physician. Dead.
HAZELL, WILLIAM LEE, McCrary, Alamance Co.: 1883–'84.
HEADEN, ISAAC BROOKS, Chatham Co.: 1835–'36. M. D., Univ. of Pa. Died 1852.
HEADEN, JAMES HUNTER, Chatham Co.: A. B., 1839; A. M., 1847.
HEADEN, SAMUEL, Liberty, Va.: A. B., 1821. Dead.
HEADEN, WILLIAM, Chatham Co.: 1821.
HEADEN, WILLIAM EDWARDS, Pittsboro: A. B., 1888. Born 1867.
HEADEN, WILLIAM JOSEPH, Chatham Co.: A. B., 1860. Teacher. Gen. Assem. Lt. C. S. A. Died 1865.

HEARN, LAWRENCE HENRY, Tarboro: 1826. Planter. Born 1810, died 1854. Fla.
HEARTT, LEOPOLD, Hillsboro: 1831-'32. Merchant.
HEARTWELL, CHARLES PAUL, Lawrenceville, Va.: A. B., 1842. Born 1821. Physician. Planter. Albany, Ga.
HEARTWELL, HARRISON J., Lawrenceville, Va.: 1838-'39. Planter. Cherry Hill, Dinwiddie Co., Va.
HECK, GEORGE CALLENDINE, Raleigh: 1886-'87. Lawyer.
HEDRICK, BENJAMIN SHERWOOD, Davidson Co.: A. B., 1851. Prof. U. N. C. Asst. Comr. of Patents. Died Sept. 2, 1886. Washington, D. C.
HEDRICK, JAMES DAWSON, Wilmington: 1884-'86.
HEILIG, JAMES DANIEL, Salisbury: 1876-'77.
HEILIG, LAWSON EDWIN, Mt. Pleasant: 1887-'88. A. B., N. C. Coll., 1887. Lawyer.
HEITMAN, NUMA FLETCHER, Lexington: A. B., 1883. Lawyer. Kansas City, Mo.
HEMKEN, BENARD B., Monroe, La.: B. S., 1858. Lawyer. Capt. C. S. A. Born 1838. Killed at Malvern Hill, 1862.
HENDERSON, ALEXANDER M., Chapel Hill: 1824. Dead.
HENDERSON, ARCHIBALD E., Granville Co.: 1820. Dead.
HENDERSON, ARCHIBALD E., Williamsboro, Granville Co.: 1859-'61.
HENDERSON, BENNETT H., Tenn.: 1821.
HENDERSON, DAVID W., Milton, Caswell Co. 1831-'35. Dead.
HENDERSON, GEORGE W., Mobile, Ala.: 1839-'42. Dead.
HENDERSON, JAMES, Kentucky: A. B., 1806. Physician. Dead.
HENDERSON, JAMES A., Chapel Hill: 1803. Physician. Dead.
HENDERSON, JOHN LAWSON, Salisbury: A. B., 1800. Dead.
HENDERSON, JOHN STEELE, Salisbury: 1862-64. Born 1846. C. S. A. Lawyer. Gen. Assem. Member Commission to Codify Laws of N. C. M. C. 1885-.
HENDERSON, LAWSON FRANK, Lincoln Co.: A. B., 1827. Physician. Dead.
HENDERSON, LEONARD, Granville Co.: 1840-'42.
HENDERSON, LEONARD A., Salisbury: 1824. Dead.
HENDERSON, LEONARD A., Granville Co.: 1859-'60. Born 1823. Capt. C. S. A. Killed in battle.
HENDERSON, MARK M., Oxford: A. B., 1816. Dead.
HENDERSON, MAURICE, Chapel Hill: 1812. Dead.
HENDERSON, PHILO P., Mecklenburg Co.: A. B., 1843. Dead.
HENDERSON, PLEASANT, Chapel Hill: 1801. Dead.
HENDERSON, PLEASANT, Chapel Hill: A. B., 1821. Physician. Dead.
HENDERSON, RICHARD, Ky.: A. B., 1804. Tutor U. N. C. Dead.
HENDERSON, RICHARD B., Granville Co.: 1850-'53. C. S. A.
HENDERSON, RICHARD BULLOCK, Warrenton: A. B., 1879. Physician. Manson, Warren Co.
HENDERSON, SAMUEL, Mecklenburg Co.: 1801. Physician. Dead.
HENDERSON, TIPPOO SAIB, Chapel Hill: A. B., 1814. Physician. Dead.
HENDERSON, WILLIAM, Chapel Hill: A. B., 1808. Tutor U. N. C. Physician. Dead.

HENDERSON, WILLIAM, Tenn.: 1833–'34. Dead.
HENDERSON, WILLIAM HENRY, Carroll Co., Tenn.: A. B., 1840. Dead.
HENDON, JOHN A., New Berne, Ala.: 1855–'56. Planter. Born 1835, died 1874.
HENDREN, JOSEPH FLANNER, Winston: 1888–.
HENDRICKS, JOHN ADDISON, Jerusalem, Davie Co.: 1885–'88. Gen. Assem., 1889–.
HENLEY, JAMES ANDREW, Franklinton, Franklin Co.: 1879–'80. Raleigh.
HENRY, EDWARD W., Charlotte Co., Va.: 1858–'59.
HENRY, ROBERT WILLIAMS, Va.: A. B., 1835. Dead.
HENRY, WALTER RICHARD, Kittrell: 1877–'78. Lawyer. Henderson.
HENRY, WILLIAM SMITH, Asheville: 1881–'82.
HENRY, WILLIAM WILD, Enterprise, Miss.: A. B., 1860. Capt. C. S. A. Lawyer. Meridian, Miss.
HENSON, JOHN MCKAMIE, Burke Co.: 1847–'49. Physician. Surg. C. S. A. Aberdeen, Miss.
HERBERT, THOMAS S., Woodville, Miss.: 1859–'60.
HERIN, JOHN A., Branson, Miss.: 1856–'57. Dead.
HERRING, JAMES JOSHUA, Lenoir Co.: A. B., 1845. C. S. A.
HERRING, JOHN ROBERT, Scotland Neck, Halifax Co.: 1881–'83. Died 1883.
HERRING, JOSHUA JAMES, La Grange: 1885–'87.
HERRING, NEEDHAM WHITFIELD, Lenoir Co.: A. B., 1838. Physician.
HERSEY, AUSTIN A., A. B., 1820.
HESTER, BENNETT FRANKLIN, Oxford: 1876–'78. Died 1882.
HESTER, JOHN M., Montgomery, Tenn.: 1854–'55. Born 1836. Travelling Salesman. Mayfield, Ky.
HESTER, ST. CLAIR, Kittrell, Vance Co.: A. B., 1888. Teacher. Raleigh.
HICKS, EDWARD HUBBELL, Oxford: A. B., 1846; A. M., 1849.
HICKS, JAMES WOOD, Granville Co.: A. B., 1847. Born 1827; M. D., Univ. of Pa. Surg. C. S. A. Tuskerton, Fla.
HICKS, JOHN HENRY, Sampson Co.: 1856–'58. Physician. Surg. C. S. A. Born 1832, died 1883.
HICKS, JOHN MILLER, Faison, Duplin Co.: A. B., 1861. Died 1868.
HICKS, JOHN SCOTCH WHITE, Warren Co.: 1878–'80. Murfreesboro.
HICKS, LOUIS, Sampson Co.: 1796. Dead.
HIGGINS, CHARLES MCLEAN, Beaufort: 1882–'83.
HIGH, JOHN T., Wake Co.: 1810. Dead.
HIGHTOWER, SAMUEL A., Homer, La.: A. B., 1860. C. S. A.
HILL, ARTHUR JAY, Wilmington: A. B., 1818. Dead.
HILL, ASHLEY THOMAS, Kinston: 1881–'82. Lawyer.
HILL, ATHERTON BARNES, Halifax Co.: A. B., 1855. Capt. C. S. A. Planter.
HILL, ATHERTON BARNES, Scotland Neck, Halifax Co.: Ph. B., 1885. Teacher. Pittsboro.
HILL, CHARLES APPLEWHITE, Franklin Co.: A. B., 1816. Gen. Assem. Dead.
HILL, CHARLES URQUHART, Scotland Neck, Halifax Co.: B. S., 1883. Dead.

HILL, CHRISTOPHER DUDLEY, Faison, Duplin Co.: A. B., 1881. M. D. Univ. of Va., 1888.
HILL, EDWARD D., Duplin Co.: 1831-'32. Dead.
HILL, EDWARD J., Faison, Duplin Co.: A. B., 1878. Gen. Assem. U. S. Consul at Montevideo, 1887-.
HILL, FREDERICK C., Wilmington: 1827. Dead.
HILL, FREDERICK J., Wilmington: 1805. Physician. Dead.
HILL, FREDERICK JONES, Wilmington: A. B., 1852. Henderson.
HILL, HENRY, Sussex Co., Va.: 1799.
HILL, ISAAC, Warrenton: 1821. Physician. Dead.
HILL, ISHAM FAISON, Faison, Duplin Co.: 1876-'78. Merchant.
HILL, JAMES HICKS, Faison, Duplin Co.: 1877-'78. Orange-grower, Ocalla, Fla.
HILL, JAMES STADLER, Stokes Co.: A. B., 1858.
HILL, JAMES W., Columbia, Texas: 1859-'60.
HILL, JOHN, Wilmington: A. B., 1814. Physician. Dead.
HILL, JOHN, Stokes Co.: 1816.
HILL, JOHN, Wilmington: A. B., 1850. Physician. Dead.
HILL, JOHN H., Wilmington: 1822. Physician. Dead.
HILL, JOHN HAMPDEN, Brunswick Co.: A. B., 1854. Druggist. Goldsboro.
HILL, JOHN S., Warsaw, Duplin Co.: 1855-'56. Dead.
HILL, JOHN SPRUNT, Faison, Duplin Co.: Ph. B., 1889. Born 1869.
HILL, JOSEPH A., Abis Spring, Calhoun Co., Ga.: A. B., 1857.
HILL, RICHARD, Dinwiddie Co., Va.: 1800. Dead.
HILL, RICHARD BRADLEY, Wilmington: A. B., 1843.
HILL, RICHARD KING, Iredell Co.: A. B., 1830. Teacher. Dead. Texas.
HILL, ROBERT DUDLEY, Faison, Duplin Co.: 1887-'88.
HILL, THOMAS, Rockingham Co.: 1810. Dead.
HILL, THOMAS, Wilmington: A. B., 1822. Dead.
HILL, THOMAS, Brunswick Co.: 1849-'51. Born 1832. M. D. Univ. of N.Y. Surg. C. S. A. Goldsboro.
HILL, THOMAS BLOUNT, Halifax Co.: A. B., 1832. Hillsboro. Dead.
HILL, THOMAS NORFLEET, Scotland Neck, Halifax Co.: A. B., 1857. Lawyer. C. S. A.
HILL, THOMAS NORFLEET, Halifax: 1886-'87. Lawyer.
HILL, THOMAS S., Wilmington: 1854-'55.
HILL, THOMAS STAFFORD, Wilmington: A. B., 1859. C. S. A. Killed in battle.
HILL, WILLIAM, Wilmington: 1804. Dead.
HILL, WILLIAM, Wilmington: A. B., 1844; A. M., 1850. Dead.
HILL, WILLIAM EDWARD, Duplin Co.: A. B., 1849.
HILL, WILLIAM G., Raleigh: 1822. Physician. Born 1806, died March 4th, 1877.
HILL, WILLIAM G., Columbia, Texas: 1859-'60.
HILL, WILLIAM H., Wilmington: 1814. Dead.
HILL, WILLIAM H., Chester, S. C.: 1837-'38. Physician. Dead.
HILL, WILLIAM LANIER, Faison, Duplin Co.: A. B., 1879. Lawyer. Warsaw.
HILLIARD, DAVID, Nash Co.: A. B., 1856. Dead.

HILLIARD, E. E., Scotland Neck, Halifax Co.: 1887–'88. A. B., Wake Forest, 1882. Lawyer.
HILLIARD, ISAAC H., Halifax Co.: 1827. Dead.
HILLIARD, JOHN, Nash Co.: 1798. Dead.
HILLIARD, LOUIS, Nash Co.: A. B., 1858. Capt. C. S. A. Gen. Assem., 1866. Judge Superior Ct., 1875. Com. Merchant. Norfolk, Va.
HILLIARD, ROBERT C., Nash Co.: 1799. Gen. Assem. Dead.
HILLIARD, ROBERT C. T. SYDENHAM, Nash Co.: A. B., 1846. Dead.
HILTON, JOHN, Raleigh: 1878–'80.
HINES, BENJAMIN S., Raleigh: 1842–'43. Dead.
HINES, EDWARD S., Raleigh: A. B., 1863. Died 1876.
HINES, ELIAS CARR, Raleigh: A. B., 1847; A. M., 1850. Lawyer. C. S. A. Born 1827, died in service April 14, 1862.
HINES, FRANK GORDON, Edenton: Ph. B., 1881. Died 1882.
HINES, HARVEY L., Raleigh: 1854–'55. C. S. A. Dead.
HINES, JESSE D., Edgecombe Co.: 1840–'41. Physician. Dead.
HINES, JOEL, Pender Co.: 1878–'79 and 1884–'85. Lawyer.
HINES, JOHN SNEAD, Raleigh: A. B., 1856. Capt. C. S. A. Planter. St. Louis, Mo.
HINES, PETER EVANS, Raleigh: A. B., 1849; A. M., 1852. Physician. Pres. N. C. Med. Soc.
HINES, PETER EVANS, Raleigh: 1882–'83.
HINES, RICHARD, Raleigh: A. B., 1850; D. D. Tutor U. N. C., 1852–'54. Minister.
HINSDALE, JOHN W., Fayetteville: 1858–'61. Col. C. S. A. Lawyer. Raleigh.
HINTON, CHARLES LEWIS, Wake Co.: A. B., 1814. Gen. Assem. State Treas. Born 1793, died 1861.
HINTON, DAVID, Raleigh: A. B., 1847. Born 1826, died 1876.
HINTON, EUGENE JOSEPH, Bertie Co.: A. B., 1845.
HINTON, JOHN HARPER, Wake Co.: A. B., 1813. Tutor U. N. C., 1814. Dead.
HINTON, JOHN W., Wake Co.: 1824. Dead.
HINTON, NOAH B., Bertie Co.: 1804. Planter. Born 1787, died 1850.
HINTON, RANSOM, Wake Co.: 1804. Physician. Dead.
HINTON, ROBERT, Wake Co.: A. B., 1815. Physician. Dead.
HINTON, SAMUEL, Wake Co.: A. B., 1798. Dead.
HINTON, SAMUEL SMITH, Wake Co.: A. B., 1825. Dead.
HINTON, WILLIAM, Bertie Co.: 1806. Born 1792, died 1840.
HINTON, WILLIAM HENRY, Bertie Co.: A. B., 1844.
HOBSON, BENJAMIN MOSELY, Milton, Caswell Co.: A. B., 1838. Minister.
HOBSON, JAMES MARCELLUS, Davie Co.: A. B., 1861. Born 1840. Lt. C. S. A. Judge Hale Co. Ct., Ala. Mem. Gen. Assem. of Ala. Greensboro, Ala.
HODGE, HENRY W., Tarboro: A. B., 1825.
HODGE, JAMES A., Wake Co.: 1861–'65. Dead.
HODGE, RICHARD DEBNAM, Raleigh: 1881–'82.
HODGE, RUFUS A., Wake Co.: 1861–'65.

HODGE, WILLIAM HENRY, Tarboro: A. B., 1825. Dead.
HODGES, JAMES MARCUS, La Grange: 1880-81. Physician.
HODGES, JOSEPH J. DURHAM, Bossier Parish, La.: 1859-'61. C. S. A. Killed at 2d Manassas.
HODGES, PAUL ARENDELL, Kinston: 1887-'89.
HODGES, THOMAS P., Okolona, Miss.: 1859-'60. Capt. C. S. A. Killed at Jonesboro, Ga., July 28, 1864.
HOFMAN, GEORGE W., Duplin Co.: 1826.
HOGAN, ALEXANDER MARTIN, Chapel Hill: A. B., 1856. Dead.
HOGAN, ALEXANDER W., Randolph Co.: 1831-'32. Dead.
HOGAN, DAVID ROSWELL, Chapel Hill: 1886-.
HOGAN, HENRY JAMES, Chapel Hill: A. B., 1861. Teacher. Mifflin, Tenn.
HOGAN, JAMES, Randolph Co.: 1818. Dead.
HOGAN, JOHN ALLEN, Randolph Co.: A. B., 1822. Dead.
HOGAN, JOHN ROSWELL, Chapel Hill: A. B., 1855. Physician.
HOGAN, WILLIAM L., Randolph Co.: 1827.
HOGG, GAVIN, Raleigh: A. B., 1807. Tutor U. N. C., 1808. Lawyer. Dead.
HOGG, JAMES, Chapel Hill: 1795. Dead.
HOGG, JAMES, A. B., 1812. Physician. Dead.
HOGG, RICHARD, Raleigh: 1825. Dead.
HOGG, THOMAS, Chapel Hill: 1817. Dead.
HOKE, JOHN FRANKLIN, Lincoln Co.: A. B., 1841. Lawyer. Capt. U. S. A. Mexican War. Col. C. S. A. Born 1821, died 1888.
HOKE, VAN WYCK, Raleigh: 1887.
HOLBROOK, LEVI, A. B., 1814.
HOLCOMB, VIRGIL ERASTUS, Rockford, Yadkin Co.: 1887-'88. Lawyer.
HOLCOMBE, FLETCHER DEEMS, Chestnut Ridge, Yadkin Co.: 1883-'84.
HOLDEN, JOSEPH WILLIAM, Raleigh: 1862-'63. Gen. Assem. Speaker H. of Com. Dead.
HOLDEN, JULIUS THOMAS, Wilmington: 1851-'52. Born 1834. Physician. Marianna, Fla.
HOLLAND, GEORGE COURTS, Dallas, Gaston Co.: 1885-'87.
HOLLAND, RALPH HERSCHEL, Charlotte: 1889-.
HOLLAND, WILLIAM A., Kinston: 1857-'58. Maj. C. S. A.
HOLLAND, WILLIAMSON, 1839.
HOLLEMAN, JOEL, Isle of Wight Co., Va.: A. B., 1822. Gen. Assem. of Va. M. C. Dead.
HOLLEMAN, SILAS ALVIN, Chatham Co.: 1881-'83.
HOLLEY, GEORGE STANLY, Bertie Co.: A. B., 1837; A. M., 1844. Lawyer. Dead.
HOLLEY, JAMES, Bertie Co.: 1830-'32. Dead.
HOLLIDAY, RICHARD WILLIAM, Clinton: 1888-.
HOLLIDAY, THOMAS C., Aberdeen, Miss.: A. B., 1860. Asst. Adj. Gen. C. S. A. Killed in battle.
HOLLIDAY, TILMAN, New Berne: 1824. Dead.
HOLMES, GABRIEL, Brunswick Co.: 1849-'51. Capt. C. S. A. Dead.

HOLMES, HARDY, Clinton: A. B., 1824; A. M., 1832. Physician. Born 1804, died 1847.
HOLMES, HARDY LUCIAN, Sampson Co.: A. B., 1817. Lawyer. Born 1795, died 1869. Wilmington.
HOLMES, JAMES, Sampson Co.: 1842-'44. Lieut. U. S. A.
HOLMES, JOHN LYON, Wilmington: A. B., 1846. Lawyer. Born 1826, died Sept. 20, 1888.
HOLMES, JOHN SIMCOX, Bowman's Bluff: 1886-'88.
HOLMES, JOHN WRIGHT, Wilmington: A. B., 1853. Dead.
HOLMES, LUCIAN, Pittsboro: 1842-'46. Minister.
HOLMES, OWEN, Clinton: A. B., 1819. Lawyer. Born 1795, died 1840.
HOLMES, OWEN DAVIS, Wilmington: A. B., 1845. Dead.
HOLMES, PETER JAMES, Southampton Co., Va.: A. B., 1842.
HOLMES, SAMUEL ALLEN, A. B., 1799. Prof. U. N. C., 1811. Dead.
HOLMES, SAMUEL ASHE, Fayetteville: A. B., 1851. Judge Superior Ct. of Cal.
HOLMES, THEOPHILUS H., Fayetteville: 1861-'62. Lieut. C. S. A. Killed at Ashland, Va., 1864.
HOLMES, THOMAS HALL, Clinton: A. B., 1848. Lawyer. Maj. C. S. A. Born 1829, died 1866.
HOLMES, WILLIAM H., Sampson Co.: 1854-'55.
HOLSHAUSER, ALLAN RODOLPHUS, Rowan Co.: 1877-'79. Minister.
HOLT, ALFRED AUGUSTUS, Orange Co.: 1821. Lawyer. Born 1804, died 1825.
HOLT, ALFRED CHARLES BRIGGS, Augusta, Ga.: 1859-'61. Born 1843. C. S. A. Lawyer.
HOLT, ARCHIBALD M., Orange Co.: 1821. Physician. Dead.
HOLT, BENJAMIN RICE, Augusta, Ga.: A. B., 1861. Lt. C. S. A. Born 1841, died 1885.
HOLT, JAMES HENRY, Graham, Alamance Co.: 1883-'84.
HOLT, JAMES M., Lexington: 1858-'59. Dead.
HOLT, JAMES RILEY, Orange Co.: 1831-'32. Minister. Born 1814, died 1871. Graham.
HOLT, LEWIS BOWEN, Orange Co.: 1841-'43. Born 1821, died 1843.
HOLT, MICHAEL WILLIAM, Orange Co.: A. B., 1832; A. M., 1837. Physician. Born 1811, died 1858.
HOLT, PLEASANT ALLEN, Orange Co.: A. B., 1845. Born 1826. Physician. Surg. C. S. A. Jacksonville, Fla.
HOLT, ROBERT LACY, Graham, Alamance Co.: 1884-'86. Manufacturer. Burlington.
HOLT, ROBERT OSCAR, Guilford Co.: A. B., 1881. Prin. Oak Ridge Inst. Oak Ridge.
HOLT, SAMUEL LOCKHART, Orange Co.: A. B., 1825; A. M., 1829. Physician. Born 1805, died 1872.
HOLT, THOMAS M., Haw River: 1849-'50. Born 1831. Gen. Assem. Speaker H. of Com., 1885. Lt. Gov., 1889-. Planter. Manufacturer.
HOLT, WILLIAM EDWIN, Graham: 1856-'58. Born 1839. Cotton Manufacturer. Lexington.

HOLT, WILLIAM IRWIN, Graham: 1887–'88.
HOLT, WILLIAM M., Lexington: 1855–'57. Lt. C. S. A. Killed in service.
HOLT, WILLIAM RAINEY, Orange Co.: A. B., 1817. Physician. Planter and Stock Raiser. Born 1798, died 1868. Lexington.
HOLTON, ARCHER BOWMAN, Bush Hill, Randolph Co.: 1869–'70.
HOOKER, ERASMUS A. ROSCOE, Hillsboro: A. B., 1848. Physician. Dead. Aurora.
HOOKER, JOSEPH JOHN, Chatham Co.: 1884–'85. Lawyer. Webster.
HOOKER, OCTAVIUS WRIGHT, Hillsboro: A. B., 1845; A. M., 1849. Physician.
HOOKER, WILLIAM DE WITT, Gulf, Chatham Co.: 1878–'79.
HOOPER, EDWARD JONES, Chapel Hill: 1833–'35. Dead.
HOOPER, JAMES HOGG, Chapel Hill: A. B., 1815. Merchant. Born 1797, died 1841. Fayetteville.
HOOPER, JOHN DEBERNIERE, Wilmington: A. B., 1831; A. M., 1834. Prof. Latin and French U. N. C., 1838–'48; Greek and French, 1875–'85. Born 1811, died Jan. 27, 1886.
HOOPER, JOSEPH CALDWELL, Chapel Hill: 1837–'38. Born 1821. Fayetteville.
HOOPER, THOMAS CLARK, Chapel Hill: A. B., 1812. Lawyer. Born 1794, died 1828.
HOOPER, WILLIAM, Chapel Hill: A. B., 1809; A. M., 1812; D. D.; LL. D., 1833. Prof. Ancient Langs. U. N. C., 1817–'22 and 1828–'37; Rhet. and Logic, 1825–'28. Prof. S. C. Coll., Columbia. Pres. Wake Forest Coll. Born 1782, died 1876.
HOOPER, WILLIAM WILBERFORCE, Chapel Hill: A. B., 1836; A. M. 1841. Physician. Dead.
HOPKINS, ARTHUR F., Ala., 1811: Judge Supreme Ct., Ala. Dead.
HOPKINS, SAMUEL G., Ky.: 1800. Dead.
HORD, BENJAMIN McC., Murfreesboro, Tenn.: 1860–'62. C. S. A. Journalist. Comm'r Agriculture. Nashville, Tenn.
HORD, GEORGE JACOB V. B., Shelby: 1884–'87.
HORN, WHITMEL D., Edgecombe Co.: 1810. Dead.
HORNE, HENRY W., Fayetteville: 1854–'55.
HORNE, JAMES W., Pittsboro: 1853–'54. Sergt. C. S. A. Killed in service.
HORNER, JAMES H., Orange Co.: A. B., 1844; A. M. Teacher. Founder and Principal Horner School. Oxford.
HORNER, WILLIAM DE WITT, Henderson: A. B., 1868.
HORNEY, WILLIAM ADAMS, Greensboro: A. B., 1861. Died 1887.
HOSKINS, JAMES W., Edenton: 1838–'39.
HOSKINS, THOMAS E., Farmville, Va.: 1816. Dead.
HOSKINS, THOMAS JONES, Durant's Neck, Perquimans Co.: 1883–'84. Edenton.
HOSKINS, THOMAS SKINNER, Edenton: A. B., 1826; A. M., 1832. Gen. Assem. Dead.
HOUSTON, ARCHIBALD C., Cabarrus Co.: 1825–'28. Dead.
HOUSTON, ROBERT BRUCE B., Catawba Co.: A. B., 1860. Lt. C. S. A.
HOUSTON, WILLIAM, Iredell Co.: A. B., 1798. Physician. Dead.

HOWARD, A. BRANSON, Iredell Co.: 1861–'63.
HOWARD, GEORGE, Tarboro, 1849–'50: Born 1829. Lawyer. Gen. Assem. Judge Superior Ct. Mem. Conven., 1861 and 1865.
HOWARD, GEORGE, Tarboro Ph. B., 1885. Lawyer.
HOWARD, LEWIS WHITFIELD, New Hanover Co.: A. B., 1857. Civ. Eng. C. S. A. Dead. Topsail.
HOWELL, GEORGE PIERCE, Goldsboro: 1886–'89. Born 1870. West Point, N. Y.
HOWELL, JOSEPH JAY, Chapel Hill: 1869–'70.
HOWELL, LOGAN DOUGLASS, Goldsboro: A. B., 1889. Born 1868.
HOWELL, ROBERT PHILIP, Goldsboro: 1856–'59. Born 1840. Capt. Q. M. C. S. A. Planter. Cashier Bank of New Hanover.
HOWELL, WILLIAM AUGUSTUS, Chapel Hill: 1869–'70.
HOWERTON, JOHN T., Nashville, Tenn.: 1855–'56. Dead.
HOWERTON, WILLIAM MATTHEW, Va.: A. B., 1847; A. M. Lawyer. Dead.
HOWZE, BENJAMIN ISAAC, Haywood, Chatham Co.: A. B., 1836. Lawyer.
HUBBARD, ALBERT GALLATIN, Leasburg: A. B., 1838; A. M., 1842. Died 1882.
HUBBELL, RANSOM, A. B., 1820.
HUCKABEE, CASWELL C., Ala.: 1839–'40. Brierfield, Ala.
HUCKABEE, JOHNSTON J., Ala.: 1839–'40. Planter. Dead.
HUFF, WILLIAM, Lawrenceville, Va.: 1862–'65. Physician. Dogwood, Brunswick Co., Va.
HUGGINS, COOPER, Jacksonville, Onslow Co.: A. B., 1859. C. S. A.
HUGGINS, WILLIAM SLOAN, Wilmington: 1888–.
HUGHES, BRICE M., Patrick C. H., Va.: 1825. Dead.
HUGHES, ISAAC WAYNE, Chocowinity, Beaufort Co.: 1884–'86.
HUGHES, JAMES BETTNER, New Berne: A. B., 1853. Physician. Surg. C. S. A.
HUGHES, LEANDER, Patrick C. H., Va.: 1824. Dead.
HUGHES, NICHOLAS COLLIN, New Berne: A. B., 1859. Lawyer. Capt. C. S. A. Born 1840. Killed at Gettysburg, 1863.
HUGHES, ROBERT HARVEY, Cedar Grove, Orange Co.: 1875–'77.
HUME, WILLIAM LOWNDES, Brevard, Transylvania Co.: 1880–'83.
HUMPHREY, PAUL CLINGMAN, Goldsboro: 1882–'83. Sect'y Wayne Agricultural Works.
HUMPHRIES, WILLIAM WASHINGTON, Columbus, Miss.: A. B., 1858; LL. B. Born 1840. Capt. C. S. A. Gen. Assem. of Miss.
HUNT, EUSTACE, Pittsylvania Co., Va.: A. B., 1857. Dead.
HUNT, GEORGE BLACKBURN, Bolivar Co., Miss.: A. B., 1861. Maj. C. S. A. Planter. Born 1839, died 1873.
HUNT, J. THOMAS, Lexington: 1852–'54. Physician. Dead.
HUNT, JAMES, Va.: 1814. Dead.
HUNT, JAMES DAVIS, Izard Co., Ark.: A. B., 1858. Lawyer. Capt. C. S. A. Born 1838. Killed at Corinth, Miss., October 4, 1862.
HUNT, JAMES GRAHAM, Oxford: 1878–'79.

HUNT, JAMES MADISON BULLOCK, Townesville, Granville Co.: A. B., 1861. Capt. C. S. A.
HUNT, NATHANIEL, Franklin Co.: 1799. Dead.
HUNT, THOMAS D., Granville Co.: A. B., 1800. Physician. Dead.
HUNT, WILLIAM C., Eutaw, Ala.: 1842-'43.
HUNT, WILLIAM ELZA, Washington Co., Miss.: A. B., 1861. Born 1840. C. S. A. Greenville, Miss.
HUNTER, BENJAMIN B., Tarboro: 1805. Physician. Dead.
HUNTER, CHARLES H., Martin Co.: 1821. Dead.
HUNTER, CLIFTON WHEAT, Enfield, Halifax Co.: 1875-'77.
HUNTER, HENRY, N. C.: 1796. Dead.
HUNTER, HERMAN W., Charlotte: 1847-'48.
HUNTER, JAMES, Halifax Co.: 1822. Physician. Dead.
HUNTER, JAMES, Guilford Co.: 1826.
HUNTER, JAMES A., Rockingham Co.: 1826.
HUNTER, JAMES McG., Raleigh: 1837-'39.
HUNTER, PATRICK, Va.: 1814. Dead.
HUNTER, PERCY ISAAC, Gates Co.: 1879-'82.
HUNTER, RICHARD BENJAMIN, Brinkleyville, Halifax Co.: 1888-.
HUNTER, WILLIAM H., Raleigh: 1817. Physician.
HUSKE, BENJAMIN ROBINSON, Fayetteville: A. B., 1850. Maj. C. S. A. Wounded at Seven Pines, June 25, and died July 15, 1862.
HUSKE, JOHN WINSLOW, Fayetteville: A. B., 1827. Lawyer. Born 1809, died 1841.
HUSKE, JOSEPH CALDWELL, Fayetteville: A. B., 1843; A. M.; D. D. Born 1822.
HUSKE, KIRKLAND, Fayetteville: 1882-'84.
HUSKE, WALTER ALVES, Fayetteville: A. B., 1839; A. M., 1843. Lawyer. Born 1818, died 1868.
HUSSEY, JOHN B., Kenansville, Duplin Co.: 1862-'63. C. S. A. Journalist. Lawyer.
HUSTED, DELANO WHITING, Raleigh: A. B., 1854. Lawyer. Lt. C. S. A. Killed at Gaines' Mill, June 27, 1862.
HUTCHINS, JAMES HILL, New Berne: A. B., 1835. Born 1815. Lawyer. Land Agent. Austin, Tex.
HUTCHINS, JOHN FABIUS, Raleigh: A. B., 1852. Dead.
HUTCHINS, JOHN RHODES, Chapel Hill: A. B., 1852. Born 1830. Planter.
HUTCHINS, TYRELL WADE, Chapel Hill: 1886-'88.
HYMAN, HERBERT SHIELDS, Scotland Neck: 1877-'78.
HYMAN, JOHN D., Edgecombe Co.: 1848-'49. Lawyer. Dead.
HYMAN, JOSEPH HENRY, Tarboro: A. B., 1855. Col. C. S. A.
HYNSON, ROBERT CRUIKSHANK, Alexandria, La.: 1858-'60. C. S. A. Druggist. Planter. Born 1838, died 1867.
INGE, HALEY L., La.: 1804. Dead.
INGE, JOHN J., Granville Co.: 1813. Dead.
INGE, WILLIAM M., Tenn.: 1819. Judge Superior Ct. Tenn.
IREDELL, JAMES JOHNSTON, Raleigh: A. B., 1848. Maj. C. S. A. Killed at Spottsylvania C. H., May, 1864.

IREDELL, SAMUEL TREADWELL, Raleigh: A. B., 1849. Physician. Dead.
IRION, ALFRED BRIGGS, Cheneyville, La.: A. B., 1855. Judge Ct. of Appeals. Marksville, La.
IRVINE, JESSE, Milton, Caswell Co.: 1841–'43. Dead.
IRWIN, HENRY, Jackson Co., Fla.: 1852–'53.
IRWIN, JAMES P., Charlotte: A. B., 1843.
ISAAC, DAN HUTCHINS, Orange Co.: 1869–'70.
ISLER, JESSE, Lenoir Co.: 1813. Physician. Dead.
ISLER, SIMMONS HARRISON, Goldsboro: A. B., 1859. Presb. Minister.
ISLER, STEPHEN WILLIAM, Kinston: A. B., 1858. Lawyer. Goldsboro.
IVEY, VIRGINIUS HENRY, Norfolk, Va.: A. B., 1845. Lawyer. Dead.
JACK, JOHN FINDLEY, Rutledge, Tenn.: A. B., 1842. Dead.
JACKSON, HERBERT WORTH, Ashboro: Ph. B., 1886. Sec. and Treas. Wetmore Shoe Co. Raleigh.
JACKSON, JONATHAN WORTH, Pittsboro: A. B., 1882. Ins. Agt. Nashville, Tenn.
JACKSON, JOSEPH JOHN, Chatham Co.: A. B., 1838; A. M., 1843. Pittsboro.
JACKSON, MAX, Fayetteville: Ph. B., 1885. Physician.
JACKSON, SAMUEL SPENCER, Chatham Co.: 1806. Dead.
JACKSON, SAMUEL SPENCER, Pittsboro: A. B., 1854; A. M. Tutor U. N. C., 1867–'69. Died 1875.
JACKSON, SAMUEL SPENCER, Pittsboro: A. B., 1886. Teacher.
JACKSON, WILLIAM M., Ala.: 1842–'43.
JACOBS, JAMES WILLIAM, Northampton Co., Va.: A. B., 1854. Lt. C. S. A. Planter. Born 1834, died 1873. Madison, Tenn.
JACOBS, JOHN CALVIN, Northampton Co., Va.: A. B., 1857 M. D. Univ. of Pa. Born 1836, died 1886.
JACOCKS, JESSE COPELAND, Perquimans Co.: 1851–'52. Capt. C. S. A. Com. Merchant. Born 1834. Dead. Hertford.
JACOCKS, THOMAS STEPHENSON, Durant's Neck, Perquimans Co.: A. B., 1836. Planter. Born 1818, died 1852.
JAMES, FERNANDO GODFREY, Greenville: 1875–'76. Lawyer.
JAMES, HINTON, Wilmington: A. B., 1798. Civ. Eng. Gen. Assem. First student entering U. N. C., 1795. Dead.
JAMES, JOHN, N. C.: 1806. Dead.
JAMES, JOHN, Greenville: 1882–'83. Lassiter's Mills.
JAMES, ROBERT ERVIN, Darlington, S. C.: A. B., 1855. Sergt. C. S. A. Died in service, May 10, 1862.
JARRATT, ISAAC AUGUSTUS, Yadkin Co.: A. B., 1861.
JARRATT, THOMAS W., Montgomery, Ala.: 1856–'59.
JASPER, JOHN B., New Berne: 1803. Dead.
JEFFERSON, JOHN WESLEY, Memphis, Tenn.: 1866–'68. Born 1849. Lawyer. San Francisco, Cal.
JEFFREYS, EDWARD L., Wake Co.: 1860–'61.
JEFFREYS, GEORGE W., Person Co.: 1813. Minister. Dead.
JEFFREYS, JACOB H., Wake Co.: 1831–'32. Dead.

JEFFREYS, J. GLENN, Caswell Co.: 1850–'52. Lt. C. S. A. Killed in service.
JEFFREYS, JAMES W., Caswell Co.: 1817. Dead.
JEFFREYS, JOHN OSBORNE, Franklinton, Franklin Co.: 1878–'82.
JEFFREYS, ZADOK MARQUIS LA FAYETTE, Fremont, Wayne Co.: 1877–'79. Com. Merchant. Goldsboro.
JENKINS, FREDERICK H., Tarboro: 1854–'55. Planter. Capt. C. S. A. Died in service, June 3, 1862.
JENKINS, JAMES DEMPSEY, Tarboro: A. B., 1862. Born 1840. Planter. Rocky Mt.
JENKINS, JAMES PERRY, Northampton Co.: A. B., 1861. Capt. C. S. A. Born 1840, died in service at Strasburg, Va., Nov. 19, 1862.
JENKINS, JAMES S., Robeson Co.: 1837–'38. Dead.
JENKINS, JOHN M., Tarboro: 1854–'57. Planter. Hamilton, Martin Co.
JENKINS, JOSEPH JOHN, Riggsbee's Store, Chatham Co.: A. B., 1886. Tally Ho, Granville Co.
JENKINS, JOSEPH VAN BUREN, Edgecombe Co.: A. B., 1861. C. S. A. Born 1840, died at Yorktown, Va., Oct. 7, 1861.
JENKINS, WILLIAM ALEXANDER, Warrenton: A. B., 1848; A. M., 1851. Gen. Assem. Atty. Gen. N. C., 1856–'62. Lt. Col. C. S. A. Born 1829, died 1869.
JENKINS, WILLIAM ALEXANDER, Warrenton: 1881–'82. Merchant. Born 1863, died 1888.
JENNINGS, JOSEPH, Elizabeth City: 1882–'83.
JENNINGS, PETER HUNTER, Richmond Co.: 1836–'37. Born 1820, died 1846.
JERKINS, ALONZO THOMAS, New Berne: 1823–'24. Born 1807. Merchant. Gen. Assem. Banker. Dead.
JERNIGAN, JOHN H., Hertford Co.: 1856–'58. Dead.
JETTON, ANDERSON C., Murfreesboro, Tenn.: 1856–'58. C. S. A. Died 1864.
JIGGITTS, DAVID EDWARD, Livingston, Miss.: 1858–'60. Planter. Vernon, Miss.
JIGGITTS, LOUIS MEREDITH, Livingston, Miss.: A. B., 1857. Surg. C. S. A. Dead.
JIMESON, JAMES ELLIOTT, Estatoe: 1886–.
JOBE, LORENZO A. T., Greensboro: A. B., 1868. Minister. Garden City, Kan.
JOHN, HENRY MOOD, Laurinburg: 1877–'78.
JOHN, MAXCY LUTHER, Laurinburg: Ph. B., 1888. Teacher.
JOHN, RODERICK BELTON, Laurinburg: A. B., 1880. Meth. Minister.
JOHNS, THOMAS J., Wake Co.: 1859–'61.
JOHNSON, A. FERDINAND, Clinton: 1862–'63. Born 1850. C. S. A. Merchant.
JOHNSON, ALVIN ROSS, Marion, McDowell Co.: 1882–'84.
JOHNSON, BENJAMIN S., Ark.: 1861–'62.
JOHNSON, CHARLES J., Bayou Sara, La.: 1858–'59.
JOHNSON, CHARLES W., Warren Co.: 1815. Dead.
JOHNSON, CLAUD RAYMOND, Livingston, Bertie Co.: 1885–'86.

JOHNSON, DANIEL WHITE, Richmond Co.: A. B., 1856. Capt. C. S. A. Born 1833. Killed at Richmond, June 27, 1862.
JOHNSON, FRANCIS MARION, Farmington, Davie Co.: A. B., 1858. Born 1837. Merchant. Farmer. Gen. Assem.
JOHNSON, HERBERT P., Lexington, Miss.: 1866–'67.
JOHNSON, ISAAC J., Miss.: 1812. Dead.
JOHNSON, JACOB COART, Johnson's Mills, Pitt Co.: Ph. B., 1887. Teacher.
JOHNSON, JAMES P., Uharton, Tex.: 1858–'59. Galveston.
JOHNSON, JOHN MONROE, Richmond Co.: 1860–'62. Born 1840. Lawyer. Civ. Eng. Teacher. Gen. Assem., S. C. Marion, S. C.
JOHNSON, JOSEPH, Louisburg: 1853–'54. Dead.
JOHNSON, LUCIUS JUNIUS, Chowan Co.: A. B., 1840. Maj. C. S. A. Died in service, April, 1865.
JOHNSON, ROBERT ARCHIBALD, Rockingham, Richmond Co.: 1867–'68. Born 1845. Civ. Eng. Lawyer.
JOHNSON, ROBERT E., Warrenton: 1825. U. S. N. Dead.
JOHNSON, THOMAS D., Clarksville, Tenn.: 1858–'59. Born 1842. Physician. C. S. A. Staff Surg. Egyptian Army, 1875–'77.
JOHNSTON, DAVID SAUNDERS, Yanceyville, Caswell Co.: A. B., 1846; A. M., 1850. Dead.
JOHNSTON, GABRIEL, Edenton: 1859–'61. C. S. A. Minister.
JOHNSTON, GEORGE BURGWYN, Edenton: A. B., 1859. Tutor U. N. C. Capt. C. S. A. Died in service, 1862.
JOHNSTON, FRANK S., Pine Bluff, Ark.: 1864–'65.
JOHNSTON, HENRY, Tarboro: 1885–'88.
JOHNSTON, JAMES ALPHONZO, Lincoln Co.: A. B., 1829. Born 1809. Merchant. Planter. Davidson College.
JOHNSTON, JAMES C., Edenton: 1851–'52.
JOHNSTON, JAMES F., Lincoln Co.: 1846–'47. Capt. C. S. A. Charlotte.
JOHNSTON, JAMES MADISON, Chowan Co.: A. B., 1849. Physician. Dead.
JOHNSTON, JAMES STERLING, Halifax Co.; A. B., 1844; A. M., 1847. Dead.
JOHNSTON, JOHN, Edenton: 1862–'63.
JOHNSTON, JOHN MCADIN, Yanceyville: A. B., 1849. Physician.
JOHNSTON, JOHN WILLIS, Halifax Co.: A. B., 1853. Gen. Assem. Weldon.
JOHNSTON, JULIUS, Ruffin, Rockingham Co.: 1875–'77.
JOHNSTON, RICHARD, N. C.: 1802. Dead.
JOHNSTON, RICHARD HALL, Tarboro: 1888–.
JOHNSTON, ROBERT BRUCE, Waynesville: A. B., 1854. Capt. C. S. A. Asheville.
JOHNSTON, ROBERT DANIEL, Lincoln Co.: A. B., 1858. Brig. Gen. C. S. A. Lawyer. Banker. Birmingham, Ala.
JOHNSTON, ROBERT PULLIAM, Asheville: 1888–'89. West Point, N. Y.
JOHNSTON, SAMUEL IREDELL, Hertford Co.: A. B., 1826; A. M., 1844. Minister. Dead.
JOHNSTON, SIDNEY XENOPHON, Lincoln Co.: A. B., 1829. M. D. Univ. of Pa. Born 1811. Mem. Conven., 1861. Gastonia.
JOHNSTON, STUART LAWSON, Plymouth: A. B., 1859. Capt. C. S. A. Lawyer. Washington, D. C.

JOHNSTON, THOMAS DILLARD, Asheville: 1858–'59. Born 1840. C. S. A. Lawyer. Mayor. Gen. Assem. Pres. Elector, 1872. M. C., 1885–'89.
JOHNSTON, THOMAS LYNN, Lincoln Co.: A. B., 1843. Physician. Dead.
JOHNSTON, THOMAS PINKNEY, Iredell Co.: A. B., 1828. Born 1808. Minister. Missionary, 1833–'54.
JOHNSTON, THOMAS WILLIAM, Orange Co.: A. B., 1857. M. D. Univ. of Pa. Born 1836, died 1860. New Berne, Ala.
JOHNSTON, THOMPSON NOAH, Bertie Co.: A. B., 1821.
JOHNSTON, WILLIAM, Franklin Co.: A. B., 1812. Dead.
JOHNSTON, WILLIAM, Lincoln Co.: A. B., 1840. Lawyer. Mayor Charlotte. Pres. C. C. & A. R. R. Charlotte.
JOHNSTON, WILLIAM ALEXANDER, Mebanesville, Orange Co.: 1877–'78.
JOHNSTON, WILLIAM HENRY, Tarboro: A. B., 1850; A. M. Born 1830. Tutor U. N. C. Lawyer.
JOHNSTON, WILLIAM HENRY, Lincoln Co.: 1858–'59. Lt. Col. C. S. A. Physician. Birmingham, Ala.
JOHNSTON, WILLIAM L., Halifax Co.: 1841–'43. Physician. Dead.
JOHNSTON, WILLIAM W., Bertie Co.: 1818.
JOHNSTON, ZEBULON MORRIS, Cabarrus Co.: A. B., 1858.
JOHNSTON, ZENAS, Rowan Co.: 1822. Born 1805, died 1824.
JOLLEE, WILLIAM B., Chapel Hill: 1857–'59. Dead.
JONES, ADDISON W., Gainesville, Ala.: 1847–'48.
JONES, ALFRED DANIEL, Cary, Wake Co.: 1876–'78. Born 1857. Lawyer. Raleigh.
JONES, ALLEN CADWALLADER, Hillsboro: A. B., 1831. Born 1811. Gen. Assem. Ala. Col. C. S. A. Planter. Dead. Eutaw, Ala.
JONES, ALPHEUS, Wake Co.: A. B., 1839; A. M., 1843. Dead.
JONES, ALSTON A., Wake Co.: 1837–'39. Dead.
JONES, ATLAS, Moore Co.: A. B., 1804; A. M., 1811. Tutor U. N. C. Gen. Assem. Planter. Dead.
JONES, AURELIUS C., Matagorda, Tex.: 1858–'61. C. S. A. Killed in service.
JONES, BARKSDALE T., Person Co.: 1837–'38. Died 1881.
JONES, CADWALLADER, Halifax Co.: 1803. Dead.
JONES, CADWALLADER, Hillsboro: A. B., 1832. Born 1813. Gen. Assem. Solicitor 5th N. C. Dist. Col. C. S. A. Rock Hill, S. C.
JONES, CALVIN, Somerville, Tenn.: A. B., 1831; A. M., 1852. Prof. Univ. of Ala., 1831–'33. Lawyer. Gen. Assem. Tenn. Chancellor West Tenn., 1847–'54. Born 1810, died March 8, 1888.
JONES, CALVIN, Princeton, Ark.: A. B., 1856. Dead.
JONES, CLARENCE DUPREE, Hillsboro: 1884–'85. Physician.
JONES, DUPONCEAU D., Chatham Co.: 1825. Dead.
JONES, EDMUND, Caldwell Co.: 1865–'68. Born 1848. C. S. A. Gen. Assem. Lenoir.
JONES, EDMUND L., Rowan Co.: 1857–'59. Died Jan., 1859.
JONES, EDMUND WALTER, Wilkes Co.: A. B., 1833. Dead.
JONES, EDWARD D., S. C.: 1807. Dead.
JONES, EUGENE THOMAS, Louisburg: 1865–'67. Raleigh.

Jones, Evan, Wilmington: 1795. Dead.
Jones, Frederick, Wilmington: 1806. Dead.
Jones, George A., Wilcox Co., Ala.: 1865–'66. Mobile.
Jones, George Dew, Matagorda, Texas: A. B., 1859. C. S. A. Planter. Died 1866.
Jones, George Washington, Granville Co.: 1832–'36.
Jones, Gustavus Adolphus, Wake Co.: A. B., 1844.
Jones, H. Francis, Thomasville, Ga.: A. B., 1860. Lt. C. S. A. Killed in service.
Jones, Halcot P., Halifax Co.: 1803. Gen. Assem. Dead.
Jones, Hamilton Chamberlain, Salisbury: A. B., 1818; A. M., 1821. Tutor U. N. C. Lawyer. Dead.
Jones, Hamilton Chamberlain, Rowan Co.: A. B., 1858. U. S. Atty.
Jones, Harwood, Northampton Co.: 1807. Dead.
Jones, Henry, Warren Co.: A. B., 1818. Dead.
Jones, Isaac, Granville Co.: 1816. Physician. Dead.
Jones, J. Cross, Livingston, Ala.: 1844–'45.
Jones, James, N. C.: 1816. Dead.
Jones, James C., Madison Parish, La.: 1860–'61.
Jones, John, Hertford Co.: 1814. Dead.
Jones, John, Salisbury: 1825. Dead.
Jones, John D., Wilmington: 1804. Gen. Assem. Speaker H. of Com. Born 1790, died 1854.
Jones, John H., Raleigh: 1825. Dead.
Jones, John T., Wilkes Co.: 1832–'36. Dead.
Jones, John Thomas, Caldwell Co.: A. B., 1861. Lt. C. S. A. Born 1841. Killed at Wilderness, 1864.
Jones, John Wesley, Edgecombe Co.: 1853–'54. M. D. Paris. Born 1831. Surg. C. S. A. Pres. N. C. Med. Soc. and N. C. Board of Health. Tarboro.
Jones, John Willie, Wake Co.: 1859–'61. C. S. A. Planter.
Jones, Johnston Blakeley, Pittsboro: 1831–'36. Physician. Born 1814, died March 1, 1889. Charlotte.
Jones, Joseph Pickett, Anson Co.: A. B., 1854. U. S. A. Col. C. S. A. Lawyer. Pensacola, Fla.
Jones, Joseph S., Warren Co.: 1824. Dead.
Jones, Kenneth R., Jones Co.: 1859–'61. Born 1842. Capt. C. S. A. Merchant. New Berne.
Jones, Montezuma, Tenn.: 1841–'43.
Jones, Nathaniel, Wake Co.: 1837–'41. Dead.
Jones, Nathaniel Crabtree, Wake Co.: A. B., 1853. Dead.
Jones, Paul, Tarboro: 1886–'88. A. B. Trinity Coll., N. C., 1885. Lawyer.
Jones, Paul L., Mooresville, Ala.: 1856–'57.
Jones, Pride, Hillsboro: A. B., 1834. Born 1815. Physician. Gen. Assem. Capt. C. S. A. Clerk Orange Co. Superior Ct. Died April, 1889.
Jones, Protheus Eppes Armistead, Granville Co.: A. B., 1833. Lawyer. Dead.
Jones, Richard S., Va.: 1817. Dead.

JONES, RICHARD THOMAS, Powellton, Va.: A. B., 1843. Dead.
JONES, ROBERT A., Halifax Co.: A. B., 1810. Dead.
JONES, ROBERT B., Va.: 1817. Dead.
JONES, ROBERT EDWARD LEE, Suffolk, Va.: 1880–'82.
JONES, ROBIN AP CADWALLADER, Hillsboro: A. B., 1844. Capt. C. S. A. Born 1826, killed at Brandy Station, 1863.
JONES, RUFUS HENRY, Wake Co.: A. B., 1843.
JONES, SETH B., Wake Co.: 1842–'45. Dead.
JONES, THOMAS, Va.: A. B., 1836. Minister. Dead.
JONES, THOMAS C., Warrenton: 1802. Dead.
JONES, THOMAS C., Wake Co.: 1829. Dead.
JONES, THOMAS FRANCIS, Perquimans Co.: A. B., 1832. Died 1856.
JONES, THOMAS WILLIAMSON, Lawrenceville, Va.: A. B., 1810. Physician. Dead.
JONES, THOMAS WILSON, Somerville, Tenn.: A. B., 1856. Capt. and Ordnance Officer C. S. A. Lawyer. Dead.
JONES, VALENTINE M., Chatham Co.: 1830–'31. Dead.
JONES, WALTER JEFFREYS, Milton, Caswell Co.: A. B., 1860. C. S. A. Teacher. Sulphur Springs, Texas.
JONES, WALTER TEMPLE, Jonesboro: 1880–'83. Dead. Carthage.
JONES, WILLIAM AMOS, Fayette Co., Tenn.: 1858. Born 1835. C. S. A. Prof. Andrew Coll. Malden, Mo.
JONES, WILLIAM CLARENCE, Camden, Ala.: A. B., 1868. Snow Hill, Ala.
JONES, WILLIAM DAVENPORT, Patterson, Caldwell Co.: 1858–'59. Born 1839. Capt. C. S. A.
JONES, WILLIAM DUKE, Granville Co.: A. B., 1822. Physician. Dead.
JONES, WILLIAM G., Warren Co.: 1809. Dead.
JONES, WILLIAM HOGAN, Wake Co.: A. B., 1849; A. M., 1852. Maj. C. S. A. Dead.
JONES, WILLIAM L., Camden, Ala.: 1866–'67.
JONES, WILLIAM S., Va.: 1803. Dead.
JONES, WILLIAM WESTWOOD, Henderson: A. B., 1862.
JONES, WILLIE WILLIAM, Halifax Co.: A. B., 1804. Dead.
JORDAN, GEORGE RYAN, Bertie Co.: A. B., 1827. Dead.
JORDAN, JAMES B., Bertie Co.: 1855–'56. A. B., Brown Univ. Lawyer. C. S. A. Born 1831, died in service 1862.
JORDAN, JOHN C., Northampton Co.: 1852–'53. Physician. Dead.
JORDAN, JOHN W., Williamson Co., Texas: 1855–'56.
JORDAN, SIMON PETER, Stokes Co.: A. B., 1819; A. M., 1822. Tutor U. N. C. Physician.
JORDAN, WILLIAM C., Greenville: A. B., 1862. Capt. C. S. A. Physician.
JORDAN, WILLIAM H., Bertie Co.: A. B., 1822. Born 1803. Minister. Dead. Oxford.
JORDAN, WILLIAM H., Bertie Co.: A. B., 1857. Tutor Wake Forest Coll. Chaplain C. S. A. Minister. Born 1833, died 1870. Thomas Co., Ga.
JOURDAN, GEORGE W., North Carolina: 1801. Dead.
JOYNER, JAMES, Pitt Co.: 1847–'48.

JOYNER, JAMES YADKIN, La Grange: Ph. B., 1881. Lawyer. Supt. of Schools. Goldsboro.
JOYNER, JOHN PUGH, La Grange: 1878–'80. Merchant.
JOYNER, JOHN R., Marlboro, Pitt Co.: 1860–'62. Chaplain C. S. A. Minister.
JOYNER, PATRICK HENRY, Johnston Co.: 1879–'80.
JOYNER, ROBERT W., Marlboro, Pitt Co: 1859–'62. Capt. C. S. A. Physician. Lawyer.
JUDD, HENDERSON D., Wake Co.: 1860–'62.
JUSTICE, ALEXANDER, New Berne: 1843–'45. Lawyer. Born 1825, died 1879.
KEARNEY, HENRY, Northampton Co.: 1795. Dead.
KEARNEY, WHITMELL H. A., Warren Co.: 1828–'29.
KEEBLE, EDWARD AUGUSTUS, Murfreesboro, Tenn.: A. B., 1827. Gen. Assem. Judge Supreme Ct. Chancellor. Died 1884.
KEECH, EDGAR JASPER, Tarboro: 1888–.
KEELS, JOHN ROBERT, Lynchburg, S. C.: 1883–'84. Lawyer.
KEIGER, A. W., Beaufort: LL. B., 1868.
KELL, BENJAMIN ELINORE, Pineville, Mecklenburg Co.: 1885–'86.
KELL, SAMUEL HICKMAN, Pineville, Mecklenburg Co.: 1885–'87.
KELLY, ANGUS ROBINSON, Moore Co.: A. B., 1841; A. M., 1847. Born 1813. Lawyer. Dead. Marion, Ala.
KELLY, JAMES, Moore Co.: A. B., 1860. Minister.
KELLY, JOHN B., Carthage, Moore Co.: A. B., 1860. C. S. A.
KELLY, JOHN M., Moore Co.: 1859–'61. Maj. C. S. A. Killed in battle.
KELLY, NEILL R., Moore Co.: 1859–'61. Lieut. C. S. A. Killed in battle.
KELLY, NICHOLAS YOUNG, Davie Co.: 1849–'52. Dead.
KENAN, DANIEL LOVE, Selma, Ala.: A. B., 1840. Born 1816.
KENAN, JAMES GRAHAM, Kenansville: A. B., 1861. Maj. C. S. A. Gen. Assem.
KENAN, THOMAS STEPHEN, Kenansville: A. B., 1857. Born 1838. Col. C. S. A. Gen. Assem., 1865–'67. Atty. Gen., 1874–'84. Clerk Supreme Ct., 1885–.
KENAN, WILLIAM RAND, Kenansville: 1860–'61. Born 1845. Sergt. Maj. C. S. A. Lawyer. Merchant.
KENNEDY, DAVID SLOAN, Magnolia, Duplin Co.: Ph. B., 1882.
KENNEDY, EDGAR BRIGHT, Lenoir Co.: 1880–'81.
KENNEDY, HYDER ALI, Claiborne Parish, La.: 1859–'61.
KENNEDY, McINTYRE, Caledonia, Moore Co.: 1883–'85.
KENNEDY, WARREN EASTON, Washington: A. B., 1833. Born 1813. Planter. Dead. Greensboro, Ala.
KENNEDY, WILLIAM LEE, Washington: A. B., 1830; A. M., 1844. Gen. Assem. Born 1810, died 1870.
KENT, ALFRED ABRAHAM, Lenoir: 1877–'79. Physician.
KENT, HORATIO MILLER, Lenoir: 1877–'78. Sheriff Caldwell Co.
KEOGH, THOMAS SAWYER, Greensboro: 1883–'85.
KERNER, ROBAH BASCOM, Kernersville, Forsyth Co.: 1877–'78. Winston.
KERNODLE, JAMES LOFTON, Morton's Store: 1888–.
KERR, JAMES EMERSON, Rowan Co.: 1826–'29. Dead.

KERR, JAMES PHILLIPS, Alamance Co.: 1881–'83. Planter. Haw River.
KERR, SAMUEL, Salisbury: A. B., 1822. Physician. Dead.
KERR, WASHINGTON CARUTHERS, Guilford Co.: A. B., 1850; A. M., 1852; Ph. D.; LL. D. Prof. Davidson Coll. Lecturer on Geol., U. N. C. State Geologist, 1869–'84. Born 1827, died 1885.
KERR, WILLIAM LA FAYETTE, Alamance Co.: A. B., 1858. Teacher. Born 1830, died 1860.
KESTLER, JOHN WESLEY, Concord: 1884–'85. Druggist. Salisbury.
KILLEBREW, JOSEPH BUCKNER, Clarksville, Tenn.: A. B., 1856; A. M. Ph. D., 1878. Born 1831. Journalist. Planter. Supt. Public Instruction. Commr. Agric., 1872–'80. Rossview, Tenn.
KILLIAN, JOHN BAXTER, Brevard, Transylvania Co.: 1877–'78.
KILPATRICK, BENJAMIN F., Jackson, Miss.: 1838–'39.
KIMBROUGH, NATHANIEL, Wake Co.: 1815. Dead.
KINCHEN, HENRY, Franklin Co.: 1795. Dead.
KINDRED, JOHN JUNIUS, Jerusalem, Va.: A. B., 1847: A. M., 1850. Lawyer. Adj. C. S. A. Dead.
KING, GEORGE BADGER, Pitt Co.: 1881–'82. Lawyer. Journalist.
KING, JAMES ALBERT, Iredell Co.: A. B., 1826; A. M., 1831. Lawyer. Gen. Assem. Died 1846.
KING, JOEL G., Louisburg: 1859–'60. Born 1841. Physician. Surg. C. S. A. Warrenton.
KING, JOHN, North Carolina: 1798. Dead.
KING, JUNIUS BAYARD, Iredell Co.: A. B., 1833. Minister. Born 1810. died 1850. Dallas Co., Ala.
KING, LEONIDAS, Anson Co.: 1822–'25. Dead.
KING, MICHAEL ANGELO, Huntsville, Ala.: A. B., 1843. Lawyer. Dead.
KING, ROBERT RUFUS, Iredell Co.: A. B., 1815; A. M., 1819. Tutor U. N. C., 1819. Minister. Born 1793, died 1822.
KING, THOMAS DEVANE, Sampson Co.: A. B., 1801. Dead.
KING, WILLIAM JOHN, Louisburg: A. B., 1860. Born 1839. C. S. A. Lawyer. Teacher. Castalia.
KING, WILLIAM RUFUS, Sampson Co.: 1801. Gen. Assem. M. C., 1810–'16. Sec'y Leg. Naples and St. Petersburg, 1816–'18. Mem. Conven. Ala., 1819. U. S. Senator from Ala., 1819–'45 and 1847–'53. President *pro tem.* U. S. Senate, 1835–'41 and 1849–'53. U. S. Minister to France, 1844–'46. Vice-President U. S., 1853. Born 1786, died 1853. Alabama.
KINGSBURY, CHARLES F., Oxford: 1855–'57.
KINGSBURY, HENRY P., Oxford: 1864–'65. Capt. 6th U. S. Cavalry.
KINGSBURY, THEODORE BRYAN, Oxford: 1847–'49. LL. D., 1888. Journalist. Wilmington.
KIRBY, JACOB S., Highland, Va.: 1820–'21.
KIRBY, MOSES A., Chapel Hill: 1818. Dead.
KIRBY, MOSES H., Virginia: 1819.
KIRBY, SAMUEL, Virginia: 1810. Dead.
KIRKLAND, ALEXANDER, Chapel Hill: 1855–'59. Minister. Whiteville.
KIRKLAND, ALEXANDER M., Hillsboro: 1823–'25. Dead.
KIRKLAND, LEONIDAS JOSEPH, Chapel Hill: 1880–'82. Durham.

Kirkpatrick, Alexander, Wilmington : 1796. Dead.
Kitchen, W. W., Scotland Neck : 1887. Lawyer.
Kittrell, Benjamin A., Oxford : 1848–'50. Dead.
Kittrell, Pleasant Williams, Chapel Hill : A. B., 1822. Physician. Dead.
Kittrell, Solomon, Granville Co. : 1809. Dead.
Kittrell, Thomas J., Chapel Hill : 1825–'26. Dead.
Kittrell, William J., Chapel Hill : 1832–'33. Dead.
Kluttz, Adam Alexander, Goldsboro : 1880–'83. Physician. Merchant. Chapel Hill.
Knapp, Edwin, Savannah, Ga. : 1856–'58. Lawyer.
Knight, Andrew C., Edgecombe Co. : 1838. Died 1840.
Knight, James Smith, Rockingham Co. : A. B., 1861. Lt. C. S. A. Killed in service.
Knight, William H., Edgecombe Co : 1851–'54. Planter.
Knox, Andrew E. B., New Orleans, La. : 1855–'58.
Knox, Hugh, Pasquotank Co. : 1813. Planter. Dead.
Knox, William B., Elizabeth City : 1834–'36. Physician. Dead.
Kolb, Reuben Francis Cameron, Eufaula, Ala. : A. B., 1859.
Koonce, Andrew Jacob, Elkin, Surry Co. : 1884–'85.
Koonce, Francis Divaul, Onslow Co. : 1855–'58. Capt. C. S. A. Lawyer. Richlands.
Koonce, Francis Divaul, Richlands, Onslow Co. : 1887–.
Koonce, William Michael, Trenton, Jones Co. : 1884–'85.
Lacey, Thomas Jefferson, Nelson, Ky. : A. B., 1821. Judge Superior Ct. Arkansas. Dead.
Lacy, James Horace, Raleigh : 1850–'52. Died 1852.
Lacy, Matthew M., Mississippi : 1850–'52. Dead.
Lamb, Charles C., Oxford : 1864–'65. Dead.
Lamb, Cornelius Gray, Camden Co. : A. B., 1853.
Lamb, Isaac N., South Carolina : 1813. Dead.
Lamb, William, South Carolina : 1819.
Lancaster, James Warren, Edgecombe Co. : A. B., 1843 ; A. M., 1846. Lawyer. Gen. Assem., 1854–'55. Wilson. Dead.
Land, John McDonald, Grenada, Miss. : A. B., 1861. C. S. A. Killed at Shiloh, April, 1862.
Land, John W., Sussex Co., Va. : 1862–'63.
Land, Thomas T., Shreveport, La. : 1858–'59.
Lane, Carma, Chatham Co. : 1857–'59. Died 1859.
Lane, Levin, Wilmington : 1810. Dead.
Lane, Thomas H., Wilmington : 1838–'39. Died 1864.
Lane, William P., Goldsboro : 1859–'61. Lt. C. S. A. Merchant.
Lane, William Walter, Wilmington : A. B., 1852. Born 1831. M. D., Univ. of N. Y.
Lanier, Thomas J., Quincy, Fla. : 1859–'61.
Lankford, Menalcus, Franklin Co. : A. B., 1847.
Lassiter, Thomas R., Lenoir Co. : B. S., 1858. Physician. Dead.
Lastrapes, Adolphe, Opelousas, La. : 1860–'61.

LATHAM, HEBER AMOS LAMAR, Greenville: Ph. B., 1885. Journalist. Washington.
LATHAM, JOSEPH NORMAN, Plymouth: 1886–'87.
LATHAM, JULIAN A., Plymouth: 1858–'61. Lt. C. S. A. Died 1880.
LATHAM, LOUIS CHARLES, Plymouth: A. B., 1859. Born 1840. Maj. 1st N. C., C. S. A. Lawyer. Mem. H. of C., 1864. State Sen., 1870. M. C., 1881–'83 and 1887–'89. Greenville.
LATHAM, THOMAS EMMETT, Ashe Co.: 1881–'82.
LATTA, GEORGE GRAY, Knoxville, Tenn.: A. B., 1868. Born 1848. Gen. Assem., Ark. Mem. Ark. Conventions, 1872, 1874 and 1876. Prosecuting Atty. Lawyer. Hot Springs, Ark.
LAUGHINGHOUSE, CHARLES O'HAGEN, Washington: 1888–.
LAW, JUNIUS A., Darlington District, S. C.: 1858–'59. Col. C. S. A. Died 1881.
LAWING, JOHN MEANS, Mecklenburg Co.: A. B., 1857.
LAWRENCE, ALEXANDER W., Raleigh: A. B., 1853. Capt. C. S. A. Dead.
LAWRENCE, THOMAS R., Bertie Co: 1856–'58. Lt. C. S. A. Teacher. Died 1884.
LAWRENCE, ADOLPHUS ALEXANDER, Statesville: A. B., 1856. M. D., Univ. Penn. Surg. C. S. A. Supt. Memphis City Hospital and U. S. Marine Hospital. Dead. Memphis, Tenn.
LAWRENCE, JOHN W., Statesville: 1862–'63.
LAZARUS, MARX E., Wilmington: 1837–'39. Columbus, Ga.
LEA, CALVIN, Caswell Co.: 1853–'56. Physician. C. S. A.
LEA, GEORGE GALLATIN, Leasburg, Caswell Co.: A. B., 1830. Dead.
LEA, HENRY C., Mobile, Ala.: 1856–'58. Fruit Grower. Talaha, Fla.
LEA, JAMES M., Leasburg, Caswell Co.: 1829–'31. Dead.
LEA, LORENZO, Leasburg, Caswell Co.: A. B., 1827; A. M., 1832. Tutor U. N. C., 1828–'29. Minister. Founder and Pres. of Jackson Female Coll. Died 1876. Jackson, Tenn.
LEA, SOLOMON, Leasburg, Caswell Co.: A. B., 1833; A. M., 1838. Tutor Randolph-Macon Coll., 1835–'37. Pres. Farmville Va. Female Seminary, 1840–'41. Pres. Greensboro Female Coll., 1846–'47. Minister.
LEA, WILLIAM, Leasburg, Caswell Co.: 1831–'32. Merchant. Dead. Petersburg, Va.
LEA, WILLIAM A., Leasburg, Caswell Co.: 1838–'39.
LEA, WILLIAM JONES, Mobile, Ala.: A. B., 1857. Born 1835. Capt. C. S. A. Planter. Daphne, Ala.
LEA, WILLIAM McNEILL, Caswell Co.: A. B., 1820. Physician. Dead.
LEA, WILLIS MONROE, Leasburg, Caswell Co.: A. B., 1821. Physician. Dead. Holly Springs, Miss.
LEACH, GEORGE T., Pittsboro: 1857–'60.
LEACH, JAMES MADISON, Lexington: Ph. B., 1881. Washington, D. C.
LEACH, JULIAN E., Randolph Co.: 1834–'35. Dead.
LEAK, JAMES AUGUSTUS, Richmond Co.: A. B., 1843. Wadesboro.
LEAK, THOMAS CRAWFORD, Richmond Co.: A. B., 1853.
LEAK, WALTER F., Rockingham: 1815. Planter. Gen. Assem. Pres. Elector, 1852. Mem. Conv., 1861. Born 1799, died 1879.

LEAK, WALTER JOHN, Salem, Miss.: A. B., 1853. Dead.
LEAK, WILLIAM P., Wadesboro: 1863–'64. Dead.
LEARY, EDGAR, Granville Co.: 1867–'68. Dead.
LEDBETTER, HENRY DAVID, Rockingham: 1886–'88.
LEDBETTER, HENRY STEELE, Richmond Co.: 1877–'79.
LEDBETTER, HENRY WALL, Wadesboro: 1854–'55. Born 1833. Civil Engineer. Planter.
LEDBETTER, JAMES MCQUEEN, Rockingham: 1888–.
LEDBETTER, WILLIAM LEAK, Anson Co.: A. B., 1854. Physician. Surg. C. S. A. Born 1831, died 1870.
LEE, ALGERNON MOSELEY, Clinton: 1857–'60. Born 1836. C. S. A. Physician.
LEE, JAMES, Dover, Tenn: 1850–'51. Memphis, Tenn.
LEE, RUCKER, 1820.
LEE, RICHARD HENRY, Clinton: 1860–'62. C. S. A. Merchant. Goldsboro.
LEE, THOMAS JEFFERSON, Clinton: 1855–'56. Born 1835. C. S. A. Journalist. Druggist.
LEE, THOMAS MOSSETTE, Clinton: 1886–.
LEECRAFT, LAFAYETTE F., Beaufort Co.: 1854–'55.
LEES, DAVID MCMICKEN, Mecklenburg Co.: A. B., 1829. Dead.
LEETCH, JAMES KNOX, Ala.: A. B., 1823. Dead.
LEGRAND, JAMES, Montgomery Co.: 1808. Dead.
LEGRAND, NASH, Norfolk, Va.: 1816–'18. U. S. N. Dead.
LEIGH, FRANK MELANCTHON, Columbus, Miss.: A. B., 1862. Born 1844. Capt. C. S. A. Manufacturer. Comm. Merchant.
LEIGH, JOHN HENRY JACOCKS, Woodville, Perquimans Co.: 1882–'85.
LEIGH, JOHN R., New Berne: 1808. State Solicitor. Dead.
LEIGH, RICHARD H., Perquimans Co.: 1860–'61. Planter. Died 1873.
LEITCH, GILES, Robeson Co.: A. B., 1851. Dead.
LEMLY, HENRY A., Salisbury: 1829–'30. Dead.
LENOIR, RUFUS T., Fort Defiance, Caldwell Co.: 1844–'45.
LENOIR, THOMAS BALLARD, Caldwell Co.: 1879–'80.
LENOIR, THOMAS I., Wilkes Co.: 1838–'39. Capt. C. S. A. Dead.
LENOIR, WALTER JAMES, Patterson, Caldwell Co.: 1880–'82.
LENOIR, WALTER WAIGHTSTILL, Wilkes Co.: A. B., 1843. Capt. C. S. A. Planter. Shull's Mills, Watauga Co.
LENTE, FREDERICK DIVOUX, New Berne: A. B., 1845; A. M., 1849. Physician. Surgeon to West Point Foundry 24 years. Professor Gynaecology N. Y. Univ., and Asst. Surg. Woman's Hospital. Founder and President American Acad. Medicine. Born 1823, died 1883.
LEONARD, JAMES RODERICK, Columbus, Ga.: 1847–'48. Born 1830. Planter. C. S. A. West Falls, Texas.
LESESNE, CHARLES, Bladen Co.: A. B., 1859. Physician. Dead.
LESTER, ROBERT E., Tallahassee, Fla.: B. S., 1859.
LEVY, LIONEL LINCOLN, New Orleans, La.: A. B., 1847.
LEWIS, AUGUSTUS MARION, Franklin Co.: 1843–'44. Born 1821. Paymaster C. S. A. Lawyer. Raleigh.

LEWIS, CHARLES KELLY, Raleigh: 1877–'78. Born 1859. Lawyer.
LEWIS, CHRISTOPHER COLUMBUS, Chapel Hill: 1855–'58.
LEWIS, DAVID W., Sparta, Ga.: 1834–'35. A. M. Mem. Confed. Cong. Pres. Ga. Agric. and Mech. Coll., 1872–'86. Died 1886.
LEWIS, EDWARD BULKLEY, Chapel Hill: A. B., 1844. Born 1822, died 1845.
LEWIS, EXUM, Chapel Hill: A. B., 1857. Died 1888.
LEWIS, HENRY, Lawrenceville, Va.: 1810. Physician. Dead.
LEWIS, HENRY WATSON, Lewiston, Bertie Co.: A. B., 1888. Teacher.
LEWIS, IVEY FOREMAN, Greensboro, Ala.: A. B., 1854. Col. C. S. A. Planter. Born 1833, died 1884.
LEWIS, JAMES MALLORY, Chapel Hill: 1844–'47. Born 1830.
LEWIS, JOHN BRYAN, Raleigh: 1875–'78.
LEWIS, JOHN CHURCHILL, Rutherfordton: 1879–'81.
LEWIS, JOHN STANBACK, Sulphur Springs: 1887–.
LEWIS, JOHN W., Chapel Hill 1842–'43. Dead.
LEWIS, JOHN W., Halifax, Va.: 1849–'50.
LEWIS, JOSEPH, Granville Co.: 1797. Dead.
LEWIS, JOSEPH VOLNEY, Rutherfordton: 1887–.
LEWIS, JOSEPH WARNER, Lawrenceville, Va.: A. B., 1852. Teacher.
LEWIS, KENELM HARRISON, Rocky Mt.: A. B., 1838; A. M., 1845. Lawyer. Born 1816, died 1866.
LEWIS, RICHARD F., Bladen Co.: 1855–'58. Physician. Gen. Assem., 1885. Lumberton.
LEWIS, RICHARD HENRY, Edgecombe Co.: A. B., 1827; A. M., 1830. Planter. Born 1806, died 1857.
LEWIS, RICHARD HENRY, Chapel Hill: A. B., 1852; A. M. Born 1832. M. D. Univ. Pa. Teacher. Kinston.
LEWIS, RICHARD HENRY, Tarboro: 1866–'68. Born 1850. Physician. Prof. Eye and Ear Diseases Savannah Med. Coll., 1875–'77. Oculist. Raleigh.
LEWIS, ROBERT GUILFORD, Louisburg: 1848–'49. Maj. C. S. A. Lawyer. Raleigh.
LEWIS, WILLIAM FIGURES, Edgecombe Co.: A. B., 1842. Dead.
LEWIS, WILLIAM FIGURES, Kinston: 1882–'83. Montana.
LEWIS, WILLIAM GASTON, Chapel Hill: A. B., 1855. Born 1835. Civil Engineer. Brig. Gen. C. S. A. Goldsboro.
LIGHTFOOT, JOHN FRAZER, Tuscumbia, Ala: A. B., 1861.
LILES, EDWARD PRENTISS, Lilesville, Anson Co.: 1880–'82.
LILES, EDWARD RUTLEDGE, Anson Co.: 1851–'52. Col. C. S. A. Gen. Assem. Journalist. Born 1832, died 1884.
LILLINGTON, GEORGE, Wilmington: 1843–'44. M. D. Univ. Pa. Born 1827, died 1851.
LILLINGTON, JOHN ALEXANDER, Wilmington: A. B., 1840. Lawyer. Gen. Assem. Born 1820, died 1854.
LINDSAY, ANDREW DICK, Greensboro: A. B., 1859. Lieut. C. S. A. Dead.
LINDSAY, EDWARD O., Greensboro: 1866–'68. Physician. Born 1849, died 1888.

LINDSAY, ERNEST, Greensboro: 1862–'63. Born 1845. St. Joseph, Mo.
LINDSAY, GAVIN HOGG, Greensboro: A. B., 1853. Lieut. C. S. A. Killed in battle.
LINDSAY, HARPER JEDUTHAN, Greensboro: 1822–'25. Born 1806. Dead.
LINDSAY, JAMES EARLY, Greensboro: B. S., 1857. Born 1836. Physician. Prof. Baltimore Med. Coll. Baltimore, Md.
LINDSAY, JEDUTHAN HARPER, Greensboro: 1856–'58. Born 1840, died 1876.
LINDSAY, JESSE HARPER, Greensboro: A. B., 1827. Gen. Assem. Pres. Nat. Bank Greensboro, 1876–'86. Born 1808, died 1886.
LINDSAY, JESSE HARPER, Greensboro: A. B., 1851. Born 1832, died 1859.
LINDSAY, ROBERT GOODLOE, Greensboro: 1832–'36. Born 1816.
LINDSAY, ROBERT HENRY, Greensboro: 1856–'58. Born 1838. C. S. A. Killed in battle, 1861.
LINDSAY, THOMAS STRANGE, Greensboro: 1860–'62. Born 1843, died 1869.
LITTLE, BLAKE, Edgecombe Co.: 1813. Physician. Dead.
LITTLE, FRANK MILTON, Wadesboro: Ph. B., 1886. Teacher.
LITTLE, JAMES LAFAYETTE, Greenville: 1880–'81.
LITTLE, JOHN, Edenton: 1831–'34. Dead.
LITTLE, JOHN RICHARD, Ansonville, Anson Co.: 1876–'77.
LITTLE, JULIAN HAMPTON, Little's Mills, Richmond Co: 1884–'85. Charlotte.
LITTLE, JULIUS ALEXANDER, Wadesboro: 1856–'58. Born 1840. C. S. A.
LITTLE, LACY LEGRAND, Little's Mills, Richmond Co.: A. B., 1889.
LITTLE, WALTER S., Ansonville, Anson Co.: 1864–'66.
LITTLE, WILLIAM, Raleigh: A. B., 1858; A. M. M. D. Univ. N. Y. Surg. C. S. A. Dead.
LITTLE, WILLIAM B., Anson Co.: 1852–'54.
LITTLE, WILLIAM G., Warsaw, Ala.: 1847–'48. Physician.
LITTLE, WILLIAM MYERS, Little's Mills, Richmond Co.: A. B., 1888. Teacher. Statesville.
LITTLEJOHN, JOSEPH B., Somerville, Tenn.: 1834–'35. Dead.
LIVINGSTON, HUGH MCGOOGAN, Robeson Co.: A. B., 1853. Pres. Austin Coll., Texas. Dead. Texas.
LIVINGSTON, JOHN KNOX, Madison, Fla.: 1867–'68. Lawyer. Gen. Assem. Ark. Bennettsville, S. C.
LIVINGSTON, LACY LEGRAND, Livingston, Fla.: 1867–'68.
LLOYD, HENRY S., Martin Co.: 1841–'42. Planter. Died 1860.
LLOYD, HENRY, Tarboro: 1875–'77.
LLOYD, JOSEPH ROSS, Tarboro: A. B., 1816. Gen. Assem. Dead.
LLOYD, SAMUEL P., Orange Co.: 1869–'70.
LOCKE, MATTHEW B., Salisbury: 1823–'25. Dead.
LOCKE, MOSES A., Salisbury: 1799. Dead.
LOCKE, ROBERT, Salisbury; A. B., 1798. Planter. Died 1818.
LOCKE, WILLIAM M., Salisbury: 1828–'29. Dead.

LOCKHART, JOHN J., Northampton Co.: 1833–'36. Planter. Dead.
LOGAN, HENRY CHARLES, Virginia: 1838–'39. Planter. Born 1819, died 1846.
LOGAN, JOHN EARLY, Greensboro: A. B., 1857. Physician.
LOGAN, RICHARD, Virginia: 1808. Dead.
LOGAN, WILLIAM, Virginia: A. B., 1840. Dead.
LOGWOOD, EDMUND, Liberty, Va.: 1822–'23. Dead.
LONDON, HENRY A., Wilmington: 1825. Dead.
LONDON, HENRY ADOLPHUS, Pittsboro: A. B., 1865. Journalist. Lawyer.
LONDON, HENRY ADOLPHUS, Pittsboro: 1884–'86.
LONDON, JOHN HAUGHTON, Pittsboro: 1886–'88. Dentist.
LONDON, JOHN R., Wilmington: 1798. Dead.
LONG, ALEXANDER, Rowan Co.: 1809. Dead.
LONG, ALPHONZO, Randolph Co.: 1838–'39. Dead.
LONG, AUGUSTUS WHITE, Chapel Hill: A. B., 1884. Prof. English Trinity Coll. N. C., and Wofford Coll., S. C. Spartanburg, S. C.
LONG, BENJAMIN SHERROD, Halifax Co.: A. B., 1825. Dead.
LONG, DANIEL A., Alamance Co.: 1866–'68; A. M.; D. D., 1886. LL. D. Pres. Antioch Coll. Yellow Springs, Ohio.
LONG, FRANK PEGUES, Jackson, Tenn.: A. B., 1859.
LONG, GEORGE WASHINGTON, Halifax Co.: A. B., 1799. Dead.
LONG, HAMILTON CRUMP, Buncombe Co.: 1881–'82.
LONG, HERVEY, 1808. Dead.
LONG, ISAAC HENRY, Graham: 1876–'78. Born 1854, died 1878.
LONG, JAMES ALLEN, Randolph Co.: A. B., 1841. Lawyer. Journalist. Born 1817, died 1864.
LONG, JAMES M., Caswell Co.: 1860–'61. C. S. A. Dead.
LONG, JOHN EDGAR, Graham: 1885–'87.
LONG, JOHN J., Halifax Co.: 1831–'32. Dead.
LONG, JOHN S., New Berne: 1851–'52. A. B. Randolph-Macon, 1851. Lawyer.
LONG, JOHN WESLEY, Randolph Co.: A. B., 1844. M. D. Univ. Pa. Born 1824, died 1863.
LONG, NICHOLAS, Louisburg: 1795. Dead.
LONG, NICHOLAS M., Halifax Co.: 1828–'29. Planter. Dead.
LONG, NICHOLAS M., Halifax Co.: 1850–'52. Capt. C. S. A. Dead.
LONG, OSMOND FITZ, Randolph Co.: A. B., 1829. M. D. Univ. Pa. Born 1808, died 1864.
LONG, RICHARD W., Salisbury, 1823–'24. Physician. Dead.
LONG, THOMAS HIRAM, Chapel Hill: 1881–'83. Planter.
LONG, THOMAS RUFFIN, Yanceyville: A. B., 1856. C. S. A. Dead.
LONG, VERNON W., Chapel Hill: Ph. B., 1887. Journalist. Winston.
LONG, WILLIAM, Rowan Co.: 1809. Dead.
LONG, WILLIAM JOHN, Randolph Co.: A. B., 1838. Gen. Assem. Mem. Conv., 1861. Lawyer. Born 1815, died 1882. Minneapolis, Minn.
LONG, WILLIAM STEPHENS, Yanceyville: A. B., 1854.
LONG, WILLIAM WILLIAMS, Weldon: 1880–'81.
LORD, FREDERICK JAMES, Wilmington: A. B., 1843.

LORD, JOHN, Wilmington: 1810. Dead.
LORD, STEPHEN F., Salisbury: 1863–'64.
LORD, WILLIAM A., Wilmington: 1853–'55.
LORD, WILLIAM CAMPBELL, Salisbury: A. B., 1858. Capt. C. S. A. Killed in battle.
LOVE, EDGAR, Gastonia, Gaston Co.: 1886–.
LOVE, JAMES LEE, Gaston Co.: Ph. B., 1884. Asst. Prof. of Math., U. N. C., 1885–. Chapel Hill.
LOVE, ROBERT E., Salisbury: 1830–'32. Dead.
LOVE, SAMUEL E., Farmville, Va.: 1813. Dead.
LOVE, STIRLING E., Lawrenceville, Va.: 1816. Dead.
LOVE, WILLIAM C., Chapel Hill: 1802. M. C., 1815–'17. Dead.
LOVE, WILLIAM JAMES, Wilmington: A. B., 1855. Physician.
LOWE, CICERO FRANKLIN, Lexington: 1885–'87.
LOWTHER, CHARLES EDEN, Edenton: A. B., 1849. Dead.
LOWTHER, WILLIAM D., Edenton: 1813. Dead.
LUCAS, JAMES S., Washington: 1859–'62.
LUCAS, JOSEPH B., Chapel Hill: 1845–'49. A. M. Tutor Anc. Langs., U. N. C., 1854–'57. Dead.
LUCAS, WILLIAM, Chapel Hill: A. B., 1847. Dead.
LUNDY, ETHELDRED H., Hicksford, Va.: 1812. Dead.
LUNSFORD, WILLIAM EWART, Durham 1886–'87.
LUSHER, GEORGE M., Memphis, Tenn.: 1856–'57. C. S. A. Engineer.
LUSHER, NATHANIEL PEARSON, Memphis, Tenn.: A. B., 1858. Lawyer. Dead.
LUTTERLOH, EDWARD BUXTON, Fayetteville: 1869–'70.
LUTTERLOH, HERBERT, Fayetteville: 1877–'78.
LUTTERLOH, JARVIS BUXTON, Fayetteville: A. B., 1860. Lt. C. S. A. Killed in battle near Kinston, 1863.
LUTTRELL, JAMES C., Knoxville, Tenn.: 1857–'59. Born 1841. Capt. C. S. A. Mayor. Merchant.
LYNCH, JAMES D., Boydton, Va.: 1855–'58.
LYNCH, JOHN BAIRD, Lombardy Grove, Va.: A. B., 1859.
LYNCH, LEANDER WILLIAMS, Cuba, Rutherford Co.: 1885–'88.
LYNCH, ROBERT BINGHAM, High Point, Guilford Co.: 1881–82.
LYNCH, WILLIAM BINGHAM, Orange Co.: A. B., 1859. Lieut. C. S. A.
LYNE, GEORGE, Granville Co.: 1814. Dead.
LYNE, HENRY, Granville Co.: 1806. Dead.
LYNE, LEONARD H., Granville Co.: 1807. Dead.
LYON, HARRISON PITTMAN, Edgecombe Co.: 1858–'61. Lieut. 33d N. C., C. S. A. Killed at the Wilderness, May 12, 1864.
LYON, JAMES THEOPHILUS, Franklinton, Franklin Co.: 1869–'70.
LYON, MARTIN ARMSTRONG, Linden, Ala.: 1845–'47. Merchant. Born 1826, died 1870. Mobile, Ala.
LYON, WILLIAM PLEASANT, Franklinton, Franklin Co.: 1869–'70.
LYTLE, ARCHIBALD, Tennessee: A. B., 1801. Dead.
LYTLE, JOHN, Tennessee: 1808. Dead.
LYTLE, WILLIAM FRANKLIN, Rutherford Co., Tenn.: A. B., 1824. Dead.

McAden, Benjamin Terry, Charlotte: 1878-'79. Died Nov., 1888.
McAden, John H., Caswell Co.: 1853-'54. Physician. Charlotte.
McAdin, Henry, Caswell Co.: 1817. M. D. Dead.
McAdoo, Albert Y., Guilford Co.: 1838-'39. M. D. Dead.
McAdoo, William C., Greensboro: 1863-'65. Dead.
McAfee, Abner A., Shelby: 1859-'61. Dead.
McAfee, Leroy Mangum, Cleveland Co.: A. B., 1858; A. M., 1866. Col. C. S. A. Dead.
McAlister, Alexander Carey, Randolph Co.: A. B., 1858. Lt. Col. C. S. A. Planter. Ashboro.
McAlister, Alexander Worth, Ashboro, Randolph Co.: A. B., 1882. Lawyer.
McAlister, Charles Colvin, Ashboro, Randolph Co.: 1887-'88. Merchant.
McAlister, David, Cumberland Co.: A. B., 1834. Tutor U. N. C., 1835. Physician. Dead.
McAlister, Hector, Cumberland Co.: A. B., 1841. Minister. Dead.
McAlpine, Andrew J., Yanceyville, Caswell Co.: 1847-'48.
McAlpine, William A., Eutaw, Ala.: 1856-'58.
Macartney, Thomas Noles, Mobile, Ala.: A. B., 1858. C. S. A. County Solicitor. Adj. Gen. Ala., 1874-'78. Born 1839, died 1883.
McAuley, John Martin, Mecklenburg Co.: 1881-'82.
McBee, Vardry Alexander, S. C.: A. B., 1841.
McBee, William Pinckney, Greenville, S. C.: A. B., 1842.
McBryde, Archibald A., Cumberland Co.: 1852-'55. Dead.
McBryde, Malcolm, Robeson Co.: 1833-'34.
McBryde, Thomas K., Robeson Co.: 1856-'58. Lt. C. S. A.
McBryde, William J., Montgomery, Ala.: 1841-'43. Lawyer. Dead.
McCabe, John, Houston, Miss: 1854-'55. Lawyer.
McCain, Nathaniel Henry, Rockingham Co.: A. B., 1830; A. M., 1841.
McCain, William A., Rockingham Co.: 1830-'31. Dead.
McCall, James M., Wilmington: 1823-'26. Dead.
McCall, Robert Sevier, North Cove, McDowell Co.: 1879-'80.
McCallum, Archibald Torrey, Shoe Hill, Robeson Co.: 1877-'78.
McCallum, James Baxter, Robeson Co.: A. B., 1860. Lt. C. S. A. Born 1839. Killed at Drury's Bluff, 1864.
McCaskey, Thomas Edward, Williamston, Martin Co.: 1883-'84.
McCaskill, Neill E., Carthage, Moore Co.: 1857-'58.
McCauley, Charles Maurice Talleyrand, Chapel Hill: A. B., 1838. Lawyer. Monroe.
McCauley, Robert W., Orange Co.: 1815. Dead.
McCauley, Samuel, Chapel Hill: 1842-'43.
McCauley, William, Orange Co.: 1813. Dead.
McClammy, Charles Washington, New Hanover Co.: A. B., 1859. Born May 29, 1839. Maj. 3d N. C., C. S. A. Planter. Gen. Assem., 1866 and 1871. Pres. Elector, 1884. M. C., 1887. Scott's Hill, Pender Co.
McClammy, Herbert, Scott's Hill, Pender Co.: 1883-'85. Lawyer.
McClamrock, William David, Cana: 1888-'89.

McCLEES, JOSEPH, Alligator, Tyrrell Co.: A. B., 1843. Gen. Assem. Lawyer. Planter. Born 1820, died 1856.
McCLELLAND, JAMES C., Iredell Co.: A. B., 1860. Teacher. C. S. A. Born 1837. Killed in service, 1862.
McCLENAHAN, JAMES T., Pittsboro: 1849–'51. Dead.
McCLUNG, JAMES WHITE, Knoxville, Tenn.: A. B., 1816. Lawyer. Speaker Gen. Assem. Ala. Born June 6, 1798, died May 30, 1848. Huntsville, Ala.
McCLUNG, MATTHEW, Knoxville, Tenn.: A. B., 1815. Merchant and Planter. Born Oct. 10, 1795, died Oct. 5, 1844.
McCLURE, WILLIAM K., Arkadelphia, Ark.: 1857–'58.
McCONNAUGHEY, GEORGE CHAMBERS, Rowan Co.: A. B., 1859.
McCONNAUGHEY, JAMES A., Rowan Co.: 1852–'54.
McCONNAUGHEY, JOSEPH LUCIEN, Rowan Co.: A. B., 1858.
McCORD, ALLISON, Ala.: 1826–'28. Dead.
McCORKLE, GEORGE, Newton: A. B., 1878. Lawyer. Washington, D. C.
McCORKLE, JAMES M., Wadesboro: 1841–'42. Dead.
McCORMICK, JAMES L., Robeson Co.: 1855–'57. Capt. C. S. A. Killed at Fort Fisher, 1864.
McCOTTER, RICHARD DAWSON, New Berne: 1858–'59. Born 1837. Lt. C. S. A. Gen. Assem., 1883. Teacher. Pamlico.
McCREERY, HAWES, Owensboro, Ky.: 1876–'77.
McCULLEN, BENJAMIN FRANKLIN, Kinston: 1878–'79.
McCULLOCH, ALEXANDER, Halifax Co.: 1796. Dead.
McCULLOCH, BENJAMIN, Halifax Co.: 1802. Dead.
McCULLOCH, JAMES C., Morton's Store, Alamance Co.: 1883–'84.
McCULLOCH, SAMUEL, Halifax Co.: 1799. Dead.
McCULLOCH, THOMAS FILLMORE, Guilford Co.: 1878–'79.
McCUTCHEN, ROBERT GEORGE, Williamsburg Dist., S. C.: A. B., 1836. Minister.
McCUTCHEN, THOMAS, S. C.: 1834–'35.
McDADE, ALPHONZO J., Chapel Hill: 1851–'55. Merchant. Mayor.
McDADE, DANIEL C., Chapel Hill: 1853–'54.
McDADE, JOHN HENDERSON, Chapel Hill: A. B., 1852. Capt. C. S. A. Killed in service.
McDADE, WAYNE H., Chapel Hill: 1852–'54. C. S. A. Dead.
McDANIEL, WILLIAM C., Fayetteville: 1860–'62. Dead.
McDERMOTT, JOSEPH ALEXANDER, Tellico Plains, Tenn.: 1860–'61. Capt. 59th Tenn. Inf., C. S. A. Born Jan. 11, 1843, killed at Vicksburg, May 28, 1863.
McDONALD, A. R., Moore Co.: 1852–'53.
McDONALD, WILLIAM, Moore Co.: A. B., 1859. Minister.
McDONALD, WILLIAM G., Greensboro, Ala.: 1839–'40. M. D. Born 1822, died 1847. Lexington, Ky.
McDONALD, WILLIAM H., Raleigh: A. B., 1887. Charlotte.
McDOUGALD, DANIEL, Cumberland Co.: A. B., 1855; A. M. Lawyer. Capt. 15th N. C., C. S. A. Born Oct. 24, 1835, killed at Malvern Hill, July, 1862.

McDOUGALD, NEILL MILLARD, Devane, Cumberland Co.: 1880–'81.
McDOWELL, CHARLES HARPER, Shufordsville, Henderson Co.: 1880–'82.
McDOWELL, CHARLES J., Camden, S. C.: 1856–'57. Sergt. C. S. A. Dead.
McDOWELL, JAMES ALLEN, Shufordsville, Henderson Co.: 1880–'82.
McDOWELL, THOMAS DAVID SMITH, Bladen Co.: A. B., 1843. Mem. Confed. Cong.
McDOWELL, WILLIAM A., Mecklenburg Co.: 1835–'36.
McDUFFIE, ARCHIBALD MURPHY, Fayetteville: 1888–.
McDUFFIE, MALCOLM JAMES, Cumberland Co.: A. B., 1851. Dead.
McEACHAN, DANIEL PURCELL, Robeson Co.: A. B., 1859.
McEACHERN, ROBERT J., Robeson Co.: 1856–'58. Capt. C. S. A. Killed in service.
McEACHIN, CALVIN ALEXANDER, Robeson Co.: A. B., 1855. C. S. A. Mem. Conven., 1875.
McEACHIN, CHARLES, Montgomery, Ala.: 1843–'47. Physician.
McEACHIN, PETER A., Robeson Co.: 1850–'53. Dead.
McEACHIN, PETER HECTOR, Montgomery, Ala.: A. B., 1848. Died 1851.
McEACHIN, WALTER DeBERNIERE, Laurinburg, Richmond Co.: 1884–'85. Planter.
McELWEE, WILLIAM HENRY, Statesville: 1881–'83. Express Agent. Greensboro.
McFADYEN, ARCHIBALD W., Cumberland Co.: A. B., 1862. Lt. C. S. A. Minister. Clarkton.
McGAVOCK, FELIX GRUNDY, Nashville, Tenn.: 1850–'51. Born 1832. Physician. Planter. Pecan Pt., Ark.
McGAVOCK, JOHN JACOB, Nashville, Tenn.: 1853–'54. Born 1835. C. S. A. Planter.
McGEHEE, LUCIUS POLK, Raleigh: A. B., 1887.
McGEHEE, MONTFORD, Person Co.: A. B., 1841; A. M., 1844. Born 1822. Lawyer. Planter. Gen. Assem., 1862–'79. Mem. Conven., 1865. Commr. Agriculture, 1880–'87. Raleigh.
McGEHEE, THOMAS JEFFREYS, Person Co.: 1837–'38. Planter. Born 1819, died 1853.
McGEHEE, WILLIAM POLK, Caswell Co.: 1882–'83. Raleigh.
McGHEE, BARCLAY, Knoxville, Tenn.: 1840–'41. Planter. Dead.
McGHEE, GEORGE W., Tenn.: 1819. Dead.
McGILVARY, JOHN H., Fayetteville: 1859–'61.
McGUIRE, JAMES, Mocksville, Davie Co.: Ph. B., 1887.
McILHENNY, JOHN, Wilmington: 1865–'67.
McILHENNY, THOMAS COWAN, Wilmington: A. B., 1845.
McINNIS, DUNCAN, Robeson Co.: A. B., 1813. Dead.
McINNIS, JOHN, South Carolina: 1807. Dead.
McINTYRE, ALEXANDER, Cameron, Moore Co.: 1880–'83. Ocala, Fla.
McINTYRE, DUNCAN THOMAS, Laurinburg, Richmond Co.: 1881–'82.
McINTYRE, PETER, Cameron, Moore Co.: 1880–'82.
McINTYRE, KENNETH M., Moore Co.: 1856–'58. Minister.
McINTYRE, WILLIAM A., Fayetteville: A. B., 1853. Dead.

McIver, Alexander, Moore Co.: A. B., 1853. Prof. Math., U. N. C., 1869–'70, and Davidson Coll. Supt. Pub. Inst. Supt. Greensboro Graded Schools. Oaks, Orange Co.

McIver, Alexander, Oaks, Orange Co.: 1886–.

McIver, Berrie Chandler, Sanford, Moore Co.: A. B., 1885. Tutor Greek, U. N. C. Teacher. Goldsboro.

McIver, Charles Duncan, Egypt, Chatham Co.: A. B., 1881. Born 1860. Teacher. Supt. of State Institutes, 1889–. Raleigh.

McIver, Duncan Evander, Sanford, Moore Co.: 1878–'81. Gen. Assem.

McIver, Evander J., Moore Co.: A. B., 1855. Col. C. S. A. Supt. Pub. Instruction, Ala.

McIver, George Wilcox, Chapel Hill: 1869–'70. Lt. 7th Inf., U. S. A.

McIver, Harman Martin, Oaks, Orange Co.: 1886–'87.

McIver, John Alton, Jonesboro, Moore Co.: A. B., 1881.

McIver, John Fenelon, Winder, Moore Co.: A. B., 1887.

McIver, John McMillan, Moore Co.: A. B., 1862. Egypt.

McIver, William Donald, Egypt, Chatham Co.: A. B., 1884. Lawyer. Sanford.

McKay, Alexander, Augusta, Ga.: A. B., 1827. Dead.

McKay, Alfred, Salisbury: 1811. Dead.

McKay, Daniel McNeill, Cumberland Co.: A. B., 1853.

McKay, James, Salisbury: 1810. Dead.

McKay, John Archibald, Cumberland Co.: A. B., 1853. Physician.

McKay, Neill, Cumberland Co.: 1835–'36. D. D. Presb. Minister.

McKay, Neill, Memphis, Tenn.: A. B., 1851. Dead.

McKay, Neill, Summerville, Harnett Co.: 1875–'76.

McKay, Prentys, Summerville, Harnett Co.: 1875–'76.

McKay, Wilson J., Harnett Co.: 1866–'68. Minister.

McKee, James, Raleigh: 1859–'61. Lt. C. S. A. Physician.

McKellar, William Hamilton, Dallas Co., Ala.: 1856–'58. Born 1838, died 1869.

McKesson, Charles Finley, Morganton: 1865–'68. Born 1849. Lawyer.

McKethan, Edwin Robeson, Fayetteville: 1887–.

McKethan, Edwin Turner, Fayetteville: A. B., 1860. Lt. C. S. A. Died 1888.

McKethan, John Campbell, Cumberland Co.: A. B., 1854. C. S. A. Physician. Dead.

McKethan, William R., Cumberland Co.: 1860–'61. C. S. A. Born 1842, died in service 1861.

McKimmon, Arthur Nelson, Raleigh: A. B., 1860; A. M., 1866. C. S. A. Dead.

McKimmon, James, Raleigh: A. B., 1860. Lt. C. S. A.

McKinnie, David E., Wayne Co.: 1867–'68. Adj. C. S. A. Teacher. Merchant. Princeton, Johnston Co.

McKinnon, Graham, Plainview, Robeson Co.: 1884–'86.

McKinnon, John, Cumberland Co.: A. B., 1857.

McKinnon, Malcolm A., Cumberland Co.: 1838–'39. Dead.

McKinnon, Malcolm McNeill, Robeson Co.: 1852–'53. Dead. Ala.

McKINNON, WILLIAM BETHUNE, Richmond Co.: 1854–'57. Surg. C. S. A. Born 1836, killed in service, 1862.

McKOY, ALLMAND A., Sampson Co.: 1846–'47. Judge Superior Ct. Died 1886.

McKOY, EDWARD, Marlboro Dist., South Carolina: 1807. Physician. Dead.

McLAUCHLIN, ARCHIBALD, Cumberland Co.: A. B., 1856. Dead.

McLAUCHLIN, JOHN CALVIN, Cumberland Co.: A. B., 1857. Lawyer. Wadesboro.

McLAUGHLIN, RICHARD B., Statesville: 1888–'89. Lawyer.

McLAURIN, JAMES, Virginia: 1815. Dead.

McLAURIN, JOSEPH, Wilmington: A. B., 1844. Born 1822. Banker.

McLAURIN, WILLIAM H., Laurinburg, Richmond Co.: 1859–'61.

McLEAN, CHARLES EDGAR, McLeansville, Guilford Co.: 1878–'79.

McLEAN, COLIN MONROE, Bladensboro, Bladen Co.: 1882–'83.

McLEAN, JOHN K., Cheraw, South Carolina: 1854–'56. Physician. Surg. C. S. A. Died 1884.

McLEAN, MURDOCK, Robeson Co.: A. B., 1812; A. M., 1820. Physician. Dead.

McLEAN, NATHANIEL, Robeson Co.: A. B., 1849. Dead.

McLEAN, NEILL ARCHIBALD, Lumberton, Robeson Co.: 1877–'78. Gen. Assem., 1883–'85.

McLEAN, WILLIAM PINKNEY, Harrison, Cass Co., Texas: A. B., 1857. Born 1836. Maj. C. S. A. Mem. Gen. Assem., 1861–'71. M. C., 1875–'77. Mem. Conven., 1875. Dist. Judge. Mt. Pleasant, Texas.

McLEMORE, JEFFERSON H., Carroll Co., Miss.: 1859–'60.

McLEMORE, ROBERT SAMUEL, Gerenton, Carroll Co., Miss.: A. B., 1857. Lawyer.

McLEOD, GILBERT, Euphronia, Moore Co.: 1877–'78.

McLEOD, WILLIS HUNTER, Johnson Co.: A. B., 1840. Dead.

McLERAN, JAMES, Fayetteville: 1814. Dead.

McLERAN, JOHN, Fayetteville: 1813. Dead.

McLIN, HENRY, New Berne: A. B., 1833; A. M., 1850. Lawyer. Druggist. Born 1815, died 1870.

McLIN, JOHN W., Haywood Co., Tenn.: 1857–'58. Dead.

McLIN, WILLIAM, Greenville Co., Va.: 1804. Dead.

McLIN, WILLIAM, Hicksford, Va.: 1822–'25. Dead.

McMILLAN, ANDREW, Richmond Co.: A. B., 1840. Minister.

McMILLAN, ARCHIBALD ALEXANDER, Robeson Co.: A. B., 1862.

McMILLAN, BENJAMIN FRANKLIN, Robeson Co.: 1878–'79.

McMILLAN, FRANKLIN B., Ashe Co.: 1846–'47. Dead.

McMILLAN, GEORGE W., New Hanover Co.: A. B., 1861. C. S. A. Killed in service.

McMILLAN, HAMILTON, Cumberland Co.: A. B., 1857. Lawyer. Gen. Assem. Teacher. Author. Wilson.

McMILLAN, HENRY, Gadsden Co., Fla.: 1858–'61.

McMILLAN, HENRY WILLIAM, Robeson Co.: A. B., 1855. Lawyer. Ark.

McMILLAN, JOHN J., Bladen Co.: 1818. Dead.

McMILLAN, JOHN LUTHER, Robeson Co.: 1878–'79.

McNabb, James Graham, Eufaula, Ala.: 1856–'57. LL. B., 1858. Died 1862.
McNabb, John M., Eufaula, Ala.: 1859–'61. C. S. A. Killed in battle, 1862.
McNair, Dugald Patterson, Robeson Co.: A. B., 1856. C. S. A. Teacher. Dead. Ala.
McNair, Duncan Elizabeth, Robeson Co.: A. B., 1855. Capt. C. S. A. Killed in service.
McNair, John, North Carolina: 1797. Dead.
McNair, John Calvin, Robeson Co.: A. B., 1849; A. M., 1852. Dead.
McNair, Malcolm, Robeson Co.: A. B., 1849. Minister. Died 1874.
McNair, Rory, Robeson Co.: A. B., 1855; A. M. Died 1868.
McNairy, Bartlett Yancy, Guilford Co.: A. B., 1843. Dead.
McNairy, Boyd, Guilford Co.: 1824–'26. Dead.
McNairy, Samuel A., Tennessee: 1801. Dead.
McNatt, Henry Wise, Robeson Co.: 1878–'79.
McNeely, Thomas Chalmers, Salisbury: 1883–'84.
McNeill, Angus Currie, Robeson Co.: A. B., 1839. Minister. Dead.
McNeill, Charles Alexander, Carthage, Moore Co.: 1876–'78.
McNeill, Daniel Hector, Cumberland Co.: 1881–'85. Minister. Marshall, Texas.
McNeill, George, Fayetteville: 1842–'44. Dead.
McNeill, Hector James, Robeson Co.: A. B., 1855. Died 1860.
McNeill, James Archibald, Robeson Co.: A. B., 1852. C. S. A. Teacher. Cameron, Milam Co., Texas.
McNeill, James H., Fayetteville: 1840–'41. Minister. Col. C. S. A. Killed in battle.
McNeill, John Pinkney, Lumberton, Robeson Co.: 1887–.
McNeill, John Quince, Wilmington: A. B., 1819. Dead.
McNeill, Malcolm, Virginia: 1813. Dead.
McNeill, Malcolm Daniel, Union, Moore Co.: 1884–'85.
McNeill, Neill Russell, Raeford: 1888–.
McNeill, Thomas A., Robeson Co.: A. B., 1868. C. S. A. Lawyer. Lumberton.
McNeill, Thomas Irby, Cheraw, S. C.: 1875–'78.
McNeill, William Hamilton, Cumberland Co.: A. B., 1887. Lawyer. Teacher.
McNider, Virginius St. Clair, Edenton: 1865–'67. M. D. Balto. Med. Coll. Jackson.
McPheeters, Samuel Brown, Raleigh: A. B., 1841; D. D. Dead.
McPheeters, William Marcellus, Raleigh: 1837–'38. Prof. Materia Medica. St. Louis, Mo.
McQueen, Archibald, Robeson Co.: A. B., 1812. Minister. Dead.
McQueen, Hugh, Chatham Co.: 1818. Mem. Conv., 1835. Atty. Gen., 1841–'42. Dead.
McQueen, James A., Robeson Co.: 1852–'56. Minister. Dead. Fla.
McQueen, James D., Lumberton, Robeson Co.: 1856–'58. Died 1858.
McQueen, John Knox, Floral College, Robeson Co.: A. B., 1862. C. S. A. Physician. Died 1885. Alabama.

McRackan, William W., Fayetteville: 1828–'29. Dead.
McRae, Aulay Sylvester, Mt. Gilead, Montgomery Co.: 1884–'85. Teacher.
McRae, Cameron Farquhar, Fayetteville: 1825–'26. Minister. Dead.
McRae, Duncan Granger, Montgomery Co.: 1856–'57. C. S. A. Born 1833. Killed in battle 1863.
McRae, Duncan Kirkland, Fayetteville: 1835–'37. LL. D., 1886. Col. C. S. A. Consul at Paris. Died 1888.
McRae, John Burgwyn, Savannah, Ga.: 1862–'63. Lawyer. Jackson.
McRae, James Patterson, Laurinburg, Richmond Co.: 1877–'79.
McRae, Montford Stokes, Mangum, Richmond Co.: 1852–'53. Sergt. C. S. A. Born 1835. Killed in battle 1862.
McRae, Roderick, Laurinburg, Richmond Co.: A. B., 1881.
McRae, Samuel Hinsdale, Fayetteville: 1884–'85. Civil Engineer.
McRae, William Plummer, Warrenton: 1880–'81. Teacher. Petersburg, Va.
McRee, Andrew Franklin, Mecklenburg Co.: A. B., 1841.
McRee, Robert C., Wilmington: 1861–'63. Sergt. C. S. A. Killed in service.
McSween, Murdock J., Richmond Co.: 1857–'59. C. S. A. Lawyer. Journalist. Died 1880.
McWilliams, Frederick Napoleon, Halifax Co.: A. B., 1836. Dead.
Maer, Abram, Bertie Co.: 1813–'17. Born 1795. Lawyer. Teacher. Dead. Georgia.
Majette, Mark, Como, Hertford Co.: 1885–'87. Lawyer.
Makepeace, Colin McRae, Franklinsville, Randolph Co.: 1882–'83.
Mallett, Edward Jones, Fayetteville: A. B., 1818; A. M., 1850 Lawyer. Consul General to Italy, 1858. Paymaster Gen. U. S. A., 1862–'65 Born 1797, died 1883. New York City.
Mallett, Edward, Fayetteville: A. B., 1849. Col. C. S. A. Killed at Bentonsville, 1865.
Mallett, George Hooper, Brooklyn, N. Y.: 1883–'84. Physician. Mexico.
Mallett, Herbert H., Chapel Hill: 1863–'65. C. S. A. Planter. Died 1878. Louisiana.
Mallett, John W., Fayetteville: 1859–'61. Adjt. C. S. A. Sumpter, S. C.
Mallett, John Walker, Chapel Hill: 1875–'76. Planter.
Mallett, Richardson, Chapel Hill: 1858–'61. Lieut. C. S. A. Killed at Gettysburg, 1863.
Malloy, Alexander, Richmond Co.: 1866–'68. Dead.
Malone, John L., Tuscumbia, Ala.: 1845–'46.
Maner, Neverson C., Edgecombe Co.: 1860–'61. C. S. A. Killed in battle.
Maness, William B., Moore Co.: 1865–'66. Dead.
Mangum, Charles Staples, Chapel Hill: 1887–.
Mangum, Ernest Preston, Chapel Hill: A. B., 1885; A. M., 1886. Teacher. Asheville.
Mangum, Priestly Hinton, Orange Co.: A. B., 1815; A. M., 1819. Tutor U. N. C., 1817. Dead.

MANGUM, WILLIAM PRESTON, Orange Co.: 1855–'57. Lieut. C. S. A. Born 1837. Killed at 1st Manassas, 1861.

MANGUM, WILLIE PERSON, Orange Co.: A. B., 1815; A. M; LL. D. Judge Superior Ct., 1819 and 1826. M. C., 1823–'26. U. S. Sen., 1837–'41, and 1841–'53. Pres. U. S. Sen., 1842–'45. Born 1792, died 1861.

MANGUM, WILLIE PERSON, Hillsboro: A. B., 1848. Tutor Wake Forest Coll. Lawyer. Mem. Royal Asiatic Soc. Consul and Consul-general to China and Japan, 1861–'81. Born May 7, 1827, died Feb. 11, 1881. Tien-Tsin, China.

MANLY, BASIL, Raleigh: 1856–'57. Maj. C. S. A. Mayor. Dead.

MANLY, CHARLES, Pittsboro: A. B., 1814; A. M. Lawyer. Atty. for Chatham Co. 30 yrs. Sec. and Treas. Bd. of Trustees, 1821–'68. Pres. Elector 1840. Governor 1849–'51. Born May 13, 1795, died May 1, 1871.

MANLY, CHARLES, Raleigh: 1841–'42. Dead.

MANLY, JOHN HAYWOOD, Raleigh: 1839–'40. Lawyer. Col. C. S. A. Dead.

MANLY, LANGDON CHEVES, Raleigh: A. B., 1845; A. M., 1849. Physician. Dead.

MANLY, MATTHIAS EVANS, Pittsboro: A. B., 1824; A. M., 1829. Judge Superior Ct., 1840–'59. Judge Supreme Ct., 1860–'65. Mem. Conv., 1865. Speaker State Sen., 1866. Elected U. S. Sen., 1867. Born 1801, died 1881. New Berne.

MANLY, WILLIAM HENRY, Raleigh: A. B., 1847. Dead.

MANN, JAMES N., Nash Co.: A. B., 1819. Gen. Assem. Dead.

MANN, JULIAN SMITH, Middleton, Hyde Co.: A. B., 1885. Lawyer.

MANN, RUFUS BROOKS, Henderson Co.: A. B., 1858. Teacher.

MANN, SAMUEL S., Lake Landing, Hyde Co.: 1888–.

MANN, THOMAS JOHN, Belvoir, Chatham Co.: 1869–'70.

MANN, THOMAS N., Nash Co.: 1815. Gen. Assem. Chargé d'Affaires Guatemala. Dead.

MANNING, FREDERICK HAUGHTON, Sunbury, Gates Co.: 1888. Lawyer.

MANNING, ISAAC HALL, Chapel Hill: 1882–'86. Chemist. Wilmington.

MANNING, JAMES SMITH, Pittsboro: A. B., 1879. Born 1859. Lawyer. Durham.

MANNING, JOHN, Edenton: A. B., 1850; A. M.; LL. D., 1883. Born 1830. Gen. Assem. Mem. Conven., 1861. M. C., 1871–'73. Commr. to codify statute laws of N. C., 1881. Prof. Law U. N. C., 1882–. Chapel Hill.

MANNING, JOHN MOORE, Pittsboro: A. B., 1879. Born 1857. Physician. Durham.

MANNING, JOSEPH ALONZO, Norfolk, Va.: A. B., 1852. Physician. Born 1832, died 1860.

MANNING, PIERRE BEAUREGARD, Sunbury, Gates Co.: A. B., 1886. Teacher. Wilmington.

MANNING, THOMAS COURTLAND, Edenton: 1842–'43. LL. D., 1878. Mem. Conven. La., 1861. Brig. Gen. C. S. A., 1863. Judge Supreme Ct., 1864. Chief Justice, 1877. Elected U. S. Sen., 1880. Pres. Elector at large, 1881. Trustee Peabody Fund. U. S. Minister to Mexico, 1886–'87. Died Oct. 11, 1887. Louisiana.

MANNY, THOMAS, Hertford Co.: 1809. Dead.
MARKHAM, HUGH PARIS, Patterson, Orange Co.: 1879–'80.
MARR, GEORGE W. L., Rockingham Co.: 1797. M. C. from Tenn. Dead. Tenn.
MARSH, DANIEL H., Chatham Co.: 1860–'62.
MARSH, JAMES ALEXANDER, Ashboro, Randolph Co.: A. B., 1858. Capt. C. S. A. Dead.
MARSH, ROBERT HENRY, Chatham Co.: A. B., 1858. Minister.
MARSH, WILLIAM H., Ashboro, Randolph Co.: 1849–'51. Dead.
MARSHALL, AQUILA JACKSON, Wilmington: 1886–'87.
MARSHALL, CALVIN Y., Greensboro, Miss.: 1860–'61. Lt. C. S. A.
MARSHALL, JAMES CLEMENT, Wadesboro: A. B., 1861.
MARSHALL, JOHN WINGFIELD, Raleigh: 1885–'86.
MARSHALL, MATTHIAS MURRAY, Pittsboro: A. B., 1863; A. M., 1866; D. D. Born 1846. Episcopal Minister. Raleigh.
MARSHALL, ROBERT L., Halifax Co.: 1802. Dead.
MARSHALL, THOMAS ASHE, Wadesboro: 1884–'85.
MARTIN, CHARLES F., Columbia, Tenn.: 1859–'61. Capt. C. S. A. Planter. Ark.
MARTIN, CLARENCE DUDLEY, Wilmington: 1860–'61. C. S. A. Born 1844. Killed in service, 1862.
MARTIN, COLEMAN A., Mississippi: 1810. Dead.
MARTIN, EDMUND LOFTIN, A. B., 1823.
MARTIN, EDWARD ALEXANDER, Richmond, Va.: A. B., 1862; A. M., 1866. Adj. C. S. A. Teacher. Born 1842, died 1870.
MARTIN, EUGENE STUART, Wilmington: A. B., 1860. Born 1840. Lt. C. S. A. Lawyer.
MARTIN, GEORGE S., Columbia, Tenn.: A. B., 1860. Lieut. and Aide-de-camp C. S. A. Born Jan. 3, 1840. Wounded in service and died Sept. 23, 1863.
MARTIN, HENRY, Granville Co.: 1799. Dead.
MARTIN, HENRY, Granville Co.: 1822–'24.
MARTIN, HUGH, Stokes Co.: A. B., 1823. Dead.
MARTIN, JAMES, Stokes Co.: A. B., 1806; A. M., 1810. Tutor U. N. C., 1806. Judge Superior Ct. Dead.
MARTIN, JAMES, Pickens Co., Ala.: A. B., 1825.
MARTIN, JAMES FRANKLIN, Stokes Co.: A. B., 1820. Physician. Dead.
MARTIN, JOHN CHASTINE, White Oak, Bladen Co.: 1886–'87. Dead.
MARTIN, JOSEPH, Stokes Co.: 1813. Dead.
MARTIN, JULIUS CÆSAR, Briar Creek, Wilkes Co.: 1884–'85. Lawyer.
MARTIN, MARTIAL T., Vermillionville, La.: 1859–'60.
MARTIN, ROBERT BRUCE, Elizabeth City: 1876–'77. R. R. Service.
MARTIN, ROBERT CAMPBELL, Assumption Parish, La.: B. S., 1859. Lt. C. S. A. Planter. Albemarle, La.
MARTIN, ROBERT GOODLOE, Granville Co.: A. B., 1822. Dead.
MARTIN, SAMUEL, Stokes Co.: 1819.
MARTIN, SAMUEL A., Stokes Co.: 1801. Dead.
MARTIN, THOMAS G., Nashville, Tenn.: 1850–'51. Planter. Maury Co., Tenn.

MARTIN, WILLIAM, Granville Co.: 1798. Dead.
MARTIN, WILLIAM FRANCIS, Elizabeth City: A. B., 1842. Physician. Col. C. S. A. Died 1880.
MARTIN, WILLIAM WHITMELL, Albemarle, La.: 1857–'58. Maj. C. S. A. Born 1840. Killed at Vicksburg, 1863.
MASON, EDMUND, Hicksford, Va.: 1822–'23. Died 1824.
MASON, EDWARD, North Carolina: 1798. Dead.
MASON, JAMES BRUCE, Davie Co.: 1867–'68. Born 1844. Lawyer. Gen. Assem. Chapel Hill.
MASON, JAMES BRUCE, Chapel Hill: 1887–'88. Durham.
MASON, JOHN R., Virginia: 1814. Dead.
MASON, JOHN R., Sussex Co., Va.: 1862–'63. Minister.
MASON, JOHN YOUNG, Hicksford, Va.: A. B., 1816; LL. D., 1845. Lawyer. Gen. Assem. Va. Judge Superior Ct. M. C., 1831–'37. Judge U. S. Dist. Ct. for Va., 1837–'44. Secretary of the Navy, 1844–'45, and 1846–'49. Atty. Gen. U. S., 1845–'46. Secretary of State, U. S. Pres. Va. Conven., 1850. Minister to France, 1853–'59. Born April 18, 1799, died Oct. 3, 1859.
MASON, LAWRENCE S., Tennessee: 1825–'26.
MASON, RICHARD HENRY, Raleigh: A. B., 1845; A. M., 1850. Minister. Dead.
MASON, ROBERT HARRISON, Hicksford, Va.: A. B., 1822. Physician. Dead.
MASON, THOMAS WILLIAMS, Brunswick Co., Va.: A. B., 1858. Born 1839. C. S. A. Lawyer. Gen. Assem. N. C. Garysburg, N. C.
MASON, WILLIAM S., Raleigh: 1845–'47. Lawyer. Died 1885.
MASSEY, CHARLES WESLEY, Durham: 1884–'86.
MASSEY, SAMUEL BUCKNER, South Carolina: 1834–'37.
MATHESON, WILLIAM MALCOLM, Montgomery Co.: 1881–'82.
MATTHEWS, AUGUSTUS, Hamilton, Martin Co.: 1881–'83. Dentist. Plymouth.
MATTHEWS, GEORGE, Farmville, Va.: 1816. Dead.
MATTHEWS, JOSIAH J., Linden, Texas: 1859–'61. C. S. A. Lawyer. Dist. Atty. Greenville, Texas.
MATTHEWS, SAMUEL P., Huntsville, Ala.: 1854–'55. Born 1837. Montgomery, Ala.
MAULTSBY, JOHN ALEXANDER, Whiteville, Columbus Co.: 1835–'39. Lawyer. Merchant. St. Louis, Mo. Born 1818, died 1887.
MAUNEY, LYCURGUS ELISHA, Murphy, Cherokee Co.: 1878–'80.
MAVERICK, GEORGE M., San Antonio, Texas: 1865–'67. Born 1845. C. S. A. Lawyer. St. Louis, Mo.
MAVERICK, LEWIS, San Antonio, Texas: A. B., 1861. Maj. C. S. A. Born 1839, died 1866, from wound received at Blair's Landing.
MAVERICK, WILLIE H., San Antonio, Texas: 1865–'68. C. S. A. Lawyer.
MAY, JAMES E., Greensboro, Ala.: 1838–'40. Dead.
MAY, JAMES T., Eutaw, Ala.: 1840–'42. Died 1856.
MAY, PLEASANT HUGH, South Carolina: A. B., 1818. Dead.
MAYFIELD, JOHN W., Warren Co.: 1853–'54. Lieut. 12th N. C., C. S. A. Killed in service.

Mayhew, Thomas William, Hyde Co.: 1878–'82. Lawyer. Engelhard.
Maynard, Ernest Patrick, Wake Co.: 1875–'78.
Means, George Washington, Concord, Cabarrus Co.: 1876–'77.
Means, James M., Concord, Cabarrus Co.: 1865–'68.
Means, Paul Barringer, Concord, Cabarrus Co.: A. B., 1868. C. S. A. State Senator. Lawyer.
Means, Robert A., Columbus, Miss.: 1857–'58.
Means, Robert Work, Concord, Cabarrus Co.: A. B., 1867. Dead.
Meares, Gaston, Wilmington: 1838–'39. Col. C. S. A. Killed in battle.
Meares, John London, Wilmington: A. B., 1843. Physician. Dead. San Francisco, Cal.
Meares, Oliver Pendleton, Wilmington: A. B., 1848. Col. C. S. A. Judge Crim. Ct., Wilmington and Charlotte.
Meares, Thomas Davis, Wilmington: A. B., 1839; A. M., 1843. Dead.
Meares, Thomas Davis, Brunswick Co.: 1864–'65.
Meares, Walker, Wilmington: A. B., 1853.
Meares, William Belvidere, Wilmington: 1802. Dead.
Meares, William Belvidere, Wilmington: A. B., 1846. Physician.
Mebane, Alexander, Orange Co.: A. B., 1831. Minister. Born 1806, died 1846.
Mebane, Benjamin Franklin, Orange Co.: A. B., 1847. M. D. Univ. Pa. Gen. Assem. Born 1823, died 1884.
Mebane, Cornelius, Orange Co.: A. B., 1860. Born 1839. Adj. C. S. A. Manufacturer. Swepsonville.
Mebane, Frank Carter, Wentworth, Rockingham Co.: 1888–.
Mebane, Freeman, Orange Co.: 1819.
Mebane, George Allen, Mebaneville, Alamance Co.: 1880–'83. Physician.
Mebane, Giles, Orange Co.: A. B., 1831. Gen. Assem. Speaker State Senate. Milton.
Mebane, James, Orange Co.: 1795. First President Dialectic Society. Mem. H. of Com., 8 terms. Speaker of the House, 1821. Born 1774, died 1857.
Mebane, James Edwin, Madison, Rockingham Co.: 1886–'87. Minister.
Mebane, John Alexander, Greensboro: 1845–'46. Lieut. U. S. A. Born 1830, died 1854.
Mebane, John Briggs, Chatham Co.: A. B., 1809. Dead.
Mebane, John Wood, Fayette Co., Tenn.: A. B., 1860. Capt. Artillery, C. S. A. Born Feb. 18, 1840. Killed at Kennesaw Mt., Ga., June 18, 1864.
Mebane, William Graves, Fayette Co., Tenn.: A. B., 1859. Born 1838. Capt. C. S. A. Macon, Tenn.
Mebane, William Kinchen, Orange Co.: A. B., 1821. Born 1801, died 1844.
Mebane, William Nelson, Greensboro: A. B., 1833; A. M., 1839. Minister. Dead.
Mebane, William Nelson, Rockingham Co.: 1860–'61. C. S. A. Mem. H. of Com., 1874–'75. State Sen., 1876–'77. Lawyer. Wentworth.
Mebane, William Thomas, Greensboro: A. B., 1845; A. M., 1850. Born 1825. M. D. Univ. of Pa. Eureka, Ark.

MELVIN, JUDGE SHATTOCK, Brandon, Miss.: 1855–'57. Born 1839. Adj. C. S. A. Planter. Pelahatchee, Miss.

MENDENHALL, JAMES RUFFIN, Jamestown, Guilford Co.: A. B., 1850.

MERCER, JOHN R., Edgecombe Co.: 1840–'42. Physician.

MERRIMON, CHARLES JOHNSTON, Raleigh: 1886–'87.

MERRITT, ABRAM HAYWOOD, Chatham Co.: A. B., 1856; A. M., 1859. Journalist. Pittsboro.

MERRITT, ALFRED GOWAN, Nashville, Tenn.: A. B., 1853. C. S. A. Gen. Assem. Judge Chancery Court.

MERRITT, EDWARD SAMUEL, Chapel Hill: 1882–'83. Druggist.

MERRITT, JAMES SHANKS, Person Co.: 1880–'81. Lawyer.

MERRITT, LEONIDAS HAYWOOD, Pittsboro: 1888–.

MERRITT, LEONIDAS JOHN, Chatham Co.: A. B., 1854. Lawyer. Lieut. C. S. A. Mem. Convention, 1861. Mem. Confed. Congress. Born 1831. Killed in battle 1862.

MERRITT, RUFUS GRANT, Pittsboro: 1875–'77. Miss.

MERRITT, WILLIAM HENRY, Orange Co.: 1869–'70.

METTS, JAMES ISAAC, Wilmington: 1860–'61. Capt. C. S. A. Broker. Chicago.

MEWBORN, WILLIAM EDGAR, Kinston: 1882–'83.

MHOON, JOSEPH J., Tuscumbia, Ala.: 1838–'41.

MHOON, WILLIAM SPIVEY, Bertie Co.: A. B., 1821. Treasurer N. C., 1830–'35. Dead.

MIAL, LEONIDAS LEMAY, Wake Co.: A. B., 1881.

MICHAUX, CHARLES EDWARD, Woodburn, Person Co.: 1886–'87.

MICHIE, WILLIAM COCHRAN, Bastrop, La.: A. B., 1861. Lawyer. St. Joseph, La.

MICKLE, JOHN M., Haynesville, Ala.: 1851–'52. Capt. C. S. A. Killed in service.

MICKLE, JOSEPH CALDWELL, Chapel Hill: 1862–'64. Born 1844. C.S.A. Minister. Teacher. Bryan, Texas.

MICKS, WENTWORTH SWIFT, Clinton: 1883–'84.

MICOU, AUGUSTIN, New Orleans, La.: A. B, 1860. Lieut. C. S. A. Dead.

MIDDLETON, ARTHUR, Virginia: 1844–'45. Dead.

MILLENDER, MARION CHARLES, Selma, Johnston Co.: 1880–'82.

MILLER, CHARLES E., North Carolina: 1829–'30.

MILLER, GEORGE, Duplin Co.: A. B., 1827. Dead.

MILLER, HENRY C., Pendleton Dist., S. C.: 1861–'62. C. S. A. Killed in service.

MILLER, HENRY WATKINS, Buckingham Co., Va.: A. B., 1834; A. M., 1837.

MILLER, HUGH LEE, Goldsboro: 1886–.

MILLER, JAMES ANDREW, Rutherfordton: A. B., 1859. Lt. C. S. A.

MILLER, JAMES DANIEL, Kinston: Ph. B., 1881. Teacher. Raleigh.

MILLER, JAMES P., Person Co.: 1809. Dead.

MILLER, JOHN F., Cleveland Co.: 1854–'55. Physician. Supt. Insane Asylum. Goldsboro.

MILLER, JOHN O., Wilmington: 1858–'59. Capt. C. S. A.

MILLER, RICHARD, Duplin Co.: 1816. Dead.
MILLER, RICHARD E., Kenansville, Duplin Co.: 1857–'59. C. S. A.
MILLER, THOMAS, Warren Co.: 1803. Dead.
MILLER, WILLIAM, Warren Co.: 1802. Gen. Assem. Atty. Gen., 1810. Speaker H. of Commons, 1812–'13. Gov. N. C., 1814–'16. Chargé d'affaires Guatemala, 1825. Died 1825.
MILLER, WILLIAM H., Virginia: 1850–'51. Dead.
MILLER, WILLIAM H., Shelby: A. B., 1867.
MILLER, WILLIAM R., Raleigh: 1844–'47. Physician. Dead.
MILLER, WILLIS L., Raleigh: 1846–'50. Minister. Dead.
MILLS, JULIUS C., Caswell Co.: 1863–'64. Physician.
MILLS, WILLIAM H. H., Nashville, Tenn.: 1860–'62.
MIMMS, THOMAS S., Todd Co., Ky.: A. B., 1860. C. S. A.
MITCHELL, AMERICUS COLUMBUS, Glennville, Ala.: 1866–'68. Born 1850. Planter.
MITCHELL, ANDERSON, Wilkes Co.: A. B., 1821; A. M., 1824. Tutor U. N. C., 1821–'22. Gen. Assem. M. C., 1842. Judge Superior Ct., 1865. Born 1800, died 1876.
MITCHELL, CHARLES ANDREWS, Chapel Hill: A. B., 1857. Surgeon C. S. A. Died 1868. Miss.
MITCHELL, GEORGE H., Hillsboro: 1837–'38. Physician. Died 1846.
MITCHELL, HUTCHINS G., Granville Co.: 1813. Dead.
MITCHELL, JAMES BILLINGSLEA, Glennville, Ala.: A. B., 1867. Born 1844. Lt. C. S. A. Lawyer. Gen. Assem.
MITCHELL, JAMES C., Chapel Hill: 1827–'28.
MITCHELL, JOHN WILLIAM X., Leesville, S. C.: 1878–'79.
MITCHELL, JULIUS CÆSAR, Glennville, Ala.: 1859–'61. Capt. C. S. A. Born 1842, died 1875.
MITCHELL, LUECO, Salisbury: 1854–'56. Dead.
MITCHELL, RANDOLPH, Glennville, Ala.: 1860–'61. C. S. A. Born 1843. Killed at Fredericksburg.
MITCHELL, ROBERT, Caswell Co.: 1799. Dead.
MITCHELL, STOCKLEY DONELSON, Rogersville, Tenn.: A. B., 1815. Clerk of Ct. Hawkins Co. Clerk of Gen. Assem., 1835–'43. Pres. Bank of Tenn. Born March 25, 1795, died June 16, 1861.
MITCHELL, WILLIAM P., Warren Co.: 1842–'43. Dead.
MOBLEY, JOHN C., Fairfield District, S. C.: 1856–'57.
MOIR, ALEXANDER FRANCISCO, Stokes Co.: 1880–'81.
MONROE, EDWARD DANIEL, Jonesboro, Moore Co.: Ph. B., 1883. Teacher.
MONROE, JAMES RANDLETT, Fayetteville: A. B., 1885. Teacher. Asheville.
MONROE, JOHN W., Rowan Co.: 1819.
MONTAGUE, ALEXANDER, Wake Co.: 1862–'65.
MONTAGUE, WALTER HENRY, Wake Co.: A. B., 1862.
MONTFORT, WILLIAM J., Onslow Co.: 1855–'56. Physician.
MONTGOMERY, JAMES ARCHIBALD, Abbeville, S. C.: A. B., 1854. Born 1830. Teacher. Planter. Anderson C. H., S. C.
MONTGOMERY, JAMES NEWTON, Caswell Co.: A. B., 1848. Dead.

MONTGOMERY, JOHN CARR, Hertford Co.: A. B., 1807. Dead.
MONTGOMERY, WILLIAM JAMES, Montgomery Co.: A. B., 1855. Born 1834. Maj. C. S. A. Solicitor 9th Dist. Concord.
MOODY, WILLIAM ALEXANDER, Robeson Co.: 1881–'82.
MOORE, ALBERT GALLATIN, Opelousas, La.: 1858–'61. Lt. C. S. A. Born 1843. Killed at Port Republic.
MOORE, ALEXANDER DUNCAN, Chapel Hill: A. B., 1845. Physician. Born 1825. Dead.
MOORE, ALFRED, Brunswick Co.: 1798. Gen. Assem. Speaker H. of Commons, 1823–'24. Lawyer. Died 1837.
MOORE, ALFRED CLEON, Surry Co.: 1825–'26. Gen. Assem. Va. Col. C. S. A. Born 1805. Dead. Wythe Co., Va.
MOORE, ALFRED M., Brunswick Co.: 1826–'27. Dead.
MOORE, ANDREW JACKSON, Pitt Co.: 1858–'61. Capt. C. S. A. Minister. Whitaker.
MOORE, AUGUSTUS, Edenton: A. B., 1824. Judge Superior Ct., 1848–'51. Died 1851.
MOORE, AUGUSTUS MINTON, Edenton: 1859–'61. Lt. C. S. A. Lawyer.
MOORE, BARTHOLOMEW FIGURES, Halifax Co.: A. B., 1820; LL. D., 1868. Mem. H. of Com. Atty. Gen., 1848–'51. Commr. to revise statutes of N. C. Mem. Conven., 1865. Born 1801, died 1878.
MOORE, BARTHOLOMEW FIGURES, Raleigh: 1854–'55. Born 1840.
MOORE, BENJAMIN FRANKLIN, Wadesboro: 1856–'58. Born 1840. Lt. C. S. A. Physician. Ashley Co., Ark.
MOORE, BENJAMIN RUSH, Person Co.: 1853–'54. Lt. Col. C. S. A. Wilmington.
MOORE, BENJAMIN TYSON, Stokes Co.: A. B., 1823. Dead.
MOORE, EUGENE DICK, Lenoir: 1886–'87.
MOORE, FURNEY T., Harnett Co.: 1880–'81.
MOORE, GABRIEL, Stokes Co.: 1822–'25. Dead.
MOORE, GEORGE BODDIE, Raleigh: 1859–'61. Born 1841. C. S. A. Planter.
MOORE, GEORGE J., Chapel Hill: 1848–'50. Dead.
MOORE, GIDEON E., Stokes Co.: 1822. Dead.
MOORE, GODWIN COTTON, St. John's, Hertford Co.: 1822. M. D. Univ. Pa. Gen. Assem. Born 1804, died 1880.
MOORE, HENRY, Louisburg: 1821. Dead.
MOORE, JAMES, Martin Co.: A. B., 1825. Dead.
MOORE, JAMES, Wilmington: 1856–'57.
MOORE, JAMES, Raleigh: 1877–'79. Born 1858.
MOORE, JAMES B., Granville Co.: 1860–'61. Dead.
MOORE, JAMES C., Jackson, Miss.: A. B., 1854. Lt. Col. C. S. A. Killed at Mumfordsville, Ky., 1862.
MOORE, JAMES EDWIN, Martin Co.: A. B., 1862. Lt. C. S. A. Gen. Assem. Lawyer. Williamston.
MOORE, JOHN D., Wilmington: 1843–'44. Dead.
MOORE, JOHN MILLER, Rock Hill, S. C.: 1883–'84.
MOORE, JOHN SWANN, Chapel Hill: A. B., 1853. Dead.

MOORE, JOHN WHEELER, Maple Lawn, Hertford Co.: A. B., 1853. Lawyer. Pres. Elector, 1860. Maj. C. S. A. Author "Heirs of St. Kilda," "History of N. C.," etc.
MOORE, JUNIUS ALEXANDER, Wilmington: A. B., 1816. Dead.
MOORE, LEVI J., Lenoir Co.: 1866–'68. Planter. Kinston.
MOORE, MATTHEW J., Platt Co., Mo.: 1859–'61. Planter. Carpenteria, Cal.
MOORE, MATTHEW M., North Carolina: 1827.
MOORE, MATTHEW REDD, Stokes Co.: A. B., 1815. Gen. Assem. Mem. Conv., 1835. Dead.
MOORE, MAURICE, Brunswick Co.: 1795. Dead.
MOORE, MOSES W., Salisbury: 1823–'25. Dead.
MOORE, ROBERT, Rowan Co.: 1796. Dead.
MOORE, ROBERT ALFRED, Bradshaw: 1888–.
MOORE, PEYTON P., Orange Co.: 1821.
MOORE, THEOPHILUS W., Person Co.: 1851–'52. Minister.
MOORE, THOMAS LAKE, Greenville, S. C.: Ph. B., 1889.
MOORE, URIAH GRANTHAM, Goldsboro: 1882–'83.
MOORE, VAN BODDIE, Raleigh: 1875–'77. Born 1855.
MOORE, WILLIAM, Rowan Co.: 1796. Dead.
MOORE, WILLIAM, Wilmington: 1807. Dead.
MOORE, WILLIAM ARMSTEAD, Edenton: 1848–'51. Judge Superior Ct. Speaker H. of Com. Dead.
MOORE, WILLIAM HARDING, Chapel Hill: 1845–'46. Physician. Supt. Insane Asylum, Goldsboro. Born 1828. Dead.
MOORE, YANCY DAVIS, Point Caswell, Pender Co.: 1884–'85.
MOREHEAD, ABRAM FORREST, Rockingham Co.: A. B., 1834. Tutor U. N. C., 1835. Lawyer. Born 1816, died 1837.
MOREHEAD, EUGENE L., Greensboro: A. B., 1868. C. S. A. Banker. Born 1845, died 1889. Durham.
MOREHEAD, HENRY J., Greensboro: 1849–'51.
MOREHEAD, JAMES TURNER, Rockingham Co.: A. B., 1819. Gen. Assem. M. C., 1852. Born 1799, died 1875.
MOREHEAD, JAMES TURNER, Greensboro: A. B., 1858. Born 1838. C. S. A. Gen. Assem. Pres. Senate, 1872.
MOREHEAD, JAMES TURNER, Greensboro: A. B., 1861. Adj. 3d N. C. Cav., C. S. A. State Senator. Mem. Conv., 1875. Leaksville.
MOREHEAD, JOHN HENRY, Greensboro: 1848–'51. Col. C. S. A. Born 1833. Killed at Gettysburg, 1863.
MOREHEAD, JOHN LINDSAY, Greensboro: A. B., 1853. Born 1833. Col. C. S. A. Banker and Manufacturer. Charlotte.
MOREHEAD, JOHN MOTLEY, Rockingham Co.: A. B., 1817; A. M., 1827. Tutor U. N. C., 1817. Mem. Conv., 1835. Governor 1841–'45. First Pres. N. C. R. R. Mem. Confed. Congress 1861. Manufacturer. Born 1796, died 1866.
MOREHEAD, JOHN MOTLEY, Charlotte: A. B., 1886.
MOREHEAD, JOHN MOTLEY, Leaksville, Rockingham Co.: 1887–.
MOREHEAD, JOSEPH M., Greensboro: 1857–'58. Born 1840. Lieut. C. S. A. Clerk and Master in Equity.

MOREHEAD, ROBERT LINDSAY, Greensboro: 1849–'51. Capt. C. S. A. Born 1831, died 1876.

MORGAN, ALEXANDER RUFUS, Oak Ridge: 1883–'84. Teacher. Minister. Yadkin College.

MORGAN, GEORGE THOMAS, Gates Co.: A. B., 1856. Teacher. C. S. A. Killed in service.

MORGAN, JESSE DAVID, Elevation, Johnston Co.: 1882–'84. Smithfield.

MORGAN, JOHN, Orange Co.: 1869–'70. Died 1886.

MORGAN, WILLIAM P., 1826.

MORING, JOHN M., Chatham Co.: 1860–'62. Gen. Assem. Speaker N. C. H. of Rep.

MORISEY, SAMUEL BUNTING, Clinton: 1848–'49. Born 1830. Physician.

MORISEY, THOMAS JUNIUS, Clinton: A. B., 1842; A. M., 1845. Born 1818. Lawyer. Gen. Assem. Planter.

MORPHIS, JAMES M., Orange Co.: 1843–'45. Lawyer. Author. Dead. Austin, Texas.

MORRIS, ALGERNON R., Orange Co.: 1855–'57.

MORRIS, JOHN MANLY, Wilton, Granville Co.: 1884–'85.

MORRIS, JOSEPH ALGERNON, Wilton, Granville Co.: A. B., 1887.

MORRIS, WILLIAM MURPHY, Orange Co.: 1869–'70.

MORRISON, ANGUS D., Richmond Co.: 1849–'52. Dead.

MORRISON, COLUMBUS, Mecklenburg Co.: A. B., 1825. Physician. Dead.

MORRISON, ELAM JOHNSTON, Mecklenburg Co.: A. B., 1818. Minister. Dead.

MORRISON, JAMES, Mecklenburg Co.: A. B., 1814; A. M., 1819. Minister. Dead.

MORRISON, JAMES ELISHA, Cabarrus Co.: A. B., 1825. Minister.

MORRISON, JOHN MURDOCK, Richmond Co.: A. B., 1854. Dead.

MORRISON, NORMAN ALLEN, Richmond Co.: A. B., 1857. Died 1859.

MORRISON, ROBERT HALL, Cabarrus Co.: A. B., 1818; D. D., 1838. Born 1798. First Pres. Davidson College. Cottage Home, Lincoln Co. Died May 13, 1889.

MORRISON, WASHINGTON, Cabarrus Co.: A. B., 1822. Born 1801, died 1836.

MORROW, ALEXANDER, Orange Co.: 1832–'36. Physician. Born 1811, died 1855.

MORROW, CALVIN NEWTON, Mebaneville, Alamance Co.: A. B., 1859. Born 1832. Minister.

MORROW, DANIEL FOUST, Alamance Co.: 1860–'61. Born 1842. C. S. A. Merchant. Oaks, Orange Co.

MORROW, EDWARD G., Minden, La.: 1857–'58.

MORROW, ELIJAH GRAHAM, Chapel Hill: A. B., 1856. Capt. C. S. A. Born 1832. Killed at Gettysburg, 1863.

MORROW, ELIJAH THEODORE, Orange Co.: A. B., 1859. Born 1839. C. S. A. Refugio, Texas.

MORROW, GEORGE W., Orange Co.: A. B., 1826. Teacher. Born 1798, died 1835.

MORROW, RICHARD ALEXANDER, Chapel Hill: 1859–'61. C. S. A. Born 1842. Killed at Fredericksburg, 1862.

MORROW, THOMAS A., Alamance Co.: 1858–'61.
MORROW, WILLIAM HENRY, Chapel Hill: A. B., 1853. C. S. A. Physician. Born 1829, died 1868.
MORROW, WILLIAM PARKS, Orange Co.: 1833–'34. Teacher. Planter. Born 1806, died 1877.
MORSE, BRIANT P., Natchitoches, La.: 1859–'61.
MORTON, WILLIAM ZENAS, Washington: 1877–'78. Lawyer. Williamston.
MOSELEY, JAMES LITTLETON, Warrenton: A. B., 1847. Dead.
MOSELEY, PALMER, Lenoir Co.: 1805. Dead.
MOSLEY, WILLIAM DUNN, Lenoir Co.: A. B., 1818; A. M., 1821. Tutor U. N. C., 1817. Pres. State Sen., 1832–'36. Mem. Gen. Assem. Fla., 1840. First Governor of Fla., 1845–'49. Born 1795, died 1863.
MOSER, ROBERT WILLIAM, Monroe, Union Co.: 1883–'85.
MOSES, SIDNEY A., Goldsboro: 1855–'56. Dead.
MOTZ, CHARLES, Lincolnton: 1861–'62.
MOYE, FRANCIS M., Stantonsburg, Wilson Co.: 1857–'58. Merchant.
MULLINS, HENRY, Fayetteville: A. B., 1857. Lawyer. Capt. C. S. A. Killed at Williamsburg, 1862.
MULLINS, WILLIAM SIDNEY, Fayetteville: A. B., 1842; A. M., 1845. Lawyer. Dead.
MUNGER, NELSON H., Darlington District, S. C.: 1835–'36.
MUNN, ANGUS, Bladen Co.: A. B., 1856. Teacher. Little River Academy.
MURCHISON, KENNETH M., Manchester, Cumberland Co.: A. B., 1853. Col. C. S. A. Merchant. New York City.
MURCHISON, WILLIAM EDWIN, Summerville, Harnett Co.. 1866–'68. Merchant. Lawyer. Jonesboro, Moore Co.
MURDOCK, ANDREW, South Carolina: 1805. Dead.
MURDOCK, JAMES H., South Carolina: A. B., 1817. Dead.
MURFREE, HARDY, Murfreesboro, Tenn.: A. B., 1848.
MURFREE, MATTHIAS, Hertford Co.: 1808. Dead.
MURFREE, WILLIAM H., Murfreesboro, Tenn.: 1843–'45.
MURFREE, WILLIAM HARDY, Hertford Co.: A. B., 1801. Lawyer. Gen. Assem. M. C., 1813. Pres. Elector. Died 1827.
MURPHEY, ARCHIBALD DEBOW, Caswell Co.: A. B., 1799. Prof. Ancient Lang., 1800. State Senator, 1812–'18. Judge Superior Ct., 1818–'20. Reporter Supreme Ct. Born 1777, died 1832.
MURPHY, CHARLES B., Cumberland Co.: 1856–'58. C. S. A. Killed in service.
MURPHY, HANSON FINLA, South Washington, Beaufort Co.: 1885–'89.
MURPHY, JAMES DIXON, Pender Co.: Ph. B., 1881. Lawyer. Greenville.
MURPHY, JOHN A., New Hanover Co.: 1858–'60. Sergt. C. S. A.
MURPHY, JOHN H., Burke Co.: 1844–'47. Born 1830. Lawyer. Planter. Asheville.
MURPHY, PETER U., Orange Co.: 1824–'25.
MURPHY, ROBERT, Bedford Co., Tenn.: 1857–'59.
MURPHY, ROBERT THOMAS, Sampson Co.: A. B., 1861. Lieut. 20th N. C., C. S. A. Clerk and Master in Equity. Died Oct. 6, 1866.
MURPHY, SMITH, Greenwood, Miss.: 1857–'59.

Murphy, Victor Moreau, Orange Co.: A. B., 1823; A. M., 1829. Physician. Dead.
Murphy, Walter, Salisbury: 1888–.
Murphy, William, Spartanburg, S. C.: 1850–'51.
Murphy, William, Salisbury: A. B., 1858. Dead.
Murphy, William Debow, Orange Co.: A. B., 1821. Dead.
Murray, Cromwell Pitt, St. George's, S. C.: 1880–'81. Lawyer.
Murray, Lemuel, Orange Co.: 1831–'32. Minister. Dead.
Muse, John B., Pasquotank Co.: 1825–'26. Planter. Gen. Assem. Dead.
Myers, George Boggan, Wadesboro: 1846–'48. Miss.
Myers, John Gray Blount, Washington: A. B., 1843. M. D. Univ. Pa. Born 1823. Planter.
Myers, Joseph D., Washington: 1851–'53. Physician. Capt. C. S. A.
Myers, R. L., Washington: 1836. Civil Engineer. Merchant. Dead.
Myrick, John Douglas, Hertford Co.: A. B., 1847; A. M., 1850. Maj. C. S. A. Dead.
Myrick, Thomas N., Hertford Co.: 1843–'44. Physician. Dead.
Nash, Frederick, Hillsboro: 1830–'33. Minister. Dead.
Nash, Frederick, Hillsboro: 1863–'64. 18th N. C., C. S. A. Born June 9, 1844; taken prisoner at Spottsylvania C. H. and died in prison Aug. 1, 1864.
Nash, Frederick Kollock, Hillsboro: 1855–'57.
Nash, George Wilcox, Pittsboro: 1869–'70.
Nash, Henry Kollock, Hillsboro: A. B., 1836; A. M., 1843. Lawyer. Gen. Assem.
Nash, Shepard K., Hillsboro: 1838–'39. Dead.
Neal, George Washington, Hertford Co.: A. B., 1852. Teacher. New Berne.
Neal, James N., Chatham Co.: 1831–'32. Born 1804, died 1832.
Neal, John, Brunswick Co.: 1804. Gen. Assem. Planter. Died 1832.
Neal, John, Louisburg: A. B., 1854. Dead.
Neal, John William, Stokes Co.: A. B., 1881. Physician.
Neal, Joseph Walter, Meadows, Stokes Co.: 1886–'87.
Neal, Nathan P., Franklin Co.: 1857–'58. C. S. A. Dead. Texas.
Neal, Richard Smith, Scotland Neck: Ph. B., 1885. Civ. Engineer.
Neal, Thomas C., Mecklenburg Co.: 1845–'46. Physician.
Neale, Henry H., Brunswick Co.: 1810. Planter. Died 1828.
Nelms, Charles G., Anson Co.: 1832–'36. Lieut. Col. C. S. A. Killed in service.
Nelms, Ebenezer, Anson Co.: 1835–'36.
Nelms, Joseph P., Anson Co.: 1841–'42.
Nesbitt, James King, Statesville: A. B., 1828. M. D. Univ. Pa. Died 1872.
Nevill, Samuel Goodman, Orange Co.: 1880–'82. Tenn.
Nevill, Whitley W., Orange Co.: 1825–'29.
Neville, Gilbert G., Bolivar, Tenn.: 1851–'53. Merchant.
Newby, Nathan, Perquimans Co.: A. B., 1852. Gen. Assem. Planter. Born 1830, died 1862.
Newby, Thomas Mullin, Perquimans Co.: A. B., 1846. Planter. Born 1825, died 1862.

NEWCOME, ROBERT A., New York: 1815. Dead.
NEWMAN, JOHN URQUHART, Suffolk, Va.: Ph. B., 1885; Ph. D. Minister. Prof. Antioch College. Yellow Springs, O.
NEWNAN, DANIEL, Salisbury: 1796. M. C. Dead.
NEWSOM, ROBERT, Virginia: 1815. Dead.
NEWTON, CHRISTOPHER COLUMBUS, Chapel Hill: 1884–'86. Baptist Missionary. Lagos, Central Africa.
NICHOLLS, JOSHUA ROBERTSON, Scotland Neck: 1879-'80. Banker. Birmingham, Ala.
NICHOLS, WILLIAM CHARLES, New Berne, Ala.: A. B., 1854. M. D. Balt. Med. Coll. Surgeon C. S. A. Editor. City Physician New Orleans. Born 1834, died 1871.
NICHOLSON, ALFRED OSBORNE POPE, Columbia, Tenn.: A. B., 1827. Gen. Assem., 1833–'39. State Sen., 1843–'45. U. S. Sen., 1840-'42 and 1859-'61. Author Compilation of Laws of Tenn. Chancellor, 1845. Pres. Bank of Tenn. Journalist. Mem. Conv., 1870. Chief Justice Supreme Ct. Tenn. Born Aug. 31, 1808, died March 23, 1876.
NICHOLSON, EDWARD A. T., Halifax Co.: 1860–'62. Capt. C. S. A. Killed at Hare's Hill, March 25, 1865.
NICHOLSON, GUILFORD, Halifax Co.: A. B., 1861. Lieut. Col. C. S. A. Planter. Died 1884. Canton, Miss.
NICHOLSON, HUNTER, Columbia, Tenn.: A. B., 1855. Born June 9, 1834. Major and A. A. G., C. S. A. Journalist. Prof. Agr. and Nat. Hist., Univ. of Tenn., 1869–'86. Planter. Knoxville, Tenn.
NICHOLSON, JAMES A., Edgefield, S. C.: 1859–'61.
NICHOLSON, J. J., Halifax Co.: 1843–'44.
NICHOLSON, JAMES MANN, Enfield, Halifax Co.: A. B., 1878. Died 1878.
NICHOLSON, ROBERT P., Montgomery Co.: 1856–'58. Minister.
NICHOLSON, THOMAS W., Halifax Co.: 1834–'36. Dead.
NICHOLSON, WILLIAM THOMAS, Halifax Co.: A. B., 1860. Capt. 37th N. C., C. S. A. Judge Advocate Wilson's Division. Killed in service.
NIXON, ALFRED, Lincoln Co.: B. S., 1881. Sheriff. Lincolnton.
NIXON, BREVARD, Lowesville, Lincoln Co.: 1885–'86. Teacher.
NIXON, HENRY BARBER, Perquimans Co.: 1875–'78. Ph. D., Johns Hopkins.
NIXON, JAMES B., Perquimans Co.: 1837–'38.
NIXON, JAMES WHEDBEE, Perquimans Co.: 1875–'77. Physician.
NIXON, JONATHAN J., Bertie Co.: 1818.
NIXON, RICHARD WILLIAM, New Hanover Co.: A. B., 1859. Lawyer. Goldsboro.
NIXON, ROBERT BURNS, New Hanover Co.: 1881–'82. New Berne.
NIXON, ROBERT J., New Hanover Co.: 1857–'58. Planter. Pender Co.
NIXON, THOMAS F., Wilmington: 1856–'59. Dead.
NOBLE, MARCUS CICERO STEPHENS, Selma, Johnston Co.: 1877–'79. Supt. of Schools. Wilmington.
NOBLE, STEPHEN W., Lenoir Co.: 1866–'68. Capt. C. S. A. Wilmington.
NORCOM, EDMUND HALSEY, Edenton: A. B., 1847. Gen. Assem. Merchant. Born 1824, died 1867.

NORCOM, FREDERICK HOSKINS, Clarkton, Bladen Co.: 1885–'86. Teacher.
NORCOM, THOMAS JAMES, Washington: A. B., 1851. Teacher. Blackwell.
NORCOTT, JOSEPH J., Pitt Co.: 1837–'39. Dead.
NORFLEET, BENJAMIN, Edgecombe Co.: 1847–'48.
NORFLEET, FRANCIS S., Bertie Co.: 1862–'63. C. S. A. Planter. La.
NORFLEET, JAMES, Tarboro: 1882–'84. Lawyer. Ft. Payne, Ala.
NORFLEET, JAMES E., Edenton: 1833–'34. Dead.
NORFLEET, JAMES KIRKPATRICK, Winston: 1887–'88.
NORFLEET, JAMES MOSES, Greenville, Pitt Co.: 1887–'88. Lawyer.
NORFLEET, M., Halifax Co.: 1822. Dead.
NORFLEET, PASCAL PAOLI, Tarboro: 1876–'78. Died 1885.
NORFLEET, STEPHEN ANDREWS, Bertie Co.: A. B., 1841. Planter.
NORFLEET, THOMAS F., Bertie Co.: 1852–'53. Died 1854.
NORFLEET, THOMAS S., Bertie Co.: 1865–'67. Planter.
NORMENT, WILLIAM S., Lumberton, Robeson Co.: A. B., 1857. Capt. C. S. A. Solicitor 3rd Dist.
NORRIS, WALTER LEE, Apex, Wake Co.: B. S., 1885. Planter.
NORTH, ERASMUS DARWIN, Connecticut: A. B., 1826; A. M., 1831. M. D. Yale, 1833. Prof. in Yale College. Died 1858.
NORVELL, FAYETTE H., Lynchburg, Va.: 1824. Dead.
NORVELL, JOHN E., Lynchburg, Va.: 1821. Dead.
NORWOOD, HAZELL, Hillsboro: A. B., 1848. Teacher.
NORWOOD, JAMES HOGG, Hillsboro: A. B., 1824; A. M. Tutor U. N. C., 1833–'34. Lawyer. Dead.
NORWOOD, JOHN, Hillsboro: 1853–'55. Physician.
NORWOOD, JOHN WALL, Hillsboro: A. B., 1824; A. M., 1827. Lawyer. Gen. Assem. Dead.
NORWOOD, JOSEPH CALDWELL, Hillsboro: 1831–'32. Planter. Dead.
NORWOOD, THOMAS LENOIR, Lenoir Co.: 1861–'62.
NORWOOD, WALTER ALVES, Hillsboro: 1823–'26. Physician. Dead.
NORWOOD, WILLIAM, Hillsboro: A. B., 1826; A. M., 1832. D. D. Minister. Died 1887. Richmond, Va.
NORWOOD, WILLIAM, Chatham Co.: 1853–'54. Dead.
NUCKOLLS, WILLIAM THOMPSON, Columbus, Ga.: A. B., 1861. Capt. C. S. A. Born 1840. Killed near Richmond, 1861.
OAKES, THOMAS JEFFERSON, Rowan Co.: A. B., 1828. Dead.
OATES, DAVID T., Charlotte: 1852–'54.
O'BRIEN, LAURENCE DENNIS GERALDUS, Edgecombe Co.: 1813. Born 1796, died 1845. Franklin, Tenn.
O'BRIEN, SPENCER, Granville Co.: A. B., 1821; A. M., 1827. Gen. Assem. Dead.
O'DANIEL, SPENCER AUGUSTUS, Chatham Co.: A. B., 1853. Dead.
ODELL, OSCAR CHARLES, Dallas, Gaston Co.: 1884–'86. Physician. Maybinton, S. C.
OGDEN, ROBERT N., New Orleans, La.: 1856–'57.
OGDEN, ROBERT NASH, La.: A. B., 1822; A. M., 1826. Judge Superior Ct. Dead.
OGILBY, NATHANIEL A., Madison, Ga.: 1859–'60. C. S. A. Killed in service.

OGLESBY, WILLIAM M., Sardis, Miss.: 1857–'59. Dead.
OLDS, FREDERICK AUGUSTUS, Raleigh: 1869–'70. Journalist.
OLIVER, JOSEPH B., Duplin Co.: 1860–'61. Lieut. C. S. A. Planter. Mt. Olive.
OLIVER, SAMUEL, North Carolina: 1829.
ORR, PERRY LEANDER, Transylvania Co.: 1879–'80.
OSBORNE, ADLAI LAURENS, Salisbury: A. B., 1802. Dead.
OSBORNE, ALEXANDER, Iredell Co.: A. B., 1798. Physician. Dead.
OSBORNE, EDWIN JAY, Salisbury: A. B., 1798; A. M., 1804. Lawyer. Dead.
OSBORNE, HENRY GRAVES, Leaksville, Rockingham Co.: 1882. Washington, D. C.
OSBORNE, JAMES WALKER, Mecklenburg Co.: A. B., 1830; A. M., 1839. Gen. Assem. Judge Superior Ct., 1859–'66. Mem. Conv., 1861. State Sen., 1868–'69. Born 1811, died 1869.
OSBORNE, JONATHAN, Oxford: 1843–'45. Born 1821. Judge Superior Ct., La. Alexandria, La.
OSBORNE, ROBERT D., Charlotte: 1861–'63.
OSBORNE, SPRUCE MCKAY, Mecklenburg Co.: A. B., 1805. Dead.
OSBORNE, THOMAS SAMUEL, Asheville: A. B., 1884. Fort Smith, Ark.
OTEY, JAMES HERVEY, Liberty, Va.: A. B., 1820; A. M., 1823. D. D. Columbia Coll., 1833. LL. D., U. N. C., 1859. Tutor U. N. C., 1820–'21. Bishop of Tenn., 1834–'63. Died 1863.
OUTLAW, DAVID, Bertie Co.: A. B., 1824. U. S. A. State Solicitor. Mem. Conv., 1835. M. C., 1847–'53. Died 1868.
OUTLAW, DAVID, Bertie Co.: 1864–'65. Merchant.
OUTLAW, EDWARD R., Windsor: 1859–'60. Born 1840. Capt. C. S. A. Planter.
OUTLAW, JOSEPH, Bertie Co.: 1817.
OUZTS, WALTER DALLAS, Edgefield, S. C.: 1878–'79. Lawyer.
OVERMAN, EDWIN ROWAN, Salisbury: 1876–'77. W. N. C. R. R. Asheville.
OVERMAN, HARRY JAMES, Salisbury: 1880–'82. Teacher.
OVERMAN, JOHN POOL, Elizabeth City: 1869–'70.
OWEN, CHAMBERS RANKIN, Salisbury: 1879–'80.
OWEN, JOHN, Bladen Co.: 1804. Lawyer. Planter. Gen. Assem. Gov. N. C., 1828–'30. Pres. Harrisburg Conv., 1840. Born 1787, died 1841.
OWEN, ROBERTSON, Halifax C. H., Va.: 1812. Dead.
OWEN, THOMAS ROBESON, Bladen Co.: A. B., 1831; A. M., 1842. Dead.
OWEN, WILLIAM HAYES, Oxford: A. B., 1833; A. M., 1838. Tutor U. N. C., 1835–'43. Prof. Wake Forest Coll. Dead.
OWENS, NAPOLEON B., Halifax Co.: 1861–'62. C. S. A. Killed in service.
OWENS, WILLIAM ALLISON, Charlotte: A. B., 1856. Col. C. S. A. Killed in service.
PAILIN, WILLIAM WHITE, Elizabeth City: 1879–'80. Died 1884.
PAINE, JAMES, North Carolina: 1796. Dead.
PAISLEY, DRURY LACY, Guilford Co.: 1880–'81.
PAISLEY, JOHN, Guilford Co.: A. B., 1835; A. M., 1840. Minister. Dead.

PALMER, JAMES, Northampton Co.: 1796. Dead.
PALMER, JAMES RUSSELL, Warren Co.: 1881–'82.
PALMER, MALVERN HILL, Greenback, Warren Co.: Ph. B., 1888. Teacher. Hertford.
PALMER, MATTHIAS BRICKELL DICKERSON, Northampton Co.: A. B., 1820. Dead.
PALMER, NATHAN MILAM, Macon, Warren Co.: 1877–'78.
PARK, JAMES, Columbia, Tenn.: A. B., 1855. C. S. A. Born 1837, died Jan. 2, 1873.
PARKE, JAMES DUKE, Anson Co.: 1837–'39. Adjt. U. S. A. Born 1822, died 1846. Troy, Ala.
PARKER, AUGUSTUS MOORE, Gatesville: A. B., 1862. C. S. A. Killed in service.
PARKER, FRANCIS MARION, Enfield: 1885–'87.
PARKER, GAITHER BENAJAH, Burnsville, Yancey Co.: 1883–'84.
PARKER, HAYWOOD, Enfield: A. B., 1887. Teacher. Bingham School.
PARKER, HERSEY, Hertford Co.: A. B., 1856. Lawyer. Planter. Minister.
PARKER, JAMES, Gatesville: A. B., 1861. Gen. Assem.
PARKER, JAMES PAGE, Haywood Co., Tenn.: A. B., 1861.
PARKER, JOHN D., Gatesville: 1858–'61. C. S. A. Planter.
PARKER, JOHN H., Tarboro: 1813. Planter. Dead.
PARKER, JOHN HAYWOOD, Tarboro: A. B., 1832; D. D. Dead.
PARKER, JUNIUS REVERDY, Graham: 1885–'87.
PARKER, ROMULUS BRAGG, Enfield: 1875–'77. Planter.
PARKER, WALTER C. Y., Hertford Co.: 1856–'58. Capt. C. S. A. Killed near Richmond, 1862.
PARKER, WILLIAM FLETCHER, Enfield, Halifax Co.: 1861–'62. Lieut. C. S. A. Treas. Halifax Co.
PARKS, OLIVER TYRRELL, Wilkes Co.: A. B., 1861. Lt. C. S. A. Killed in service.
PARKS, SIDNEY LEE, Wilkes Co.: 1880–'81.
PARROTT, WILLIAM H., Georgetown, D. C.: 1818. Dead.
PARSONS, BENJAMIN, Granville Co.: 1796. Dead.
PARSONS, HILLIARD CRAWFORD, Wadesboro, Anson Co.: 1883–'84. Druggist.
PARSONS, JOHN H., Hinds Co., Miss.: 1860–'61.
PARTRICK, WILLIAM SULLIVAN, Clinton: 1885–'86. Merchant.
PASCHALL, CHARLES LESLIE, Oxford: 1877–'78.
PASTEUR, EDWARD GRIFFITH, New Berne: A. B., 1821; A. M., 1824. Judge Ala. Supreme Ct. Dead.
PASTEUR, THOMAS JEFFERSON, New Berne: 1820–'22. Born 1800. State Senator, 1840–'45. Collector Customs, 1845–'49. Anthony Place, Fla.
PATE, PRESTON BROOKS, Laurel Hill, Richmond Co.: 1886.
PATE, THOROUGHGOOD, Laurel Hill, Richmond Co.: 1880–'82. Lawyer.
PATRICK, ABNER T., North Carolina: 1827–'28.
PATRICK, DAVID SETTLE, Rockingham Co.: A. B., 1856. Prof. U. N. C., 1869–'70.

PATRICK, GEORGE LANE, Kinston: B. S., 1886. Civ. Engineer.
PATRICK, JAMES, Guilford Co.: 1815. Dead.
PATRICK, WILLIAM, North Carolina: 1821.
PATTERSON, A. HILL, Milton, Caswell Co.: 1858–'61.
PATTERSON, ANDREW HENRY, Salem: 1887–.
PATTERSON, FRANK FRIES, Salem: 1882–'85. Lawyer. Lewiston, Idaho.
PATTERSON, GILBERT BROWN, Shoeheel, Robeson Co.: A. B., 1886. Elizabeth City. Teacher.
PATTERSON, HENRY HOUSTON, Chapel Hill: 1866–'67. Born 1844. C. S. A. Merchant.
PATTERSON, JAMES A., Tuscumbia, Ala.: 1858–'60.
PATTERSON, JESSE LINDSAY, Salem: 1878–'79. Lawyer.
PATTERSON, JOHN, North Carolina: 1807. Dead.
PATTERSON, JOHN, Richmond Co.: A. B., 1816; A. M., 1820. Tutor U. N. C. Minister. Dead.
PATTERSON, LOUIS MOREHEAD, Salem: 1878–'81. Teacher. Died 1886.
PATTERSON, MALLOY, Richmond Co.: A. B., 1855.
PATTERSON, RUFUS LENOIR, Caldwell Co.: A. B., 1851. Mem. Conv., 1861 and 1865. Merchant. Manufacturer. Born 1830, died 1879. Salem.
PATTERSON, SAMUEL LEGERWOOD, Patterson, Caldwell Co.: 1867–'68. Born 1850. Planter.
PATTON, JAMES ALFRED, Asheville: A. B., 1851. Dead.
PATTON, JOHN WEBSTER, Company Shops (now Burlington): 1884–'86. Minister.
PATTON, PETER WARLICK, Table Rock, Burke Co.: 1883–'84. Teacher.
PAYNE, ROBERT LEE, Lexington: 1852–'53. Born 1834. M. D. Univ. of Pa. Pres. N. C. Med. Soc., 1877. Journalist.
PAYNE, ROBERT LEE, Lexington: 1875–'78. Physician.
PEACE, LEONIDAS VASSAR, Granville Co.: 1878–'80.
PEACE, WILLIAM, Raleigh: 1796. Founder of Peace Institute. Merchant. Director Bank of State and Bank of N. C. 45 years. Born 1773, died 1865.
PEARCE, OLIVER WINFIELD, Fayetteville: A. B., 1860. C. S. A. Planter.
PEARCE, LUCIUS R. A., Canton, Miss.: 1857–'58. C. S. A. Killed at Mumfordsville, Ky.
PEARSALL, MATTHEW JAMES, Clinton: 1889–.
PEARSON, FRANCIS MARION, Anson Co.: A. B., 1841. Lawyer. Born 1818, died 1861. Little Rock, Ark.
PEARSON, JOHN W., Brandon, Miss.: 1857–'60. Merchant. Died 1883.
PEARSON, JOHN W., Yadkin Co.: 1865–'66. Lt. C. S. A. Died 1883.
PEARSON, RICHMOND, Rowan Co.: 1799. Dead.
PEARSON, RICHMOND MUMFORD, Rowan Co.: A. B., 1823; A. M., 1826. Gen. Assem., 1829–'33. Judge Superior Ct., 1836–'48. Judge Supreme Ct., 1848–'58. Chief Justice Supreme Ct., 1858–'78. Born 1805, died 1878.
PEARSON, RICHMOND NICHOLAS, Anson Co.: A. B., 1841. Born 1820. Physician. Dead. Cool Springs, Ga.
PEARSON, ROBERT CALDWELL, Morganton: 1855–'57. Born 1836. M. D., N. Y. Med. Coll. Surg. C. S. A.
PEARSON, WILLIAM G. B., Bladen Co.: 1856–'58.

PEARSON, WILLIAM SIMPSON, Morganton: A. B., 1868. Born 1849. U. S. Consul at Palermo, 1873. Lawyer. Editor. Author.
PEEBLES, ATLAS J., Northampton Co.: 1837-'38. Dead.
PEEBLES, HENRY BRUCE, Jackson, Northampton Co.: 1878-'82.
PEEBLES, HENRY W., Hicksford, Va.: 1812. Dead.
PEEBLES, ROBERT BRUCE, Northampton Co.: 1859-'62. Adj. Gen. C. S. A. Lawyer. Gen. Assem., 1869. Jackson.
PEEBLES, WILLIAM W., Jackson, Northampton Co.: A. B., 1853. State Senator.
PEELE, WILLIAM JOSEPH, Jackson, Northampton Co.: A. B., 1879. Lawyer. Raleigh.
PEGRAM, HENRY B., New Orleans, La.: 1857-'58.
PEGUES, JAMES B., Marengo Co., Ala.: 1854-'56.
PEGUES, WILLIAM, Cabarrus Co.: 1805. Dead.
PELHAM, ATKINSON, Kentucky: 1817. Dead.
PELL, EDWARD LEIGH, Chapel Hill: 1877-'80. Minister.
PELL, ROBERT PAINE, Chapel Hill: A. B., 1881. Asst. Prof., 1881-'83. Minister. Wilson.
PEMBERTON, WILLIAM DAVID, Albemarle, Stanly Co.: Ph. B., 1881. Born 1859. Physician.
PENDER, HERBERT WARD, Tarboro: 1879-'81.
PENDER, JAMES, Tarboro: 1879-'80. Lawyer.
PENDER, JOSIAH, Edgecombe Co.: 1838. Capt. U. S. A. Died 1846.
PENDER, LEWIS C., Wayne Co.: 1808. Dead.
PENDER, LORENZO DOW, Tarboro: A. B., 1848; A. M., 1851. Lawyer. Dead.
PENDER, ROBERT W., Tarboro: 1845-'46. Dead.
PENDER, SAMUEL TURNER, Tarboro: 1876-'77.
PENN, ABRAM, Patrick C. H., Va.: 1822. Minister.
PENN, COLUMBUS, Patrick C. H., Va.: 1825-'26. Dead.
PENN, EDMUND, Patrick C. H., Va.: 1827-'28. Dead.
PENN, PETER L., Patrick C. H., Va.: 1825-'26. Dead.
PEOPLES, JOHN J., Chatham Co.: 1864-'65.
PERKINS, CONSTANTINE W., Tuscaloosa, Ala.: 1844-'45. Physician. Born 1824, died 1868.
PERKINS, JAMES BLAKELEY, Columbus, Miss.: A. B., 1859. Lawyer. Austin, Miss.
PERKINS, JAMES J., Greenville, Pitt Co.: 1853-'56. Planter.
PERKINS, JOHN T., Burke Co.: 1837-'38. Dead.
PERKINS, MINUTIUS ANGELO, Newport, Carteret Co.: 1882-'84.
PERKINSON, MATTHEW R., Virginia: 1818.
PERRY, BENJAMIN L., Beaufort Co.: 1859-'61. Asst. Adj. Gen., C. S. A. Hotel-keeper. Wilmington.
PERRY, DAVID BARLOW, Tarboro: 1885-'87.
PERRY, EDWARD FOREST, Wake Forest: 1883-'84.
PERRY, HUGH H., Marshall, Tex.: 1863-'64. C. S. A. Dead.
PERRY, JOHN J. CLIFFORD, Newbegun Creek, Perquimans Co.: 1882-'83. Physician.

PERRY, JOHN MERRITT, Beaufort Co.: A. B., 1858. Gen. Assem. Lawyer. Tarboro. Died 1878.
PERRY, JOSHUA, Franklin Co.: 1838–'40. Dead.
PERRY, JOSHUA P., Marshall, Tex.: 1855–'56. Born 1839, died 1856.
PERRY, SAMUEL, Franklin Co.: 1842–'43. Physician.
PERRY, THEOPHILUS, Harrison, Tex. A. B., 1854. Maj. C. S. A. Killed in service.
PERRY, WILLIE J., Harrison Co., Tex.: 1856–'57.
PERSON, JESSE H., Louisburg: 1860–'61. Lieut. C. S. A. Killed in service.
PERSON, SAMUEL J., Rowan Co.: 1818. Dead.
PERSON, SAMUEL JONES, Moore Co.: A. B., 1843. Judge Superior Ct. Dead.
PERSON, THOMAS JEFFERSON, Northampton Co.: A. B., 1848. Gen. Assem. Died 1885.
PERSON, WILLIE MANGUM, Franklinton, Franklin Co.: 1883–'86. Lawyer.
PESCUD, PETER FRANCISCO, Raleigh: 1867–'68. Ins. Agt. New Orleans, La.
PETERS, WASHINGTON, Portsmouth, Va.: 1865–'67. Physician.
PETERSON, MATTHEW RANSOM, Clinton: 1883–'85. 2nd Lieut. U. S. A.
PETERSON, SOLON SCOTT, Morganton: 1878–'79.
PETERSON, WILLIAM CANOVA, Wallace, Duplin Co.: 1878.
PETTIGREW, CHARLES LOCKHART, Tyrrell Co.: A. B., 1836. Planter. Born 1816, died 1873.
PETTIGREW, EBENEZER, Lake Phelps, Tyrrell Co.: 1795. State Sen., 1809–'10. M. C., 1835–'37. Planter. Born 1783, died 1848.
PETTIGREW, JAMES JOHNSTON, Tyrrell Co.: A. B., 1847. Asst. Prof. Naval Observatory, Washington, D. C., 1848. Secty. Spanish Legation, 1850. Author. Gen. Assem. S. C., 1856. Brig. Gen., C. S. A. Born 1828; mortally wounded at Falling Waters, July 14, died at Bunker Hill, Va., July 17, 1863.
PETTIGREW, JOHN, Lake Phelps, Tyrrell Co.: 1797. Dead.
PETTIGREW, WILLIAM SHEPARD, Tyrrell Co.: 1834–'37. A. M., 1868. Born 1818. Episc. Minister. Mem. Conv., 1861. C. S. A. Ridgeway.
PETTY, GEORGE EDWARD, Archdale: 1888–.
PHARR, HENRY NEAL, Charlotte: 1888–'89. Lawyer.
PHARR, WALTER WELLINGTON, Cabarrus Co.: A. B., 1840. Minister.
PHELPS, WILLIE HERMAN, Catawba Co.: 1878–'79.
PHIFER, CHARLES W., Mississippi: A. B., 1854. U. S. A. Brig. Gen. C. S. A. Coffeeville, Miss.
PHIFER, GEORGE, Cabarrus Co.: 1790. Dead.
PHIFER, JOHN, Concord: A. B., 1799. Gen. Assem. Planter. Died 1845.
PHIFER, JOHN FULENWEIDER, Cabarrus Co.: 1805. Planter. Born 1786, died 1828.
PHIFER, JOHN N., Cabarrus Co.: 1812. Planter. Born 1795, died 1856. Miss.
PHIFER, MARTIN LOCKE, Cabarrus Co.: 1836–'38. Lawyer. Planter. Born 1818, died 1853.
PHILBECK, JOSEPH BEATTIE, Shelby, Cleveland Co.: 1883–'86 and 1888–.

PHILIPS, CHARLES, Marianna, Fla.: 1856–'57.
PHILIPS, FREDERICK, Edgecombe Co.: A. B., 1858. Capt. C. S. A. Judge Superior Ct., 1883–. Tarboro.
PHILIPS, JAMES JONES, Edgecombe Co.: 1863–'64. C. S. A. Mortally wounded at Lynchburg; died Aug. 20, 1865.
PHILIPS, JAMES JONES, Tarboro: 1886–. Born 1870.
PHILIPS, JOHN W., Edgecombe Co.: 1866–'68. Planter. Battleboro.
PHILIPS, WALTER EVERETT, Battleboro, Edgecombe Co.: A. B., 1881. Planter.
PHILLIPS, ALEXANDER LACY, Chapel Hill: A. B., 1880. Presb. Minister. Birmingham, Ala.
PHILLIPS, ALONZO, Hillsboro: 1865–'67. Born 1845. Merchant. Dead. Chicago.
PHILLIPS, CHARLES, Chapel Hill: A. B., 1841; A. M., 1844; D. D.; LL. D. Born 1822. Tutor, 1844–'54. Prof. Engineering U. N. C., 1854–'60, and Math., 1861–'68 and 1875–'79. Prof. Davidson Coll., 1869–'75. Died May 10, 1889.
PHILLIPS, EDGAR TOBIAS, Johnston Co.: 1881–'82. Teacher.
PHILLIPS, ETHELDRED, Edgecombe Co.: 1817. Dead.
PHILLIPS, JOHN LEIGHTON, Washington, D. C.: 1878–'80. Surg. U. S. A.
PHILLIPS, SAMUEL FIELD, Chapel Hill: A. B., 1841; A. M., 1844; LL. D. Lawyer. Prof. Law, 1854–'59. Gen. Assem. Speaker H. of Com. Sol. Gen. U. S., 1873–'85. Washington, D. C.
PHILLIPS, THOMAS CALDWELL, Yadkinville: 1877–'78. Lawyer.
PHILLIPS, WILLIAM BATTLE, Chapel Hill: Ph. B., 1877; Ph. D. Prof. Agr. Chem. and Mining U. N. C., 1885–'88. Chemist and Mining Engineer. Birmingham, Ala.
PHILPOTT, JOHN W., Providence, La.: 1852–'53.
PICKENS, ISRAEL LEONIDAS, Greensboro, Ala.: A. B., 1842.
PICKENS, SAMUEL, Cabarrus Co.: A. B., 1814. Comptroller Ala. Planter. Born 1791, died 1855. Greene Co., Ala.
PICKETT, JAMES F., Pike Co., Ala.: 1857–'59.
PICKETT, WILLIAM DICKSON, Anson Co.: A. B., 1822. Judge Superior Ct. Ala. Dead.
PICOT, PETER OLIVER, Plymouth: A. B., 1818; A. M., 1827. Physician. Dead.
PILLOW, GEORGE M., Columbia, Tenn.: A. B., 1859. Lawyer. Lt. C. S. A. Dead.
PILLOW, GIDEON JEROME, Columbia, Tenn.: A. B., 1855. Dead.
PINCKARD, THOMAS CICERO, Tuskegee, Ala.: 1845–'46. Lawyer. Teacher. Minister. Opelika, Ala.
PINKSTON, JOHNSON, Chowan Co.: A. B., 1812. Physician. Dead.
PINNIX, MARSHALL HENRY, Caswell Co.: A. B., 1859; A. M., 1877. Born 1835. Lawyer. Gen. Assem., 1875–'77. State Senator, 1881–'83. Lexington.
PIPKIN, THOMAS HARE, Murfreesboro: A. B., 1825. Dead.
PITCHFORD, THOMAS JEFFERSON, Warren Co.: A. B., 1831. Born 1810. Physician. Gen. Assem., 1856–'65. Dead.

PITT, MARK B., Edgecombe Co.: 1859-'61. Lt. C. S. A. Physician.
PITTMAN, REDDIN GRESHAM, Halifax Co.: A. B., 1860. Top. Eng. C. S. A. Engineer. Rocky Mount.
PITTMAN, WILLIAM H., Marianna, Fla.: 1856-'57. Born 1838, died 1857.
PITTS, JOHN HENRY, Catawba Station: 1869-'70.
PLUMMER, EDWARD HALL, Warrenton: A. B., 1855. C. S. A. Lawyer. Manufacturer. Carter, Tenn.
PLUMMER, HENRY LYON, Warrenton: A. B., 1815. Physician. Planter. Dead.
PLUMMER, WALTER G., Warrenton: 1859-'60.
PLUMMER, WILLIAM, Warrenton: 1815. Lawyer.
PLUMMER, WILLIAM T., Warrenton: 1856-'59. Merchant. Petersburg, Va.
POE, FRANK CALDWELL, Pittsboro: 1877-'78.
POLK, ALEXANDER HAMILTON, Raleigh: 1825. Born 1811, died 1830.
POLK, ALLEN J., Tennessee: 1840-'43. Planter. Dead.
POLK, ANDREW JACKSON, Raleigh: 1840-'41. Capt. C. S. A. Born 1824, died 1870.
POLK, CADWALLADER, Columbia, Tenn.: A. B., 1857. Kentucky.
POLK, FRANKLIN E., Tenn.: 1823-'25. Dead.
POLK, GEORGE W., Raleigh: 1833-'37. Born 1818. Dead. Maury Co., Tenn.
POLK, HORACE MATTHEW, Bolivar, Tenn.: A. B., 1841. Lawyer. Planter. Gen. Assem. La. Gen. Assem. Tenn. Born 1819. Dead.
POLK, JAMES H., Maury Co., Tenn.: 1858-'61. Capt. C. S. A. Planter. Miss.
POLK, JAMES KNOX, Tennessee: A. B., 1818; A. M., 1822; LL. D., 1845. Gen. Assem. of Tenn., 1823-'25. M. C., 1825-'39. Speaker H. of Rep., 1835-'39. Gov. Tenn., 1839-'41. Pres. United States, 1845-'49. Born Nov. 2, 1795, died June 15, 1849.
POLK, LEONIDAS, Raleigh: 1821. D. D.; LL. D. Bishop of La. and Ark., 1838-'64. Lt. Gen. C. S. A. Born April 10, 1806. Killed on Pine Mountain near Marietta, Ga., June 14, 1864.
POLK, LUCIUS JUNIUS, Raleigh: A. B., 1822; A. M., 1844. Planter. Adj. Gen. of Tenn. Born 1808, died 1869. Maury Co., Tenn.
POLK, MARSHALL TATE, Columbia, Tenn.: A. B., 1825. Planter. Dead.
POLK, RUFUS J., Columbia, Tenn.: 1860-'61. Planter. Arkansas.
POLK, THOMAS G., Columbia, Tenn.: 1840-'41. Capt. C. S. A. Decatur, Ala.
POLK, THOMAS GILCHRIST, Mecklenburg Co.: A. B., 1809; A. M., 1816. Dead.
POLK, WILLIAM, Rowan Co.: 1837-'38.
POLK, WILLIAM H., Tennessee: 1832-'33. Chargé d'affaires at Naples. Dead.
POLK, WILLIAM JULIUS, Raleigh: A. B., 1813; A. M., 1816. Physician. Dead. Columbia, Tenn.
POLK, WILLIAM L., Raleigh: 1813.
POLLOCK, WILLIAM DURWARD, Kinston: Ph. B., 1885.
POOL, ANDERSON J., Marion, Ala.: 1840-'42.

POOL, CHARLES CARROLL, Elizabeth City: A. B., 1860; A. M., 1866. Mem. Conv., 1868. Judge Superior Ct.
POOL, GEORGE D., Elizabeth City: 1859–'61.
POOL, JAMES L., Marion, Ala.: 1843–'44.
POOL, JOHN, Elizabeth City: A. B., 1847. Lawyer. Gen. Assem. Mem. Conven., 1865. U. S. S., 1867–'73. Born 1826, died 1884.
POOL, JOHN HERSEY, Pasquotank Co.: 1854–'57. Physician. South Mills.
POOL, SAMUEL P., Elizabeth City: 1858–'61. C. S. A. Dead.
POOL, SOLOMON, Elizabeth City: A. B, 1853; A. M.; D. D. Tutor and Adjunct Prof. Math. U. N. C., 1853–'66. Pres. U. N. C., 1868–'71. Meth. Minister. N. C. Conference.
POOL, STEPHEN FARMER, Marion, Ala.: A. B., 1846.
POOL, WALTER FRESHWATER, Elizabeth City: 1869–'70.
POOL, WILLIAM GASKINS, Elizabeth City: A. B., 1849; A. M. Physician. Died 1887.
POPE, B. A., Weldon: 1838–'39. Dead.
POPE, WILLIAM B., Halifax Co.: 1836–'37. Capt. C. S. A. Dead.
POPE, WILLIAM HENRY, Pittsboro: 1887–'88.
POPLESTON, SAMUEL WASHINGTON, Edenton: A. B, 1825. Dead.
PORTER, FRANKLIN, Tarboro: 1864–'68. Lawyer. St. Joseph, Mo.
PORTER, THOMAS J., Maury Co., Tenn.: 1825. Dead. Bolivar Co., Miss.
POTEAT, JOHN M., Caswell Co.: 1857–'59.
POTTER, HENRY H., Granville Co.: 1825.
POTTS, JOHN W., Washington: 1820. Physician. Gen. Assem. Dead.
POU, EDWARD WILLIAM, Smithfield: 1881–'84. Lawyer. Pres. Elector 1888.
POWELL, AUGUSTUS, Coahoma, Miss.: 1861–'62.
POWELL, BENJAMIN T., Camden, Ark.: 1860–'62.
POWELL, EDGAR, Roxobel, Pitt Co.: 1878–'79.
POWELL, GEORGE TATE, Catawba Co.: 1865–'66. Born 1845. Physician. Planter.
POWELL, JAMES MARSHALL, Greensboro: 1877–'78.
POWELL, JOSEPH CLAY, Tarboro: B. S., 1877. Planter.
POWELL, JOSEPH W., Edgecombe Co.: 1866–'68. Planter.
POWELL, LEMUEL BROWN, Warren Co.: A. B., 1831; A. M., 1837. Physician.
POWELL, ROBERT J., Richmond Co.: 1858–'59.
POWELL, WILLIAM H., Bertie Co.: A. B., 1853. Dead.
PRICE, HARRY HILL, New Orleans, La.: 1860–'61. Born 1842. Adj. C. S. A.
PRICE, JAMES A., Caswell Co.: 1838–'39. Physician.
PRICE, JAMES MADISON, Leaksville, Rockingham Co.: 1881–'83. Physician. Died April, 1888.
PRICE, JAMES VALENTINE, Madison, Rockingham Co.: 1880–'81.
PRICE, NYMPHAS EDGAR, Pitt Co.: 1859–'62. Born 1841. C. S. A. Minister. Bath.
PRICE, THOMAS JEFFERSON, Monroe: 1881–'82.

PRICE, THOMAS S., Martin Co.: 1854-'56.
PRICE, WASHINGTON, North Carolina: 1826.
PRICE, WILLIAM W., Danville, Va.: 1842-'43.
PRINCE, NICHOLAS W., Tuscaloosa, Ala.: 1836-'37. Fruit-grower. Born 1816, died 1880. Apopka, Fla.
PRINCE, OLIVER HILLHOUSE, Tuscaloosa, Ala.: A. B., 1840. Lawyer. Capt. C. S. A. Born Aug. 8, 1819. Killed at Chickamauga, Sept. 21, 1863. Demopolis, Ala.
PRINCE, THOMAS McCARREL, Pitt Co.: A. B., 1827. Dead.
PRIVOTT, HAYWOOD COLLINS, Edenton: 1884-'85.
PROCTOR, ALBERT G., Elizabeth City: 1836-'37. Gen. Assem. Died 1842.
PROCTOR, SAMUEL JOSEPH, Elizabeth City: A. B., 1840.
PROUT, EDMUND GREGORY, Williamsboro, Granville Co.: A. B., 1865. Minister.
PROUT, WILLIAM CURTIS, Williamsboro, Granville Co.: A. B., 1865. Minister.
PRUDHOMME, JAMES A., Natchitoches, La.: 1858-'60.
PRUDHOMME, MITCHELL S., St. Landry, La.: 1857-'58.
PUGH, FRANK SLADE, Hamilton, Martin Co.: 1884-'85.
PUGH, ROBERT LAURENCE, Assumption Parish, La.: A. B., 1861. Lt. C. S. A. Lawyer. Planter. Albemarle, La.
PUGH, THOMAS, Bertie Co.: 1815. Dead.
PUGH, THOMAS J., Bertie Co.: 1821. Dead.
PUGH, WHITMELL S., Bertie Co.: 1841-'42. Dead.
PUGH, WILLIAM A., Bertie Co.: 1833-'34.
PUGH, WILLIAM WHITMELL HILL, Bertie Co.: 1828-'29. Born 1811. Gen. Assem. of La. Mem. La. State Conven., 1852. Planter. Dead. Assumption, La.
PULLIAM, ALFRED BARNETT, Somerville, Tenn.: 1855-'57. Born 1838. M. D. Univ. of Pa. Surg. C. S. A.
PULLIAM, JOEL LANE, La Grange, Tenn.: 1880-'81.
PURCELL, ARCHIBALD, Robeson Co.: A. B., 1840. Planter. Died 1867. Maxton.
PURCELL, J. EDWIN, Robeson Co.: A. B., 1868. C. S. A. State Senator. Purcepolis.
PURCELL, JOHN, Robeson Co.: 1881-'82.
PURCELL, JOHN G., Robeson Co.: 1855-'58. Lt. C. S. A. Killed in service.
PURCELL, MALCOLM GILCHRIST, Robeson Co.: A. B., 1820. Gen. Assem. Dead.
PURCELL, WILLIAM H., Robeson Co.: 1866-'68. Columbia, Ala.
PURNELL, MUNGO T., Grenada, Miss.: 1860-'61.
PURNELL, THOMAS R., Halifax Co.: 1834-'36. Dead.
PUREFOY, GEORGE WASHINGTON, Orange Co.: 1869-'70. Physician.
PURYEAR, HENRY SHEPHERD, Huntsville, Yadkin Co.: 1857-'59. Born 1841. Lawyer. Concord.
PUTTICK, JOHN MARSHALL, Raleigh: A. B., 1855. C. S. Navy. Dead.
QUARLES, GEORGE McD., Minden, La.: A. B., 1860. C. S. A. Killed in service.

QUARLES, WILLIAM LOWNDES, Minden, La.: A. B., 1863.
QUINCE, JOHN B., Wilmington: 1846-'47. Dead.
QUINCE, NATHANIEL HILL, Wilmington: A. B., 1842. Dead.
QUINCE, WILLIAM, Wilmington: 1818. Dead.
RADCLIFFE, THOMAS, Wilmington: B. S., 1881.
RAGSDALE, THOMAS L., Raleigh: 1814. Dead.
RAIFORD, MARSHALL DEMETRIUS, Goldsboro: 1863-'64. Physician. Hockley, Tex.
RAINEY, JAMES, Caswell Co.: 1816. Dead.
RAINS, JOHN, New Berne: A. B., 1823; A. M., 1826. Gen. Assem. Lawyer. Born 1804, died 1834. Alabama.
RAMSAY, JUNIUS NAPOLEON, Northampton Co.: A. B., 1857. Physician. C. S. A.
RAMSAY, JOHN AMBROSE, Moore Co.: A. B., 1811; A. M., 1816. Gen. Assem. Dead.
RAMSEY, GEORGE A., Columbus, Miss.: 1860-'62. Dead.
RAMSEY, NATHAN ALEXANDER, Pittsboro: A. B., 1848.
RAND, OSCAR RIPLEY, Alabama: A. B., 1854. Capt. C. S. A. Planter. Raleigh.
RANDALL, WILLIAM GEORGE, Burke Co.: A. B., 1884. Prof. Univ. of S. C. Prin. of Institute. McKinney, Tex.
RANDOLPH, JOHN, Northampton Co.: 1837-'38. Lawyer. Dead.
RANKIN, ALBERT MCQUINSTIAN, Greensboro: 1879-'80. Cheraw, S. C.
RANKIN, CHARLES ALEXANDER, Fayetteville: 1888-.
RANKIN, JOHN CHAMBERS, Guilford Co.: 1835-'36. D. D. Born 1816. Missionary to India. Baskinridge, N. J.
RANKIN, JOHN D., Gaston Co.: 1853-'54. Sergt. C. S. A. Killed in service.
RANKIN, JOHN TAYLOR, Wilmington: 1862-'63. Born 1845. Lt. C. S. A.
RANKIN, JOSEPH K., Lenoir: 1867-'68.
RANSOM, GEORGE, Garysburg, Northampton Co.: 1887-.
RANSOM, HENRY HUNT, New Berne: 1883-'86. Teacher.
RANSOM, JOSEPH E., Northampton Co.: 1876-'79.
RANSOM, MATT WHITAKER, Warren Co.: A. B., 1847; LL.D. Born Oct. 8, 1826. Lawyer. Planter. Maj. Gen. C. S. A. Atty. Gen. of N. C., 1852-'55. Pres. Elector, 1852. Gen. Assem., 1858-'60. Peace Commr. to Cong. of Southern States, Montgomery, Ala., 1861. U. S. Sen., 1872-. Garysburg.
RANSOM, PATRICK EXUM, Weldon: 1886-'88.
RANSOM, ROBERT, Northampton Co.: A. B., 1880. Lawyer.
RANSOM, THOMAS ROBERT, Northampton Co.: 1881-'84 and 1886-'87. A. B. Georgetown Coll., D. C., 1885. Lawyer.
RAY, LAVENDER R., Newnan, Ga.: 1860-'61. Born 1842. Lieut. C. S. A. Lawyer. Gen. Assem. of Ga.
RAY, WILLIAM E., Franklin Co.: 1859-'60. C. S. A. Dead. Marshall, Texas.
READ, CHARLES L., Virginia: 1810. Dead.
READ, CLEMENT CARRINGTON, Smithville, Va.: A. B., 1819. Dead.
READ, HOWELL L., Virginia: 1810. Dead.
READ, THOMAS E., Smithville, Va.: A. B., 1820. Dead.

REDD, EDMUND B., Martinsville, Va.: 1825. Died 1851.
REDD, OVERTON, Martinsville, Va.: 1808. Dead.
REDFEARN, WILSON, Wadesboro, Anson Co.: 1886–'87.
REDMOND, FRANK P., Tarboro: 1862–'64. Dead.
REECE, DARRETT MANLY, Booneville, Yadkin Co.: 1883–'85. Lawyer.
REECE, JOSHUA MONTGOMERY, Booneville, Yadkin Co.: 1880–'81.
REECE, WINSON LLEWELLYN, Booneville, Yadkin Co.: 1884–'85. Lawyer.
REESE, JOHN JAMES, Knoxville, Tenn.: A. B., 1843. Lawyer. Planter. Capt. U. S. A., Mex. War. Lt. Col. C. S. A. Born July 4, 1823, died April 9, 1880. Jasper, Tenn.
REEVES, WILLIAM H., Somerville, Tenn.: A. B., 1867. C. S. A. Born 1843, died 1871.
REGAN, ONSLOW, Robeson Co.: 1863–'64. Physician. Texas.
REGISTER, EDWARD CHANCY, Duplin Co.: 1881–'82. Physician. Charlotte.
REICH, THOMAS WILLIAM, Mocksville, Davie Co.: 1878–'79.
REID, GEORGE PINCKNEY, Cuba, Rutherford Co.: 1885–'86.
REID, JOHN, Virginia: 1809. Dead.
REID, JOHN T., Mecklenburg Co.: 1840–'42. Dead.
REID, REUBEN DAVID, Wentworth: 1877–'79.
REID, SAMUEL G., Marion, Ala.: 1854–'55.
REID, THOMAS J., Macon, Tenn.: 1856–'57. Physician. Surg. C. S. A.
RENCHER, ABRAHAM, Chatham Co.: A. B., 1822; A. M., 1831. Lawyer. Gen. Assem. M. C. Chargé d'affaires to Portugal. Gov. New Mex. Ter. Born 1798, died July 6, 1883. Chapel Hill.
RENCHER, JOHN GRANT, Santa Fé, New Mex.: A. B. 1862; A. M., 1866. Capt. C. S. A. Lawyer. Pittsboro.
RENCHER, WILLIAM CONWAY, Santa Fé, New Mex.: A. B., 1866; A. M., 1881. Lawyer. Journalist. Pittsboro.
REPITON, A. PAUL, Wilmington: 1857–'59. Dead.
RESPESS, RICHARD W., Williamston: 1859–'61. C. S. A. Dead.
REYNOLDS, CHARLES A., Leaksville, Rockingham Co.: 1867–'68.
REYNOLDS, NATHANIEL AUGUSTUS, Asheville: 1878–'80.
RHEA, JOHN H., Lawrenceville, Va.: 1812. Dead.
RHEM, JOSEPH FRANKLIN, New Berne: 1888–.
RHODES, EUGENE C., Bladen Springs, Ala.: 1858–'61. Capt. C. S. A. Died 1866.
RHODES, JAMES, Waynesboro, Wayne Co.: 1824–'25. Dead.
RHODES, JOSEPH T., Duplin Co.: 1826.
RHODES, PAUL RUFUS, Avoca, Bertie Co.: 1882–'83.
RHODES, RICHARD C., Lumberton: 1819.
RHODES, WILLIAM, Moore Co.: 1857–'58.
RHODES, WILLIAM HENRY, Comfort, Jones Co.: 1883–'84.
RHODES, WILLIAM JAMES, Sampson Co.: 1860–'61. C. S. A. Died in service, 1864.
RIAL, TIMS, Columbus, Miss.: A. B., 1860. C. S. A.
RICE, HENRY WILLIAM, Raleigh: A. B., 1886. Teacher. Louisburg.
RICE, JEMISON W., Eutaw, Ala.: 1841–'43.

RICE, WILLIAM D., Eutaw, Ala.: 1841–'42.
RICHARDSON, ALFRED SMITH, Whiteville: 1884–'85, 1887–'88.
RICHARDSON, CLEMENT LANIER, Anson Co.: 1858–'61. Surg. C. S. A. Physician. St. Mary's Parish, La.
RICHARDSON, EDMUND ERNEST, Reidsville: 1878–79.
RICHARDSON, EDWARD L., Johnston Co.: 1861–'62. C. S. A. Died in service, Danville, Va., 1864.
RICHARDSON, GEROSS, Craven Co.: 1878–'79.
RICHARDSON, LUNSFORD, Johnston Co.: 1828–'29. Gen. Assem. Planter. Died 1856.
RICHARDSON, MILTON C., Chatham Co.: 1862–'65. Lawyer. Clinton.
RICHARDSON, SAMUEL N., Bladen Co.: 1860–'61. C. S. A.
RICHARDSON, SHAHANE, Craven Co.: 1878–'81. Died 1881.
RICHARDSON, WILLIAM, Johnston Co.: 1860–'62. Lieut. C. S. A. Smithfield.
RICHARDSON, WILLIAM H., Pickens Co., Ala.: 1855–'58.
RICHARDSON, WILLIAM MARSHALL, Anson Co.: A. B., 1851. Lt. C. S. A. M. D. Jeff. Med. Coll. Jeanerette, La.
RICHARDSON, WILLIAM S., Anson Co.: 1854–'55.
RICHMOND, CALEB H., Milton, Caswell Co.: 1860–'61.
RICHMOND, JAMES L., Fairfield, S. C.: 1860–'61.
RICHMOND, JOHN MCCRORTEY, Fairfield, S. C.: A. B., 1858.
RICHMOND, ROMAN EUGENE, Memphis, Tenn.: 1886–'88.
RICHMOND, STEPHEN D., Milton, Caswell Co.: 1857–'58. Lieut. C. S. A. Killed in service.
RICKS, BENJAMIN SHERROD, Halifax Co.: A. B., 1823. Dead.
RICKS, WILLIAM BENJAMIN, Nashville, Nash Co.: 1885–'87 and 1889–.
RIDDICK, CHARLES E. C., Gates Co.: 1858–'59. Lieut. C. S. A. Mortally wounded at Williamsburg, May 5, 1862.
RIDDICK, DAVID E., Gates Co.: 1856–'57.
RIDDICK, EDWARD LIVINGSTON, Gates Co.: A. B., 1859. C. S. A. Killed in service.
RIDDICK, WALLACE CARL, Raleigh: A. B., 1885.
RIDDICK, WILLIAM T., Gates Co.: 1855–'58.
RIDDLE, CHARLES LUCIAN, Egypt, Chatham Co.: A. B., 1883; 1885–'86. Lawyer. Elizabeth City.
RIDDLE, THOMAS, Chatham Co.: A. B., 1825. Dead.
RIDDLE, WILLIAM ALVIS, Eutaw, Ala.: 1854–'58. Born 1842, died 1867.
RIDLEY, BROMFIELD LEWIS, Oxford: A. B., 1824; A. M., 1827. Prof. Lebanon Law School, Tenn. Judge, Mid. Tenn. Born 1803, died 1868.
RIDLEY, CHARLES LEWIS, Oxford: 1824–'27. Physician. Planter. Gen. Assem. of Ga. Born 1805. Dead. Bibb Co., Ga.
RIDLEY, JAMES, Granville Co.: 1799. Dead.
RIDLEY, JOHN C., North Carolina: 1830–'31.
RIDLEY, ROBERT ARCHIBALD THOMAS, Oxford A. B., 1827; A. M., 1830. Physician. Speaker H. of Com. of Ga. Died 1863.
RIDLEY, ROBERT B., Oxford: 1835–'36. Dead.

RIEGER, AUGUSTIN W., Beaufort Co.: 1865-'68. LL.B. Lawyer. Planter. Wilmington.
RIGGS, WILLIAM T., De Soto, La.: 1861-'62.
RIGGSBEE, ADOLPHUS, Chapel Hill: 1882-'84.
RIGGSBEE, ATLAS JUDSON, Chapel Hill: 1869-'70.
RIGGSBEE, RUFUS, Chapel Hill: 1882-'84.
RIGGSBEE, STANLEY S., Chatham Co.: 1860-'61. Sergt. Maj., C. S. A.
RIGGSBEE, WILLIAM HENRY, Chapel Hill: 1869-'70.
RIGHTON, WILLIAM, Edenton: A. B., 1802. Dead.
RINGO, JOSEPH, Fayetteville, Tenn.: 1854-'58. Born Sept. 10, 1836, died Nov. 10, 1864. Micanopy, Fla.
RINTELS, DAVID WALLACE, Charlotte: 1884-'85.
RISQUE, FERDINAND WILLIAM, Lynchburg, Va.: A. B., 1826. Dead.
RIVES, HEBER THOMPSON, Beaufort Co.: 1881-'82.
RIVES, JAMES P., Edgecombe Co.: 1866-'68. Farmer. Nash Co.
ROACH, JAMES W., Hinds Co., Miss: 1860-'62.
ROAN, FELIX R., Yanceyville: A. B., 1857. Capt. C. S. A. Register of Deeds for Caswell Co.
ROAN, NATHANIEL K., Yanceyville, Caswell Co.: 1862-'65. C. S. A. Died June 26, 1882.
ROAN, PRESTON, Yanceyville, Caswell Co.: A. B., 1861; A. M., 1866. Surg. C. S. A. Physician. Died 1882. Winston.
ROAN, ROBERT L., Yanceyville, Caswell Co.: 1867-'68. Reidsville.
ROBARDS, HENRY J., Granville Co.: 1831-'34. Physician.
ROBARDS, HORACE LAWRENCE, Granville Co.: A. B., 1835; A. M., 1839.
ROBARDS, THOMAS S., Granville Co.: 1824.
ROBARDS, WILLIAM H., Granville Co.: 1824-'27. Dead.
ROBARDS, WILLIAM J., Granville Co.: 1859-'61.
ROBBINS, ALEXANDER WEATHERLY, Jamestown, Guilford Co.: 1880-'81.
ROBBINS, FRANK LEE, Statesville: 1888-.
ROBBINS, FRANKLIN CHILDS, Randolph Co.: A. B., 1859; A. M., 1877.
ROBBINS, GASTON AHI, Lexington: 1877-'78. Lawyer. Selma, Ala.
ROBBINS, JAMES LAFAYETTE, Randolph Co.: A. B., 1859. C. S. A. Killed in service.
ROBBINS, JULIUS ALEXANDER, Randolph Co.: A. B., 1857. Capt. C. S. A. Killed at Mt. Sterling, Ky., 1864. Selma, Ala.
ROBBINS, MARMADUKE SWAIN, Randolph Co.: A. B., 1856. Gen. Assem., 1883-'85.
ROBERSON, WILLIAM STONE, Chapel Hill: A. B., 1889.
ROBERTS, CHARLES M., Gates Co.: 1853-'55. Lt. C. S. A.
ROBERTS, FRANK WILLIAM, Flat River, Orange Co.: 1877-'79.
ROBERTS, FREDERICK C., New Berne: 1851-'52. Lawyer.
ROBERTS, ISAAC, Carbonton, Moore Co.: A. B., 1859.
ROBERTS, JACOB MORRIS, Dallas, Gaston Co.: 1882-'83. Lincolnton.
ROBERTS, JAMES COLE, New Berne: Ph. B., 1884. Banker. Anniston, Ala.

ROBERTS, JOHN JONES, New Berne: A. B., 1838; A. M., 1841; D. D. Born 1819. Prof. U. N. C. Minister. New York.
ROBERTS, STEPHEN CHESTER, New Berne: A. B., 1852. Minister.
ROBERTSON, HENRY J., Winchester, Tenn.: 1860–'61.
ROBESON, CORNELIUS, Fayetteville: 1819. Dead.
ROBESON, DAVID GILLESPIE, Bladen Co.: A. B., 1854.
ROBINSON, CHARLES, Anson Co.: 1810. Dead.
ROBINSON, CHARLES CORNELIUS, Autauga Co., Ala.: 1858–'60. C. S. A. Elmore Co., Ala.
ROBINSON, CHARLES PHILLIPS, Wadesboro, Anson Co.: 1886–'87.
ROBINSON, CORNELIUS, Hayneville, Ala.: 1852–'53. Capt. C. S. A. Merchant. Montgomery, Ala.
ROBINSON, GILBERT MOTTIER, Lowndesboro, Ala.: A. B., 1856. Died 1885.
ROBINSON, JAMES H., Goldsboro: 1855–'57. Dead.
ROBINSON, JAMES S., Halifax Co.: 1829. Dead.
ROBINSON, SAMUEL B., Cabarrus Co.: 1813. Dead.
ROBINSON, THOMAS JEFFERSON, Fayetteville: 1846–'49. Prof. U. S. Naval Acad. C. S. A. Born 1827, died 1879.
ROBINSON, WILLIAM, Anson Co.: 1815. Dead.
ROBINSON, WILLIAM ALFRED, Warren Co.: A. B., 1853.
ROBY, AUGUSTUS H., Decatur, Ala.: 1837–'38. Dead.
RODGERS, JOHN J. F., Pike Co., Ala.: 1858–'59.
RODMAN, JOHN CROOM, Washington: 1888–.
RODMAN, WILLIAM BLOUNT, Washington: A. B., 1836; A. M. Col. C. S. A. Mem. Conv., 1868. Judge Supreme Ct., 1868–'78.
RODMAN, WILLIAM BLOUNT, Washington: 1878–'80. Lawyer. Journalist.
RODWELL, JAMES ROBERT, Macon, Warren Co.: 1877–'78.
ROGERS, ALEXANDER, Rockingham Co.: 1803. Dead.
ROGERS, BENJAMIN A., Marlboro Dist., S. C.: 1858–'60. Capt. C. S. A.
ROGERS, HYDER ALI, Stokes Co.: 1812.
ROGERS, JOHN P., Granville Co.: 1861–'64. Died May 6, 1886.
ROGERS, JUNIUS FOSTER, Granville Co.: 1878–'79.
ROGERS, ROBERT M., Darlington Dist., S. C.: 1859–'61.
ROGERS, SION HART, Wake Co.: A. B., 1846; A. M., 1849. Lawyer. Gen. Assem. Attorney Gen. M. C. Dead.
ROGERS, WILLIAM JUNIUS, Northampton Co.: A. B., 1859.
ROGERS, WILLIAM T., Marlboro Dist., S. C.: 1859–'61.
ROLLINS, WALLACE EUGENE, Asheville: 1888–.
ROSCOE, JOHN T., Windsor, Bertie Co.: 1842. Physician. Dead.
ROSE, CHARLES GRANDISON, Person Co.: A. B., 1820. Lawyer. Born 1800, died 1827.
ROSE, GEORGE MCNEILL, Fayetteville: A. B., 1867. Adj. C. S. A. Gen. Assem. Speaker H. of Com., 1883–'85. Lawyer.
ROSE, JOHN MCADAM, Fayetteville: 1867–'68. Presb. Minister. Greenville, S. C.
ROSE, WILLIAM ALEXANDER, Stokes Co.: A. B., 1835. Dead.

ROSEBOROUGH, RUFUS MILTON, Iredell Co.: A. B., 1832. Dead.
ROSENTHAL, ALBERT, Goldsboro: 1886–'88.
ROSS, EUGENE CLIFTON, Edward's Mills: 1888–.
ROSS, JESSE GOODWIN, De Soto Parish, La.: A. B., 1861. C. S. A. Killed in service.
ROTHROCK, ROBAH BENJAMIN, Davidson College: 1881–'84.
ROULHAC, JOHN GRAY, Martin Co.: A. B., 1813. Born 1797, died 1858. Florida.
ROULHAC, JOSEPH B., Martin Co.: 1812. Dead.
ROULHAC, JOSEPH BLOUNT GREGORY, Bertie Co.: A. B., 1812. Dead.
ROULHAC, WILLIAM, Martin Co.: 1806. Dead.
ROUNSAVILLE, BENJAMIN DUSENBERRY, Lexington: A. B., 1808. Lawyer. Born 1785, died 1832.
ROUNSAVILLE, PETER KING, Lexington: A. B., 1844; A. M., 1847. Lawyer. Died 1867. Covington, Ind.
ROUNTREE, HERBERT, Wilson: 1881–'82.
ROUSE, NOAH JAMES, La Grange: Ph. B., 1881. Teacher. Lawyer. Kinston.
ROUSE, THOMAS RICHARD, La Grange: Ph. B., 1884. Teacher. Lawyer. Kinston.
ROUTH, ANDREW S., Lake St. Joseph, La.: 1858–'61.
ROUTH, STEPHEN M., Lake St. Joseph, La.: 1858–'60.
ROWE, HOWARD MAY, Black Creek, Wilson Co.: 1884–'85.
ROWLAND, JAMES H., Granville Co.: 1867–'68. Lawyer. Dead.
ROYALL, WILLIAM, Virginia: A. B., 1820. Dead.
ROYSTER, HORACE T., Henderson: 1856–'57.
ROYSTER, IOWA M., Raleigh: A. B., 1860. Tutor U. N. C., 1860–'62. Lt. C. S. A. Wounded at Gettysburg, died July 15, 1863.
ROYSTER, WILLIAM D., Granville Co.: 1859–'61. Dead.
RUDISILL, SAMUEL L. P., Gaston Co.: 1852–'55.
RUFFIN, EDMUND, Hanover C. H., Va.: Ph. B., 1883. Old Church, Va.
RUFFIN, ETHELDRED, Franklin Co.: A. B., 1851. C. S. A. Dead.
RUFFIN, GEORGE M., Marengo Co., Ala.: 1843–'45. Died 1853. Raleigh.
RUFFIN, GEORGE WASHINGTON, Franklin Co.: A. B., 1842. Dead.
RUFFIN, HAYWOOD, Greene Co.: 1795. Physician. Dead.
RUFFIN, HENRY J. G., Greene Co.: 1803. Gen. Assem. Mem. Conv., 1835. Dead.
RUFFIN, JACOB, North Carolina: 1835–'36.
RUFFIN, JAMES HIPKIN, Rockingham Co.: A. B., 1819; A. M., 1823. Dead.
RUFFIN, JAMES HIPKIN, Hillsboro: Ph. B., 1881. Rocky Mount.
RUFFIN, JAMES STERLING, Orange Co.: A. B., 1846. Physician. Demopolis, Ala.
RUFFIN, JOHN KIRKLAND, Alamance Co.: A. B., 1854. Physician. Surg. C. S. A.
RUFFIN, LAMON, Franklin Co.: A. B., 1853. C. S. A. Killed in service.
RUFFIN, PETER B., Orange Co.: 1838–'39.
RUFFIN, SAMUEL H., Louisburg: A. B., 1835. Dead.

RUFFIN, STERLING, Orange Co.: 1834-'35.
RUFFIN, STERLING, Wilson 1882-'85. Washington, D. C.
RUFFIN, THOMAS, Franklin Co.: A. B., 1841; A. M., 1846. Atty. 9th Dist. Mo., 1844-'48. M. C., 1853-'61. Col. C. S. A. Wounded near Fairfax C. H., Va., died at Alexandria, Va., Oct. 1863.
RUFFIN, THOMAS, Orange Co.: A. B., 1844. Col. C. S. A. Judge Superior Ct. Judge Supreme Ct. Died May 23, 1889. Hillsboro.
RUFFIN, THOMAS, Hillsboro: 1878-'81. Warrior Station, Ala.
RUFFIN, WILLIAM CAIN, Hillsboro: 1884-'85. Merchant. Warrior Station, Ala.
RUFFIN, WILLIAM H., Louisburg: 1833-'36. Physician.
RUFFIN, WILLIAM KIRKLAND, Orange Co.: A. B., 1830. Dead.
RUFFIN, WILLIAM T., Orange Co.: 1826.
RUGELEY, HENRY LOWNDES, Matagorda, Tex.: A. B., 1859. Physician. Surg. C. S. A.
RUMBOUGH, HENRY THOMAS, Warm Springs, Madison Co.: B. S., 1881.
RUMM, HENRY C., North Carolina: 1806. Dead.
RUMPH, GEORGE MERRICK, St. George, S. C.: 1879-'80. Lawyer.
RUSS, SIMPSON, Bladen Co.: A. B., 1859. Physician. Surg. C. S. A. Greenville.
RUSSELL, DANIEL L., Wilmington: 1860-'61. Judge Superior Ct. M. C.
RUSSELL, EDWIN H., Warren Co.: 1860-'61. Planter. Boydton, Va.
RUSSELL, MONTGOMERY D., Lincoln Co., Tenn.: 1858-'59. Died 1863.
RUSSELL, ROBERT G., Granville Co.: 1860-'61. Dead.
RUSSELL, THOMAS, North Carolina: 1820.
RUSSELL, WILLIAM F., Oxford: 1824. U. S. N. Dead.
RYAN, DAVID STONE, Chapel Hill: 1855-'59. Telegrapher. Journalist. St. Louis, Mo.
RYAN, JOSEPH A., Windsor, Bertie Co.: 1822. Dead.
RYAN, SAMUEL GARLAND, Chapel Hill: 1859-'61. C. S. A. Lawyer. Raleigh.
SALTER, WASHINGTON, North Carolina: 1796. Dead.
SAMPSON, JAMES, Sampson Co.: A. B., 1816. Dead.
SAMUELS, THOMAS L., Enterprise, Miss.: 1858-'59. Dead.
SANDERS, BENJAMIN W., Lexington, Miss.: 1855-'56. Died 1870.
SANDERS, BRYAN, North Carolina: 1822.
SANDERS, CLAUDIUS BROCK, Johnston Co.: A. B., 1851. Dead.
SANDERS, DAVID W., Lexington, Miss.: 1853-'56. Maj. C. S. A.
SANDERS, EDWARD BENJAMIN, Onslow Co.: A. B., 1860. C. S. A. Lawyer.
SANDERS, EDWIN SMITH, Johnston Co.: A. B., 1870. Capt. C. S. A. Killed in service.
SANDERS, FLEMING, Rocky Mount, Va.: 1799. Judge Gen. Ct. Va. Dead.
SANDERS, GARNER, Sumpter C. H., S. C.: 1811. Dead.
SANDERS, ISAAC BENJAMIN, Onslow Co.: A. B., 1849. Dead.
SANDERS, JOHN, Sumpterville Dist., S. C.: 1817. Dead.
SANDERS, LUCIAN HOLMES, Johnston Co.: A. B., 1845. Died 1875.
SANDERS, MARION, Sumpterville Dist., S. C.: A. B., 1822.

SANDERS, RANSOM, Johnston Co.: 1814.
SANDERS, ROBERT ALEXANDER, Johnston Co.: A. B., 1844; A. M., 1848. Dead.
SANDERS, WILLIS HENRY, Pleasant Grove, Johnston Co.: A. B., 1843. Born 1823. Gen. Assem. Lt. Col. C. S. A. Dead.
SANDFORD, E. DOUGLAS, Fayetteville: 1860–'61. C. S. A. Telegrapher.
SANDFORD, JOHN WILLIAM, Fayetteville: A. B., 1854. Surg. U. S. A., 1857–'60. Surg. C. S. A. Born 1834, died 1881.
SANDFORD, ROBERT HALLIDAY, Fayetteville: A. B., 1850. Born 1832. C. S. A. Teacher. Dead.
SANSOM, RICHARD, Tennessee: 1845–'46. Dead.
SAPP, OSCAR LEMAY, Kernersville: 1887–.
SAPP, ROBERT LEE, Jamestown, Davidson Co.: 1886.
SASSER, JAMES H., Waynesboro, Wayne Co.: 1824. Dead.
SASSER, LEWIS LAFAYETTE, Wayne Co.: 1880–'81. Physician. Smithfield.
SASSER, PHILEMON H., Raleigh: 1858–'59. Lt. C. S. A. Dead.
SATTERFIELD, EDWARD FLETCHER, Roxboro, Person Co.: A. B., 1859. C. S. A. Killed in service.
SATTERTHWAITE, LEWIS EDWARD, Pitt Co.: 1857–'59. Capt. C. S. A. Lawyer. Journalist. Born 1837, died 1872.
SATTERTHWAITE, WILLIAM EDWARD, Pitt Co.: 1858–'60. Lt. C. S. A. Born 1842, died 1866.
SATTERWHITE, HORACE B., Salisbury: 1805. Physician. Dead.
SATTERWHITE, SOLOMON GREEN, Henderson: 1880–'82.
SAUNDERS, DAVID MITCHELL, Tennessee: A. B., 1824; A. M., 1827.
SAUNDERS, DAVID W., Lexington, Miss.: 1853–'56. Maj. C. S. A. Lawyer.
SAUNDERS, ELIJAH BEATTIE, Lilesville, Anson Co.: 1883–'85.
SAUNDERS, HENRY WATSON, Brunswick Co.: 1856–'58. Born 1840, died 1858.
SAUNDERS, JAMES, Caswell Co.: A. B., 1836. Lawyer. Born 1816, died in service in Mexican War, 1847.
SAUNDERS, JAMES BURRELL, Lewiston, Bertie Co.: 1883–'85.
SAUNDERS, JOSEPH HUBBARD, Chowan Co.: A. B., 1821; A. M., 1824. Tutor U. N. C., 1821–'25. Episc. Minister. Born 1800, died 1839.
SAUNDERS, JOSEPH HUBBARD, Chapel Hill: A. B., 1860; A. M., 1866. Lt. Col. 33d N. C., C. S. A. Planter. Born 1839, died 1885. Pitt Co.
SAUNDERS, NORFLEET SMITH, Pactolus, Pitt Co.: 1885. Died 1885.
SAUNDERS, REUBEN TROY, Johnston Co.: A. B., 1827. Dead.
SAUNDERS, RICHARD BENBURY, Chapel Hill: A. B., 1854. Capt. C. S. A. Durham.
SAUNDERS, RICHARD BENBURY, Oxford: 1886–'88. Durham.
SAUNDERS, ROMULUS MITCHELL, Caswell Co.: 1809–'11. Speaker H. of Com., 1819. M. C., 1821–'27 and 1841–'46. Atty. Gen. N. C., 1828. Commr. of French Claims, 1833. Judge Superior Ct., 1835–'40 and 1852–'67. Min. to Spain, 1850. Born 1791, died 1867.
SAUNDERS, THEODORE H., Wake Co.: 1816. Dead.
SAUNDERS, WILLIAM JOHNSON, Raleigh: A. B., 1856; A. M. Maj. C. S. A. Lawyer. Planter.

SAUNDERS, WILLIAM LAURENCE, Chapel Hill: A. B., 1854; LL. B., 1858; LL. D., 1889. Col. C. S. A. Journalist. Secretary of State, N. C. Editor of Colonial Records. Raleigh.
SAVAGE, THOMAS P., Nansemond Co., Va.: 1860-'61.
SAWYER, CHARLES WILLIAM, Perquimans Co.: 1880-'82. Physician. Coinjock.
SAWYER, ENOCH MATHIAS, Norfolk, Va.: 1833-'34. Dead.
SAWYER, FREDERICK, Camden Co.: 1820. Gen. Assem. Dead.
SAWYER, JOHN HEYWOOD, Elizabeth City: 1875-'76. Lawyer.
SAWYER, JULIAN EDMUND, Elizabeth City: A. B., 1833; A. M., 1836. Minister. Dead.
SAWYER, LEMUEL, Camden Co.: 1799. M. C. Dead.
SAWYER, MATHIAS ENOCH, Edenton: A. B., 1823. Physician. Dead.
SAWYER, WILSON, Camden Co.: 1798. Dead.
SCALES, ALFRED MOORE, Rockingham Co.: A. B., 1823; A. M., 1826. Dead.
SCALES, ALFRED MOORE, Rockingham Co: 1845-'46. LL. D., 1889. Lawyer. Gen. Assem. Brig. Gen. C. S. A. M. C., 1857-'59, 1875-'85. Pres. Elector, 1860. Gov. N. C., 1885-'89. Banker. Greensboro.
SCALES, ALFRED MOORE, Greensboro: 1888-.
SCALES, ERASMUS DECATUR, Rockingham Co.: A. B., 1860. Capt. C. S. A.
SCALES, JAMES PINCKNEY, Rockingham Co.: A. B., 1849. Gen. Assem. Miss. Dead.
SCALES, JAMES TURNER, Henry Co., Va.: A. B., 1858.
SCALES, JOHN L., Madison, Rockingham Co.: 1846-'47.
SCALES, JOSEPH H., Henry Co., Va.: 1859-'62. Elizabeth City.
SCALES, JUNIUS IRVING, Rockingham Co.: A. B., 1853. Gen. Assem. Col. C. S. A. Died 1880.
SCALES, NATHANIEL ELDRIDGE, Madison, Rockingham Co. A. B., 1855. Born 1833. Civ. Eng. Maj. C. S. A. R. R. Contractor.
SCALES, PETER PERKINS, Henry Co., Va.: A. B., 1855. Capt. C. S. A. Killed in service.
SCALES, THOMAS SIDNEY, Lowndes Co., Miss.: A. B., 1862; A. M., 1868.
SCHENCK, DAVID, Greensboro: 1884-'85.
SCHENCK, JOHN FRANKLIN, Cleveland's Mills, Cleveland Co.: Ph. B., 1886.
SCHULKIN, JAMES BION, Whiteville, Columbus Co.: 1878-'80.
SCOTT, EDWARD M., Hillsboro: 1844-'45. Capt. C. S. A. Killed in service.
SCOTT, HENRY WILLIAM, Graham: 1886-'87.
SCOTT, JAMES EDWIN, Alamance Co.: 1877-'78. Died 1888.
SCOTT, JAMES GRAHAM, Hillsboro: A. B., 1844. Dead.
SCOTT, LAURENCE WILLIAMS, New Berne: A. B., 1836. Physician. Lawyer. Born 1816, died 1845.
SCOTT, ROBERT WALKER, Alamance Co.: 1877-'78.
SCOTT, RUFUS, Greensboro: A. B., 1854.
SCOTT, THOMAS BATUP, Halifax C. H., Va.: A. B., 1814. Dead.
SCOTT, WILLIAM LAFAYETTE, Guilford Co.: A. B., 1854. Lawyer. Lt. Col. C. S. A. Born 1828, died 1872.

SCULL, ST. LEON, Gates Co.: B. S., 1885; 1886–'87. Lawyer.
SEARCY, E. H. W., Forsyth Co., Ga.: 1866. Stenographer. Griffin, Ga.
SEAWELL, AARON ASHLEY FLOWERS, Jonesboro, Moore Co.: Ph. B., 1889.
SEAWELL, JOSEPH J., Raleigh: 1821. Dead.
SEAWELL, JOSEPH JACOB, Alabama: A. B., 1851. Dead.
SEAWELL, LEONARD H., Raleigh: 1823–'25. Dead.
SEAWELL, RICHARD B., Raleigh 1836–'38. Dead.
SEAWELL, ROBERT W., Raleigh: 1833–'34.
SEAWELL, WILLIAM, Raleigh: A. B., 1825; A. M., 1832. Born 1808. Gen. Assem. Ala. Dead. Montgomery, Ala.
SELF, WILLIAM AUGUSTUS, Hickory: A. B., 1886. Lawyer. Newton.
SELLARS, DUNCAN, New Hanover Co.: A. B., 1840. Minister.
SELLERS, CALVIN C., Wilcox, Ala.: 1854–'56. Teacher. Randolph, Ala.
SESSIONS, COLEMAN, New Orleans, La.: A. B., 1856. Died 1860.
SESSIONS, HENRY WRIGHT, New Orleans, La.: A. B., 1857. Died 1865.
SESSOMS, PRESTON H., Bertie Co.: 1861–'62. Sergt. C. S. A. Teacher. Windsor.
SESSUMS, LEMUEL D., Edgecombe Co.: 1799. Died 1804.
SESSUMS, SOLOMON D., Nash Co.: 1839–'40. Planter.
SETTLE, DAVID A., Rockingham Co.: 1856–'58. Col. C. S. A. Gen. Assem.
SETTLE, THOMAS, Rockingham Co.: A. B., 1850. Lawyer. Gen. Assem., 1854–'59. Pres. Elector, 1856. Capt. C. S. A. Speaker State Senate, 1865. Judge Supreme Ct., 1868–'71, 1873. U. S. Minister to Peru, 1871. Pres. Rep. Nat. Conven., 1872. Judge U. S. Dist. Ct., Fla., 1877–'88. Born 1831, died Dec. 1, 1888.
SEVIER, AMBROSE H., Little Rock, Ark.: 1861–'62.
SEXTON, COLL HECTOR, Harnett Co.: 1879–'81. Raleigh.
SEYMOUR, FLETCHER T., Somerville, Tenn.: 1858–'61. C. S. A. Planter. Haywood Co., Tenn.
SHANNON, NICHOLAS BIDDLE, Okolona, Miss.: A. B., 1859. Dead.
SHANNONHOUSE, FRANK McREE, Charlotte: 1888–.
SHAFFNER, HENRY FRIES, Salem: Ph. B., 1887.
SHAFFNER, WILLIAM FRANCIS, Salem: 1886–.
SHARP, GEORGE W., Iredell Co.: 1817. Dead.
SHARP, HUNTER, Hertford Co.: 1879–'81.
SHARP, JOHN PIKE, Edgecombe Co.: A. B., 1840. Dead.
SHARP, JOHN S., Rockingham Co.: 1838–'39.
SHARP, THOMAS H., Hertford Co.: 1856–'57.
SHARP, THOMAS I., Columbus, Miss.: 1843–'45. Capt. C. S. A. Killed in service.
SHARP, THOMAS PEARSON, Tyro Shops, Davidson Co.: 1889–.
SHARP, WILLIAM, Hertford Co.: 1857–'58.
SHARPE, BENJAMIN CHARLES, Tarboro: A. B., 1880. Lawyer. Greensboro.
SHARPE, EDWARD P., Tarboro: 1858–'60. C. S. A. Farmer. Dead.
SHARPE, GEORGE W., North Carolina: 1820. Dead.

SHAW, ALEXANDER CLIFTON, Rockingham, Richmond Co.: 1884–'86.
SHAW, ANGUS, Richmond Co.: 1859–'61. Physician.
SHAW, ANGUS BARRY, Rockingham, Richmond Co.: 1886–'87.
SHAW, ANGUS ROBERTSON, Robeson Co.: 1880–'82.
SHAW, COLIN, Fayetteville: A. B., 1838; A. M., 1841. Minister. Dead.
SHAW, DANIEL, Montgomery Co.: 1842–'43.
SHAW, HENRY ELIAS, Willard: 1887–'88. Lawyer. La Grange.
SHAW, HENRY M., Currituck Co.: 1866–'68. Physician.
SHAW, HOWARD BURTON, Tarboro: 1886–.
SHAW, JOHN DUNCAN, Richmond Co.: A. B., 1854.
SHAW, NORMAN LESLIE, Harrellsville, Hertford Co.: 1859–'61. Born 1842. Capt. C. S. A. Merchant. Editor. Edenton.
SHAW, THOMAS JEFFERSON, Robeson Co.: 1880–'81.
SHAW, WILLIAM ANDREW, Raleigh: A. B., 1821; A. M., 1831. Minister. Physician. Dead.
SHEPARD, CHARLES BIDDLE, New Berne: A. B., 1827; A. M., 1830. Gen. Assem., 1832–'33. M. C., 1837–'41. Born 1808, died 1843.
SHEPARD, EGBERT, Orange Co.: 1812. Dead.
SHEPARD, FREDERICK, New Berne: 1822. Dead.
SHEPARD, FREDERICK CHARLES, Raleigh: 1849–'51. Born 1832. Dead. Birmingham, Ala.
SHEPARD, GEORGE EDWARD, Wilmington: A. B., 1859. Planter. Pender Co.
SHEPARD, JAMES BIDDLE, New Berne: A. B., 1824; A. M., 1833. Gen. Assem., 1842. U. S. Dist. Atty. Born 1815, died 1871.
SHEPARD, JOHN ROBERT DONNELL, Raleigh: A. B., 1865. Born 1845. Paris, France.
SHEPARD, JOSEPH C., Wilmington: 1855–'58. Born 1840. M. D. Univ. of Pa. Surg. C. S. A. Physician. Scott's Hill.
SHEPARD, RICHARD MUSE, New Berne: A. B., 1829. Lawyer. New Orleans, La. Born 1813, died 1844.
SHEPARD, WILLIAM BIDDLE, New Berne: 1813. Gen. Assem. M. C., 1829–'37. Banker. Born 1799, died 1852. Edenton.
SHEPHERD, FREDERICK AUGUSTUS, Anson Co.: A. B., 1846.
SHEPHERD, GEORGE GOODRIDGE, Charleston, S. C.: 1887–'88. Lawyer.
SHEPHERD, JAMES E., Wilson: 1867–'68. Lawyer.
SHEPHERD, JESSE GEORGE, Cumberland Co.: A. B., 1841. Speaker H. of Com., 1856–'57. Judge Superior Ct., 1858. Born 1821, died 1869.
SHEPPARD, ABRAM, Matagorda, Texas: 1846–'48.
SHEPPARD, WILLIAM, 1796. Dead.
SHEPPERD, WILLIAM BONAMY, Bristol, Fla.: 1881–'82.
SHERARD, CHRISTOPHER C., Livingston, Ala.: A. B., 1852. C. S. A. Physician.
SHERARD, JOHN VICKAR, Wayne Co.: A. B., 1846. Lawyer. State Solicitor. Goldsboro.
SHERRILL, FRANKLIN AVERY, Catawba Co.: 1879–'82.
SHERROD, BENJAMIN, Halifax Co.: 1797. Dead.
SHERROD, CHARLES T., Courtland, Ala.: 1846–'47.

SHERROD, JOHN HENRY, Hamilton, Martin Co.: 1875–'76.
SHERROD, JOHN MAYO, Hamilton, Martin Co.: 1888–.
SHERROD, WILLIAM C., Spring Creek, Ala.: 1851–'52.
SHIELDS, MALCOLM MCGILVARY, Carthage: A. B., 1886.
SHIPP, ALBERT MICAJAH, Lincoln Co.: A. B., 1840; A. M., 1845; D. D. Prof. French and History, U. N. C. Pres. Wofford Coll., S. C.
SHIPP, BARTLETT, Charlotte: B. S., 1883. Lawyer. Greensboro.
SHIPP, WILLIAM MARCUS, Lincoln Co.: A. B., 1840. Judge Superior Ct.
SHOBER, CHARLES ERNEST, Salisbury: 1881–'82.
SHOBER, CHARLES EUGENE, Salem: A. B., 1847. Dead.
SHOBER, FRANCIS EDWIN, Salem: A. B., 1851. Born 1831. Lawyer. Gen. Assem. M. C. Chief Clerk, U. S. Senate.
SHORTER, CHARLES STEWART, Columbus, Ga.: 1858–'59. Capt. C. S. A. Planter. Walla Walla, W. T.
SHORTER, ELI SEMMES, Columbus, Ga.: 1858–'60. M. D. Univ. of Pa. Druggist. New York City.
SHORTER, HENRY RUSSELL, Eufaula, Ala.: A. B., 1853. Lawyer. R. R. Commissioner.
SHORTER, REUBEN CLARKE, Irvinton, Ala.: A. B., 1845. Dead.
SHORTER, REUBEN CLARKE, Montgomery, Ala.: 1866–'68.
SHORTER, WILLIAM A., Eufaula, Ala.: 1866–'68.
SILER, ALBERT W., Macon Co.: 1851–'52. Dead.
SILER, DAVID W., Macon Co.: 1844–'45. Dead.
SILER, JESSE W., Franklin, Macon Co.: 1858–'59. Lt. C. S. A. Killed in service.
SILER, LEONIDAS FIDELIO, Macon Co.: A. B., 1852. Lawyer. Journalist. Dead.
SILER, QUINTUS PARK, Orion, Ala.: 1866–'67. Born 1849. Merchant. Troy, Ala.
SILER, RUFUS S., Macon Co.: 1858–'59. Lt. C. S. A. Killed in service.
SILER, THADDEUS P., Macon Co.: 1844–'45.
SILLERS, WILLIAM WALTER, Clinton: A. B., 1859. Lawyer. Lieut. Col. C. S. A. Born 1838, killed in service, 1863.
SILLS, GRAY, Nash Co.: 1822. Physician. Dead.
SIMESON, JAMES H., Virginia: A. B., 1817. Dead.
SIMMONS, ALBERT MARCHANT, Fairfield, Hyde Co.: A. B., 1887; 1889–.
SIMMONS, BENJAMIN TAYLOR, Fairfield, Hyde Co.: 1888–.
SIMMONS, DAVID WARE, Onslow Co.: A. B., 1861. Lt. C. S. A. Killed in service.
SIMMONS, EDWARD STANLY, Washington: 1876–'77.
SIMMONS, ENOCH SPENCER, Hyde Co.: 1877–'78. Lawyer. Journalist.
SIMMONS, WILLIAM GASTON, Montgomery Co.: 1854–'55. Prof. Physics and Math., Wake Forest Coll., N. C. Born 1830, died March 3, 1889.
SIMMONS, WILLIAM SILAS, Anderson's Store: 1886–'87.
SIMRAL, GEORGE B., Woodville, Miss.: 1863–'64.
SIMS, ALEXANDER D., Lawrenceville, Va.: 1819. Col. U. S. A. M. C. from S. C.

SIMS, EDWARD DROMGOOLE, Lawrenceville, Va.: A. B., 1824; A. M., 1827. Tutor U. N. C., 1825–'27. Meth. Minister. Prof. Ancient Langs. and Eng. Lit., Randolph-Macon Coll., Va. Prof. Math., Nat. Philosophy and Eng. Lit., Univ. of Ala., 1841–'45. Died 1845.
SIMS, G. GORDON, Woodville, Miss.: 1857–'59.
SIMS, JAMES B., Louisburg: A. B., 1843. Dead.
SIMS, RICHARD, Warren Co.: 1795. Dead.
SIMS, RICHARD H., Brunswick, Va.: 1861–'62.
SIMS, RICHARD S., Lawrenceville, Va.: 1833–'37. Physician.
SIMS, ROBERT N., Albemarle, La.: B. S., 1859.
SIMS, WILLIAM, Albemarle, La.: B. S, 1859.
SIMS, WILLIAM DROMGOOLE, Halifax C. H., Va.: A. B., 1825. Dead.
SINCLAIR, NEAL ANGUS, Plainview, Robeson Co.: 1882–'83. Teacher. Fayetteville.
SINGELTARY, RICHARD H., Raleigh: 1853–'54.
SINGELTARY, RICHARD WILLIAMS, Pitt Co.: A. B., 1858. Lt. Col. C. S. A. Gen. Assem. Mem. Conv., 1875. Lawyer. Leasburg, Fla.
SINGELTARY, SAMUEL J., South Carolina: 1835–'36.
SINGELTARY, THOMAS CHAPEAU, Greenville: 1855–'57. Col. C. S. A. Born 1840, died 1873.
SINGLETON, T. J., Craven Co.: 1806. Gen. Assem. Dead.
SITGREAVES, JOHN S., South Carolina: 1817.
SKINNER, FREDERICK NASH, Edenton: A. B., 1882. Minister.
SKINNER, HENRY A., Edenton: 1827. Dead.
SKINNER, JOHN LUDLOW, Raleigh: 1888–.
SKINNER, THOMAS EDWARD, Hertford, Perquimans Co.: A. B., 1847; D. D. Born 1825. Bapt. Minister. Raleigh.
SKINNER, THOMAS GREGORY, Hertford, Perquimans Co.: 1858–'61. Born 1843. C. S. A. Lawyer. M. C., 1883–'87.
SKINNER, TRISTRIM L., 1837. Maj. C. S. A. Born 1820. Killed in battle, 1862.
SLADE, ALFRED M., Martin Co.: 1815. U. S. Consul Buenos Ayres. Dead.
SLADE, JAMES BOG, Martin Co.: A. B., 1822. Physician. U. S. A. Dead.
SLADE, JAMES BOG, Martin Co.: A. B., 1852.
SLADE, JAMES JEREMIAH, Ga.: A. B., 1852. Capt. C. S. A. Teacher.
SLADE, JAMES JEREMIAH, Columbus, Ga.: 1887–'88.
SLADE, JEREMIAH, Martin Co.: A. B., 1855.
SLADE, THOMAS BOG, Martin Co.: A. B., 1820; A. M., 1823; D. D. Pres. Columbus Fem. Inst., Ga., 1842–'63. Born 1800, died 1882.
SLADE, THOMAS BOG, Columbus, Ga.: A. B., 1856. Teacher.
SLADE, THOMAS TURNER, Lincolnton: A. B., 1845. Physician. Capt. C. S. A. Killed in service.
SLADE, WILLIAM, Martin Co.: 1824. Dead.
SLADE, WILLIAM BONNER, Columbus, Ga.: A. B., 1879.
SLATER, DAVID, North Carolina: 1799. Dead.
SLATER, HENRY, Raleigh: 1869–'70.
SLAUGHTER, LEWIS GILCHRIST, Salisbury: A. B., 1827. Dead
SLOAN, HENRY, Sampson Co.: 1875–'76.

SLOAN, JAMES A., Greensboro: 1863-'64. Dead.
SLOAN, JOHN ALEXANDER, Greensboro: A. B., 1859. Capt. C. S. A. Author. Born 1839, died 1885.
SLOAN, JOHN D., Pike Co., Ala.: 1866-'68.
SLOAN, ROBERT MODERWELL, Greensboro: A. B., 1854. Cashier Bank of Reidsville. Died 1888.
SLOCUMB, JOHN CHARLES, Clinton: 1880-'84.
SLOCUMB, WILLIAM RUFUS KING, Clinton: 1884-'86.
SLOVER, GEORGE, New Berne: A. B., 1866; A. M. Born 1843. Physician.
SMALL, JOHN ANDERSON, Elizabeth City: 1869-'70.
SMALL, JOSEPH WILLIAM, Pittsboro: A. B., 1850. Dead.
SMALL, NATHAN B., Elizabeth City: 1855-'57. Dead.
SMALLWOOD, EDWARD FLEET, New Berne: 1839-'40. Born 1822. Physician. Dead.
SMEDES, ABRAHAM KIERSTED, Raleigh: 1861-'62. C. S. A. Lawyer. Born 1845, died 1880. Goldsboro.
SMEDES, CHARLES WATTS, Raleigh: A. B., 1883.
SMEDES, EVERT BANCKER, Raleigh: A. B., 1883. New York.
SMEDES, LYELL, Raleigh: 1852-'53. Born 1832, died 1861.
SMITH, ALBERT, Tuskegee, Ala: 1859-'60. Born 1841.
SMITH, ALEXANDER HALL, Halifax Co.: 1863-'64. Born 1845. C. S. A. Lawyer. Martin Co.
SMITH, ALEXANDER R., Halifax Co.: 1865-'67.
SMITH, ALEXANDER ROBESON, Cumberland Co.; A. B., 1852.
SMITH, ANDREW JONES, Wilmington: 1876-'77.
SMITH, ARCHIBALD AARON TYSON, Fayetteville: A. B., 1831; A. M., 1833.
SMITH, AUGUSTUS, Columbus Co.: 1859-'60. Dead.
SMITH, BENJAMIN B., Brunswick Co.: 1814. Dead.
SMITH, BENJAMIN MEN, Granville Co.: A. B., 1844.
SMITH, BENJAMIN GORDON, Scotland Neck, Halifax Co.: A. B., 1858.
SMITH, BURTON, Hillsboro, Miss.: A. B., 1855. Physician. Born 1832, died 1856.
SMITH, CLAUDIUS FERDINAND, Coxville, Pitt Co.: A. B., 1887.
SMITH, DAVID P., Decatur, Ga.: 1857-'59.
SMITH, EDWARD CHAMBERS, Raleigh: 1882-'83. A. B., Davidson Coll., N. C., 1881. Lawyer.
SMITH, FARQUHAR, Harnett Co.: A. B., 1860. C. S. A.
SMITH, FELIX GRUNDY, Gonzales Co., Tex.: A. B., 1857. Engineer. C. S. A. Dead.
SMITH, FRANCIS JONES, Hillsboro: 1832-'36. Physician. Born 1816, died 1877.
SMITH, FRANKLIN LAFAYETTE, Charlotte: A. B., 1829. Dead.
SMITH, GEORGE A., Scotland Neck, Halifax Co.: 1852-'53. Planter. C. S. A. Dead.
SMITH, GEORGE C., Charlotte Co., Tex.: 1858-'60.
SMITH, GEORGE WORTHINGTON, Raleigh: 1879-'81. Texas.
SMITH, GERARD J., Cumberland Co.: 1833-'34. Dead.

SMITH, HAMPDEN SIDNEY, Raleigh: 1878–'79.
SMITH, HENRY, Granville Co.: 1816. Dead.
SMITH, HENRY, North Carolina: 1821.
SMITH, ISAAC HALL, Scotland Neck, Halifax Co.: 1866–'68. Born 1848. C. S. A. Planter.
SMITH, JAMES A., Robeson Co.: 1866–'68. C. S. A. Bap. Minister. Fair Bluff.
SMITH, JAMES C., Fayetteville: 1858–'60.
SMITH, JAMES CAMPBELL, Cumberland Co.: A. B., 1835; A. M., 1839. Physician. Dead.
SMITH, JAMES CAMPBELL, Cumberland Co.: A. B., 1852.
SMITH, JAMES H., Johnston Co.: 1815. Dead.
SMITH, JAMES M., Anson Co.: 1858–'59. C. S. A. Killed in service.
SMITH, JAMES MADISON, Anson Co.: A. B., 1855.
SMITH, JAMES SYDNEY, Hillsboro: 1833–'35. Born 1819, died 1867.
SMITH, JAMES T., Anson Co.: 1832–'33. Born 1813, died 1833.
SMITH, JAMES TILLMAN, Anson Co.: 1864–'65. Born 1843. Gen. Assem. Tex.
SMITH, JESSE POTTS, Fayetteville: A. B., 1845. Dead.
SMITH, JOHN ALEXANDER, Cumberland Co.: 1854–'55. Born 1836, died 1855.
SMITH, JOHN BAPTIST, Granville Co.: A. B., 1842. Dead.
SMITH, JOHN C., Cumberland Co.: A. B., 1826. Dead.
SMITH, JOHN G., Anson Co.: 1847–'48. Physician. Viney Grove, Ark.
SMITH, KIRBY HOBTON, Goldsboro: 1886–'88.
SMITH, LUBY STEPHENS, Goldsboro: 1881–'83. Physician.
SMITH, MAURICE THOMPSON, Granville Co.: 1851–'52. Lt. Col. C. S. A. Killed in service.
SMITH, NORFLEET, Halifax Co.: A. B., 1860. Born 1839. Lt. C. S. A. Planter.
SMITH, PETER EVANS, Scotland Neck, Halifax Co.: A. B., 1851.
SMITH, RICHARD A., Chatham Co.: 1847–'48. Dead.
SMITH, RICHARD HENRY, Scotland Neck, Halifax Co.: A. B., 1832. Born 1812. Gen. Assem. Mem. Conv., 1861. Planter.
SMITH, RICHARD HENRY, Halifax Co.: 1859–'62. Born 1841. C. S. A. Lawyer. Scotland Neck.
SMITH, RICHARD IVY, Caswell Co.: A. B., 1820. Dead.
SMITH, RICHARD LAWRENCE, Halifax Co.: A. B., 1850. Capt. C. S. A. Born 1827. Dead.
SMITH, ROBERT, Cabarrus Co.: 1795. Dead.
SMITH, ROBERT A., Halifax Co.: 1830–'32. Dead.
SMITH, ROBERT B., York Co., S. C.: 1854–'55.
SMITH, ROBERT LEE, Norwood, Stanly Co.: Ph. B., 1888. Teacher.
SMITH, ROBERT WALTER, Hertford, Perquimans Co.: 1888–.
SMITH, RUFUS H., Rockingham Co.: 1842–'43.
SMITH, SAMUEL CLAUDE, Goldsboro: 1881–'83. Lawyer. Smithfield.
SMITH, SAMUEL F., North Carolina: 1821.
SMITH, SAMUEL HENRY, Granville Co.: A. B., 1821.

SMITH, SAMUEL PERRY, Mecklenburg Co.: A. B., 1856.
SMITH, SAMUEL W., Granville Co.: 1837–'38. Dead.
SMITH, SAMUEL W., Dallas Co., Ark.: 1859–'61. Born 1839. Merchant. Malvern, Ark.
SMITH, SYDNEY, Marengo Co., Ala.: 1856–'59. Born 1839. Merchant. Dallas, Texas.
SMITH, THOMAS C. C., Bladen Co.: 1824–'26. Dead.
SMITH, THOMAS LUCIUS, Newport, Tenn.: A. B., 1860. C. S. A. Killed in service.
SMITH, THOMAS McG., Milton, Caswell Co.: 1851–'52. Maj. C. S. A. Killed in battle.
SMITH, WALTER J., Averysboro, Cumberland Co.: 1858–'60. Born 1840. C. S. A. Planter.
SMITH, WILLIAM HENRY, Halifax Co.: A. B., 1852.
SMITH, WILLIAM J., Maury Co., Tenn.: 1859–'61. Dead.
SMITH, WILLIAM RUFFIN, Halifax Co.: A. B., 1824. Planter. Dead.
SMITH, WILLIAM T., Cumberland Co.: A. B., 1832. Planter. Born 1810, died 1855.
SMITH, WILLIAM T., Wadesboro: 1860–'61. Sergt. C. S. A.
SMITH, WILLIE HENRY, Reidsville: 1885.
SNEAD, JAMES W., New Berne: 1830–'32. Gen. Assem. U. S. Dist. Atty. Born 1813, died 1846.
SNEAD, NATHAN I., Johnston Co.: 1861–'62. C. S. A. Killed in service.
SNEED, ARCHIBALD H., Granville Co.: 1802. Maj. U. S. A. Dead.
SNEED, JAMES, Granville Co.: A. B., 1804. Physician. Dead.
SNEED, JUNIUS, Granville Co.: 1808. Dead.
SNEED, RICHARD, Granville Co.: 1807. Dead.
SNEED, SAMUEL FARRAR, Williamsboro, Granville Co.: A. B., 1824. Dead.
SNEED, STEPHEN KUTUSOFF, Williamsboro, Granville Co.: A. B., 1815. Dead.
SNEED, WILLIAM M., Granville Co.: 1860–'61.
SNEED, WILLIAM MORGAN, Granville Co.: A. B., 1799. Dead.
SNIPES, WILLIAM FLETCHER, Chatham Co.: 1853–'54.
SNIPES, WILLIAM SEATON, Lambsville, Chatham Co.: 1886–.
SNOW, HENRY A., Halifax Co.: 1858–'61. C. S. A. Dead.
SNOW, SAMUEL, Raleigh 1859–'61. New York City.
SNOW, SAMUEL T., Halifax Co.: 1858–'61. Lieut. C. S. A. Killed in service.
SOMERVELLE, GEORGE G., Tipton Co., Tenn.: 1860–'61. Died 1862.
SOMERVELLE, JAMES, Warrenton: 1798. Dead.
SOMERVELLE, JOHN, Tipton Co., Tenn.: A. B., 1859. Sergt. Maj. C. S. A. Lawyer. Supt. City Schools. Dead. Memphis, Tenn.
SOMERVILLE, WILLIAM JONES, Haywood Co., Tenn.: A. B., 1859. Dead.
SORSBY, STEPHEN SILLS, Nash Co.: A. B., 1832. Dead.
SOUTHALL, FRANCIS A., Halifax Co.: 1833–'35.
SOUTHALL, JAMES, Murfreesboro: 1824. Dead.
SOUTHALL, JOSEPH J. B., Enfield, Halifax Co.: 1831–'32. Dead.
SOUTHER, WILLIAM D., Edenton: 1813. Dead.
SOUTHERLAND, CLAUDIUS BONNER, Wilmington: 1885–'86.

SOUTHGATE, JAMES HAYWOOD, Durham: 1876–'78. Born 1859. Ins. Agt.

SPAIGHT, ASHLEY WOOD, Selma, Ala.: A. B., 1842. Gen. Assem., Tex. Brig. Gen. C. S. A. Mem. Conv., 1866. Sect'y State, Tex. Comm'r of Ins.

SPAIGHT, CHARLES GEORGE, New Berne: A. B., 1820; A. M., 1823. Lawyer. Gen. Assem. Born 1800, died 1831.

SPAIGHT, RICHARD DOBBS, New Berne: A. B., 1815; A. M. M. C., 1823–'24. State Sen., 1824–'34. Mem. Conv., 1835. Gov. N. C., 1835–'37. Born 1796, died 1850.

SPANN, JOHN J., Henderson Co.: 1854–'55.

SPEAR, WILLIAM WALLACE, Hillsboro: A. B., 1831; A. M., 1838; D. D. Born 1812. Philadelphia, Pa.

SPEARS, HENRY TURNER, Lillington, Harnett Co.: 1875.

SPEIGHT, JOHN F., Edgecombe Co.: 1859–'61. Planter. Died 1885.

SPEIGHT, RICHARD H., Edgecombe Co.: 1866–'68. Physician.

SPEIGHT, SETH B., Livingston, Ala.: 1860–'61. C. S. A. Killed in battle, 1862.

SPELLER, CHARLES B., Windsor, Bertie Co.: 1858–'60. Lieut. C. S. A. Planter. Dead.

SPELLER, JAMES J., Bertie Co.: 1852–'53. Lieut. C. S. A. Dead.

SPELLER, THOMAS H., Bertie Co.: 1817. Dead.

SPENCER, JAMES M., Greene Co., Ala.: A. B., 1853. Lawyer. Born 1827, died 1861.

SPENCER, PETER PICKET, Hyde Co.: 1839–'41. Planter. Born 1818, died 1880.

SPENCER, SAMUEL, Anson Co.: 1805. Dead.

SPENCER, WILLIAM HENRY, Hyde Co.: A. B., 1854. Born 1831. Lawyer. Terre Haute, Ind.

SPENCER, WILLIAM M., Greene Co., Ala.: 1849–'52. Died 1856.

SPICER, JOHN DANIEL, Onslow Co.: 1855–'57. Physician. Goldsboro.

SPIVEY, AARON JOSHUA, Bertie Co.: A. B., 1830. Minister.

SPOON, WILLIAM LUTHER, Hartshorn: 1887–.

SPRAGGINS, LAFAYETTE B., Virginia: 1836–'37.

SPRAGGINS, THOMAS M., Virginia: 1836–'37.

SPRAGGINS, THOMAS S., Virginia: 1808. Dead.

SPRINGFIELD, BLOUNT, Madison Co., Tenn.: 1840–'41.

SPRINGS, ADAM, Mecklenburg Co.: A. B., 1798. Dead.

SPRINGS, ALVA CONNELL, Charlotte: A. B., 1879.

SPRINGS, JOHN M., Charlotte: 1852–'55. Capt. C. S. A. Died 1865.

SPRINGS, LEROY, Fort Mill, S. C.: 1878–'80.

SPRUILL, CHARLES WHITMELL, Warrenton: 1855–'57. C. S. A. Born 1838, died 1873.

SPRUILL, FRANK SHEPHERD, Littleton, Halifax Co.: 1881–'83. Lawyer. Louisburg.

SPRUILL, GEORGE EVANS, Warren Co.: 1845–'46. M. D. Univ. of Pa. Born 1828. Dead.

SPRUILL, PETER EVANS, Warrenton: A. B., 1855. Tutor U. N. C. Lawyer. C. S. A. Born 1836, died in service at Richmond, 1862.

SPRUILL, THOMAS HILL, Warren Co.: A. B., 1840. Lawyer. Born 1820, died 1845.
STAFFORD, JAMES, Rowan Co.: A. B., 1821. Minister. Dead.
STAFFORD, JAMES MADISON, Cheneyville, La.: 1853–'54. Born 1833, died 1875.
STALLINGS, JOHN M., Duplin Co.: 1853–'56. Minister. Pres. Thomasville Fem. Coll. Mem. Conven., 1875. Thomasville.
STALLINGS, JOSIAH, Duplin Co,: A. B., 1833.
STAMPS, PRESTON, Milton, Caswell Co.: A. B., 1883. Raleigh.
STAMPS, THOMAS, Virginia: A. B., 1836. Dead.
STAMPS, WILLIAM LIPSCOMB, Virginia: A. B., 1836. Physician.
STANBACK, DAVID CHANDLER, Richmond Co.: 1875–'76.
STANCILL, MILLARD F., Northampton Co.: 1865–'68. Physician.
STANCILL, REUELL ANDERSON, Carrollton, Miss.: A. B., 1862. C. S. A. Dead.
STANCILL, REUELL M., Carrollton, Miss.: A. B., 1857. C. S. A. Killed in service.
STANCILL, ROBERT HENRY, Margaretsville, Northampton Co.: 1888.
STANFIELD, STEPHEN ADDISON, Virginia: A. B., 1844. Minister.
STANLEY, EDWARD, North Carolina: 1829.
STANLY, FRANK, New Berne: 1825. Meth. Minister. Died 1862.
STAPLES, MADISON L., Virginia: 1848–'49.
STAPLES, WALTER R., Virginia: 1842. Judge Va. Ct. of Appeals.
STARBUCK, HENRY REUBEN, Winston: A. B., 1887. Lawyer.
STARKE, JOHN MALONE, South Carolina: A. B., 1820. Dead.
STATON, ARCHIBALD T., Hamilton, Martin Co.: 1858–'60. Lt. C. S. A. Killed in service.
STATON, HENRY, Tarboro: 1887–.
STATON, HENRY LOGAN, Edgecombe Co.: 1867–'68. Lawyer. Tarboro.
STATON, JAMES RODERICK, Tarboro: 1876–'77. Physician. Died 1885.
STATON, SIMMONS B., Tarboro: 1859–'61. C. S. A. Died 1863.
STEDMAN, CHARLES MANLY, Fayetteville: A. B., 1861; A. M., 1866. Born 1841. Maj. C. S. A. Lawyer. Lt. Gov. N. C., 1885–'89. Wilmington.
STEDMAN, ELISHA B., Pittsboro: A. B., 1830. Physician. Dead.
STEDMAN, FRANK HAYWOOD, Fayetteville: 1877–'80. Wilmington.
STEDMAN, JAMES OWEN, Fayetteville: A. B., 1832. Minister.
STEDMAN, JOHN MADISON, Fayetteville: A. B., 1830.
STEDMAN, ORAN A., Cumberland Co.: 1830.
STEELE, EDWIN DOUGLAS, Greensboro: 1875–'77.
STEELE, GEORGE SPENCER, Rockingham, Richmond Co.: 1884–'87.
STEELE, THOMAS W., Richmond Co.: 1845–'46.
STEELE, WALTER LEAK, Richmond Co.: A. B., 1844; A. M., 1847. Lawyer. Manufacturer. Gen. Assem. M. C.
STEELE, WILLIAM LITTLE, Rockingham, Richmond Co.: 1883–'84.
STEPHENS, SAMUEL BARROW, New Berne: A. B., 1832. Dead.
STEPTOE, EDWARD J., Liberty, Va.: 1832–'33. U. S. A.
STERLING, EDWARD G., Greensboro: A. B., 1860. C. S. A. Killed in service.

STERRETT, ROBERT H., Columbiana, Ala.: 1865–'66. Born 1846. Lieut. C. S. A. Birmingham, Ala.
STEVENSON, JOSEPH W., New Berne: A. B., 1856. Lawyer. Lieut. C. S. A. Born 1834, died 1865.
STEVENSON, MARK DEWOLF, New Berne: 1862–'63 and 1866–'67. Born 1845. C. S. A. Lawyer.
STEVENSON, WILLIAM, North Carolina: 1804. Dead.
STEWART, AZARIAH COBURN, Taylorsville, Alexander Co.: 1858–'60. C. S. A. Mem. Conv., 1861. Born 1836, died 1861.
STEWART, CHARLES, Harnett Co.: 1878–'80.
STEWART, DANIEL, Richmond Co.: A. B., 1858. Lieut. C. S. A. Killed in service.
STEWART, GABRIEL L., Plymouth: 1806. Dead.
STEWART, JONATHAN LAFAYETTE, Monroe Co., Miss.: A. B., 1857. Minister. Lawyer. Clinton, North Carolina.
STEWART, SAMUEL, Chatham Co.: A. B., 1823; A. M., 1829. Dead.
STEWART, WILLIAM BELFIELD, Clinton: A. B., 1881.
STICKNEY, FENNER SATTERTHWAITE, Washington: 1876–'77. Wilson.
STICKNEY, JOHN COBB, Greensboro, Ala.: A. B., 1855. Born 1832. Surg. C. S. A. Physician. New Orleans, La.
STICKNEY, JOSEPH B., Washington: 1847–'48. Gen. Assem. Merchant. Wilson.
STIREWALT, JOHN, Cabarrus Co.: 1828–'29.
STITH, ABNER, Lawrenceville, Va.: A. B., 1813. Tutor U. N. C., 1814–'16. Dead.
STITH, WILLIAM, Lawrenceville, Va.: 1817. Dead.
STOCKARD, JAMES KIVETTE, Graham: 1879–'80.
STOCKTON, FRANCIS DAUGHTRY, Statesville: A. B., 1859. Lieut. C. S. A. Lawyer. Dead.
STOKES, HUGH MONTGOMERY, Wilkes Co.: A. B., 1815. Dead.
STOKES, JOHN RICHMOND, Wilkes Co.: A. B., 1809. Dead.
STOKES, THOMAS DUDLEY, Richmond, Va.: B. S., 1882. Merchant.
STOKES, THOMAS WILLIAM, Ruffin, Rockingham Co.: 1883–'84.
STONE, DAVID WILLIAMSON, Raleigh: 1818–'20. Dead.
STONE, DEWITT CLINTON, Louisburg: A. B., 1845; A. M., 1849. Pres. Galveston, Tex., Cotton Exchange. Mayor Galveston. Born 1825, died Aug., 1884.
STONE, JOHN H., Dayton, Ala.: 1843–'44. C. S. A. Killed in service.
STONEY, THOMAS P., Charleston, S. C.: 1855–'56. Merchant.
STOWE, SAMUEL TATE, Lodo: 1885–'86.
STRAIN, JAMES, Orange Co.: 1819.
STRANGE, ALEXANDER RAVENSCROFT, Fayetteville: 1846–'49. Born 1830, died 1851.
STRANGE, JOHN KIRKLAND, Fayetteville: A. B., 1848. Born 1828, died 1852.
STRANGE, JOSEPH HUSKE, Wilmington: 1877–'79. New York.
STRANGE, ROBERT, Fayetteville: A. B., 1841. Lawyer. Maj. U. S. A. in Mexican War. Gen. Assem., 1852. Mem. Conv., 1861. Maj. C. S. A. Born 1823, died 1877.

STRANGE, ROBERT, Wilmington: A. B., 1879. Episc. Minister.
STRAYHORN, ISAAC R., Hillsboro: A. B., 1868. Solicitor 5th Dist.
STRAYHORN, JOHN THOMAS, Hillsboro: 1880–'83. Roxboro.
STREET, NATHANIEL HEATH, New Berne: B. S., 1878. Physician.
STREET, WILLIAM B., Hillsboro: 1822. Dead.
STRICKLAND, EDWARD FOUNTAIN, Bliss, Surry Co.: 1883–'85.
STRICKLAND, JAMES THOMAS, Surry Co.: 1878–'80. Physician. Thomasville.
STRICKLAND, MELVILLE C., Bliss, Surry Co.: 1885–'86.
STRICKLAND, WILLIAM G., Wake Co.: 1854–'56. C. S. A. Hotel-keeper. Wake Forest.
STRONACH, ALEXANDER, Raleigh: Ph. B., 1889.
STRONG, GEORGE VAUGHAN, Sampson Co.: A. B., 1845; LL. D., 1889. Born 1827. Judge Crim. Ct. Raleigh.
STRONG, HUGH, Chester, S. C.: 1860. C. S. A. Minister. Dead.
STRONG, WILLIAM ALEXANDER, Sampson Co.: 1842–'43. Lawyer. Born 1823, died 1867. Kansas.
STROWD, ROBERT LEE, Chapel Hill: 1883–'84. Planter.
STROWD, THOMAS WILSON, Chapel Hill: 1885–.
STRUDWICK, FREDERICK NASH, Hillsboro: 1849–'51. Solicitor 5th Dist. Pres. Elector, 1888.
STRUDWICK, SAMUEL, Orange Co.: 1814. Dead.
STRUDWICK, WILLIAM F., Hillsboro: 1828. Physician. Dead.
STRUDWICK, WILLIAM S., Hillsboro: 1849–'51. Physician.
STUBBS, HARRY WILLIAM, Williamston: 1875–'77. Lawyer. Gen. Assem.
STUBBS, JOHN J., Bennettsville, S. C.: 1822. Dead.
STUBBS, LEWIS E., South Carolina: 1822. Dead.
STURDIVANT, ARMISTEAD B., Boydton, Va.: 1845–'46.
STURDIVANT, CHARLES, Virginia: 1817.
STURDIVANT, FABIUS D., Wake Co.: 1861–'62.
SUGG, CHARLES, Chapel Hill: 1869–'70.
SUGG, EDWARD JONES, Chapel Hill: 1869–'70.
SUGG, JAMES B., Springfield, Tenn.: 1854–'55. Capt. C. S. A. Dead.
SUGG, JOHN, Chapel Hill: 1869–'70.
SUGG, OSBURN, Wake Co.: 1826.
SUGG, REDDING S., Sparta: 1852–'53. Lt. C. S. A. Druggist. King's Mountain.
SUGG, WILLIAM M., Chapel Hill: 1887–'89.
SULLIVAN, MILTON A., South Carolina: 1848–'50. Capt. C. S. A. Killed in service.
SULLIVAN, RUFUS BEAUREGARD, Lincolnton: 1884–'85.
SUMMERELL, JOSEPH JOHN, Northampton Co.: A. B., 1842; A. M., 1845. M. D. Univ. of Pa. Pres. N. C. Med. Assoc. Salisbury.
SUMMERVILLE, JAMES, South Carolina: A. B., 1838.
SUMMERVILLE, JOHN, Granville Co.: 1797. Dead.
SUMMERVILLE, ROBERT V., Granville Co.: 1810. Dead.
SUMNER, BENJAMIN, Gates Co.: A. B., 1822; A. M., 1827. Gen. Assem. Dead.

SUMNER, DAVID E., Hertford Co.: 1809. Gen. Assem. Dead.
SUMNER, DUKE W., Tennessee: 1798. Dead.
SUMNER, EDMOND BLOUNT, Perquimans Co.: 1844–'45. Lt. C. S. A. Born 1825, died 1880.
SUMNER, JAMES EDWARD, Oxford: A. B., 1856. Miss.
SUMNER, THOMAS, Hertford Co.: A. B., 1823. Dead.
SUMNER, THOMAS JETHRO, Oxford: A. B., 1845. Born 1827. Civil Engineer.
SUTHERLAND, WILLIAM R., Orange Co.: 1832–'36. Dead.
SUTTON, JOHN MEBANE, Bertie Co.: 1858–'60. Capt. C. S. A. Born 1842, died 1866.
SUTTON, KIRBY EDWARD, LaGrange: 1885–'86.
SUTTON, SANFORD ELLSBERRY, LaFayette, Ala.: 1859–'60. Born 1840, died 1860.
SUTTON, STARK ARMISTEAD, Bertie Co.: A. B., 1855. Capt. C. S. A. Born 1837, killed in service 1864.
SUTTON, WILLIAM G. M., Bertie Co.: 1824.
SUTTON, WILLIAM MORING, Bertie Co.: A. B., 1857. Died 1884.
SUTTON, WILLIAM THOMAS, Bertie Co.: 1832–'33. Born 1810.
SUTTON, WILLIAM THOMAS, Bertie Co.: A. B., 1858.
SWAIN, DAVID LOWRY, Buncombe Co.: 1821–'22. LL. D. Lawyer. Gen. Assem., 1824–'29. State Solic., 1827. Judge Superior Ct., 1830. Gov. N. C., 1832–'35. Member Conv., 1835. Pres. U. N. C., 1835–'68. Born Jan. 4, 1801, died Sept. 3, 1868. Chapel Hill.
SWAIN, JOSEPH JORDAN, Bertie Co.: 1858–'59. C. S. A. Planter. Dead. Wilcox Co., Ala.
SWAIN, RICHARD CASWELL, Chapel Hill: A. B., 1858. Physician. Born 1837, died 1872.
SWANN, ALEXANDER D., Wilmington: 1833–'37. Dead.
SWANN, FREDERICK D., Wilmington: 1808. Dead.
SWANN, FREDERICK W., Wilmington: 1831–'32. Dead.
SWANN, JOHN, Wilmington: 1803. Dead.
SWANN, SAMUEL, Wilmington: 1796. Dead.
SWAYZE, CALDWELL CALHOUN, Opelousas, La.: A. B., 1858. Lawyer.
SWINDELL, JAMES H., Washington: 1855–'57.
SYDNOR, HENRY A., Halifax, Va.: 1838–'39. Dead.
SYKES, EDWARD TURNER, Columbus, Miss.: A. B., 1858. Born 1838. A. A. Gen. C. S. A.
SYKES, LAWSON W., Aberdeen, Miss.: 1858–'61. Capt. C. S. A. Killed in service.
SYKES, RICHARD LYCURGUS, Columbus, Miss.: A. B., 1860. Born 1840. C. S. A. M. D. Univ. of N. Y.
SYKES, S. TURNER, Aberdeen, Miss.: A. B., 1858.
TALBOT, MATTHEW, Matagorda, Tex.: A. B., 1857. Born 1838. C. S. A. Lawyer. Teacher.
TALLEY, JUNIUS BRUTUS, Ore Hill, Chatham Co.: 1884–'85. Died 1885.
TALTON, WILLIAM RANSOM, Selma: 1885–'87.

TANKERSLEY, FELIX, Livingston, Ala.: 1859-'61. Lt. C. S. A. Born 1843, killed in service 1865.
TANKERSLEY, WILLIAM LITTLE, Chapel Hill: 1880-'81.
TARRY, EDWARD, Virginia: 1812. Dead.
TARRY, GEORGE, Virginia: A. B., 1822. Dead.
TARRY, GEORGE PATRICK, Boydton, Va.: 1858-'60. Tarry's Mills, Va.
TATE, ALEXANDER COLVIN, Ashton, Pender Co.: 1881-'83.
TATE, CHARLES SIDNEY, Ashton, Pender Co.: 1881-'83.
TATE, HENRY HUMPHRIES, Gaston Co.; A. B., 1858. Greensboro.
TATE, JAMES T., Gaston Co.: A. B., 1864.
TATE, JOHN WEBSTER, Gaston Co.: A. B., 1858. Died 1862.
TATE, ROBERT HUNTER, New Hanover Co.: A. B., 1847. Physician. Gen. Assem. Born 1826, died 1864.
TATE, SAMUEL C. W., Cherokee Co.: 1846.
TATE, THOMAS H., New Hanover Co.: 1842-'45.
TATUM, JOHN DUDLEY, Milledgeville, Ga.: A. B., 1858. C. S. A. Killed in service.
TATUM, WESLEY, Henderson, Tex.: 1859-'60. Teacher. Dead.
TAYLOE, DAVID THOMAS, Washington: A. B., 1846. Physician. Surg. C. S. A.
TAYLOR, ALEXANDER, Shine, Greene Co.: 1888-.
TAYLOR, ALFRED M., Hillsboro: 1839-'41. Dead.
TAYLOR, BENJAMIN F., Marshall, Tex.: 1859-'60. C. S. A.
TAYLOR, DRURY S., Virginia: 1829. Dead.
TAYLOR, GEORGE A., Covington, Tenn.: 1848-'51. Planter. Macon, Tenn.
TAYLOR, GEORGE DAVID, Dysartville: 1885-'86.
TAYLOR, GEORGE L., Mecklenburg Co.: 1820. Planter. Died 1885.
TAYLOR, GEORGE W., Homer, La.: A. B., 1860. Surgeon. C. S. A.
TAYLOR, HANNIS, Raleigh: 1867-'68. Born 1851. Lawyer. Mobile, Ala.
TAYLOR, HENRY H., Knoxville, Tenn.: 1860-'61. Born 1841. Capt. C. S. A. Lawyer. Clerk U. S. Circuit Ct.
TAYLOR, ISAAC MONTROSE, Chapel Hill: Ph. B., 1879. Asst. Surg. Insane Asylum. Morganton.
TAYLOR, JAMES COLE, Chapel Hill: B. S., 1877. Cambridge, O.
TAYLOR, JAMES FAUNTLEROY, Chatham Co.: A. B., 1810; A. M. Lawyer. Atty. Gen. N. C., 1825-'28. Dead.
TAYLOR, JAMES FAUNTLEROY, Raleigh: A. B., 1841; A. M., 1844.
TAYLOR, JAMES H., Chapel Hill: 1827. Dead.
TAYLOR, JAMES H., Granville Co.: 1856-'59. C. S. A. Killed in service.
TAYLOR, JAMES HARVEY, Granville Co.: A. B., 1821. Dead.
TAYLOR, JAMES PEYTON, Pittsboro: A. B., 1859.
TAYLOR, JAMES SPOTTISWOODE, University of Va.: 1887-'89.
TAYLOR, JOHN, Orange Co.: 1795. Dead.
TAYLOR, JOHN, Granville Co.: 1820. Dead.
TAYLOR, JOHN CAMILLUS, Granville Co.: A. B., 1820; A. M., 1827. Dead.
TAYLOR, JOHN DOUGLASS, Wilmington: A. B., 1853. Col. C. S. A. Planter. Gen. Assem.

TAYLOR, JOHN LEWIS, Chatham Co.: A. B., 1807; A. M., 1810. Chief Justice of Supreme Ct. Dead.

TAYLOR, JOHN LEWIS, Chapel Hill: A.B., 1828; A.M., 1832. Physician. Dead.

TAYLOR, JOHN TILLINGHAST, Granville Co.: A. B., 1853. Capt. C. S. A. Killed in service.

TAYLOR, JOHN W., Hillsboro: 1828–'32. Dead.

TAYLOR, JOHN Y., Mecklenburg Co., Va.: 1824–'28.

TAYLOR, LEONIDAS, Oxford: A. B., 1845. Physician.

TAYLOR, LEONIDAS HENDERSON, Oxford: A. B., 1837; A. M., 1843. Physician. Dead.

TAYLOR, LEWIS, Granville Co.: A. B., 1813. Dead.

TAYLOR, MASSILLON FIELD, Townesville, Granville Co.: A. B., 1861. Capt. C. S. A. Killed in service.

TAYLOR, OLIVER P., Oxford: 1853–'55. Capt. C. S. A.

TAYLOR, PHILIP A., Tennessee: 1841–'42.

TAYLOR, SAMUEL B., Hillsboro: 1831–'34. Dead.

TAYLOR, SIMON HENDERSON, Marksville, La.: 1858–'61. C. S. A. Born 1840, killed at Culpeper C. H., Va., 1861.

TAYLOR, THOMAS, North Carolina: 1805. Dead.

TAYLOR, THOMAS EDWIN, Chapel Hill: A. B., 1832; A. M., 1841. Dead.

TAYLOR, THOMAS W., Townesville, Granville Co.: 1858–'61.

TAYLOR, WILLIAM ANDERSON, North Carolina: A. B., 1824. Dead.

TAYLOR, WILLIAM HAMNER, Dysartville: 1886–'87.

TEMPLE, RUFUS HENRY, Wake Co.: 1881–'82. Lawyer.

TEMPLE, WILLIAM OSCAR, Pasquotank Co.: 1877–'78. Lawyer.

TENNEY, ABDEL KADER, Chapel Hill: 1863–'65. Druggist.

TENNEY, JOHN, Chapel Hill: 1869–'70.

TENNEY, OREGON BURNS, Chapel Hill: 1869–'70.

TERRY, ABNER W. C., Pittsylvania, Va.: 1835–'36.

TERRY, BENJAMIN FRANKLIN, Virginia: A. B., 1830; A. M., 1838.

TERRY, CHARLES CORNELIUS, Richmond Co.: A. B., 1851. Gen. Assem. of Miss. Born 1830, died 1879. Mississippi.

TERRY, JOSEPH M., Virginia: 1830–'32.

THARPE, WILLIAM A., Paris, Tenn.: 1852–'53.

THIES, ERNEST AUGUST, Concord: 1887–'88.

THIGPEN, ANDREW M., Edgecombe Co.: A. B., 1861. Lt. C. S. A. Dead.

THIGPEN, WILLIAM A., Edgecombe Co.: 1856–'58. Farmer. Dead.

THOM, ADDI EDWIN DONNEL, Greensboro: A. B., 1833. Minister. Dead.

THOMAS, CHARLES RANDOLPH, Beaufort: A. B., 1849. Mem. Conv., 1861. Sect'y State, 1864–'66. Judge Superior Ct. M. C., 1871–'75. New Berne.

THOMAS, CHARLES RANDOLPH, New Berne: A. B., 1881. Lawyer. Gen. Assem. Beaufort.

THOMAS, FREDERICK DUNCAN, New Berne: 1884–'86.

THOMAS, GEORGE GILLETT, Wilmington: 1864–'66. M. D. Univ. of Md. Born 1848.

THOMAS, JAMES, New Berne: A. B., 1886. Lawyer.
THOMAS, MARCUS CICERO, Beaufort: A. B., 1855. Meth. Minister.
THOMAS, PHILIP HUNGERFORD, Milton, Caswell Co.: A. B., 1820; A. M., 1827. Physician. Dead.
THOMAS, THOMAS E., Beaufort: 1855–'56. Physician. New York City.
THOMAS, WARREN, Milton, Caswell Co.: 1821.
THOMAS, WASHINGTON, Washington: 1861–'62.
THOMAS, WILLIAM LEWIS, Bennettsville, S. C.: 1879–'80. Lawyer.
THOMPSON, BASIL MANLY, Pittsboro: A. B., 1852. Died 1854.
THOMPSON, CHARLES, Edenton: 1855–'57. C. S. A. Killed at Gettysburg, 1863.
THOMPSON, CHARLES A., Robeson Co.: 1857–'59. Physician. Died 1876.
THOMPSON, EDWIN G., Orange Co.: 1836–'38. Physician. Born 1812, died 1841.
THOMPSON, GEORGE, North Carolina: 1827.
THOMPSON, GEORGE NICHOLAS, Leasburg, Caswell Co.: A. B., 1853. Physician. County Atty., 1860–'65. U. S. Commissioner, 1868–'69.
THOMPSON, GEORGE SIDNEY, Chapel Hill: 1858–'60. Maj. C. S. A. Born 1839, died 1876.
THOMPSON, GEORGE W., Chapel Hill: 1821. Physician. Dead.
THOMPSON, GEORGE W., Pittsboro: 1843–'44.
THOMPSON, HENRY CLAY, Chapel Hill: A. B., 1857. Born 1835. Teacher.
THOMPSON, HENRY ERWIN, Moore Co.: A. B., 1883.
THOMPSON, JACOB, Leasburg, Caswell Co.: A. B., 1831. Tutor U. N. C., 1831–'33. Lawyer. M. C. from Miss., 1839–'53. U. S. Sect'y Interior, 1857–'61. Com'r from Miss. to N. C., 1860. Inspector Gen. C. S. A. Gov. Miss., 1862–'64. Confidential Agt. C. S. A. to Canada, 1864–'65. Born May 15, 1810, died at Memphis, Tenn., March 24, 1885.
THOMPSON, JACOB A., Leasburg, Caswell Co.: 1854–'57.
THOMPSON, JAMES BEDFORD, Cedar Creek, Cumberland Co.: 1882–'83.
THOMPSON, JAMES NICHOLAS, Leasburg, Caswell Co.: A. B., 1861. C. S. A. Killed in service.
THOMPSON, JAMES YOUNG, Caswell Co.: A. B., 1827. Physician. Dead.
THOMPSON, JOHN, Leasburg, Caswell Co.: 1835–'36. Surg. U. S. A. Surg. C. S. A. Physician. Died 1876.
THOMPSON, JOHN C., Alabama: 1857–'58.
THOMPSON, JOHN CARNES, Port Tobacco, Md.: A. B., 1835. Dead.
THOMPSON, JOHN F., Davidson Co.: 1856–'57. C. S. A. Killed in service.
THOMPSON, JOHN R., Raleigh: 1840–'42. Physician.
THOMPSON, LEWIS, Bertie Co.: A. B., 1827; A. M., 1832. Gen. Assem. Mem. Conv., 1865. Born 1808, died 1867.
THOMPSON, LEWIS THOMAS, Clinton, Miss.: A. B., 1856. Dead.
THOMPSON, LEWIS W., Bertie Co.: 1830–'31. Dead.
THOMPSON, M. DeKAY, Salem, Va.: 1864–'65.
THOMPSON, NOAH, Bertie Co.: 1827. Dead.
THOMPSON, OSCAR GARD, Wilmington: 1875–'76. Goldsboro.
THOMPSON, SAMUEL M., Florence, Ala.: A. B., 1860. Col. C. S. A.
THOMPSON, SEYMOUR COLUMBUS, Cedar Cliff: 1887–.

THOMPSON, THOMAS C., Wharton, Tex.: 1857–'59. Druggist.
THOMPSON, THOMAS W., Bertie Co.: 1850–'51. Planter. Windsor.
THOMPSON, TRISTRAM BETHEA, Little Rock, S. C.: 1880–'81.
THOMPSON, WELLS, Matagorda, Tex.: A. B., 1859. Born 1837. Capt. C. S. A. Pres. Tex. Senate. Lieut. Gov. Tex.
THOMPSON, WILLIAM, Leasburg, Caswell Co.: A. B., 1840. U. S. A., Mexican War. C. S. A. Oxford.
THOMPSON, WILLIAM, Edenton: A. B., 1854. Capt. C. S. A. Dead.
THOMPSON, WILLIAM A., Chapel Hill: 1864–'65. Died 1876.
THOMPSON, WILLIAM C., Linden, Ala.: 1843–'45.
THOMPSON, WILLIAM C., Bertie Co.: 1854–'55. Planter. Lewiston.
THOMPSON, WILLIAM HENRY, Chapel Hill: A. B., 1824. Physician. Dead.
THOMPSON, WILLIAM HENRY, Sampson Co.: A. B., 1854. Born 1830. Capt. C. S. A. Merchant. Clinton.
THOMPSON, WILLIAM SILLERS, Clinton: 1886–'87.
THOMPSON, WILLIE GASTON, Moore Co.: 1881–'83.
THOMSON, ALFRED GRAYSON, Franklin Parish, La.: A. B., 1861. C. S. A. Died 1863.
THOMSON, RUFFIN, Hinds Co., Miss.: 1859–'61. Jackson, Miss.
THORNE, EDWARD A., Halifax Co.: 1845–'46. Physician.
THORNE, WILLIAM H., Halifax Co.: 1842.
THORNTON, FRANCIS A., Warren Co.: 1813. Dead.
THORNTON, GEORGE WASHINGTON, Franklin Co.: A. B., 1802. Physician. Dead.
THORNTON, JOHN A., Virginia: 1801. Dead.
THORP, BENONI, Berea, Granville Co.: B. S., 1888. Chemist. Raleigh.
THORP, HENRY ROAN, Nash Co.: A. B., 1857. Physician. Surg. C. S. A. Dead.
THORP, JOHN HOUSTON, Nash Co.: A. B., 1860. Capt. C. S. A. Gen. Assem. Lawyer. Planter.
THORP, PETERSON, Granville Co.: 1856–'58.
THURMOND, G. EDWARDS, Early Grove, Miss.: 1859–'61. Carpenteria, Cal.
THWEATT, ELISHA B., Virginia: 1812. Dead.
THWEATT, HENRY C., Halifax C. H., Va.: 1824. Dead.
TIGNOR, JAMES, 1808.
TILLERY, HENRY L., Halifax Co.: 1858–'60. C. S. A. Manufacturer.
TILLERY, JOHN RICHARD, Halifax Co.: 1856–'58. Planter. Manufacturer. Tillery's.
TILLETT, HENRY AUGUSTUS, Cypress Creek, Bladen Co.: 1879–'81.
TILLETT, ISAAC NEWTON, Elizabeth City: A. B., 1839. Lawyer. Died 1849.
TILLETT, ISAAC NEWTON, Camden Co.: A. B., 1857. Lt. C. S. A. Teacher. Lawyer. Dead. St. Louis, Mo.
TILLEY, GEORGE VANCE, Chapel Hill: 1886–.
TILLINGHAST, JOHN HUSKE, Fayetteville: 1853–'55. Chaplain C. S. A. Minister.
TILLMAN, BENJAMIN S., New Berne: 1813. Dead.
TIMBERLAKE, WILLIAM POINDEXTER, Lexington, Tenn.: A. B., 1861.

TOMLINSON, JAMES MILTON, Johnston Co.: 1857-'59. Sergt. C. S. A. Died of wounds received at Williamsburg, May, 1862.
TOMLINSON, RUFFIN WIRT, Johnston Co.: A. B., 1842. Dead.
TOMPKINS, JOHN B., Nash Co.: 1840-'41. Physician. Dead.
TOMPKINS, MATTHEW W., Albany, Ga.: 1858-'60.
TOMS, CLINTON WHITE, Hertford, Perquimans Co.: Ph. B., 1889. Born 1868.
TOOLE, HENRY I., Tarboro: 1795. Dead.
TOOLE, HENRY IRWIN, Edgecombe Co.: A. B., 1828; A. M., 1839. Born 1810, died 1850. Wilmington.
TOOMER, ALEXANDER DUNCAN, Pittsboro: 1841-'43. Dead.
TOOMER, FREDERICK ARMAND, Pittsboro: A. B., 1851. Physician. Dead.
TOOMER, JOHN D., Wilmington: 1798. Judge Superior Ct. Dead.
TOOMER, LEWIS H., Wilmington: 1802. Dead.
TORRANS, RICHARD N., New Berne: 1821. Planter. Born 1804, died 1830.
TORRENCE, CHARLES LAW, Salisbury: A. B., 1821. Dead.
TORRENCE, HENRY TOOMER, Pittsboro: A. B., 1853. Lawyer. Died 1858.
TORRENCE, HUGH, Mecklenburg Co.: 1827.
TORRENCE, RICHARD ALLISON, Mecklenburg Co.: A. B., 1855. Charlotte.
TOWLES, DANIEL THOMAS, Raleigh: A. B., 1849; A. M., 1852. Minister. Dead.
TOWNES, JAMES EDMUND, Townesville, Granville Co.: 1858-'61. Born 1843. C. S. A.
TOWNSEND, JOSEPH WHITE, Perquimans Co.: 1826. Gen. Assem. Judge Ark. Born 1808, died 1852.
TOWNSEND, RICHARD WALTER, Lumberton: 1881-'82.
TRAVIS, WILLIAM, Rowan Co.: 1819.
TREADWELL, OLIVER WOLCOTT, Connecticut: A. B., 1826. Tutor U. N. C., 1826-'29. Dead.
TREADWELL, WILLIAM LOWNDES, Lamar, Miss.: A. B., 1851. Dead.
TRIGG, WILLIAM STEPHEN, Alabama: A. B., 1847.
TRIPP, JOHN BRYANT, Greenville: 1885-'87.
TROY, EDWARD, Columbus Co.: 1881-'82.
TROY, JOHN CLARK, Fayetteville: 1875-'77.
TROY, MATTHEW, Salisbury: A. B., 1803; A. M. Dead.
TROY, ROBERT E., Columbus Co.: 1836-'37. Lawyer. Dead.
TUCKER, GEORGE, Virginia: 1817.
TUCKER, JAMES HENRY, Greenville: 1880-'84. Lawyer.
TUCKER, JOHN C., La Fourche, La.: 1857-'59.
TUCKER, JOSEPH JOEL WASHINGTON, Raleigh: A. B., 1847; A. M., 1850. M. D. Univ. of Pa. Born 1827, died 1856.
TUCKER, RUFUS SYLVESTER, Raleigh: A. B., 1848; A. M., 1868. Born 1829. Maj. C. S. A. Merchant. Planter.
TUCKER, WILLIAM RUFUS, Raleigh: Ph. B., 1887. Lawyer. Banker.
TULL, JOHN GRAHAM, Lenoir Co.: A. B., 1836; A. M., 1839. Physician. Dead.
TUNSTALL, WHITMELL PEYTON, Chatham, Va.: A. B., 1827. Dead.
TUNSTALL, WILLIAM, Halifax Co.: 1817. Dead.

TUNSTALL, THOMAS TATE, Baldwin Co., Ala.: 1839–'41. Born 1823. U. S. Consul to Cadiz, 1856, and to San Salvador, 1888. Tensaw, Ala.

TURLINGTON, IRA THOMAS, Elevation, Johnston Co.: Ph. B., 1883. Teacher. Smithfield.

TURLINGTON, WILLIS EDGAR, Johnston Co.: 1879–'80. Physician. Elevation.

TURNER, BAILEY P., Hendersonville, Tenn.: 1856–'57. Dead.

TURNER, JAMES C., North Carolina: 1825.

TURNER, JAMES NEILL, Cumberland Co.: A. B., 1855. Capt. C. S. A. Born July 22, 1835, mortally wounded at Petersburg, died Sept. 29, 1864.

TURNER, JOSIAH G., Hillsboro: 1842–'43. Lawyer. Journalist.

TURNER, SAMUEL JEFFERSON, Marion, McDowell Co.: 1880–'81. Lawyer. Gen. Assem., 1887–'89. Bakersville.

TURNER, THOMAS HENRY CLAY, Hillsboro: A. B., 1844. Physician. Dead.

TURRENTINE, JOHN A., Hillsboro: 1848–'50. Dead.

TURRENTINE, SAMUEL BRYANT, Hillsboro: A. B., 1884; A. M., 1887. Minister. King's Mountain.

TWITTY, WILLIAM JOHNSTON, Warrenton: A. B., 1824. Dead.

TWITTY, WILLIAM LEWIS, Rutherford Co.: A. B., 1858. Dead.

TYLER, WILLIAM P., Bertie Co.: 1848–'49. Lawyer. Dead.

TYSON, BENJAMIN FRANKLIN, Greenville: 1884–.

TYSON, LUCIAN P., Carthage, Moore Co.: 1859–'61.

URQUHART, LEWIS THOMPSON, Lewiston: 1888–.

URQUHART, RICHARD ALEXANDER, Lewiston: 1888–.

UZZELL, JOHN RANDOLPH, Goldsboro: 1880–'81.

UZZELL, KIRBY SMITH, Goldsboro: B. S., 1886. Lawyer. Journalist. Garden City, Ark.

UZZELL, ROBERT LEE, Goldsboro: B. S., 1886. Teacher. Roanoke, Va.

VALENTINE, THOMAS WOOD, Bowman's Bluff: 1886–'88.

VAN AMRINGE, STACEY, Wilmington: 1886–'87. Lawyer. Born Sept. 26, 1865, died 1887.

VANCE, DAVID MITCHELL, Charlotte: 1875–'76. Born 1857. Lawyer. Journalist. New Orleans, La.

VANCE, JAMES NOEL, Asheville: 1881–'82.

VANCE, THOMAS MALVERN, Charlotte: 1879–'81. Lawyer. Pres. Elector, 1888. Seattle, Washington.

VANCE, ZEBULON BAIRD, Buncombe Co.: 1851–'52. LL. D. Born May 13, 1830. Lawyer. County Solic., 1852. Gen. Assem., 1854. M. C., 35th and 36th Congs. Col. C. S. A. Gov., 1862, 1864, 1876. Elected U. S. Sen., 1870. U. S. Sen., 1879–. Black Mountain.

VAN DERVEER, WILLIAM BLACKSHEAR, Montgomery, Ala.: 1859–'61. Born 1840. C. S. A. Planter. Clio, Texas.

VANDIVER, WALTER WIGHTMAN, Asheville: 1881–'83.

VANN, ENOCH JASPER, Groveville, Ga.: A. B., 1854. Pres. Fla. Sen. State Attorney. Judge Cir. Ct. Madison, Florida.

VANN, LIVINGSTON, Madison, Fla.: 1881–'84. Lawyer.

Van Wyck, Augustus, Pendleton, S. C.: A. B., 1864; A. M., 1868. Born 1844. Judge Brooklyn City Ct. Brooklyn, N. Y.
Van Wyck, William, Pendleton, S. C.: A. B., 1861; A. M., 1866. Lawyer. Born 1840, died May 28, 1887. New York City.
Varner, Herbert M., Macon, Ga.: 1858–'60.
Vaughan, James Atlas, Richmond Co.: 1827. Born 1810. Dead. Little Rock, Ark.
Vaughan, Latimer Clark, Warrenton: A. B., 1879. Journalist. Orlando, Fla.
Vaughan, Leonidas Polk, Sparta, Alleghany Co.: 1883–'86.
Vaughan, Robert, North Carolina: 1796.
Vaughan, Vernon Henry, Mt. Meigs, Ala.: A. B., 1860. Adj. C. S. A. Prof. Math. Univ. Ala., 1868. Gov. Utah, 1869. Planter and Miner. Died Dec. 4, 1878. San Francisco, Cal.
Vaughn, Robert Galloway, Madison, Rockingham Co.: 1887–.
Venable, Joseph, Oxford: A. B., 1857.
Vines, Charles, Edgecombe Co.: 1860–'61. Lieut. C. S. A. Born Oct. 30, 1842, killed at Cedar Creek, Oct. 19, 1864.
Vines, Charles Carson, Edgecombe Co.: 1875–'76.
Vinson, James D., Northampton Co.: 1867–'68. Dead.
Viser, James Hervey, Florence, Alabama: A. B., 1841; A. M., 1848. Lawyer.
Von Schweinitz, Emile Alexander, Salem: A. B., 1882; Ph. D., 1885. Washington, D. C.
Waddell, Alfred, Brunswick Co.: 1824. Dead.
Waddell, Alfred Moore, Hillsboro: 1850–'53. Lawyer. Lieut. Col. C. S. A. M. C. Pres. Elector, 1888. Wilmington.
Waddell, Alfred Moore, Wilmington: 1877–'78.
Waddell, Edward B., 1827. Dead.
Waddell, Francis N., Wilmington: 1813. Dead.
Waddell, George H., Chapel Hill: 1846–'47. Dead.
Waddell, Hugh, Hillsboro: A. B., 1818. Lawyer. Pres. N. C. Sen. Dead.
Waddell, Hugh Y., Wilmington: 1821. Dead.
Waddell, James Fleming, Pittsboro: 1841–'43. Capt. C. S. A.
Waddell, Legh Richmond, Pittsboro: A. B., 1852. Dead.
Waddell, Maurice Quince, Wilmington: 1821. Lawyer. Dead.
Waddell, Owen Alfred, Pittsboro: 1851–'52. Maj. C. S. A. Born 1833, killed at Altoona, Ga., 1864. Warrensburg, Mo.
Waddell, Theodore Dehon, Pittsboro: 1853–'55. Born 1838. C. S. A. New York City.
Waddill, John Cooper, Selma, Ala.: A. B., 1856. Born 1833. Minister. Matagorda, Tex.
Waddill, John R., Hertford Co.: A. B., 1851. Capt. C. S. A. Killed in battle.
Wade, Clement W., Spring Hill, Tenn.: 1855–'57. Planter. Dead.
Wade, Thomas Berryman, Spring Hill, Tenn.: A. B., 1858. Planter. Dead.

WAITT, MALCOLM GRAHAM, Raleigh: 1869-'70.
WALDO, JOSEPH T., Hamilton, Martin Co.: 1855-'56. Lawyer. Gen. Assem.
WALDROP, OTIS THERON, Wilmington: 1885-'86.
WALKER, JAMES ALVES, Wilmington: A. B., 1858.
WALKER, JAMES C., Caswell Co.: 1837-'38. Physician. Dead.
WALKER, JAMES H., Wilmington: 1813.
WALKER, JOEL PATON, Lauderdale Springs, Miss.: A. B., 1861. Capt. C. S. A. Lawyer. District Atty. Gen. Assem.
WALKER, JOHN M., Hillsboro: 1840-'42.
WALKER, JOHN MOSELEY, Hickory: A. B., 1881. Charlotte.
WALKER, JOSHUA COCHRAN, Wilmington: A. B., 1854. Born 1833. Surg. C. S. A. Physician. Dead.
WALKER, JOHNSON, Coffeeville, Upshur Co., Texas: 1858-'60.
WALKER, JULIUS, Wilmington: 1807. Dead.
WALKER, LUCIAN HOLMES, Hickory: A. B., 1881. Charlotte.
WALKER, MIMS B., Uniontown, Ala.: 1858-'59. Born 1838. Capt. C. S. A. Gen. Assem. Planter. Faunsdale, Ala.
WALKER, NICHOLAS L., Milton, Caswell Co.: 1845-'47. Dead.
WALKER, PETER, Hillsboro: 1834-'35.
WALKER, PLATT D., Wilmington: 1865-'67. Lawyer. Charlotte.
WALKER, THOMAS OWEN DAVIE, Wilmington: A. B., 1843. Lawyer. R. R. Director. Born 1822, died 1865.
WALKER, WILLIAM MEARES, Wilmington: A. B., 1852. Capt. C. S. A. Born 1829, killed in battle 1864.
WALKER, WILLIAM RICHMOND, Caswell Co.: A. B., 1838; A. M., 1858.
WALKUP, HENRY C., Union Co.: 1864-'65.
WALKUP, SAMUEL HOEY, Mecklenburg Co.: A. B., 1841; A. M., 1844. Col. C. S. A. Dead.
WALL, HENRY CLAY, Richmond Co.: 1858-'61. Born 1841. Author. Merchant. Rockingham.
WALL, JAMES M., Fayette Co., Tenn.: 1856-'58. C. S. A.
WALL, JAMES MARSHALL, Anson Co.: A. B., 1867. Born 1839. Teacher. Planter.
WALL, JOHN, North Carolina: 1826.
WALL, JOHN POYTHRESS, Rockingham, Richmond Co.: 1852-'54. Born 1835, died 1855.
WALL, JOHN T., Hicksford, Va.: 1823. Dead.
WALL, JOSEPH G., Hicksford, Va.: 1807. Dead.
WALL, RICHARD ROBERT, Rockingham Co.: A. B., 1829. Physician. Dead.
WALL, WILLIAM MILLARD, Mt. Airy, Surry Co.: 1887-'88.
WALLACE, GEORGE W., Norfolk, Va.: 1862-'64. Physician. Beckley, Va.
WALLACE, JAMES ALBERT, Pitt Co.: A. B., 1860. C. S. A.
WALLIS, WILLIAM BANE ALEXANDER, Stokes Co.: A. B., 1816.
WALSER, FREDERICK TAYLOR, Yadkin College: 1862-'63. Born 1849. Journalist.
WALSER, JOSEPH GAITHER, Yadkin College: 1888-.

WALSER, ZEBULON BAIRD, Yadkin College: 1880–'84. Gen. Assem. **Lexington.**
WALSH, CHARLES, Mobile, Ala.: 1857–'59. Capt. C. S. A. Dead.
WALTON, TIMOTHY, Dayton, Ala.: A. B., 1859.
WARD, ALFRED DECATUR, Joford, Duplin Co.: Ph. B., 1885. Kenansville.
WARD, EDWARD W., Memphis, Tenn. 1847–'48.
WARD, FRANCIS, Greene Co.: 1809. Dead.
WARD, GASTON, Chapel Hill: 1869–'70.
WARD, JAMES RIDDLE, Chatham Co.: A. B., 1846; A. M., 1849. Physician. Dead.
WARD, NATHAN PERRY, Franklin Co.: A. B., 1857. Dead.
WARD, SAMUEL MILTON, Chapel Hill: 1869–'70.
WARD, WYATT MACON, Wilson Co.: 1881–'82.
WARE, JAMES N., Perry Co., Ala.: 1859–'60.
WARE, JOHN J., Brownsville, Tenn.: 1857–'59. Surg. C. S. A. Physician. Dead.
WARE, WILLIAM H., Perry Co., Alabama: 1859–'60.
WARLICK, LEE MARTIN, Lincolnton: A. B., 1884. Roxboro.
WARREN, JOSEPH EDWARD JOHNSON, Rosedale: 1887–.
WASHBURN, DANIEL MOSES, Mica: 1886–'87.
WASHINGTON, AUGUSTIN, 1822. Dead.
WASHINGTON, AUGUSTINE BURKETTE, Memphis, Tenn.: A. B., 1858. LL. B. C. S. A. Killed at Chickamauga, Sept. 19, 1863.
WASHINGTON, GEORGE, Wayne Co.: A. B., 1848.
WASHINGTON, G. LAWRENCE, Kinston: 1859–'62.
WASHINGTON, JAMES AUGUSTUS, Lenoir Co.: A. B., 1823. Physician. Born 1803, died 1847. New York City.
WASHINGTON, JAMES AUGUSTUS, Wayne Co.: A. B., 1851. Col. C. S. A. Physician. Goldsboro.
WASHINGTON, JOHN, 1821. Dead.
WATKINS, HENRY THOMAS, Milton, Caswell Co.: 1847–'49. Merchant. Born 1830, died 1871.
WATKINS, HENRY THOMAS, Henderson: A. B., 1878. Lawyer.
WATKINS, JOEL T., Mecklenburg, Va.: 1835–'36.
WATKINS, SAMUEL VENABLE, Farmville, Va.: 1814–'16. Dead.
WATKINS, STEPHEN H., Virginia: 1836–'37.
WATKINS, STEPHEN K. S., Somerville, Tenn.: 1858–'59. Born 1839. Lieut. C. S. A. Planter. Williston, Tenn.
WATKINS, THOMAS R., Somerville, Tenn.: 1859–'61. Born 1840. C. S. A. Physician. Buntyn, Tenn.
WATKINS, WARNER MERIWETHER, Milton, Caswell Co.: A. B., 1863.
WATLINGTON, JAMES SCOTT, Milton, Caswell Co., A. B., 1858.
WATSON, CHARLES E., Chapel Hill: 1864–'66. Durham.
WATSON, EDWARD THOMAS, Chapel Hill: 1844–'46. Physician. Dead.
WATSON, GEORGE WASHINGTON, Moulton, Ala.: A. B., 1851. C. S. A. Dead.
WATSON, JAMES A., Chapel Hill: A. B., 1868. Physician. Arkansas.
WATSON, JOHN B., Johnston Co.: 1828. Dead.

WATSON, JOHN H., New Berne: 1832–'35. Born 1816. Lawyer. Dead. St. Louis, Mo.

WATSON, JOHN THOMAS, Nash Co.: A. B., 1843; A. M., 1850. Physician. Dead.

WATSON, NATHANIEL HUGH, Chapel Hill: A. B., 1857. Dead.

WATSON, THOMAS LOWE, Chapel Hill: A. B., 1859. Lieut. C. S. A. Born June 7, 1839. Killed at Chickamauga, 1863. Texas.

WATSON, WILLIAM H., Smithfield, Wayne Co.: 1827. Dead.

WATT, ROBERT B., Rockingham Co.: 1833–'34. Dead.

WATT, RUFUS L., Rockingham Co.: 1840–'41. Dead.

WATT, WILLIAM P., Rockingham Co.; 1834–'36. Dead.

WATTERS, HENRY W., Wilmington: 1805. Dead.

WATTERS, JOHN WILLIAMS, Brunswick Co.: A. B., 1825. Physician. Dead.

WATTERS, JOSEPH H., Brunswick Co.: 1801. Dead.

WATTERS, SAMUEL PAXSON, Wilmington: A. B., 1855. Episc. Minister. Morganton.

WATTERS, WILLIAM, Brunswick Co.: 1847–'51. Planter. Dead.

WATTS, LEANDER ALBERTUS, Iredell Co.: A. B., 1826. Minister. Born 1801, died 1855.

WATTS, THOMAS WYNN, Williamston, Martin Co.: A. B., 1826.

WAUGH, JESSE ALBERT, Stokes Co.: A. B., 1831. Dead.

WEAVER, LUTHER JONES, Orange Co.: 1869–'70.

WEAVER, RICHARD THOMAS, Jackson, Northampton Co.: A. B., 1846. Physician. Dead.

WEAVER, WILEY CROMWELL, Orange Co.: 1869–'70.

WEBB, BENJAMIN D., Halifax Co.: 1863–'64. C. S. A. Planter.

WEBB, CHARLES AURELIUS, Warren Plains: A. B., 1889. Teacher. Asheville.

WEBB, HENRY, Hillsboro: 1823. Dead.

WEBB, HENRY YOUNG, Hillsboro: 1803–'06. A. M. Gen. Assem. Judge 3d Dist. Ala. Ter. Born 1784, died 1823. Greene Co., Ala.

WEBB, HENRY YOUNG, Eutaw, Ala.: 1841–'44. Born 1822. M. D. Jefferson Coll. Pres. Bd. of Censors and Health officer, Greene Co.

WEBB, JAMES, Hillsboro: 1795. Dead.

WEBB, JAMES LOUIS ADRIAN, Maury Co., Tenn.: A. B., 1857. Planter. Hood, Miss.

WEBB, JOHN, Tallyho, Granville Co.: 1877–'79. Oxford.

WEBB, JOHN M., Alamance Co.: 1866–'68. A. M., 1878. Prin. Webb School. Bellbuckle, Tenn.

WEBB, JOSEPH C., Hillsboro: 1865–'68.

WEBB, RICHARD STANFORD, Alamance Co.: A. B., 1859; A. M., 1866. Born 1837. Chaplain C. S. A. N. C. Conference.

WEBB, ROBERT DICKENS, Marion, Ala.: 1828. Physician. Born 1808, died 1845.

WEBB, THOMAS, Granville Co.: 1799. Dead.

WEBB, THOMAS, Hillsboro: A. B., 1847; A. M., 1851. Gen. Assem. Pres. N. C. R. R.

WEBB, THOMAS SHAPARD, Memphis, Tenn.: 1858–'61. Born 1840. Major C. S. A. Lawyer. Knoxville, Tenn.

WEBB, WILLIAM EDWARDS, Granville Co.: A. B., 1812; A. M., 1815. Prof. Anc. Langs., U. N. C. Dead.

WEBB, WILLIAM HENRY GRAHAM, Granville Co.: 1860–'61. Lieut. C. S. A. Born Dec. 2, 1842. Mortally wounded at Gettysburg.

WEBB, WILLIAM PETER, Tuscaloosa, Ala.: A. B., 1835. Lawyer. Judge. Eutaw, Ala.

WEBB, WILLIAM ROBERT, Alamance Co.: 1860–'61, and 1863–'64. A. B., 1867; A. M., 1868. Born 1842. Capt. C. S. A. Prin. Webb School. Bellbuckle, Tenn.

WEBB, WILLIAM SMITH, Hillsboro: A. B., 1799. Physician. Born 1778, died 1866. Williamson Co., Tenn.

WEEKS, STEPHEN BEAUREGARD, Nixonton, Pasquotank Co.: A. B., 1886; A. M., 1887; Ph. D., 1888. Tutor U. N. C., 1887–'88. Chapel Hill.

WEILL, SOLOMON COHEN, Wilmington: A. B., 1885; LL. B., 1886. Acting Prof. Greek, 1885–'86. Lawyer.

WEIR, SAMUEL P., Greensboro: A. B., 1860. Lieut. C. S. A. Born Oct. 12, 1839, killed at Fredericksburg, 1862.

WELLBORN, OLIN, Dalton, Ga.: 1860–'61. Col. C. S. A.

WESSON, BENJAMIN J., Calloway Co., Ky.: 1858–'61. A. M., 1878. Teacher. Fulton, Ky.

WEST, JESSE FELIX, Waverly, Va.: Ph. B., 1885. Lawyer.

WEST, JOHN WALTER, Waverly, Va.: 1882–'83.

WEST, JUNIUS EDGAR, Waverly, Va.: 1882–'84.

WEST, LOUIS, Woodville, Miss.: 1858–'59.

WESTRAY, SAMUEL EDWARD, Nash Co.: A. B., 1858. Planter.

WETMORE, GEORGE BADGER, Fayetteville: A. B., 1844; D. D. Episc. Minister. Born 1823, died June 10, 1888. Banner's Elk.

WETMORE, THOMAS BADGER, Fayetteville: A. B., 1841. Born 1821. Lawyer. Maj. C. S. A. Livingston, Ala.

WETMORE, WILLIAM ROBARDS, Fayetteville: A. B., 1854. Born 1834. Tutor U. N. C. Chaplain C. S. A. Episc. Min. Lincolnton.

WHARTON, JOHN ELISHA, Guilford Co.: A. B., 1857. Capt. C. S. A. Sherman, Tex.

WHARTON, JESSE RANKIN, Guilford Co.: A. B., 1855. Supt. Pub. Instruct.

WHARTON, SAMUEL DAVIES, Guilford Co.: A. B., 1845. Dead.

WHARTON, HENRY WATSON, Greensboro: 1887–.

WHARTON, TURNER ASHBY, Greensboro: 1880–'83. Minister.

WHEAT, JOHN THOMAS, Chapel Hill: A. B., 1851; A. B. Univ. of Nashville, 1849. Lawyer. Sec. Conv. La., 1861. Capt. 1st Louisiana, C. S. A. Born Dec. 3, 1830, killed at Shiloh, April 6, 1862. New Orleans, La.

WHEAT, LEONIDAS POLK, Chapel Hill: 1858–'60. Born 1841. Planter. Berryville, Va.

WHEDBEE, JOSHUA LEE, Hertford Co.: 1876–'77. Planter.

WHEDBEE, THOMAS C., Hertford Co.: 1887–'88. Lawyer.

WHEELER, JUNIUS BRUTUS, Lincoln Co.: 1849–'51. Col. U. S. A. Prof. Engineering U. S. Mil. Acad. Author. Born 1830, died 1886. West Point, N. Y.

WHITAKER, BENJAMIN FRANKLIN, Halifax Co.: A. B., 1846. Physician.
WHITAKER, CAREY, Halifax Co.: A. B., 1802.
WHITAKER, CAREY, Halifax Co.: 1850–'52. Capt. C. S. A. Killed in battle, 1864.
WHITAKER, CHARLES, Halifax Co.: A. B., 1855.
WHITAKER, DAVID C., Davenport, Iowa: B. S., 1858. Lieut. C. S. A. Born Nov. 30, 1838, died in service at Jamestown, Apr. 21, 1865.
WHITAKER, DE BERNIERE HOOPER, Raleigh: 1887–.
WHITAKER, EXUM LEWIS, Halifax Co.: A. B., 1844. Capt. U. S. A. Died in Mex. War, 1847.
WHITAKER, JAMES FLETCHER, Enfield, Halifax Co.: 1878–'79.
WHITAKER, JAMES HUNTER, Halifax Co.: A. B., 1853. Capt. C. S. A.
WHITAKER, JOHN C., Halifax Co.: 1833–'34. Dead.
WHITAKER, JOHN HENRY, Halifax Co.: A. B., 1847. Lawyer. Planter. Maj. 1st N. C. Cav., C. S. A. Born June 19, 1827, wounded at Fairfax C. H. and died June 27, 1863.
WHITAKER, LEWIS B., Halifax Co.: 1816.
WHITAKER, MATTHEW, Enfield, Halifax Co.: 1838–'40. Physician. Dead.
WHITAKER, NATHANIEL J., Wake Co.: 1853–'54.
WHITAKER, RICHARD H., Tallahassee, Fla.: 1850–'51. Dead.
WHITAKER, SPIER, Halifax Co.: 1817. Gen. Assem. Atty. Gen. N. C., 1842–'47. Dead. Davenport, Iowa.
WHITAKER, SPIER, Davenport, Iowa: A. B., 1861. Adj. C. S. A. Lawyer. Chm'n State Dem. Com., 1888–. Raleigh, N. C.
WHITAKER, THOMAS D., Scotland Neck: 1884–'85. Lawyer.
WHITAKER, WILLIAM H., Davenport, Iowa: A. B., 1858. Lawyer. C. S. A. Born Dec. 20, 1836, died in service, Oct. 20, 1862. California.
WHITAKER, WILSON CARY, Tallahassee, Fla.: A. B., 1851. Physician.
WHITAKER, WILSON WILLIS, Caswell Co.: A. B., 1838; A. M., 1841. Dead.
WHITE, BENJAMIN FRANKLIN, Bertie Co.: Ph. B., 1884.
WHITE, CHAPMAN G., Columbia, Tenn.: 1854–'56. Died 1859.
WHITE, GEORGE MONTGOMERY, Bladen Co.: A. B., 1853. Died 1860.
WHITE, JAMES WILLIAM, Clinton, Sampson Co.: 1887–.
WHITE, JOHN M., York District, S. C.: 1852–'53.
WHITE, JOSEPH MASTERS, Marianna, Fla.: A. B., 1858. Born 1837, died 1867.
WHITE, RICHARD STREET, Elizabethtown, Bladen Co.: B. S., 1886. Lawyer.
WHITE, STUART, Raleigh: A. B., 1856. Dead.
WHITE, THOMAS, Petersburg, Va.: 1845–'48. Capt. C. S. A.
WHITE, WALTER WALLACE, Boykin's, Va.: 1885–'86.
WHITE, WILLIE HILL, Smithfield, Wayne Co.: 1810. Physician. Dead.
WHITE, WILLIAM HILL, Salisbury: 1881–'83.
WHITE, WILLIAM J., Warrenton: 1859–'61. Merchant.
WHITEHEAD, ROBERT BYNUM, Wilson: 1888–.

WHITEHEAD, WILEY WHITEFOOT, Kenansville: A. B., 1858. Died 1863.
WHITEHURST, JAMES B., Tarboro: 1888. Lawyer.
WHITEHURST, WILLIAM WARREN, Straits, Carteret Co.: 1882–'84.
WHITESIDE, GEORGE M., Rutherford Co.: 1867–'68. Lawyer. Died 1880.
WHITFIELD, ALLEN, Lenoir Co.: 1812.
WHITFIELD, ANTHONY D., Columbus, Miss.: 1859–'60.
WHITFIELD, BOAZ, Demopolis, Ala.: A. B., 1858; A. M., 1861. Born 1838. C. S. A. Lawyer. Physician. Planter.
WHITFIELD, BRYAN, Tallahassee, Fla.: A. B., 1854. Physician. Capt. C. S. A. Born 1833, killed in battle, 1861. Greenville, Ala.
WHITFIELD, BRYAN WATKINS, Demopolis, Ala.: A. B., 1849. Born 1828. Physician. Planter.
WHITFIELD, CICERO, Lenoir Co.: A. B., 1860. Sergt. C. S. A. Physician.
WHITFIELD, EDWARD H., Wayne Co.: 1817. Dead.
WHITFIELD, GAIUS, Demopolis, Ala.: 1853–'56. Born 1837. C. S. A. Planter.
WHITFIELD, GEORGE, Lenoir Co.: 1822. Dead.
WHITFIELD, GEORGE, Lenoir Co.: A. B., 1823. Dead.
WHITFIELD, GEORGE, Tallahassee, Fla.: 1850–'52. Surg. C. S. A. Dead.
WHITFIELD, GEORGE WILLIAM, Linden, Ala.: 1845–'47. Lawyer. Gen. Assem. Born 1829, died 1871. Wilson, N. C.
WHITFIELD, JAMES B., Lenoir Co.: 1824. Dead.
WHITFIELD, JAMES GEORGE, Lenoir Co.: A. B., 1859. Born 1840. Black Bluff, Ala.
WHITFIELD, JAMES HERVEY, Gainesville, Ala.: A. B., 1855. Brandon, Miss.
WHITFIELD, JOHN ALEXANDER, Lowndes Co., Miss.: A. B., 1849. Capt. C. S. A. Killed in battle.
WHITFIELD, NATHAN B., Lenoir Co.: 1813. Dead.
WHITFIELD, NATHAN B., Lenoir Co.: 1853–'56. Col. C. S. A. Judge.
WHITFIELD, NATHAN B., Wayne Co.: 1857–'59. Capt. C. S. A. Killed in battle.
WHITFIELD, NATHAN BRYAN, Demopolis, Ala.: A. B., 1857. Born 1835. C. S. A. Civ. Engineer. San Francisco, Cal.
WHITFIELD, NEEDHAM G. BRYAN, Demopolis, Ala.: A. B., 1849. Born 1830. C. S. A. Lawyer.
WHITFIELD, NEEDHAM J., Aberdeen, Miss.: 1848–'50.
WHITFIELD, OWEN HOLMES, Aberdeen, Miss.: A. B., 1846. Lawyer. Dead.
WHITFIELD, RICHARD A., Lenoir Co.: 1849–'52.
WHITFIELD, RICHARD HENRY, Demopolis, Ala.: A. B., 1850. Born 1830. M. D. Univ. Pa. Surg. C. S. A. Meridian, Miss.
WHITFIELD, ROBERT A., Gainesville, Ala.: 1856–'57.
WHITFIELD, SAMUEL, Wayne Co.: 1816. Dead.
WHITFIELD, SAMUEL ERWIN, Aberdeen, Miss.: A. B., 1850.
WHITFIELD, SAMUEL GODWIN, Enfield, Halifax Co.: 1878–'79.
WHITFIELD, THEODORE, Hinds Co., Miss.: A. B., 1850. Born 1834. D. D. Charlotte, N. C.

WHITFIELD, WILLIAM A., Wayne Co.: 1834–'37. U. S. Navy.
WHITFIELD, WILLIAM BLACKLEDGE, Jefferson Co., Fla.: 1859–'61. C. S. A. Born 1842, killed at Seven Pines, 1862.
WHITFIELD, WILLIAM COBB, La Grange, Lenoir Co.: 1880–'81. Physician.
WHITFIELD, WILLIAM W., Mississippi: 1843–'44.
WHITNER, ALONZO CHURCH, Madison C. H., Fla.: A. B., 1861; A. M. Judge Superior Court.
WHITNER, BENJAMIN FRANKLIN, Madison C. H., Fla.: 1860–'61. Capt. C. S. A.
WHITSETT, WILLIE T., Gibsonville, Guilford Co.: 1886–'88.
WHITSETT, GEORGE WALTER, Graham, Alamauce Co.: Ph. B., 1882. Dentist. Greensboro.
WHITTED, ANDERSON, Hillsboro: 1807. Dead.
WHITTED, HENRY, Virginia: 1817. Dead.
WHITTED, JAMES, Orange Co.: 1803. Dead.
WHITTED, JOHN McK., Bladen Co.: 1857–'60. C. S. A.
WHITTED, THOMAS, Bladen Co.: 1853–'56. C. S. A.
WHITTED, THOMAS SMITH, Bladen Co.: A. B., 1858. Elizabethtown.
WHITTED, WILLIAM DAVIS, Hendersonville: 1869–'70.
WHITTINGTON, HIRAM ALLEN, Burnsville, Yancey Co.: 1886–'88.
WHYTE, THOMAS EDWARD, Chapel Hill: A. B., 1845. Born 1827. Surg. C. S. A. Physician. Clarke Co., Ga.
WHYTE, WILLIAM JOSEPH, Chapel Hill: A. B., 1850. Born 1831. Teacher. Dead. Mobile, Ala.
WIGGINS, MASON L., Halifax Co.: 1815. Gen. Assem. Dead.
WIGGINS, OCTAVIUS A., Halifax Co.: 1860–'62. Lieut. C. S. A. Wilmington.
WIGGINS, RICHARD A., Alabama: 1827.
WIGGINS, THOMAS J. M., Halifax Co.: 1860–'61. Dead.
WIGGINS, WILLIAM H., Halifax Co.: 1851–'52. Dead.
WIGGINS, WILLIAM R., Oxford: 1848–'49. Lawyer.
WILCOX, JOHN, Greysville, Ky.: 1857–'59.
WILCOX, MAURICE HOLTON, Warrenton: 1878–'79. Died 1879.
WILDER, GASTON HILLARY, Johnston Co.: A. B., 1838; A. M., 1843. Planter. Gen. Assem. U. S. A. Dead.
WILDER, HILLARY MADISON, Wake Co.: A. B., 1846. Dead.
WILDER, THOMAS BONNER, Louisburg, Franklin Co.: 1884–'85.
WILEY, CALVIN HENDERSON, Guilford Co.: A. B., 1840; A. M., 1845; D. D., 1881. State Supt. Pub. Instruction. Died 1887.
WILKERSON, THOMAS BENTON, Granville Co.: 1853–'55. Born 1837. M. D. Univ. Pa. Surg. C. S. A. Author.
WILKES, BURWELL BASSETT, Lawrenceville, Va.: A. B., 1825. Dead.
WILKES, ELI ASHTON, Chester, S. C.: 1881–'82.
WILKES, JOHN FRANCIS, Charlotte: Ph. B., 1881. Manufacturer.
WILKES, PAUL, Charlotte: 1882–'83.
WILKINS, AMOS J., Edgecombe Co.: 1818. Dead.
WILKINS, BENJAMIN F., Virginia: 1812. Dead.

WILKINS, EDMUND T., Hicksford, Va.: A. B., 1814. Dead.
WILKINS, EDMUND WEBB, Eastville, Va.: A. B., 1851.
WILKINS, JOHN J., Hicksford, Va.: 1822.
WILKINS, JOHN L., 1818. Dead.
WILKINS, WILLIAM, Hicksford, Va.: 1817. Dead.
WILKINS, WILLIAM W., Brunswick Co., Va.: 1862–'63.
WILKINSON, FRANKLIN SMITH, Edgecombe Co.: A. B., 1857. Teacher. Tarboro.
WILKINSON, NATHANIEL, 1807. Dead.
WILKINSON, WILLIAM STRONACH, Tarboro: A. B., 1887. Teacher. Enfield.
WILLCOX, FREDERICK LEROY, Carbonton, Moore Co.: 1888–.
WILLCOX, JOSEPH MARTIN, Carbonton, Moore Co.: 1888–.
WILLCOX, LEWIS BARGE, Hawkinsville, Ga.: 1879–'80.
WILLEFORD, MARANDY R., Upshur Co., Texas: 1859–'61.
WILLEY, CLAUDE C., Gatesville: 1879–'80.
WILLIAMS, ABNER F., Elizabeth City: 1838–'39. Dead.
WILLIAMS, ALBERT SIDNEY, Wilmington: 1887–.
WILLIAMS, ALEXANDER, Surry Co.: 1813. Physician.
WILLIAMS, CYRUS WELLMON, Polk Co.: 1879–'81.
WILLIAMS, DAVID, Martin Co.: 1816. Dead.
WILLIAMS, DUNCAN MURCHISON, Wilmington: 1876–'78.
WILLIAMS, FRANCIS RUSH, Davie Co.: 1854–'56. M. D. Univ. Pa. Born 1835, died 1868.
WILLIAMS, GABRIEL LONG, Montgomery Co., Tenn.: 1854–'56. Born 1834. Merchant. Clarksville, Tenn.
WILLIAMS, GREEN DUKE, Nut Bush, Granville Co.: 1824. Dead.
WILLIAMS, HENRY, Tennessee: 1802. Dead.
WILLIAMS, HENRY, Williamston, Martin Co.: 1853–'55.
WILLIAMS, HENRY CHRISTMAS, Warren Co.: A. B., 1820. Born 1801, died 1828.
WILLIAMS, HENRY G., Northampton Co.: 1803. Dead.
WILLIAMS, HENRY G., Franklin Co.: 1844–'46. Gen. Assem.
WILLIAMS, HENRY GASTON, Warren Co.: A. B., 1861. Ensign C. S. A. Born 1841, killed at Malvern Hill, 1862.
WILLIAMS, HENRY HORACE, Sunbury: A. B. and A. M., 1883. Prof. Trin. Coll., N. C., 1884–'85. B. D. Yale, 1888.
WILLIAMS, JAMES HENDERSON, Cumberland Co.: A. B., 1841. Dead.
WILLIAMS, JAMES HILLIARD, Warrenton: A. B., 1856. Born 1835. C. S. A. Teacher. Planter. Dead.
WILLIAMS, JOHN BRANCH, Tallahassee, Fla.: 1851–'53. Planter. Born 1834, died 1873. Carroll Parish, La.
WILLIAMS, JOHN BUXTON, Warren Co.: 1831–'33. Planter. Born 1815, died 1877.
WILLIAMS, JOHN BUXTON, Warren Co.: A. B., 1864. Born 1844. C. S. A. Physician. Oxford.
WILLIAMS, JOHN CALHOUN, Cumberland Co.: A. B., 1841; A. M., 1846. Dead.

WILLIAMS, JOHN CAMPBELL, Cumberland Co.: A. B., 1809. Dead.
WILLIAMS, JOHN D., Fayetteville: 1865–'67. Merchant. Wilmington.
WILLIAMS, JOHN G., Washington, Beaufort Co.: 1832–'34. Born 1815. Planter. Dead.
WILLIAMS, JOHN GODFREY, Raleigh: 1882–'84. Baltimore, Md.
WILLIAMS, JOHN ROBERT, Apex, Wake Co.: 1886–.
WILLIAMS, JOHN T., Surry Co.: 1827.
WILLIAMS, JOSEPH, Surry Co.: 1827. Dead.
WILLIAMS, JOSEPH, Panther Creek, Yadkin Co.: A. B., 1858. Born 1836. Planter.
WILLIAMS, JOSEPH ADRIAN, Pitt Co.: A. B., 1859. Capt. C. S. A. Killed in battle, 1863.
WILLIAMS, JOSEPH AUGUSTUS, Chatham Co.: 1878–'79.
WILLIAMS, JOSIAH, Franklin Co.: 1803. Dead.
WILLIAMS, LEWIS, Surry Co.: A. B., 1808; A. M., 1812. Tutor U. N. C., 1810–'12. Gen. Assem., 1813–'14. M. C., 1815–'42. Born Feb. 1, 1786, died at Washington, D. C., Feb. 20, 1842.
WILLIAMS, LEWIS L., Nashville, Tenn.: 1838–'40. Dead.
WILLIAMS, MONROE RICHARD, Farmington, Davie Co.: 1854–'55. Born 1833. C. S. A. Planter.
WILLIAMS, NATHANIEL T., Jerusalem, Va.: 1824. Dead.
WILLIAMS, NATHANIEL W., Tennessee: 1797. Judge Superior Ct. Dead.
WILLIAMS, NICHOLAS, Pitt Co.: 1851–'52. Planter. Dead.
WILLIAMS, NICHOLAS GLENN, Panther Creek, Yadkin Co.: 1882–'84.
WILLIAMS, NICHOLAS LANIER, Yadkin Co.: 1816. Planter. Mem. Council of State. Born 1799, died July 3, 1886.
WILLIAMS, NICHOLAS LANIER, Yadkin Co.: A. B., 1861. Dead.
WILLIAMS, OLIVER LaFAYETTE, Farmington: 1887–'88.
WILLIAMS, PATRICK HENRY, Elizabeth City: 1887–'88.
WILLIAMS, PHILIP K., Warren Co.: 1865–'66.
WILLIAMS, RICHARD F., Pitt Co.: 1851–'52.
WILLIAMS, ROBERT, Surry Co.: 1809. Adj. Gen. N. C. M. C. Dead.
WILLIAMS, ROBERT, Warren Co.: 1817. Dead.
WILLIAMS, ROBERT DANIEL, Elizabeth City: 1880–'81. Merchant.
WILLIAMS, ROBERT WILLOUGHBY, Tallahassee, Fla.: 1861–'62. Born 1845. C. S. A. Planter. Carroll Parish, La.
WILLIAMS, SAMUEL, Halifax Co., Va.: A. B., 1834.
WILLIAMS, SAMUEL ALSTON, Warren Co.: A. B., 1832.
WILLIAMS, SAMUEL G., Louisburg, Franklin Co.: 1834–'36. Dead.
WILLIAMS, SHERWOOD H., Pitt Co.: 1859–'60.
WILLIAMS, SOLOMON, Martin Co.: 1799. Dead.
WILLIAMS, SOLOMON BUXTON, Warren Co.: 1863–'64. Born 1846. Planter.
WILLIAMS, THOMAS C., Warren Co.: 1845–'47. Lawyer. Died 1884.
WILLIAMS, THOMAS DAVIS, Warrenton: A. B., 1855. Lawyer. C. S. A. Dead.
WILLIAMS, THOMAS JASPER, Halifax Co., Va.: A. B., 1834. Physician.

WILLIAMS, THOMAS LANIER, Surry Co.: A. B., 1808; A. M., 1812. Gen. Assem. Tenn. Judge Supreme Ct., Tenn. Chancellor Tenn., 1836–'52. Born Feb. 1, 1786, died Dec. 3, 1856. Knoxville, Tenn.
WILLIAMS, THOMAS LANIER, Greenville, Tenn.: 1858–'59.
WILLIAMS, WILLIAM, 1809. Dead.
WILLIAMS, WILLIAM, Surry Co.: 1813. Dead.
WILLIAMS, WILLIAM DICKSON, Greenville, Tenn.: 1846–'47. Born 1826.
WILLIAMS, WILLIAM H., 1805. Dead.
WILLIAMS, WILLIAM HENRY, Greene Co.: A. B., 1857. Warsaw.
WILLIAMS, WILLIAM L., Cumberland Co.: 1831–'32.
WILLIAMS, WILLIAM S., Charlotte: 1857–'58.
WILLIAMS, WILLIAM T., Virginia: 1807. Dead.
WILLIAMS, WILLIAM W., Raleigh: 1886–'88.
WILLIAMSON, GEORGE H., Cincinnati, Ohio: 1860–'61.
WILLIAMSON, JAMES COLON, Cerro Gordo: 1887–'88.
WILLIAMSON, JAMES MONROE, Person Co.: A. B., 1831. Lawyer. Gen. Assem. Tenn. Born 1810, died 1877. Memphis, Tenn.
WILLIAMSON, JOHN G. A., Person Co.: 1813. Chargé d'Affaires Venezuela. Dead.
WILLIAMSON, JOHN LEA, Caswell Co.: A. B., 1843; A. M., 1847.
WILLIAMSON, JOHN REED, Lincoln Co.: A. B., 1827. Dead.
WILLIAMSON, JOHN WILLIAM, Caswell Co.: A. B., 1858. Surg. C. S. A. Physician.
WILLIAMSON, ROBERT PAINE, Roxboro, Person Co.: A. B., 1823; A. M., 1827. Physician. Born 1804, died 1849.
WILLIAMSON, RUSSELL M., Columbia, Tenn.: 1823–'25.
WILLIAMSON, THOMAS LEA, Yanceyville, Caswell Co.: A. B., 1852.
WILLIAMSON, WALTER S., Caswell Co.: 1858–'59.
WILLIAMSON, WELDON E., Caswell Co.: 1850–'52. Dead.
WILLIS, HENRY M., San Francisco, Cal.: 1854–'55. Lawyer.
WILLS, GEORGE STOCKTON, Greensboro: Ph. B., 1889. Teacher. Oak Ridge.
WILLS, WILLIAM HENRY, Greensboro: 1887–'88.
WILLS, WILLIAM LOUDON, Edenton: A. B., 1823. Dead.
WILSON, ADOLPHUS ERWIN, Morganton: 1882–'85.
WILSON, ADOLPHUS R., Blackman's Mills: 1869–'70.
WILSON, ALBERT ROBERT, Greensboro: 1877–'80. Physician.
WILSON, ALEXANDER ERWIN, Cabarrus Co.: A. B., 1822. D. D. M. D. Missionary to China.
WILSON, CHARLES CRAWFORD, New Berne: A. B., 1832. Physician. Dead.
WILSON, DELONZA TATE, Hobton: A. B., 1887. Teacher.
WILSON, GEORGE GREGORY, Greensboro: A. B., 1882. Dead.
WILSON, GEORGE LOVICK, New Berne: A. B., 1860. C. S. A. Dead.
WILSON, HENRY ASBURY, Yadkinville: 1886–'87. Died 1887.
WILSON, JAMES WILLIAM, Alamance Co.: A. B., 1852. Born 1832. Maj. C. S. A. Pres. W. N. C. R. R. Civil Engineer. Morganton.
WILSON, JOHN, Milton, Caswell Co.: A. B., 1848; A. M., 1852. Physician.

Wilson, John Nestor, Greensboro: 1878–'79. Physician.
Wilson, John R., Danville, Va.: 1837–'38.
Wilson, John W., Chatham Co.: 1846–'47.
Wilson, John W., Guilford Co.: 1857–'59. Lieut. C. S. A. Killed in battle.
Wilson, Nathan Hunt Daniel, Greensboro: A. B., 1886. Meth. Minister.
Wilson, Peter Mitchell, Warrenton: 1865–'67. Born 1848. A. M. Univ. Edinburgh. Teacher. Lawyer. Journalist. Com. Agr. N. C., 1880. Raleigh.
Wilson, Richard Don, Caswell Co.: A. B., 1842. Lawyer. Teacher. C. S. A. Born 1819, died 1883. McDowell Co.
Wilson, Robert Willis, Hillsboro: A. B., 1848; A. M., 1852. Teacher. Born 1828, died 1868.
Wilson, Stephen Pender, Shawboro, Guilford Co.: 1883–'85.
Wilson, William Albert, Sutherland, Ashe Co.: A. B., 1889.
Wilson, William Edward, Elizabeth City: A. B., 1857. 17th N. C., C. S. A. Killed at Roanoke Island, Feb. 7, 1862.
Wimberly, George Lewis, Edgecombe Co.: A. B., 1857.
Wimberly, George Lewis, Battleboro: 1879–'81. Physician. Rocky Mount.
Wimbish, James Alexander, Virginia: A. B., 1844. Dead.
Winborne, Peter Parker, Barnitz, Chowan Co.: 1887–.
Winborne, Robert Henry, Hertford Co.: A. B., 1847; A. M., 1850. Physician. Planter. Barnitz.
Winborne, Robert Warren, Murfreesboro: A. B., 1881. Lawyer. Gen. Assem.
Winborne, Samuel Pretlow, Murfreesboro: 1886–'87. Planter. Como.
Winder, John Henry, Raleigh: 1877–'78.
Winder, John William, Warsaw, Duplin Co.: 1883–'84.
Windham, Thomas K., Pickens Co., Ala.: A. B., 1856. C. S. A. Planter.
Windsor, William Sanford, Williamsburg: 1884–'85.
Winslow, John T., Fayetteville: 1852–'53. Lawyer. Died 1863.
Winslow, Warren, Fayetteville: A. B., 1827. Lawyer. Gen. Assem. Gov. N. C., 1854–'55. M. C., 1855–'61. Mem. Conv., 1861. Born 1810, died 1862.
Winstead, Stephen, Princeton, Ark.: 1860–'61. Capt. C. S. A. Born 1842, died 1873.
Winston, Francis Donnell, Windsor, Bertie Co.: A. B., 1879. Lawyer. Gen. Assem.
Winston, George D., 1823.
Winston, George Tayloe, Windsor, Bertie Co.: 1866–'68. Lit. B. Cornell, 1874. A. M. Davidson Coll. Instruct. Math. Cornell, 1874–'75. Assist. Prof. Literature, U. N. C., 1875–'76; Prof. Lat. and Ger., 1876–'85; Prof. Lat., 1885–. Pres. N. C. Teachers' Assembly, 1879 and 1888. Chapel Hill.
Winston, John A., Gainesville, Ala.: 1859–'61.
Winston, John Camm, Richmond, Va.: 1878–'80. Merchant. Minneapolis, Minn.

Winston, John Nelson, DeKalb Co., Ala.: 1859–'60. Born 1840. M. D. Louisville Med. Coll.
Winston, John Winslow, Fayetteville: A. B., 1827; A. M., 1832. Lawyer. C. S. A. Born 1807, died 1863. Jefferson, Tex.
Winston, Patrick Henry, Rockingham Co.: 1818. Lawyer. Reporter Supreme Ct. Dead.
Winston, Patrick Henry, Bertie Co.: 1844–'45. A. B. Columbian Univ. Lawyer and Planter. Gen. Assem., 1850–'54. Commr. Board of Claims, 1861. Finan. Agt. between N. C. and Confed. States, 1863. Pres. Council of State, 1864. Mem. Conv., 1865. Born 1820, died 1886.
Winston, Patrick Henry, Windsor, Bertie Co.: A. B., 1867. Born 1847. Lawyer. Spokane Falls, Washington.
Winston, Robert Watson, Windsor, Bertie Co.: A. B., 1879. Tutor U. N. C., 1880–'81. Lawyer. Gen. Assem. Oxford.
Winston, Stephen P., Tuscumbia, Ala.: 1846–'47.
Winston, William E., Gainesville, Ala.: 1859–'61. Lieut. C. S. A.
Wise, M. William, Murfreesboro, Hertford Co.: 1850–'51.
Withers, Elijah Benton, Caswell Co.: A. B., 1859. Maj. C. S. A. Lawyer. Danville, Va.
Withers, Eugene Percival, Danville, Va.: Ph. B., 1888. Lawyer.
Withers, William M., Caswell Co.: 1846–'47.
Witherspoon, John, New Berne: A. B, 1810; A. M.; D. D.; LL. D. Pres. Miami Coll. Dead.
Wittich, Ernest Leroy, Tuskegee, Ala.: 1860–'61. Color Sergt. C. S. A. Born 1843. Killed at Cold Harbor, 1864.
Wolfe, Rowland Vance, Asheville: 1883–'85.
Womack, Francis, Pittsboro: 1883–'85. Druggist. Smithfield.
Womack, James Green, Pittsboro: A. B., 1837; A. M., 1840. M. D. Univ. Pa. Born 1818, died 1874. Jackson, Tenn.
Womack, Sidney, Eutaw, Ala.: 1859–'61. Born 1842, died 1868.
Wood, Ben Franklin, Claiborne, Ala.: 1833–'34.
Wood, Frank, Edenton: 1876–'78.
Wood, Henry Gilliam, Edenton: Ph. B., 1889.
Wood, John Quincy Adams, Elizabeth City: 1869–'70.
Wood, John Whitaker, Scotland Neck: LL. B., 1885.
Wood, Julian, Edenton: Ph. B., 1884. Lawyer.
Wood, William B., 1815. Dead.
Wood, William H. R., Fort Claiborne, Ala.: 1830–'33. Dead.
Woodard, Leonidas Polk, Wilson Co.: 1883–'85.
Woodard, Paul Lee, Black Creek, Wilson Co.: 1886–.
Woodard, Sidney Albert, Black Creek, Wilson Co.: 1880–'85. Lawyer.
Woodburn, John Allen, Guilford Co.: A. B., 1859.
Wooding, William Hill, Pittsylvania Co., Va.: A. B., 1827.
Woodley, Daniel Edgar, Columbiana, Tyrrell Co.: 1884–'87.
Woodley, Theophilus Henry, Creswell: 1888–.
Woods, James, Nashville, Tenn.: A. B., 1853. Lawyer. Died 1859.
Woodson, Byron, Richmond, Va.: 1883–'85. Lawyer.

WOODSON, ROBERT SCOTT, Plymouth, Washington Co.: 1885–'87. M. D. Vanderbilt Med. Coll., 1889. Day's Gap, Ala.
WOOSTER, JOHN LEWIS, Wilmington: A. B., 1851.
WOOSTER, WILLIAM A., Wilmington: A. B., 1860. Capt. C. S. A. Killed in battle.
WOOTEN, THOMAS CHRISTIAN, Kinston, Lenoir Co.: 1882–'84. Lawyer.
WORMELY, JOHN R., Claiborne, Ala. 1857–'58.
WORTH, CHARLES WILLIAMS, Wilmington: A. B., 1883.
WORTH, DAVID GASTON, Ashboro: A. B., 1853. Born 1831. Merchant. Wilmington.
WORTH, GEORGE CLARKSON, Wilmington: 1888–.
WORTH, JAMES SPENCER, Wilmington: 1888–.
WORTH, SHERBAL G., Montgomery Co.: 1852–'54. Capt. C. S. A. Killed in battle.
WORTHAM, GEORGE W., Oxford: 1841–'43. Born 1828. Lawyer. Capt. C. S. A. Dead.
WORTHAM, JAMES L., Granville Co.: 1814. Dead.
WORTHINGTON, BENJAMIN T., Greenville, Miss.: 1860–'61. Born 1844. C. S. A. Planter. Leota, Miss.
WORTHINGTON, ROBERT, Greenville, Pitt Co.: 1886–'87.
WRIGHT, ADAM EMPIE, Wilmington: A. B., 1853. Physician. Born 1833, died 1879.
WRIGHT, CHARLES JEWKES, Wilmington: A. B., 1812. Born 1792, died 1821.
WRIGHT, CLEMENT GILLESPIE, Bladen Co.: A. B., 1843; A. M., 1853. Lawyer. Gen. Assem., 1861. Lieut. Col. C. S. A. Born Oct. 15, 1824. Killed in battle, 1865. Fayetteville.
WRIGHT, CLEMENT GILLESPIE, Greensboro: 1882–'86. Lawyer.
WRIGHT, ELISHA ELDRIDGE, Memphis, Tenn.: A. B., 1861. Capt. C. S. A. Killed at Murfreesboro, 1863.
WRIGHT, JAMES ALLAN, Wilmington: A. B., 1854; A. M., 1857. Lawyer. Clerk Superior Ct. Capt. C. S. A. Born April 13, 1836. Killed at Mechanicsville, 1862.
WRIGHT, JAMES MOREHEAD, Bladen Co.: A. B., 1826; A. M., 1832. Dead.
WRIGHT, JOHN LEWIS, Wilmington: A. B., 1824. Physician. Born 1805, died 1834.
WRIGHT, JOSEPH HILL, Wilmington: A. B., 1854. Dead.
WRIGHT, JOSHUA G., Wilmington: 1825. Dead.
WRIGHT, JOSHUA GRAINGER, Wilmington: A. B., 1861. Born 1840.
WRIGHT, JULIUS WALKER, Wilmington: A. B., 1858. Lawyer. C. S. A. Dead.
WRIGHT, THOMAS HENRY, Wilmington: A. B., 1820. Physician. Pres. Bank of Cape Fear. Born 1800, died 1861.
WRIGHT, WILLIAM AUGUSTUS, Wilmington: A. B., 1825. Dead.
WRIGHT, WILLIAM AUGUSTUS, Wilmington: 1864–'66.
WRIGHT, WILLIAM BECK, Duplin Co.: A. B., 1825; A. M., 1830. Lawyer. Gen. Assem. Born 1804, died 1880. Fayetteville.

Wyche, Bevil G., Lawrenceville, Va.: 1816. Dead.
Wyche, John Jenkins, Granville Co.: A. B., 1825; A. M., 1828. Tutor U. N. C., 1826–'28. Prof. Jeff. Coll., Miss. Born 1800, died 1870.
Wynns, James M., Murfreesboro, Hertford Co.: 1851–'53. Col. C. S. A.
Yager, William L., Contra Costa Co., Cal.: 1859–'61. C. S. A. Killed in battle.
Yancey, Algernon S., Caswell Co.: 1831–'33. Dead.
Yancey, Bartlett, Caswell Co.: 1804. Lawyer. Speaker Sen. N. C. eleven years. M. C., 1813–'17. Born 1775, died 1828.
Yancey, Garland M., Chapel Hill: 1857–'60. C. S. A. Teacher. Key West, Fla.
Yancey, Rufus Augustus, Caswell Co.: A. B., 1829. Dead.
Yancey, Tryon Milton, Caswell Co.: A. B., 1814; A. M., 1817. Dead.
Yarborough, Fenner, Louisburg: 1875–'77.
Yarborough, Henry, Hillsboro: A. B., 1827; A. M., 1833. Physician. Dead.
Yarborough, James Hart, Louisburg: 1877–'79. Kansas.
Yarborough, John B., Louisburg: 1852–'53. Dead.
Yarborough, Neill Smith, Sumpter Co., Ala.: A. B., 1856. Dead.
Yarborough, Richard Fenner, Louisburg: 1851–'53.
Yarborough, Richard Fenner, Raleigh: 1888–.
Yarborough, Wiley, Salisbury: 1808. Dead.
Yates, William James, Charlotte: 1887–'88.
Yeargin, Morgan, Orange Co.: 1807. Dead.
Yellowley, Charlton Whitaker, Jackson: A. B., 1855. Lawyer. Prin. Seminary, Texas. C. S. A. Born July 26, 1831, died in service, May 12, 1864. San Marcos, Texas.
Yellowley, Edward Clements, Pitt Co.: A. B., 1844. Lawyer. Gen. Assem. Col. C. S. A. Died 1885.
Yellowley, James B., Williamston: 1815. Dead.
Yellowley, James Brownlow, Greenville, Pitt Co.: 1866–'68. Born 1848. Lawyer. Gen. Assem. Miss. Madison, Miss.
York, Richard W., Chatham Co.: 1865–'66. Lawyer.
Young, Augustus P., Louisburg: 1859–'61. Lawyer. Selma, Ala.
Young, Boaz Walton, Wake Co.: A. B., 1862.
Young, David Jones, Oxford: A. B., 1858. C. S. A. Killed in battle.
Young, George Valerius, Mississippi: A. B., 1849.
Young, Henry, Granville Co.: 1798. Dead.
Young, James, Granville Co.: 1802. Physician. Dead.
Young, John, Granville Co.: 1812. Dead.
Young, John G., Charlotte: A. B., 1867.
Young, John N., Iredell Co.: 1829.
Young, John S., North Carolina: 1804. Dead.
Young, Samuel D., Oxford: 1853–'54. Physician. Died 1888. Henderson.
Young, William Hamilton, Oxford: A. B., 1858. Died 1885. Henderson.

HONORARY DEGREES.

1799-1889.

1799	Joseph Caldwell, *North Carolina*	A. M.
"	James Smiley Gillespie, *North Carolina*	A. B.
"	Charles Wilson Harris, *North Carolina*	A. M.
"	Joseph Blount Littlejohn, *North Carolina*	A. M.
1810	David Caldwell, *North Carolina*	D. D.
"	Samuel Craighead Caldwell, *North Carolina*	A. M.
"	James Hall, *North Carolina*	D. D.
"	James McRee, *North Carolina*	D. D.
"	John Robinson, *North Carolina*	A. M.
"	William Leftwich Turner	A. M.
"	James Wallis	A. M.
"	John McKamie Wilson	A. M.
1811	William Richardson Davie, *North Carolina*	LL. D.
"	Elias Haws	A. M.
"	William McPheeters, *North Carolina*	A. M.
"	Samuel Miller, *New Jersey*	D. D.
"	Charles Gotthold Reichell, *Pennsylvania*	D. D.
"	Andrew Rhea, *Pennsylvania*	A. M.
1812	George Addison Baxter, *Virginia*	D. D.
"	Ashbel Green, *New Jersey*	LL. D.
"	James Patriot Wilson, *Pennsylvania*	D. D.
1813	Jeremiah Atwater, *Pennsylvania*	D. D.
1814	Levi Holbrook	A. M.
1815	Anthony Forster	A. B.
1816	Joseph Caldwell, *North Carolina*	D. D.
1818	John McDowell, *Virginia*	D. D.
"	Thomas Pollock Devereux, *North Carolina*	A. M.
1819	William McPheeters, *North Carolina*	D. D.
1820	Ransom Hubbell	A. M.
1823	John Stark Ravenscroft, *North Carolina*	D. D.
1825	Charles Bailey	A. M.
"	John Henry Eaton, *Tennessee*	A. M.
"	William Glascock, *Virginia*	A. B.

1825	NATHANIEL MACON, North Carolina	LL. D.
1828	WILLIAM GLASCOCK, Virginia	A. M.
"	JOHN HILL WHEELER, North Carolina	A. M.
1829	JOHN ROBERTSON	D. D.
"	JOHN McKAMIE WILSON	D. D.
1830	ADAM EMPIE, Virginia	D. D.
"	JAMES PHILLIPS, North Carolina	A. M.
"	NICHOLAS MARCELLUS HENTZ, North Carolina	A. M.
"	CORNELIUS VERMEULE, New Jersey	D. D.
1831	JOHN TATE, North Carolina	A. M.
1832	JARVIS BARRY BUXTON, North Carolina	A. M.
"	SAMUEL LYLE GRAHAM, Virginia	A. M.
1833	PHILIP BRUCE WILEY, North Carolina	A. M.
"	JOHN AVERY, North Carolina	D. D.
1834	GEORGE EDMUND BADGER, North Carolina	LL. D.
"	LEVI SILLIMAN IVES, North Carolina	LL. D.
"	THOMAS RUFFIN, North Carolina	LL. D.
"	SAMUEL SMITH	A. M.
"	ANDREW SYME, Virginia	D. D.
1836	ALEXANDER WILSON, North Carolina	A. M.
1837	BASIL MANLY, Alabama	D. D.
1838	GEORGE HOWE, South Carolina	D. D.
"	JOHN AUGUSTUS GRETTER, North Carolina	A. M.
1839	ROBERT ALLISON EZZELL, North Carolina	A. M.
"	GEORGE WASHINGTON FREEMAN, North Carolina	D. D.
"	JOHN HAMPTON	A. M.
"	DRURY LACY, North Carolina	A. M.
"	ALEXANDER WILSON, North Carolina	D. D.
1841	NEHEMIAH H. HARDING, North Carolina	D. D.
1844	ALBERT BALDWIN DOD, New Jersey	D. D.
"	ROBERT BRENT DRANE, North Carolina	D. D.
"	CHARLES PITMAN	D. D.
1845	JOHN RANDOLPH CLAY, Kentucky	A. M.
"	WILLIE PERSON MANGUM, North Carolina	LL. D.
"	JOHN YOUNG MASON, Virginia	LL. D.
"	JEREMIAH WILLIAM MURPHY, North Carolina	A. M.
"	JAMES KNOX POLK, Tennessee	LL. D.
1846	JOHN KIMBERLY, North Carolina	A. M.
1847	MATTHEW FONTAINE MAURY, Virginia	A. M.
"	BENJAMIN PEIRCE, Massachusetts	LL. D.
1848	MICHAEL TUOMEY, Alabama	A. M.
1849	WILLIAM ALEXANDER GRAHAM, North Carolina	LL. D.
1850	JAMES BOGARDUS DONNELLY, North Carolina	A. M.
1851	BENJAMIN CRAVEN, North Carolina	A. M.
"	WILLIAM NORWOOD, Virginia	D. D.
"	JAMES PHILLIPS, North Carolina	D. D.
1852	MOSES ASHLEY CURTIS, North Carolina	D. D.
"	DRURY LACY, North Carolina	D. D.

Honorary Degrees.

Year	Name	State	Degree
1852	Matthew Fontaine Maury	Virginia	LL. D.
1853	Walker Anderson	Florida	LL. D.
"	William Horn Battle	North Carolina	LL. D.
"	Joseph Cross	South Carolina	D. D.
"	Thomas F. Davis	South Carolina	D. D.
"	Cyrus Johnson	North Carolina	D. D.
"	Frederick Nash	North Carolina	LL. D.
"	Richmond M. Pearson	North Carolina	LL. D.
1854	Eli W. Caruthers	North Carolina	D. D.
"	John Randolph Clay	Kentucky	LL. D.
"	Aldert Smedes	North Carolina	D. D.
1856	Samuel H. Wiley	North Carolina	A. M.
1857	Aaron V. Brown	Tennessee	LL. D.
"	Lucien Holmes	North Carolina	A. M.
"	William Hooper	North Carolina	D. D.
"	William S. Mason	North Carolina	A. M.
1859	Robert R. Heath	North Carolina	A. M.
"	James Buchanan	Pennsylvania	LL. D.
"	Mitchell King	South Carolina	LL. D.
"	James Hervey Otey	Tennessee	LL. D.
1861	Abraham Caruthers	Tennessee	LL. D.
"	Nathan Green	Tennessee	LL. D.
1862	Thomas Atkinson	North Carolina	LL. D.
"	Stewart Lawson Johnston	North Carolina	A. M.
"	Matthias Evans Manly	North Carolina	LL. D.
1864	Francis W. Hilliard	North Carolina	A. M.
"	Norval W. Wilson	North Carolina	A. M.
1866	Andrew Johnson	Tennessee	LL. D.
"	Edwin G. Reade	North Carolina	LL. D.
"	Numa F. Reid	North Carolina	D. D.
1867	Richard Hines	Tennessee	D. D.
"	William Henry Seward	New York	LL. D.
1868	Edmund Burke Haywood	North Carolina	A. M.
"	Bartholomew Figures Moore	North Carolina	LL. D.
"	Charles Phillips	North Carolina	D. D.
"	Thomas H. Pritchard	North Carolina	D. D.
"	Thomas H. Seymour	Connecticut	LL. D.
"	Alfred Augustin Watson	North Carolina	D. D.
1877	Charles Force Deems	New York	LL. D.
"	J. C. Hiden	North Carolina	D. D.
"	John Kerr	North Carolina	LL. D.
"	George Patterson	North Carolina	D. D.
"	Jacob Henry Smith	North Carolina	D. D.
1878	William M. Brooks	North Carolina	A. M.
"	James Grant	Iowa	LL. D.
"	Joseph Buckner Killebrew	Tennessee	Ph. D.
"	Thomas Courtland Manning	Louisiana	LL. D.
"	John Jones Roberts	New York	D. D.

Honorary Degrees. 241

1878	JAMES M. SPRUNT, *North Carolina*	D. D.
"	BENJAMIN J. WESSON, *Kentucky*	A. M.
1879	THOMAS SAMUEL ASHE, *North Carolina*	LL. D.
"	FABIUS HAYWOOD BUSBEE, *North Carolina*	A. M.
"	JOHN H. DILLARD, *North Carolina*	LL. D.
"	F. H. KERFOOT, *Maryland*	D. D.
"	WASHINGTON CARUTHERS KERR, *North Carolina*	Ph. D.
"	SAMUEL FIELD PHILLIPS, *District of Columbia*	LL. D.
"	J. T. PICKETT, *Mississippi*	D. D.
"	DAVID T. SANDERSON, *Alabama*	D. D.
"	ARISTIDES S. SMITH, *North Carolina*	D. D.
"	JOHN M. WEBB, *Tennessee*	A. M.
1880	JOSEPH M. ATKINSON, *North Carolina*	D. D.
"	ALBERT MIRABEAU BOOZER, *South Carolina*	A. M.
"	ISAAC W. CLARKE, *Texas*	A. M.
"	W. H. HALL, *New York*	A. M.
"	THOMAS WEST HARRIS, *North Carolina*	A. M.
"	D. MCGILVARY, *Siam*	D. D.
"	EDWARD RONDTHALER, *North Carolina*	D. D.
"	DAVID SCHENCK, *North Carolina*	LL.D.
"	WILLIAM N. H. SMITH, *North Carolina*	LL. D.
"	THOMAS G. STARR, *Virginia*	D. D.
1881	ROBERT W. BOYD, *North Carolina*	A. M.
"	CHARLES ALSTON COOK, *North Carolina*	A. M.
"	FRANK M. DEEMS, *New York*	Ph. D.
"	JOSEPH H. FOY, *Missouri*	D. D.
"	WILLIAM MERCER GREEN, *Mississippi*	LL. D.
"	ANDREW DOZ HEPBURN, *North Carolina*	LL. D.
"	MATT WHITAKER RANSOM, *North Carolina*	LL. D.
"	WILLIAM CONWAY RENCHER, *North Carolina*	A. M.
"	THOMAS RUFFIN, *North Carolina*	LL. D.
"	CALVIN H. WILEY, *North Carolina*	D. D.
1882	ROBERT BURWELL, *North Carolina*	D. D.
"	THOMAS LANIER CLINGMAN, *North Carolina*	LL. D.
"	GEORGE DAVIS, *North Carolina*	LL. D.
"	NELSON M. FEREBEE, *North Carolina*	A. M.
"	ALBERT R. LEDOUX, *New York*	M. Sc.
"	DANIEL A. LONG, *North Carolina*	A. M.
"	E. F. ROCKWELL, *North Carolina*	D. D.
"	JETHRO RUMPLE, *North Carolina*	D. D.
1883	ALEXANDER GRAHAM, *North Carolina*	A. M.
"	JOHN MANNING, *North Carolina*	LL. D.
"	S. MENDELSSOHN, *North Carolina*	LL. D.
"	HENRY E. SHEPHERD, *South Carolina*	LL. D.
"	ALBERT MICAJAH SHIPP, *Tennessee*	LL. D.
"	JOHN E. C. SMEDES, *North Carolina*	D. D.
1884	WILLIS ALSTON, *North Carolina*	A. M.
"	N. COLLIN HUGHES, *North Carolina*	D. D.

1884	Thomas J. Jarvis, North Carolina	LL. D.
"	Augustus S. Merrimon, North Carolina	LL. D.
"	Edward Warren, France	LL. D.
"	John S. Watkins, North Carolina	D. D.
"	M. L. Wood, North Carolina	D. D.
1886	John R. Brooks, North Carolina	D. D.
"	John Lemuel Carroll, North Carolina	D. D.
"	A. W. Chapman, South Carolina	LL. D.
"	Marcus V. Lanier, North Carolina	LL. D.
"	Daniel A. Long, Ohio	D. D.
"	Luther McKinnon, North Carolina	D. D.
"	Duncan Kirkland McRae, North Carolina	LL. D.
"	H. W. Ravenell, South Carolina	LL. D.
1887	John G. Bacchus, New York	D. D.
"	Joseph J. Davis, North Carolina	LL. D.
"	Morris H. Henry, New York	LL. D.
"	Theodore Benedict Lyman, North Carolina	LL. D.
"	Hunter McGuire, Virginia	LL. D.
"	L. C. Vass, North Carolina	D. D.
1888	Robert Paine Dick, North Carolina	LL. D.
"	E. R. Hendrix, Missouri	LL. D.
"	Theodore Bryan Kingsbury, North Carolina	LL. D.
"	Samuel Rothrock, North Carolina	D. D.
1889	Alphonso Calhoun Avery, North Carolina	LL. D.
"	William George Brown, Washington and Lee Univ.	Ph. D.
"	W. B. Burney, University of South Carolina	Ph. D.
"	Paul Carrington Cameron, North Carolina	LL. D.
"	John Franklin Crowell, Trinity College	Litt. D.
"	Daniel G. Fowle, North Carolina	LL. D.
"	Daniel Coit Gilman, Johns Hopkins University	LL. D.
"	Edmund Burke Haywood, North Carolina	LL. D.
"	William Joseph Martin, Davidson College	LL. D.
"	William Royall, Wake Forest College	LL. D.
"	William Laurence Saunders, North Carolina	LL. D.
"	Alfred Moore Scales, North Carolina	LL. D.
"	James E. Shepherd, North Carolina	LL. D.
"	George Vaughan Strong, North Carolina	LL. D.
"	Charles Elisha Taylor, Wake Forest College	Litt. D.
"	Crawford H. Toy, Harvard University	LL. D.
"	Charles S. Venable, University of Virginia	LL. D.
"	F. C. Woodward, South Carolina University	Litt. D.

ADDITIONS AND CORRECTIONS.

Page 49. For WM. H. C. WEBB read WM. H. G. WEBB.
" 77. A. D. BETTS. Strike out * and 1889.
" 81. After JAMES RANDLETT (third line from bottom) insert MONROE.
" 92. H. B. BATTLE. For Ph. B. (first line) read B. S.
" 92. MARMADUKE BATTLE. Add Died June 16, 1889.
" 92. R. H. BATTLE, A. B., 1854. Insert LL. B., 1858.
" 94. JOSEPH BENJAMIN. Strike out Dead. Add: Planter. Puerto Cortez, Spanish Honduras.
" 95. A. D. BETTS. Strike out Died May, 1889.
" 100. A. G. BROWN. Strike out Dead. Add Los Angeles, Cal.
" 102. WM. C. BULLOCK. Add date of death, March 23, 1873.
" 109. Insert CLARK, JOHN THOMAS, Halifax Co., Va.: 1829. Episc. Minister. Born 1809, died 1886.
" 111. H. E. COLEMAN, 1862-'63, and J. C. COLEMAN. Strike out Dead.
" 123. WM. T. ENNETT. Add Born Nov. 19, 1839, died June 14, 1889.
" 128. S. M. FROST. Strike out Dead.
" 134. R. H. GRAVES, 1867-'68. Add Born 1851, died July 10, 1889.
" 140. S. HASSELL. Strike out Wilson (at end).
" 142. F. P., G. W. and W. D. HAYWOOD. Strike out Dead.
" 143. LEOPOLD HEARTT. Add Died 1888.
" 158. A. R. KELLY. Strike out Dead.
" 160. J. W. LANCASTER. Strike out Dead.
" 163. WM. F. LEWIS, A. B., 1842. Strike out Dead.
" 166. J. L. LOVE. For Asst. Prof. read Assoc. Prof.
" 168. W. H. MCDADE. Strike out Dead.
" 174. JOHN MANNING. For 1882- (twelfth line from bottom) read 1881-.
" 176. RICHARD H. MASON. Strike out Dead.
" 186. Insert OGILBY, HUGH J., Madison, Ga.: 1859-'60.

It is earnestly requested that additions and corrections of any kind be sent to President K. P. BATTLE, Chapel Hill, N. C.

www.ingramcontent.com/pod-product-compliance
Lightning Source LLC
Chambersburg PA
CBHW031959230426
43672CB00010B/2208